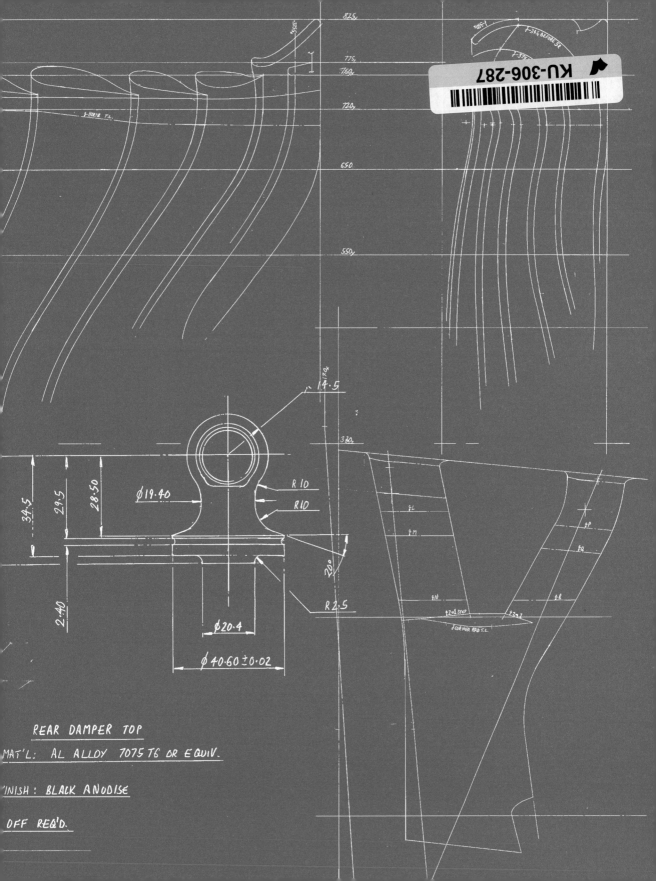

825.

775.
760.

720.

650.

550.

1·HORIZ T.L.

14.5

330.

Ø19.40

R 10

R 10

34.5

29.5

28.50

20°

R 2.5

2·40

Ø20·4

Ø 40·60 ±0·02

REAR DAMPER TOP

MAT'L: AL ALLOY 7075 T6 OR EQUIV.

FINISH: BLACK ANODISE

OFF REQ'D.

Dear Dad,

Save this and remembered fun – and sometimes frustrating! – time spent fixing the car with you. Thank you, and I hope you enjoy this!

All my love,

HOW TO
BUILD A
CAR

HOW TO BUILD A CAR

Adrian Newey

HarperCollins*Publishers*

HarperCollins*Publishers*
1 London Bridge Street
London SE1 9GF

www.harpercollins.co.uk

First published in 2017
2

MIX
Paper from
responsible sources
FSC™ C007454

This book is produced from independently certified FSC™ paper
to ensure responsible forest management.

For more information visit: www.harpercollins.co.uk/green

CONTENTS

PROLOGUE

Clouds were gathering that day. Rain was forecast. Feeling scrutinised, I lowered myself creakily into the cockpit of the FW15, painfully aware that at 35, after 10 years in the business, and with two constructors' championships under my belt, I was about to take my first proper spin in a Formula One car – in fact, my first real drive on a race track, period.

It was 1993, and I was chief designer at Williams. Frank Williams, owner of the team, had been talked into letting a journalist take one of our cars for a spin. What you might call a promotional drive. With that idea gaining traction, co-founder and technical director, Patrick Head, thought that the senior engineers, him, me and Bernard Dudot, who was in charge of Renault engine development, should also have a go.

And so here I was, sitting in the car at the Paul Ricard circuit in the South of France, absorbing from a driver's angle all the things I'd paid so little attention to as an engineer: the procedure for the ignition sequence; the whine and howl of the engine – a feeling of being cocooned but alone in the cockpit, as though the sheer volume and bone-shaking drama of it is physically holding you in place. Nerves suddenly give a feeling of intense claustrophobia.

'You've got to be smooth on the clutch or you'll stall it,' I'd been warned.

I didn't want to do that. Just the pride talking here: after all I'd designed it; I really didn't want to stall it – like some kind of competition winner.

I stalled it. Those carbon clutches are so aggressive. You have to give the engine about 5,500rpm, which is like trying to move off at the rev limit for a normal road car. Even then you're barely touching the throttle.

They wound it up again and this time I managed to get off the line, tentative but wanting to give a good account of myself. Taking to the straight, I had the traction control wound up high for stability, but even so it felt like I was wrestling with the car rather than driving it. I was wearing my motorcycle helmet, which was in constant danger of being sucked off my head, the chin strap throttling me. I'd thought the constant howling noise was immense at a standstill, but on the track it's like World War III breaking out in the cockpit. The airbox is above your head so it felt as though the V10 was screaming at me, while the sheer forward thrust, the sense of the car wanting to break free of my puny control, was breathtaking. We're used to having absolute dominion over our machines, but not me over this one: the FW15 had around 780bhp in a car weighing 500kg plus the driver; so me with kit on, say 580kg, gave a very, very high power-to-weight ratio. And it was stunning.

The clutch at that time was still a left-foot pedal – these days it's on the steering wheel. Even so, you only use the clutch once, to get rolling, the rest of the time your left leg is unemployed. The right, of course, is trying to stay on the accelerator, though the monkey brain is telling it to get back on the brake pedal. The shift itself was the flappy paddle, still a relatively new feature that had not yet spread on to road cars. Lights on the dash – green, green, amber – indicated the build-up of revs. My limit was 14,000.

At 13,500rpm, the green light goes on. You get ready.

The second green blinks on at 13,700rpm. Almost there.

Amber at 13,900rpm.

Change.

That little sequence takes about half a second.

Gradually becoming accustomed to the noise and beginning to feel as though I was controlling the car and not the other way around, I thought how intuitive the driving controls are. Green. Green. Amber. Change. It made me see Paul Ricard from a new vantage point, and the act of piloting a Formula One car from a fresh perspective. I was in my forties when the bug to actually race rather than just design the cars bit deep – but it first nibbled at that moment.

It began to rain – *chucking* it down with rain. I'd started to get a bit cocky but the combination of inexperienced (but gathering in confidence) driver and the rain was not a good one, and as my engineer's brain began to think about that redundant left leg, and whether it could be positioned differently to allow a narrower and more aerodynamically efficient front to the chassis, I lost a little focus. Before you knew it, I'd spun the FW15.

Good thing about Ricard: there are lots of run-offs. You have to be going some to hit anything at Ricard and I wasn't, so I didn't, and no, I wasn't quick with the clutch, so yes, I stalled it again.

There's no on-board starter on the car. If you spin and don't manage to keep the engine running, you have two problems: first, the engine's stopped, so you'll need mechanics armed with a pit starter motor to get back in business; second, it's stuck in whatever gear you were in at the time, and because the gear shift is hydraulically powered, it's not until the engine is running that you can then go back down through the gears. But, of course, the mechanics can't start the car in gear, because it would race off away from them. They need to come to the car with a little ratchet spanner and manually rock the car backwards and forwards while working the spanner on the

First drive in an F1 car, at the end of '93. Surprisingly, I don't look scared witless!

end of the gear-shift barrel until it gets back down to neutral. Only then can they put the starter in and restart the car and off you go again.

So there I waited. After five minutes or so, the mechanics arrived in a hire car. This had brightened their day, and yes, I was on the receiving end of some light-hearted banter. When everything was safe I took off again, clocking up more laps, really getting into it now, feeling a bit more at one with the car. Speeds? Now you're asking. At Monza, cars reach speeds of 220mph. Me at Ricard, I got it up to 175mph that day, which obviously is not what Alain Prost or Damon Hill would have settled for in that car, but still, for a 34-year-old engineer on his first outing, it was fast enough.

Indeed, by the following June, when I raced the FW15 against Christian Fittipaldi and Martin Brundle 'up the hill' at the Goodwood Festival of Speed, I felt comfortable simply driving it. After all, it's actually relatively easy to drive a Formula One car. Throttle, Green, Green, Amber. Change. Brake, turn the wheel, point it at a corner, accelerate. Simple. It's like an arcade game.

The challenge is doing it faster than everybody else without losing control. That is an entirely different level.

ON THE GRID

CHAPTER 1

Born in 1958, I came of age in a world infatuated with the motorcar: Scalextric, Formula One, The Monte Carlo Rally. At 10 years old I watched a Lamborghini tumble down a mountainside and Mini Coopers pull off *The Italian Job*. And when Kowalski slapped his Dodge Charger into fifth and accelerated away from the cops in *Vanishing Point*, I yelled in amazement, 'He's got another gear!' and then slid down in my seat as what felt like the whole of the cinema turned to glare at me.

I devoured *Autosport*, the weekly 'bible' for all things motorsport. I was glued to the radio during the 1968 London-to-Sydney Marathon. By the age of six I'd decided my future lay in motor sport. I was 12 when I knew I wanted to design racing cars.

Playing with Scalextric.

My passions were forged at home. Situated at the end of a rural lane on the outskirts of Stratford-upon Avon, our house backed onto a smelly pig farm, and it was from there that my father, Richard, ran a veterinary practice with his business partner, Brian Rawson. The practice combined pet surgeries with farm visits for bigger animals, and from an early age I was a dab hand at passing buckets of water and lengths of rope. I've seen enough newborn livestock to last me a lifetime.

My mother, Edwina, was attractive; quite the catch. She'd been an ambulance driver during the war and met my dad when she brought her unwell Pyrenean Mountain Dog into his practice. Her father had taken an instant dislike to her new beau. 'That man will only cross my doorstep over my dead body,' he said. The day before he and my dad were due to visit for the first time, he died of a heart attack.

I was born on Boxing Day. The rather far-fetched tale I was told involved my mother and father driving around Colchester, complete with a midwife in the back of the car, when my mother's waters broke. Different times, of course, but I'm not sure that even in those days you were assigned a midwife just in case you gave birth, and why on earth she would have been with them on Boxing Day, I couldn't possibly say. But anyway, my father knocked on a door, they were taken in by strangers, and my mother gave birth there and then. My very first crib was in a chest of drawers.

As the 1960s wore on, the hippy lifestyle appealed to my mum and she dressed accordingly, which made her pretty exotic for Stratford. Unusually for a time when divorce was less common, she had a son, Tim, from a previous marriage. Tim is seven years older than me and our interests were different. *Top of the Pops* and *Thunderbirds*, broadcast at the same time but on BBC1 and ITV respectively, was always a lively battle of channel switching. That age gap meant he soon left for Repton boarding school, and then university, eventually settling in Spain where he teaches English to local kids. We have fond reunions once a year over the course of the Spanish Grand Prix in Barcelona.

Both my parents had tempers, and in my early teens I'd witness some terrible arguments between the two. Mum would drag me in and try to enlist my support, which in retrospect was a bit naughty.

On one occasion I cycled off to escape the feuding pair. After about an hour I thought I'd better return, but as I pedalled back down the lane I saw our red Lotus Elan (registration number: UNX 777G) driving very, very slowly towards me. At first I thought there was nobody inside. It was only as I came closer that I realised my mum was driving. God knows how. She was slouched so low into the driver's seat she must have been navigating by the telephone poles.

My mother would from time to time hit the bottle to get herself through, though she firmly denied this, claiming that she never poured her own drink, always waiting for my father to get in from evening veterinary surgery at around 7pm.

Our African Grey parrot, Goni, lived in his evening cage just by the drinks cabinet. One evening, as my dad made my mum her usual tipple, Goni started to mimic the sounds: 'click' as the sweet Martini cork was pulled, followed by 'glug-glug' as the drink was poured, 'squeak-squeak' as the gin bottle lid was undone, followed by 'glug-glug', 'chink-chink' as the ice went in, followed by my mother's voice: 'Aah, that's better!' Rumbled by the parrot.

One thing was for sure, though: you never knew what to expect from them; orthodox they were not. I was 13 when my brother, Tim, home from Bath University, suggested a family outing to see *A Clockwork Orange*. My parents were happy for me to dress up as an X-appropriate 18-year-old, complete with hat, glasses and my brother's trench coat, and steal into the cinema, but then were angry with Tim for recommending the film, their liberal-parenting sensibilities falling at some point in between the two stools.

The film, meanwhile, seeped into my subconscious, and 40 years later, when I finally saw it for the second time, I found I could remember almost every single frame: its sleek lines, stylised hyper-realism and violence set to a soundtrack of synthesised Beethoven made an impression on me in ways I had never fully comprehended at the time.

We weren't frightfully rich, but neither were we poor. Supplementing the money from the practice were my father's shares in the family business, Newey Bros of Birmingham.

Established in 1798, Newey Bros had risen to become one of the country's biggest manufacturers of hooks and eyes, dress fasteners and military and tent hooks, and by 1947 had added 'Sta-Rite' hair pins and 'Wizard' bodkins to the range. To this day you can buy fasteners bearing the Newey name. No doubt it was thanks to that extra income that my father was able to indulge his interest in cars, not just driving them, although he did an awful lot of that, but tinkering, modifying and maintaining them.

It was where his true interest lay. Despite specialising in the life sciences for his career, his heart lay in physical science. He read maths books like other dads read John le Carré, he had a huge passion for engineering and he liked nothing better than a challenge: *how can I do this differently? How can I do this better?* Each year in Formula One we pore over the regulations for the next year, and part of my job, perhaps even the part I relish most, involves working out what the regulations actually say, as opposed to what their intent is and whether this subtle difference allows any new avenues. I'm basically saying, 'How can I use these regulations to try something that hasn't been done before?'

It's a process that seems to come naturally to me, I guess because I effectively started at an early age, and I had an excellent mentor in my father.

Fittingly, it was a combination of Dad's need to think outside the box, his love of cars and a compulsion to tinker that led to one of my earliest memories: five years old, looking out of the landing window – to see smoke billowing from the windows of the garage below.

Our garage at that time was an annex to the main house, an Aladdin's cave for a five-year-old. Dad would spend hours in there, working on cars and dreaming up solutions to problems.

For instance: how do you thoroughly creosote fence posts? The world at large would knuckle down to giving them a second coat. My dad, on the other hand, had a better idea. He cut the ends off several empty tins of Castrol GTX before soldering them together to make one long tube. Into that went the posts, then the creosote. It was, or should have been, an easy and efficient way to creosote the fence posts. Mad, but ingenious, like the elaborate, custom-fitted boxes he built to store veterinary equipment in the boot of his cars, or the gardening equipment he made; or the fact that he used to prepare for camping trips to the Brecon Beacons or Scotland by dedicating a bedroom to the endeavour for a month in advance, taking a pair of scales in there and weighing everything obsessively, even going so far as to cut the handle off a toothbrush. He had an eye for detail, which is another characteristic that's rubbed off on me. I wouldn't say I was tidy – it was a standing joke in our family that my father and I were as messy as each other – but when it comes to the research and design of racing cars, attention to every little detail is imperative.

Chief among Dad's many quirks was a disregard for most things health-and-safety, which brings me back to his revolutionary method for creosoting fence posts. What he'd failed to take into account when he left his contraption to marinade in the garage was the paraffin heaters he used to stop the sumps freezing on his Riley RMF (registration VCD 256 – a very pretty car, I loved it), and his red Saab 2 Stroke (a car I despised for the disgusting noise it made).

And you can guess what happened. Left upright, the fence posts had fallen over, the creosote met the paraffin and *boom*.

The Riley that suffered when the garage caught fire.

I had two thoughts on seeing the flames. I'm not sure in which order they came but, for the record, let's say they were: (1) I must alert my parents and the fire brigade, and (2) I hope the Saab is destroyed, not the Riley.

With objective number one achieved we ran out to try and extinguish the flames, before – very exciting – the fire brigade arrived, and we were told to stand at a safe distance and let the professionals do their job. I was concerned about the damage, of course, but also in that rather nice position of knowing I wasn't responsible.

However, Murphy's Law prevailed; it was the Riley that was damaged, not the Saab.

CHAPTER 2

I have a driver who ferries me to and from work. If that sounds terribly flash, I apologise, but it's an arrangement born out of practicality, because as well as giving me the chance to go over emails (I have them printed out for me, which I know is not very green but it allows me to scribble and make notes more easily on them), it affords me valuable extra thinking time. My thoughts naturally default to shape and form, problems and solutions, and I can easily be lost in them. Many were the times I'd arrive late, having taken a wrong turn or missed my junction, deep in thought. So now, for reasons of effective time management and a desire for punctuality, I have a driver.

My office at Red Bull in Milton Keynes overlooks the car park and is at one corner of the main engineering office, home to some 200 engineers. I try to keep meetings and administrative duties to a minimum, so that most of my working day is spent at my drawing board, where I'll work on next year's car or refinements to the current model. Whatever I'm working on, it's always with the same aim, the one defining goal of my entire career: to increase the performance of the car.

Computer-aided design (CAD) systems weren't around when I began in the industry, and although most, if not all, of my colleagues have long since converted, I've stuck with my drawing board. Call me a dinosaur, but I think of it as my first language; for me it represents a state of continuity and I like continuity; it's something I strive for. If I were to convert to CAD I'd have to learn something new, and not only is there a time penalty to doing that, but there's the question of whether I'd be as fluent in my new language as I was in my old.

Besides, what I value about the drawing board is that you can have everything at scale in front of you, whereas on a CAD system you're limited by the size of the monitor. I also like the fact that I can sketch freeform and change it quickly. It's an illustration of how fast I can work that when I'm flat-out I keep at least two people occupied taking my paper drawings and turning them into CAD drawings. And these are just the ones I think are worth transcribing. It's usually taken several iterations to get to that point; my consumption of erasers is only just behind my consumption of pencil lead.

I'm happiest when working on a big regulation change. Drawing the RB7, the 2011 car, was just such a time: an overhaul that included the incorporation of the KERS system (it stands for 'kinetic energy recovery system'), which stores energy in a battery under braking and then releases it during acceleration.

Other designers were saying that the best place to put the battery was under the fuel tank: it's nice and central, it's in a relatively cool location and it's easy to connect from a wiring point of view. But aerodynamically, I wanted to get the engine as far forward in the chassis as possible so as to allow a very tight rear end to the bodywork, and the best way to achieve that was to take the heavy KERS battery and put it near the back of the car, which in turn would allow the engine to be moved forward to keep the weight distribution balanced. My suggestion was that we put the battery behind the engine, in front of the gearbox.

Initially I proposed this to Rob Marshall, our chief designer. His reaction was a deep breath. You want to take the batteries, which we know are a difficult thing to manage, very sensitive to vibration, prone to short-

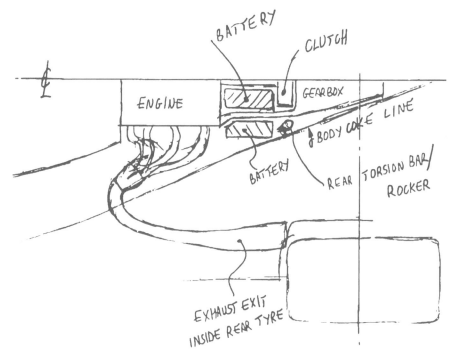

Figure 1: Placement of the KERS system in the RB7.

ing out, sensitive to temperature – you want to take these and put them between the engine and the gearbox, one of the most hostile environments on the car? Really?

I was insistent. I said, 'Look, Rob, I'm sorry, and I know it's difficult, but not only does putting them in this location give us a good advantage, but it's an advantage we'll have locked in, because it'll be impossible for a team to copy that within a season, it's such a fundamental part of the architecture of the car.'

So Rob went away and started talking to his engineers in the design office, and came back and said, 'No, everybody agrees, it's just not possible, we can't do it.'

My feeling was that it ought to be possible, so I drew some layouts that split the battery into four units, two mounted inside the gearbox case just in front of the clutch and two mounted alongside but on the outside of the gearbox case. I drew some ducting to put the batteries into their own little compartments with cold air blowing over them in addition to the water-cooling they have anyway.

Fortunately Rob is not only a very creative designer but also a designer who understands that if there is an overall performance benefit to be had, and if it looks viable, you've got to give it a go. It was a brave, I guess you could argue an irresponsible decision, in that if we hadn't got it to work it would have compromised our season.

It took longer than I hoped. During the early part of the season, the KERS system was in the habit of packing up and was constantly in danger of catching fire. But once we made it reliable, we had this underlying baked-in package advantage that we were able to carry for the balance of that season and the next two, a key part of the 2011, 2012 and 2013 championship-winning cars. Which, as you can imagine, appealed to my inner love of continuity.

If the fact that I still use a drawing board and pencil sounds old-fashioned, that's nothing compared to my start in education. At four I was sent to the local convent school where I was told that being left-handed was a sign of the devil. The nuns made me sit on the offending hand, as though I could drive out the demon using the power of my godly bum.

It didn't work. I'm still left-handed. What's more, when I went from that school to Emscote Lawn prep school in Warwick, I still couldn't write. As a result I was placed in the lower set. And what do kids in the lower set do? They mess around.

My earliest experiments in aerodynamics came during a craze for making darts out of felt-tip pens and launching them at the blackboard. We'd have competitions, and I was getting pretty good until one particular French lesson, when for reasons best known to my 12-year-old self I launched my dart straight up into a polystyrene ceiling tile. The teacher turned from the blackboard, alerted by suppressed laughter that fluttered across the room, and what he saw was a classroom full of boys with their hands clamped over their mouths and one, me, sitting bolt upright with an expression like butter wouldn't melt.

Sure enough, he made his way through the desks to mine, about to demand what was going on, when the dart above our heads chose that moment to come unstuck from the ceiling, stall, turn sideways and bank straight into the side of his neck. Statistically, it was a one in a thousand chance. It was poetry.

That wasn't my only caning. The other one was for rigging up a pea-shooter from a Bunsen burner tube and accidentally tagging a science teacher instead of the mate I was aiming at.

Speech days were especially boring. On one particular occasion, me and my friend James had been playing in the woods, found some aerosol cans and lobbed them on the school incinerator. Expecting them to blow up straightaway, we took cover behind some trees, only to be frustrated by a distinct lack of pyrotechnics. Eventually we got tired of waiting and wandered off.

Shortly after that, speech day commenced, parents assembled and we took our seats, ready to be bored rigid, when suddenly from the woods came a series of booms and the stage was showered in ash. James and I looked at each other gleefully, but we counted ourselves lucky not to be caught and punished for it.

When it came to the challenge of making a hot-air balloon, I was able to put to good use my interest in building things. By this time I was beginning to understand the concept that if you want something to go up, you need to make it big in order to achieve a good volume-to-surface-area ratio, so I made a large balloon out of tissue and bent coat-hangers, complete with solid-fuel pellets for heat. Unfortunately the pellets didn't generate enough oomph to get the balloon airborne, so I carted my dad's propane burner into school and used that instead. The headmaster came out to see what was going on, leant on the burner and burnt his hand, which cemented his dislike of me.

At home I continued messing about with motor cars. In 1968 Dad bought a red Lotus Elan in kit form (other families had large saloons, we had sporty two-seaters), which according to Lotus you could build yourself – 'in a weekend', although even Dad could never manage that – and save on car purchase tax. Manna from heaven for an obsessive tinkerer like my dad, and I was his willing helper, happy to put up with his occasional, volcanic loss of temper in order to watch a car being built from a kit.

Meanwhile, I'd started building model kits. Most of my friends were making Messerschmitts and Spitfires but naturally I preferred cars, and my favourite was a one-twelfth-scale Tamiya model of a Lotus 49, as driven by Jim Clark and Graham Hill.

This was the first year that Lotus and their founder Colin Chapman had introduced corporate sponsorship, so the model was liveried in red, white and gold and had all the right details, moving suspension, the works. It was a great model by any standard, but what was especially noteworthy from my point of view was that the parts were individually labelled. Suddenly I was able to put a name to all the bits and pieces I'd see on the floor of the garage. 'Ah, that's a lower wishbone. That's a rear upright.' This, to me, was better than French lessons.

By 12 I began to get bored of putting together other people's designs and started sketching my own. I was drawing constantly by then – it was the one thing I was good at, or, rather, the one thing I knew I was good at – as well as clipping pictures out of *Autosport* and copying them freehand, trying to reproduce them but also customise them at the same time, adding my own detail.

Needless to say, as I look back on my childhood now, I can identify where certain seeds were planted: the interest in cars, the fascination with tinkering – both of which came from my dad – and now the first flowerings of what you might call the design engineer's mind, which even more than a mathematician's or physicist's involves combining the artistic, imaginative left side of the brain – the 'what if?' and 'wouldn't it be interesting to try this?' bit – with the more practical right side, the bit that insists everything must be fit for purpose.

For me, that meeting of the imagination with practical concerns began at home. In the garden was what my father called a workshop but what was in fact a little timber hut housing some basic equipment: a lathe, bench drill, sheet-metal folding equipment and a fibreglass kit. In there I set up shop, and soon I was taking my sketched-out designs and making them flesh.

I'd fold up bits of metal to make a chassis and other bits out of fibreglass. Parts I couldn't make, like the wheels and engine, I'd salvage from models I'd already put together. None of my school friends lived close by, so I became like a pre-teen hermit, sequestered in the shed (sorry Dad, 'the workshop'), beavering away on my designs with only our huge Second World War radio for company. I spent so much time in there that on one occasion I even passed out from the chloroform I used to clean the parts with.

Back at school, I employed my models for a presentation, which was well received considering how mediocre I was in every other aspect of school life. 'Can do well when he is sensible. I regret that his behaviour in class has too often been extremely silly,' blustered my traumatised French teacher in a school report. 'Disinterested, slapdash and rather depressing,' wrote another teacher.

The problem was that I shared traits inherited from both my mother and my father. My mum was vivacious and often flirtatious, a very good artist but mostly a natural-born maverick; my dad was an eccentric, a veterinarian Caractacus Potts, blessed or maybe cursed with a compulsion to think outside the box. No doubt it's an equation that has served me well in later life, but it's not best-suited to school life.

I distinctly remember a science lesson on the subject of friction. 'So, class, who thinks friction is a good thing?' asked the teacher. I was the only one who raised his hand.

'Why, Newey?'

'Well, if we didn't have friction, none of us would be able to stand up. We'd all slip over.'

The teacher did a double-take as though suspecting mischief. But despite the titters of my classmates, I was deadly serious. He rolled his eyes. 'That's ridiculous,' he sighed, 'friction is clearly a bad thing. Why else would we need oil?'

Right then I knew I had a different way of looking at the world. Thinking about it now, I'm aware that I'm also possessed of an enormous drive to succeed, and maybe that comes from wanting to prove I'm not always wrong, that friction can be a good thing.

EMSCOTE LAWN SCHOOL,
WARWICK.

TERMINAL REPORT

Name........A.M.NEWEY (ma)................

Autumn Term, 1971

Name.......A. M. NEWEY....................... Class.....CE 5.......

ENGLISH REPORT

Number of Boys in Class	19
Place at End of Term	3

He has some flair. He would excel if he could only raise the energy.

Signature........................

Name.......A. Newey....................... Class.....CE J.......

FRENCH REPORT

Number of Boys in Class	19
Place at End of Term	6

Can do well when he is sensible. I regret that his behaviour in class has too often been extremely silly; this will stop at once, please.

Signature........................

A selection of school reports.

Name _____ Newey ma. _____ Class. Common Entrance.

SCRIPTURE REPORT

Number of Boys in Class	19
Place at End of Term	8=

Frequently competent:
occasionally illogical.

Signature _____ JSRidley _____

Name _____ Newey ma _____ Class _____ C.E.V.

MUSIC REPORT

Number of Boys in Class	
Place at End of Term	

Disinterested and expresses it in a
slapdash attitude in class. Rather
depressing.

Signature _____ M.C.Pons _____

Name _____ A. Newey.

HEADMASTER'S REPORT

Adrian has the ability and the opportunity to do really well
next term. At the moment he prefers frivolous mediocrity to
excellence. I do hope that he can grow up and concentrate
far harder in his day to day classwork; too often I have
grumbles from staff about his silliness in class.

Signature _____ J.H. Riley _____

CHAPTER 3

Dad loved cars but he wasn't especially interested in motorsport. Meanwhile my passion in that area had only intensified through my early years. As a young lad I persuaded him to take me to a few races.

One such meet was the Gold Cup at Oulton Park in Cheshire in 1972, and it was there, thanks to some judicious twisting of my dad's arm, that we'd taken the (second) yellow Elan CGWD 714K one early summer morning: my very first motor race.

At the circuit we wandered around the paddock – something you could often do in those days – and I was almost overwhelmed by the sights but mainly the sounds of the racetrack. It was like nothing I'd ever heard before. These huge, full-throated, dramatic-sounding V8 DFV engines, the high-pitched BRM V12 engines; the mechanics tinkering with them, fixing what, I didn't know, but I was fascinated to watch anyway, inconceivably pleased if I was able to identify something they were doing. 'Dad, they're disconnecting the rear anti-roll bar!'

I'd seen real racing cars before. In another act of supreme arm-twisting, I'd persuaded my dad to take me to the Racing Car Show at Olympia in London. But Oulton Park was the first time I'd seen them in the wild, in their natural habitat and, what's more, actually *moving*. It's an undulating track and the cars were softly sprung in those days. I found myself trans-fixed by watching the ride-heights change as cars thundered over the rise by the start/finish line. I was already in love with motor racing but I fell even harder for it that day.

My second race was at Silverstone for the 1973 Grand Prix, where Jackie Stewart was on pole, and the young me was allowed a hamburger. Stewart on pole was par for the course in those days, but the hamburger was some-thing of a rarity, as another of my father's many foibles was his absolute hatred of junk food. He was always very Year Zero about things like that. When the medical profession announced that salt was good for you, he

Posing with the Cosworth DFV engine at the Racing Car Show.

would drink brine in order to maintain his salt levels on a hot summer day. When the medical profession had a change of heart and decided that salt was bad for you after all, he cut it out altogether, wouldn't even have it in the water for boiling peas.

That afternoon, for whatever reason, perhaps to make up for the fact that we didn't wander around the paddock as we had done at the Gold Cup, Dad relaxed his no-junk-food rule and bought me a burger from a stall at the bottom of the grandstand at Woodcote, which in those days was a very fast corner at the end of the lap, just before the start/finish line.

We took our seats for the beginning of the race, and I sat enthralled as Jackie Stewart quickly established what must have been a 100-yard lead on the rest of the pack as he came round at the end of the first lap.

Then, before I knew it, two things happened. One: the young South African Jody Scheckter, who had just started driving for the McLaren team, lost control of his car in the quick Woodcote corner, causing a huge pile-up. It was one of the biggest crashes there had ever been in Formula One, and it happened right before my very eyes.

And two: I dropped my burger from the shock of it.

My memory is of the whole grandstand rising to its feet as the accident unfolded, of cars going off in all directions, and an airbox hurtling high in the air, followed by dust and smoke partly obscuring the circuit. It was very exciting but also shocking; was somebody hurt or worse? It seemed inconceivable they wouldn't be. I recall the relief of watching drivers clamber unhurt from the wreckage (the worst injury was a broken leg). Once the excitement subsided it became obvious we'd now have to wait an age for marshals to clear the track. There was only one thing for it, I clambered underneath the bottom of the grandstand, retrieved my burger and carried on eating it.

At 13 I was packed off to Repton School in Derbyshire. My grandfather, father and brother had all attended Repton, so it wasn't a matter for debate whether I went or not. Off I went, a boarder for the first time, beginning what was set to be another academically undistinguished period of my life.

Except this time it was worse, because the immediate and rather dismaying difference between Emscote Lawn and Repton was that at Emscote Lawn I was popular with other pupils, which meant that even though I wasn't doing well in lessons, at least I was having a decent time. But at Repton, I was much more of an outcast.

The school was and maybe still is very sports orientated, but I was average at football, hopeless at cricket and even worse at hockey. The one team sport I was decent at was rugby, but at that time they didn't play rugby at Repton, and never bothered with it for some reason. I had to satisfy myself with being fairly good at cross-country running, which isn't exactly the surest path to adulation and popularity. I was bullied, only once physically, by two of the boys in the year above, which made my life in the first two years at Repton pretty tough. But boredom became the biggest killer, and the way I dealt with it was by retreating into sketching and painting racing cars, reading books on racing cars and making models, as well as something new – karting.

Shenington kart track. I remember it well, having persuaded my dad to take me there, aged 14. During our first visit, Dad and I stood watching other kids with their dads during an open practice day. What we quickly learnt was that there were two principal types of kart: the 100cc fixed-wheel with no gearbox or clutch, and those fitted with a motorcycle-based engine and gearbox unit.

The thing about the fixed-wheel karts was that you had to bump-start them, which involved the driver running by the side of the kart while some other poor patsy (a dad, usually) ran along behind holding up the back end, the two of them then performing a daring drop-and-jump manoeuvre. For me, it was intimidating to watch, with dads letting go of the rear end while the kids missed their footing, the driverless karts fired and then carried on serenely at about 15mph until they crashed into the safety barrier at the end of the paddock as onlookers scattered, followed by much shouting, kids in tears and so forth.

It was proper slapstick, but given my dad's short temper I decided to go for the more expensive but easier-to-start second option.

Meanwhile, my father was making a few observations of his own. 'As far as I can see,' he said thoughtfully, 'most of these boys are here not because they want to be, but because their dads want them to be.'

What could he mean? I was already sold on wanting a kart. No doubt about it. But Dad was insistent. I was going to have to prove my hunger and dedication. So he made a proposal: I had to save up and buy my own kart. But for every pound I earned, he would match it with one of his own.

During the summer holidays I worked my arse off. I canvassed the neighbourhood looking for odd jobs. I mowed lawns, washed cars and sold plums from our garden. I even managed to get a commission from an elderly neighbour to do a painting of her house and front garden. And gradually I raised enough money to buy a kart from the back pages of *Karting Magazine*. The kart itself was a Barlotti (made by Ken Barlow in Reading, who felt his karts needed an Italian-sounding name) with a

Villiers 9E motorcycle engine of 199cc. It was in poor condition but it was a kart and, importantly, came with a trailer.

I managed to go to two practice outings at Shenington, but the stopwatch showed the combination of me and the kart to be hopelessly slow, way off even the back of the grid. In the meantime, back at Repton for a second unhappy academic year, I was at least getting on well with the teacher who ran the workshop in which we had two lessons a week. I persuaded him to allow me to bring the kart so that I could work on it at evenings and weekends. And so it was that in January 1973 my dad and I arrived at school in the veterinary surgery minivan (registration PNX 556M) with kart and trailer.

Now I could fill the long, boring periods of 'free time' at boarding school much more usefully – I stripped and rebuilt the engine, rebuilt the gearbox with a new second gear to stop it jumping out, serviced the brakes, etc.

The next summer holiday we returned to Shenington but, after a further two outings, the kart and I were still too slow. Simply rebuilding and fettling it had not made it significantly quicker; more drastic action was required – the engine was down on power and the tube frame chassis was of a previous generation compared to the quick boys' karts. For the engine I needed a 210cc piston and an aluminium Upton barrel to replace the cast-iron one, funded by more washing of cars, etc., with my dad continuing to double my money. To make a new chassis was more ambitious, and for that I needed welding and brazing skills. So I booked myself on a 10-day welding course at BOC in the aptly named Plume Street, north Birmingham.

Every morning I got up at six, took the bus from Stratford to Birmingham to arrive by nine, spent the day with a bunch of bored blokes in their thirties, most of whom were being forced to take the course by their employers, and then returned home about nine.

I seemed to be quite good at welding and brazing, which meant that I progressed more quickly through the various set tasks than many of the others on the course. Some of them got quite resentful about this and started grumbling, while also taking the mickey out of my public school voice. I learnt that in circumstances such as this, I needed to fit in and began to modify my voice to have more of a Brummie accent, which was valuable when I started college. Shame it is such an unpleasant nasal drone though; I have since slowly tried to drop it again!

Armed with my new super-power, I returned to school and constructed a chassis. Over the Christmas holiday I rebuilt the engine using the Upton barrel, as well as making an electronic ignition cribbed from a design in an electronics magazine, with the help of a friend.

Come the summer term it was ready, so I rolled it out of the workshop hoping to get it going. The first time, no dice. I wheeled it back inside. Tinkered some more. I'd got the ignition timing wrong.

Another afternoon I tried again. This time, with two friends enthusiastically pushing the kart, I dropped the clutch and, with an explosion of blue smoke from the exhaust, it fired up.

Jeremy Clarkson was a pupil at Repton at the time and he remembers the evening well, having since told flattering stories to journalists, saying that I'd built the go-kart from scratch (I hadn't) and that I drove it around the school quad at frighteningly high speeds (I didn't).

In truth, it was more of a pootle around the chapel, but one that had disastrous consequences when one of the pushing friends took a turn, pranged it and bent the rear axle. It was annoying, because it meant I had to save for a new one, but at least he contributed towards it.

Almost worse than that, though, was the fact that the headmaster came to see what the kerfuffle was all about. It was hardly surprising. My kart was a racing two-stroke. No silencer. And the din was like a sudden assault by a squadron of angry android bees. Distinctly unimpressed, the head banned me from bringing it back to school. As it turned out, it didn't matter; I would not be returning for another term.

There's another story that Jeremy tells journalists. He says there were two pupils expelled from Repton in the 1970s: he was one, and I was the other . . .

Which brings me to . . .

CHAPTER 4

Coming up to my O-levels (GCSEs in today's language), I shuffled in to see a careers advisor, who cast a disinterested eye over my mock results, coughed and then suggested I might like to pursue History, English and Art at further education. I thanked him for his time and left.

Needless to say, I had different plans. Working on my kart had taught me two things: first, that I probably wasn't cut out to be a driver, because despite my best efforts, not to mention my various mechanical enhancements, the combination of me and kart just wasn't that fast.

And second, it didn't matter that I wasn't cut out to be a driver, because although I enjoyed driving the kart it wasn't where my true interest lay. What I *really* wanted to do – what I spent time thinking about, and what I thought I might conceivably be quite good at – was car design, making racing cars go faster.

So, much to my father's relief, as the school fees were hefty, I decided to leave Repton for an OND course, equivalent to A-levels, at the Warwickshire College of Further Education in Leamington Spa.

I couldn't wait. At Repton I'd been caught drinking in the local Burton-on-Trent pubs, which had earned me a troublemaker reputation that I was in no particular hurry to discard. My attitude to the school ranged from ambivalence all the way to apathy (with an occasional touch of anarchy) and the feeling was entirely mutual. We were never destined to part on good terms anyway. And so it proved.

At the end of each term, the sixth form would arrange a concert for the whole school. As usual, this was to be held in the Pears' School, a venerable building boasting oak panelling and ornate stained-glass windows dating back to its construction in 1886. The survivor of two world wars and God knows how many other conflicts, the building was a justifiable source of great pride for the school, and it was in these historic surroundings that the prog rock band Greenslade had been booked to play.

Like many kids of the time, my tastes leaned towards the hippy end of things: long(ish) hair, voluminous Oxford bags, loon pants and psychedelic music: Santana, Genesis (Peter Gabriel's Genesis, to be precise), Supertramp, Average White Band and of course Pink Floyd.

Repton disapproved. In an effort to stop the dangerous viral spread of platform shoes, the school had passed an edict banning any shoe under which you could pass a penny on its end. Being a smart Alec I'd used a piece of aluminium to bridge the gap between heel and sole, thus allowing me to wear my platform boots while still abiding by the letter of the law (no prizes for spotting the connection between that and what I do now). Unsurprisingly, the powers that be at Repton took a dim view of this particular act of rule-bending, but it enhanced my reputation in the teachers' common room for being a troublemaker.

Anyway. I digress. The advantage of the fashion, in particular the forgiving trousers, was their suitability for hiding bottles of booze. Sure enough, what we fifth-formers did was tape half-bottles of gin, vodka and whatever other spirits we could purloin to our shins, then swish into the concert with the contraband safely hidden beneath our flapping trouser legs.

Greenslade began their performance. To be honest, you probably had to be on acid to enjoy it, but we settled for surreptitiously mixing our smuggled alcohol with innocent-looking glasses of Coke and getting slowly smashed.

It's a dangerous and combustible combination: a hot summer, the end of term, lots of boys, booze and the pernicious, corrupting effects of dual-keyboard prog rock. Pretty soon, the atmosphere had turned rowdy. And no one was more rowdy than yours truly.

As with most concerts, the mixing desk was located in the middle of the auditorium. I sat close by and, seeing that the soundman had nipped off for a leak, I darted over to the mixer and slid all of the sliders to max.

The band played on. The noise, a mix of distortion, bass, shrieking keyboards and sheer, unexpected volume, was immense. Without a care for the tinnitus we would all suffer the following day, the hall erupted and for a moment, before the headmaster arrived and the soundman returned, absolute anarchy ruled.

Years later, Jeremy Clarkson said it was the loudest thing he'd ever heard. As we've already established, Jeremy is prone to exaggeration, but on this occasion he's probably right. It was very, very loud.

My punishment? I was dragged to the school sanatorium and forced to endure a stomach pump. Completely unnecessary, of course, not even ethical. Simply a way of punishing me for what had happened.

The next day it was discovered that the loud noise had loosened the leading and cracked the ceramics holding the stained-glass windows in place. It was the last straw. My parents were contacted and summoned to the school.

My mother arrived in her Porsche (registration WME 94M). Quintessentially Mum: dressed in her usual white, with white boots and carrying a potted lily. She knew the headmaster had a taste for lilies and she was never one to pass up an opportunity to charm the birds from the trees. 'Hello, Lloyd, how lovely to see you; here's a gift,' she said, placing it before him and taking a seat. 'Is this about Adrian? He's such a good boy, isn't he?'

On this occasion her charms were wasted. 'Indeed, this is about Adrian,' she was told flatly. 'But I'm afraid he hasn't been a good boy. In fact, he has been a very bad boy. So bad, in fact, that I'm afraid you are going to have to take him away. He is no longer welcome at Repton.'

My mother looked from the headmaster to me and then back again. She raised her chin. 'Well if that's your attitude, Lloyd, I'll have my plant back,' she said. 'Come on Adrian, let's go.'

I know nothing about Jeremy's expulsion, but that's how I got my marching orders. I left Repton under a cloud, relieved to finally wave the place goodbye (flicking it the Vs at the same time).

I've been back since, mind you. Just the once, when my father and I competed in a 'boys versus old Reptilians' cross-country run. But other than that, it was a not-particularly-fond final farewell. The irony is that I am told photographs of Jeremy and me are among other noteworthy old Reptonians in their Hall of Fame.

CHAPTER 5

Post-Repton, life improved and things started to click into place: I finally raced the kart at Shenington, and though the kart and I didn't exactly set the world alight, at least we could race towards the back of 'the pack', and were several seconds faster than we had been 12 months earlier.

By accident it turned out that the chopper blade I had made to go on the end of the crankshaft, to give the electronic ignition its signal to spark, happened to be of a width that meant it also gave about the right ignition timing if the engine ran backwards. And so the most notable feature of my race weekend was when I spun at the hairpin during practice and must have pressed the clutch while still going backwards. When I let the clutch back out I found I suddenly had four reverse gears instead of four forward! The look of disbelief from onlookers as I completed the rest of the lap into the paddock backwards, looking over my shoulder, still brings a smile to my face. The chief steward was less impressed with my efforts, however.

I also began work on a 'special', which was a road-going sports car that I planned to build from my own drawings. It was an ambitious project, and although it was one I ultimately abandoned, a couple of valuable things emerged from the experience. The first thing was that in the course of researching it, I read of a guy called Ian Reed of Delta Racing Cars in Surrey who'd built such a car, so – figuring he might be a useful source of information – I wrote to him.

One exchange of letters later and Ian invited me along to the factory, spent about half a day looking over my drawings, and gave me tips on how to develop and design the car, as well as a bit of useful careers advice.

Second, I was putting in the hours. Apparently, in order to attain expert status at any given activity, be it tennis, violin, cooking, whatever, you need to clock up at least 500 hours' practice, ideally from the age of eight through your teens, when you're much more receptive and can learn more quickly.

Me in my modified pedal go-kart.

Unknowingly, that's exactly what I was doing. I was practising, just as I always had. For my combined eighth birthday-and-Christmas present (a dreaded combination familiar to anyone who has a birthday near Christmas), I'd received a pedal go-kart, and sure enough I customised it by adding on my own bodywork parts in order to make it look like a Formula One car. Later came my 10-speed Carlton bicycle that I lightened by drilling holes in it and swapping the supplied steel saddle post for my own aluminium design. I was very proud of that – until the day it snapped.

So even though my plans for 'the special' didn't quite get off the ground, it was still a valuable exercise. And anyway, there's only so much time you can spend in the workshop. The poor old special was competing with my new life of college, girlfriends and, most especially, as soon as I reached my seventeenth birthday, motorbikes.

For the first term at college I had cycled the three miles to the bus station in Stratford and then taken the bus to Leamington. Many of the guys on the course (about 15 of us in total, no girls) had Yamaha FS1E or Puch mopeds, while one of the guys, Andy, being slightly older, had a Norton Commando, making him supercool. Bikes were the main topic of interest between lessons and at lunch, and I immediately felt drawn. Luckily for me, it turned out my dad also had a passion for bikes, having ridden as a despatch rider in the army. Such was his enthusiasm, he offered to buy me a brand-new bike for Christmas/birthday (I guess that combo can come in handy sometimes), which left me very happy but somewhat dumbfounded at the time after the kart experience. Initially I fancied a Ducati 250 but then, reading *Bike* magazine, read a road test on a relatively new bike, a Moto Morini 350 Sport. My dad agreed and hence at exactly 17 I became the proud owner of one. Just one small problem: the law only allowed learners to ride bikes under 250cc. So for £25 I acquired a very tired 1958 BSA C15 to learn to ride and pass my test on, while my dad kindly took it upon himself to do around a thousand miles on the Morini to 'run it in'.

The summer of 1976 was a wonderful long hot summer, perfect for my newfound love of riding motorbikes, despite the melted tar on the road that caught out so many of my mates. I became an enthusiastic member of the local bike club, Shakespeare's Bikers, which met at The Cross Keys every Wednesday at seven, and enjoyed many weekend outings. Suddenly I had a new passion, a group of friends from all walks of life (through college and the bike club), and – thanks to this new network – an introduction to a social life that included girls. Added to these was the advent of punk, a welcome backlash from the slushy music of Donny Osmond *et al.* House parties featuring this new anarchic music allowed me to indulge in the only form of dancing I'm any good at – pogoing.

I loved my bike. There was a real camaraderie among us bikers, a feeling of freedom that a car simply does not bring to the same extent. There was even a brief period in which I thought my future should be as a bike designer, but in my heart of hearts I knew this was the flush of a new romance; I should stay true to my equally unlikely ambition of becoming a racing car designer.

My maternal grandmother, Kath, lived on gin and Martini – a habit inherited by my mother – and I was very fond of her, which made it doubly upsetting when gangrene took her leg, after which she seemingly lost the will to live and passed away in a nursing home a few months later, in the summer of 1977.

No, I was told by my parents, you can't spend your grandmother's inheritance on another motorbike. You should put it in the building society. And anyway, what's wrong with the Moto Morino?

But I'd been close to Kath, so I insisted it's what she would have wanted. Manipulative, I know. But who among us is above a bit of strategic emotional blackmail at times? It worked and I got what 'we' both wanted: a Ducati 900SS (registration number CNP 617S), which was a very smart bike for an 18-year-old.

I loved British-made cars, mainly Lotus, but when it came to bikes, I lived *la dolce vita*. During my OND course we visited the Triumph and Norton factories, and what struck us was their arrogant belief that they were still the best in the world. They were determined to carry on doing what they were doing, making the same old Commandos and Tridents, seemingly oblivious to the fact that the Italians were making more attractive and better-quality bikes, while the Japanese were also manufacturing better-quality bikes at far lower prices.

The Triumph factory in particular was a dirty, union-run relic of a bygone age. One detail that stayed with me was a room in which the distinctive Triumph pinstripe was applied to the petrol tank. A pot of gold paint sat in one corner of the room. On a table in the centre was a petrol tank, and somewhere between the two was a Triumph worker, an old boy clad in grey overalls. The paintbrush in his hand shook as he approached the tin, dipped and slowly returned to the petrol tank, splattering gold paint on the floor as he came.

We watched, agape, convinced we were about to witness an act of vandalism, but at the very last moment his hand steadied and with a flick of the wrist and a smooth flourish he applied a perfect gold pinstripe to the tank.

A second, younger man would lift the tank away and replace it with a new one as the old boy shambled back to the paint pot and the whole process began again. It was incredibly inefficient. You dread to think what the white-coated engineers of Suzuki and Kawasaki would have made of it. But it was also strikingly beautiful. No doubt there's a metaphor in there somewhere.

Like many of their generation, my mum and dad were vehemently opposed to Japanese-made products. 'Jap crap', my dad called them. So it was inevitable that I'd be drawn towards Italian bikes. The trouble was I was *too* drawn towards them (and girls, music and booze), and I almost flunked my end-of-first-year exams. Ian Reed had told me that in order to make it in motorsport I'd need a degree, and there was no degree without my OND. After that, and for the first time in my life, I truly applied myself academically, as well as setting about finding a university.

One thing I learnt from almost flunking those exams was that distraction is the enemy of performance: I thought I was revising in the lead-up but in fact I was listening to music while reading notes. I learnt the words to ELO songs, not my material.

Of the unis I considered, Southampton was the one calling out to me. I knew from reading *Autosport* that the racing teams Brabham and March used the wind tunnel in Southampton to develop their cars, and I figured that being a Southampton student might give me a chance to ingratiate myself with them.

The course itself was Aeronautics and Astronautics, and I didn't – and still don't, really – have an interest in aircraft. By rights I should have been aiming for a mechanical engineering degree, and if I'd wanted to end up in the automotive industry working on production-line cars then that's what I'd have done.

But I didn't want a career in the automotive industry. I wanted a career in racing. My thinking was that an Aeronautics course would teach me aerodynamics and about the design of lightweight structures, about materials and control theory. I decided that because of that parallel technology with aircraft, and because of the lure of the wind tunnel, I'd aim for Southampton.

I worked hard to get into Southampton and I succeeded. But the problem was that even though I'd apparently got the highest OND mark in the country, the maths content of the course was the same maths I'd learnt at advanced Maths O-level. At Southampton, all the lecturers assumed that students were educated to A-level standard.

With engineering, and particularly aeronautical engineering, being so maths orientated, I was woefully out of my depth and struggling to keep up with the lecturers, who would simply skip through the derivations of equations, assuming we all knew what they considered to be the basics.

At weekends I studied. Not socialising, not tinkering with 'the special', not even gallivanting around on my motorbike, just trying to get myself up to snuff with my maths. But however hard I worked, I always seemed to be two steps behind everybody else. To make matters worse, I shared Halls with a bunch of 'ologist students who did nothing but party – not exactly the perfect environment for the kind of crash-course study I needed. By Christmas I was seriously thinking of throwing in the towel.

Finally, in desperation, I did two things: first, I returned to see Ian Reed, who by now was at March, a production racing car company making Formula One and Formula Two cars, a sizeable outfit by the standards of the day.

'Look,' said Ian, 'if you want a job as a draughtsman then it's yours, but you'll only ever be a draughtsman. If you want to be a proper design engineer, you need to get your degree. What I suggest you do is get your head down and keep battling.'

Second, my tutor, the late Ken Burgin, who was always very supportive, noted that I was struggling and helped me with extra tutorials. In addition, he instilled in me the need to keep going. That was the mantra. Ken and Ian both said it: get your head down, Adrian; keep battling.

So I did. And although I never really caught up with the maths – to this day, it's my Achilles' heel – I did manage to overcome the problem by memorising mathematical derivations parrot fashion. Put simply, I never understood them, but I knew how to fake them. It hasn't held me back in the long term and, in a perverse way, it instilled in me a determination that when the going gets tough you need to get your head down and find a way through it. I also formed the ability to really and truly concentrate when studying, which has certainly helped me in my career, though I have to admit, not socially. Particularly at race weekends I tend to suffer from tunnel vision, not seeing left or right, only what is right in front of me.

The second year at Southampton was a bit more interesting, geared as it was towards the more practical side of things, which was my strength. The lectures were no longer all about background theory; we started to learn about applied engineering as well as gearing up for what would prove to be my favourite element of the course: the final-year project.

Fate, luck and chance were also playing their part. I started at Southampton in 1977 and graduated in 1980. Those three years just happened to be a time of seismic change in Formula One.

Which is where it starts to get really interesting.

CHAPTER 6

To make a racing car accelerate and achieve a higher top speed you need more power, less weight and less aerodynamic drag. And if that sounds like a simple set of goals, it probably would be, if not for the troublesome mechanics of cornering.

This is where downforce comes in. Downforce is what we call the pressure that pushes the car downwards, effectively suckering it to the track. And because the generation of downforce is something that happens as a result of the aerodynamic shaping of the car, you can increase grip without it involving a significant increase in weight. In other words, you get to have your cake and eat it: more grip without a loss of acceleration.

Thus, the aim of the chassis designer is to:

One: ensure that the tyres are presented to the ground in an even and consistent manner through the braking, cornering and acceleration phases.

Two: ensure the car is as light as possible.

Three: ensure that the car generates as little drag as possible.

> Four: ensure that the car is generating as much downforce as possible in a balanced manner throughout the phases of the corner.

Downforce was a still relatively poorly researched area in motorsport in 1977. Having sat out the 1940s and 1950s altogether, it then played a small part in the 1960s when teams began fitting spoilers to sports cars, typically at Le Mans where the inherent lift of the cars' body shapes had led to drivers complaining of instability on the long, fast straights and kinks of that circuit. With the introduction of a very large rear wing by Jim Hall of Chaparral in 1967, cars started generating significant downforce for the first time, having literally looked to the skies for inspiration – to aircraft.

An aeroplane lifts because the contours of its wing cause air to flow at different speeds across the two sides, low pressure on the topside, high on the other, with the wing moving in the direction of the low pressure and giving us what we call 'positive lift' as a result.

The wing on a racing car works the same way, but in reverse: 'negative lift', or 'downforce', pressing the car into the ground and hence allowing the tyres to generate more grip.

With this blindingly simple solution established, wings on racing cars became a common feature of the 1970s, with teams continually seeking to create more downforce, but with little further progress, until 1977.

To explain what happened in 1977, please first allow me to offer a brief lesson in aerodynamics. The pressure difference across the surface of the wing creates a distortion of the flow field as it passes through the air, known as circulation. In the case of a racing car, this means that air behind the car is thrown upwards, creating a rooster tail of air behind the car that can clearly be seen when Formula One cars run in the wet. However, the air on the high-pressure side of the wing is also able to leak around the tips of the wing, reducing the low pressure on the suction side and hence reducing the wing's efficiency. This tip leakage, when combined with the forward motion of the vehicle, sets up a spiral, tornado-like structure known as the tip vortex. These tip vortices can be seen spilling from the rear wing when a Formula One car runs on a damp day or indeed on the wings of aircraft as they come in to land in the same conditions.

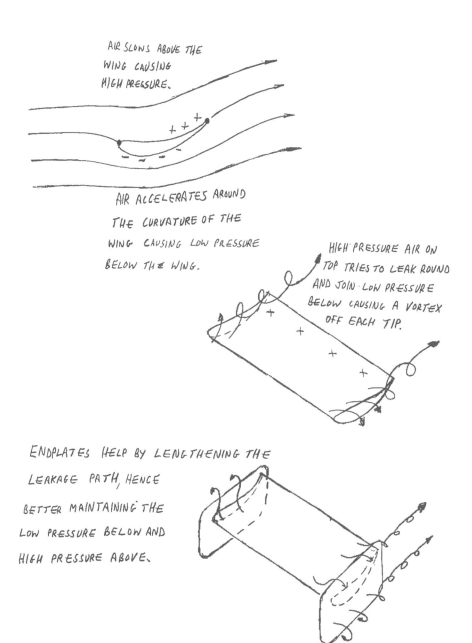

Figure 2: How a wing works and how it forms a vortex at its tips.

Aircraft (and birds) reduce this loss of efficiency of their wings by increasing span, exemplified by sailplanes, which have very long slender wings. However, in 1968, following a spate of accidents in Formula One caused by the long span, high wings used during the period collapsing, regulations were introduced to restrict their span. Teams responded by fitting plates to the ends of their chopped-down wings, which helped to create a more tortuous leak path between the upper and lower surfaces of the wing, but overall efficiency was reduced. This, simplistically, remained state-of-the-art technology in Formula One from 1968 to 1977.

But nature, as is so often the case, had already worked out an efficient solution to the problem of how to make a wing of a given span much more efficient. If you watch a heavy river bird such as a swan, it will often fly just

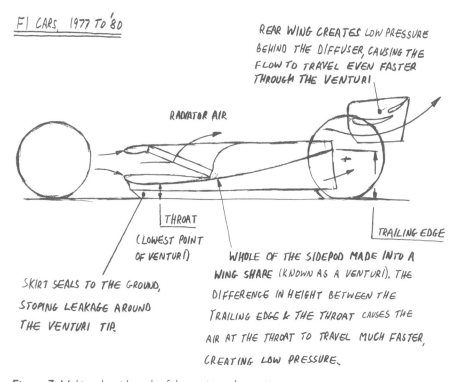

F1 CARS, 1977 TO '80

REAR WING CREATES LOW PRESSURE BEHIND THE DIFFUSER, CAUSING THE FLOW TO TRAVEL EVEN FASTER THROUGH THE VENTURI

RADIATOR AIR

THROAT
(LOWEST POINT OF VENTURI)

TRAILING EDGE

WHOLE OF THE SIDEPOD MADE INTO A WING SHAPE (KNOWN AS A VENTURI). THE DIFFERENCE IN HEIGHT BETWEEN THE TRAILING EDGE & THE THROAT CAUSES THE AIR AT THE THROAT TO TRAVEL MUCH FASTER, CREATING LOW PRESSURE.

SKIRT SEALS TO THE GROUND, STOPING LEAKAGE AROUND THE VENTURI TIP.

Figure 3: Making the sidepods of the car into a huge wing.

above the water, with the tips of its wings on the edge of dipping in. In doing so, it harnesses two powerful effects:

(1) If its wing tips just touch the water's surface, the leak path is sealed, the low pressure on the suction surface is not compromised and the wing hence becomes much more efficient.
(2) The downwash of air behind the wing (created by circulation) reacts against the river's surface, creating a higher pressure underneath the wing – a phenomenon known as 'ground effect'.

Turn this upside down, so that you have a downforce-generating wing with its endplate rubbing on the ground, and suddenly you have a massively effective solution. This is exactly what Lotus did in 1977, using much of the underside of the car to create an enormous wing, sealed to the ground at its tips by 'sliding skirts'.

It was an innovation that today we'd call a 'disruptive technology', a game-changer that pushed aerodynamics firmly to the forefront of racing car design.

Which is where I come in, because while all this was happening in the late 1970s, I was at university studying aerodynamics and hoping for a career in Formula One – a sport that had suddenly recognised the importance of aerodynamics.

You have to remember that at this time, racing teams were quite small – a staff of around 30 compared to the 800 or so we have at Red Bull today – and designers were mainly mechanical engineers; very few had studied aeronautics. They were trying to teach themselves, and, as such, development was somewhat haphazard.

It's not a criticism. Far from it. If I could go back to design at any point in the sport's history, it would be then, because if you look at the cars on the grid from the early to late 1970s, they all looked very different to each other. The rulebook then was small; they had a huge amount of freedom, but relatively little understanding of the end product, purely because they didn't have the research tools that we benefit from today; they were only just waking up to the possibilities of wind tunnels and the kind of simulation tools we now use routinely.

But they were pioneers. They'd be trying new suspension geometries, 'anti-dive', 'anti-lift' or adaptable suspension that ended up flexing like bits of chocolate. Great ideas that somebody came up with in the shower or standing at their drawing board staring off into space. All of them released to great fanfare and acclaim. Most of them abandoned almost immediately. Giddy times.

Of all these early pioneers, the most buccaneering was Colin Chapman, founder and boss at Lotus and the closest thing I have to a design hero.

Chapman was one of the few who did in fact have aeronautical training, which he used to great effect. He had a tendency, though, to start afresh rather than build on past success, so having won the championship with a car powered by a Cosworth DFV engine in 1968 – the first car to feature that engine – Colin then decided to invest heavily in four-wheel drive, a lame duck of an idea that resulted in cars that were way too heavy to be competitive.

Another blind alley in the form of an inefficient gas turbine car meant that by 1970 Lotus were still racing the same car that had won the 1968 championship and were struggling to catch up. The Lotus 72 of mid-1970 was a gem that held them high through to 1972, followed by a further series of blind alleys. It wasn't until the Lotus 78, the ground-effect car, that they became competitive again. And though they didn't win the championship that year, the following year's car, the Lotus 79, dominated 1978.

After that, however, Lotus returned to blind alleys. When Gordon Murray of Brabham introduced pullrod suspension to replace the old rocker system, and John Barnard at McLaren replied with a pushrod set-up – both of which helped cars cope with the huge loads generated by downforce – the Lotus answer was to develop a chassis with a separate aerodynamic shell linked directly to the wheels, so it transmitted all its downforce straight to the wheels, not through the suspension. It didn't really work and, to add insult to injury, it was banned.

Personally, I would have been intrigued to meet Chapman. He was a fascinating character, a real innovator. It was he who espoused the idea that

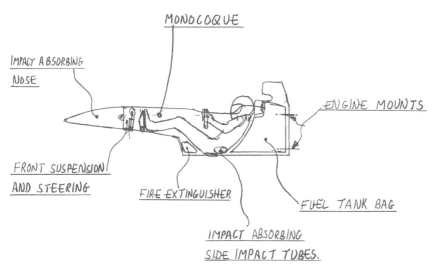

Figure 4: The monocoque with its many components.

high power was less important than good handling. He had a talent for applying advances made in disciplines other than F1. So, for example, he's often credited as being the first to introduce monocoque construction, where instead of constructing a chassis from steel tubes, you make it out of sheets of aluminium. It was a revolution in Formula One, but the Jaguar D-type of 1954 was the car that had really introduced this construction technique to motor racing. Same with bolting the engine straight to the chassis instead of to a sub-frame.

Sadly, the ground-effect car was Chapman's last hurrah. Not long afterwards, he teamed up with John DeLorean to design the DeLorean, the *Back to the Future* car, after which there were allegations of murky dealings, which were followed soon afterwards by an upcoming court case and an untimely fatal heart attack in 1982, when Chapman was aged just 54.

Mario Andretti, the driver of the ground-effect car during that championship-winning season, always maintained that Chapman had faked his own death and fled to Brazil in order to escape trial, a claim that would be absurd if it were anybody else but Chapman.

Meanwhile, back at Southampton University, I noticed that even though all the Formula One teams had cottoned on to the benefits of ground effect (marking the end of the era of crazy ideas in the shower and the beginning of a time when the design of cars began to converge into a generic shape), sports cars were lagging behind.

So for my final-year project I chose to study 'ground-effect aero-dynamics as applied to a sports car'.

I set to work. I made a wing out of aluminium. This would go on the underside of my car, which was to be a road-going sports model. I tested it on its own using pressure taps to develop the shape in a small wind tunnel until I was happy with it. I designed a one-quarter-scale model of the car, which incorporated the underside wing shape, made it, and then took that into the main 7ft × 5ft tunnel.

It's fair to say, I've spent a good part of my life in wind tunnels, under-standably so when you consider the huge benefit they offer to someone who designs performance cars for a living. A wind tunnel allows you to measure how much downforce and drag you're generating, and how that downforce is distributed; how much is on the front axle, how much is on the rear. You

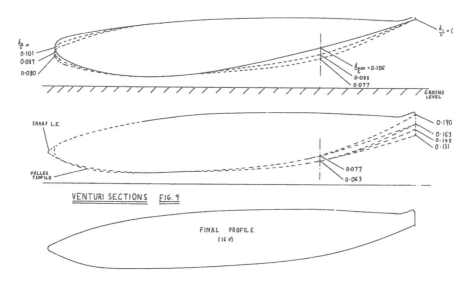

Figure 5: Technical drawing from my university project, illustrating 2D sections of the underside wing shape (venturi).

can also measure side, yaw and roll forces. With various caveats, you can measure the full aerodynamic performance of a car without actually having to build the car itself.

Truth be told, I put more work into my project than I should have done for what, after all, counted for just 25 per cent of the final degree. But I loved doing it. It felt like going back to my roots, like being back at home during the summer holidays, only now I had a wind tunnel in which to test my sketches and the models I built from them. It was my school-summer-holiday upbringing applied at university.

The finished article certainly created a lot of downforce. What I'd done was to make use of the Lotus innovation by featuring a skirt that sealed to the ground and stopped the leakage of air, coupled to a full-width under-wing, but at the same time I had proposed a mechanical package that would allow this aerodynamic shape. True, as a road car it wouldn't have been terribly practical due to the fact that in order to deal with the downforce the car's suspension would have had to be very stiff and therefore very uncomfortable. So I proposed a variable geometry spring system linked to car speed – what would later become known as active suspension. It was, as far as I know, the first properly researched study of ground-effect aerodynamics applied to a sports car.

More importantly, as well as leaving me with a good understanding of ground-effect aerodynamics, it gave me something I could show to prospective employers. And it contributed to my achieving a first-class honours degree, the very idea of which would have caused me to utter a four-letter expletive had it been suggested at Christmas of my first year.

CHAPTER 7

While at university I'd written to Gordon Murray, chief designer at Brabham, telling him how highly I thought of him, as well as outlining an idea I'd had for a suspension system that kept the camber of the wheels upright in cornering.

I loved Brabham. I'd got to know a few of their guys from using the Southampton wind tunnel, and I thought the idea was a good one. Moreover, since Brabham was the only team apart from Ferrari to use a transverse gearbox, which was more suitable for my suspension system idea than a conventional longitudinal gearbox, they were the perfect recipients for it.

With hindsight, the concept wasn't so great. It would have been difficult to get it stiff enough without compromising the structure of the chassis. Gordon, who all these years later still remembers me writing to him, replied in characteristically polite terms, letting me down gently but offering me encouragement for the future. Along with March, where Ian Reed had ended up, Brabham had gone to the top of my hit list when it came to looking for a job post-graduation.

But when I enquired, neither of them had an opening. Nor did any of the other dozen or so teams in both Formula One and Two that I subsequently wrote to – a large and costly carpet-bombing operation that involved sending photocopied extracts from my university project in order to convince them of my brilliance.

Roughly half simply ignored me. Most of the rest replied with the 'Catch 22' answer that they wanted someone with experience. Tyrell Racing offered me an interview, and subsequently a job subject to sponsorship. But the sponsorship didn't come through so the job didn't either, although they were impressed with the extract.

As were Tiga, a Formula Two team out of Caversham near Reading. Theirs was a nice, tidy workshop run by a couple of Aussies, Tim Schenken and Howden Ganley. During my interview with Schenken, Ganley returned from a trip to Reading library laden down with books, apparently hoping to understand how to design and build his own wind tunnel. I admired his can-do spirit, but building a wind tunnel after a visit to Reading library felt somewhat optimistic.

Still, they were a likeable pair, and they too offered me a job subject to sponsorship. Which never arrived, meaning neither did the job.

In desperation I went for an interview at British Leyland, an all-day thing where I joined a bunch of other applicants. The worker in charge of my group told us he'd spent the previous year performing stress-analysis tests on the tailgate of a Morris Ital estate car, and I thought to myself, *I don't think I can do that – spend a whole year performing stress-analysis tests on a tailgate.*

We went for lunch and, gazing out of the canteen windows, we could see a car shrouded in what looked like black bin liners doing circuits of a test track. There was great excitement among the other candidates. Could it be . . .? Was this the exciting new British Leyland car? The Metro. That confirmed my worry: I definitely cannot do this job and remain sane!

Way more encouraging was a job offer from Lotus, except that, typical of my luck at the time, it wasn't Lotus the racing team but Lotus road cars. And while I had personal history with Lotus road cars, and there was always a chance I might be able to attract attention from the team, their big hit of the time was the Lotus Esprit, which I thought was an ugly, awful thing enjoying unwarranted popularity thanks to its appearance in *The Spy Who Loved Me.*

Arriving for an interview I was struck by the fact that the factory was an utter pigsty. As well as the Esprit, bits of which I saw were made of thick, poorly contoured fibreglass, they were deep into research and design for the DeLorean, which had all the hallmarks of the design monstrosity it would later prove to be.

Still, it was a job offer, the best I had, and I was about to accept – on the verge of doing so, in fact – when the phone rang.

At the other end was Harvey Postlethwaite, technical director at Fittipaldi Automotive and already on the road to becoming a design legend, with a later stint at Ferrari sealing the deal in that regard.

Harvey liked the project sample I'd sent. Would I come for an interview?

A day or so later I rode into the Fittipaldi HQ at Reading, which turned out to be a small factory unit, a couple of Portacabin offices and a herring-bone car park. Sitting in reception, still in my biking leathers, I was greeted by Harvey, hair a mess, big grin on his face.

'You're a biker,' he said, delighted by the sight of my leathers. 'What have you got?'

'Ducati 900SS,' I told him.

'Fantastic,' he said, 'mine's a Moto Guzzi Le Mans.'

This was a time when one of the hot points of discussion in the bike magazines was about which was the superior Italian bike, Moto Guzzi or Ducati. Harvey was eager for first-hand experience and asked if he could take my Ducati out for a spin.

'Sure,' I said, and stood in the car park for what felt like an age as he took my bike for a run God knows where, returning and taking off his helmet to reveal even messier hair and an even bigger grin.

'Right,' he said, 'when can you start?'

As interviews go, it beat sitting in the British Leyland canteen.

HOW TO BUILD A
MARCH 83G

CHAPTER 8

I began at Fittipaldi with the title of 'junior aerodynamicist', but because they didn't have any other aerodynamicists, I was senior aerodynamicist as well.

It was that sort of place, teeming with early 1980s chaos and run on a diet of cigarettes, coffee and beige polyester. A team of around 35 was split between the factory and Portacabin offices, but although it was a respectable size for the time – a bit smaller than Lotus but not by much – its problem was that there were more chiefs than Indians thanks to the fact that it was comprised of two teams that had merged: the original Fittipaldi Automotive, founded by driver-brothers Wilson and Emerson, and Wolf Racing, whose main driver was Keke Rosberg (father of Nico).

Parachuted into the middle of the post-merger manoeuvring, I managed to steer clear of the various office politics, stepped-on toes and egos that had been bruised by the fusion. Being junior meant I could move easily between the Portacabins in the gravel car park and the factory, where on Fridays, after the traditional lunchtime in the pub, workers sat down to an afternoon of hard-core pornography. I didn't care. I was just happy to be in Formula One at last.

One day, the atmosphere in the Portacabins was more than usually fevered thanks to the expected arrival of Emerson.

Never being one to idolise drivers, my own fires were under control, but I was intrigued because I hadn't yet crossed paths with the great man, his visits to base camp being somewhat infrequent.

Then, as now, my office overlooked the car park, and as the morning wore on I noticed that somebody had left a chassis stand in Emerson's parking space. As I say, he hardly ever came in, so whoever put it there probably thought it was a safe place. Except on this particular occasion it wasn't, because Emerson came haring into the car park, typical racing driver, going way too fast and coming in blind, sideways into his parking spot in a spray of gravel . . . slap-bang into the chassis stand.

It would have been a pretty impressive bit of driving if not for the crash at the end of it. The chassis stand went flying through the hedge, having stoved in the front of Emerson's Rover – one of those awful wedge-shaped Rovers, only now it had steam rising from where the chassis stand had burst the radiator.

As I stood watching Emerson emerge, gesticulating wildly and swearing loudly in Portuguese, and saw everybody run from the offices to witness the commotion, I remember thinking that they were all so human. Even Emerson, this hugely respected driver, was just as fallible as the rest of us.

CHAPTER 9

In 1981, the skirts that Lotus had introduced for their ground-effect car were lifted. New FIA regulations insisted they be at least 6cm off the ground, and could no longer slide up and down, which of course would hugely reduce their effectiveness since they'd no longer be sealed to the track.

In response, teams fitted rubber skirts to the cars, but they didn't work nearly as well because they flexed in a poorly controlled way and wore out – which is something that rubber does when it slides along the ground.

Those 1981 cars were really 1980 cars with these much less effective skirts. It was my first taste of a major regulation change, and I felt the aero needed to be fundamentally redesigned to re-optimise to this new limitation.

My idea was simple: to raise the underwing and make it longer, so that the leakage under the rubber skirts would be, as a percentage of the overall flow under the car, smaller. It was a sound principle, but to accommodate it meant significantly redesigning the rear suspension.

Straightaway, I was into something I find fascinating: the integration of mechanical and aerodynamic design (something I had tried to bear in mind with my project at Southampton).

We started to develop it through 1981 with the intention of it being the car for 1982. Once a month we'd load a Vauxhall Chevette van with the model and any other tools we needed, and then Pip, our fabricator, and I would drive to the wind tunnel at Imperial College in Kensington.

They were early morning starts, the whole operation conducted in a hurry. On one particularly icy morning I span the Chevette across the slip road onto the M4, clouting the barrier on the outside. Together, we pulled the wheel arch back out to stop it rubbing on the wheel, clambered shivering back inside and kept on going.

Once at the tunnel, we'd do a run on the model, measure how much downforce and drag it produced, and then make alterations to it – for example, by changing the front wing altogether, varying the angle of the existing wing, or doing the same to the sidepods or the diffuser.

Nowadays, there's almost no adlibbing on the model; everything on it is a pre-manufactured part and test schedules are followed because that's the best way to be efficient. Back then, though, we'd come armed with all sorts of bits and pieces, with Pip and the model-maker on hand to make alterations, and me recording the results and making calls on what to do next. We had limited resources and there was a lot of improvisation, but if we had an interesting direction we'd make a part on the spot, stick it on and try it.

Our numbers were good, a big improvement on the 1981 car. Bearing in mind we had no idea what other teams were getting from their own cars – you rarely do, of course – we were quietly confident that we had a decent design on our hands. Joining Williams years later, I compared notes with Patrick Head, and based on what he told me about the 1982 Williams car, ours would have been very competitive.

But it's by no means an easy feat to translate wind tunnel results to the finished article. You need sufficient resources for engineering, detailed design and manufacturing, and in that respect Williams always had a head start. But on paper at least, our Fittipaldi was championship material. We could have been a contender.

The ifs and buts of motor racing. In the event, the rug was pulled . . .

I'd started at Fittipaldi in August 1980, but by Christmas 1981 it became apparent that there was something rotten in the state of Reading. When I first began, the team was sponsored by Skol beer, and there was, if you will excuse the pun, a fair bit of money swilling about for development and a can-do atmosphere. At the end of that year Skol pulled out, to be replaced by Avis for 1981, meaning much less finance available.

Work continued on the 1982 car. We'd begun designing a rear suspension to complement the aerodynamics – to the point that drawings were ready to go off for manufacturing the components – when suddenly the whole thing was stopped because there was no money left to build the car. We were told we would have to use the 1981 car in 1982.

Staff began leaving. Harvey joined Ferrari. One of the team managers, Peter Warr, left for Lotus and the other, Peter Mackintosh, joined March. That positive, can-do attitude evaporated.

It was with a heavy heart that I found myself looking for something new.

CHAPTER 10

In those days, every motor racing team effectively had three engineering disciplines: the design and aerodynamics offices, and race engineering, though the race engineers would be doubling up with working in the design office during the week.

Since then, the industry has mushroomed, and nobody crosses from one department to another. You'll have, let's say, 90 people in aerodynamics, another 70 in the design office, and perhaps 30 in race engineering and simulation, the latter being a relatively new area.

Me, I'm known chiefly as an aerodynamicist, but that's a product of the fact that aerodynamics is the biggest single performance differentiator. Therefore, I tend to spend most of my time looking at aerodynamics, with the mechanical layout a close second, in order to make sure the two complement one another in a package. In fact, my sole interest lies in improving the ability of the car to score points, and what helps me do that is my experience across the disciplines.

Which brings me back to early 1982, when of the three key areas – aerodynamics, mechanical design and race engineering – I only had experience of the first. With Fittipaldi I had been loosely involved in the design of the rear suspension for the axed 1982 car, but not in the detail. I'd been to the track a grand total of once, and that was for a cold test at Donington where I just stood and watched the car do a few shakedown laps. I'd never even worn a set of headphones.

At its simplest level, what a race engineer does is work with the driver to get as much performance from the car as he can. It incorporates basics like issuing instructions to the mechanics on how much fuel to put in and which set of tyres to fit for each outing, as well as ensuring that the set-up is correct depending on the conditions: the weather, of course, but also the track.

The tools the race engineer has at his disposal are what we call the set-up parameters: that's the front and rear spring rates, the roll bar stiffness, the damper settings, the wing settings, the ride-heights, the camber, caster and toe-in or toe-out of the wheels, gear ratios, etc. It's all about trying to find the right set-up for the car, the driver – each driver has his own race engineer – and the circuit.

What attracted me to race engineering, besides the chance to learn something new, was the opportunity to combine that with being a designer and an aerodynamicist. I could influence the development of a car based on first-hand knowledge of its performance at the track.

So say, for example, the driver was complaining of a handling problem. In the first instance I could talk to him in a race-engineering capacity and perhaps reduce the problem through the set-up of the car. But with an engineer's eyes I could also hope to understand whether that problem was inherent to the mechanical design or the aerodynamic characteristics of the car. My understanding of the car would be complete.

So when Peter Mackintosh, having left Fittipaldi to take charge of the March Formula Two team, offered me a job, and that job was the chance to work as a race engineer at the weekends, then in the drawing office during the week as a draughtsman, I was sorely tempted, and probably would have signed immediately if not for the fact that Peter Warr offered me a post at Lotus as an aerodynamicist.

Now I had some real thinking to do. Should I stay in Formula One and go to Lotus, 'my' team? Or should I take the opportunity to learn the two missing disciplines in my CV at March, albeit with a drop to the lower categories?

In truth there wasn't a huge amount of deciding to be done. You might say I'm lacking in sentimentality, but I prefer to think of it as taking a clear-eyed view of the future. I really wanted to add that race-engineering-and-design-draughtsman string to my bow. I chose March.

I began work. Feeling awfully wet behind the ears, and only too aware that I'd be race engineering drivers a few years older than I was, I grew a beard. Peter Mackintosh, the team manager, with no engineering back-ground but lots of experience, was race engineering Corrado Fabi, while Ralph Bellamy, the Aussie veteran engineer who designed the Formula Two car, engineered Johnny Cecotto. I was given the third car, driven by Christian Danner.

My first race of the Formula Two season was at Silverstone, on 21 March 1982. And it was straight in at the deep end, having joined too late to attend any of the pre-season tests. It was raining, so I saw to it that the wet tyres were on and correctly pressured, and I made sure that there was fuel in the car. Simple stuff, I know, but I wanted to at least get through the weekend having got the basics right.

Christian took the lead. He was good in the wet, and he was leading the race with two laps to go when, to our horror, he drew to a stop. His car had run out of fuel.

I got the blame. Christian ranted that I didn't know what I was doing (partly true), and that I was useless (objection, your honour), and with emotions running high, before he was in possession of all the facts, Christian fired me as his race engineer.

I would later be absolved – it turned out there was a leak – but the damage was done; our relationship was terminal after that first weekend and it appeared my race engineering was, at the very least, on temporary hold. However, to my everlasting gratitude, and for reasons that I have never understood, Johnny suggested we do a swap, with Ralph engineering Christian, and me learning the ropes with Johnny.

Johnny was a cheerful, curly-haired Venezuelan; a real character. He was already a world champion in motorcycle racing, but after some distressing accidents had moved into racing cars. His plan was to prove himself in Formula Two with the aim of progressing into Formula One. That being the case, taking on an inexperienced race engineer was something of a gamble.

But that's the kind of chap he was; on one occasion he'd noticed that the silencers on my Ducati were rusty and he used his contacts in Ducati to get me a new set. He just had that in him, and I owe him a great deal for giving me a second chance.

What's more, he was a great driver, and as the season wore on he won at Thruxton and remained competitive for other races. Meanwhile I concentrated on finding my feet, as well as developing an understanding of Johnny and gradually changing the set-up of the car to suit his driving style.

In its simplified form, the essence of motor racing is to link together as quickly as possible the sequence of corners that form all racing tracks. However, all drivers have subtly different styles and all racing cars have different inherent characteristics; changing the set-up is a process that involves customising the car to the individual driver and finding the best relationship between the car and the style of the driver. This involves tweaking the 'set-up parameters' mentioned earlier.

As far as springs went, we worked to a system evolved by Ralph: 1600lbs/in on the front and 1500lbs/in on the rear, which was a fairly stiff set-up that we ran on all three cars.

Until, that was, we got to the seventh race, at Pau in the South of France, a street track. Johnny and I walked the track. 'Christ,' I said, 'this is a bumpy track. I think we need to go soft on the springs; get a bit more compliance in the suspension. What do you think: fit the softer springs now, or wait until after the first session?'

Johnny had faith in me. 'Straightaway,' he said.

So I went and had a rummage in the truck, found some soft springs and fitted them, taking it down 200lbs/in each end.

The benefit of doing this, of course, is that the car will absorb the bumps more effectively. With stiff springs on a bumpy track, the car tends to leap from bump to bump, meaning the load on the tyres at the contact patch changes too much, causing the car to continually grip and slide between crest and hollow. If you've ever driven an overly stiff road car, you'll know what I mean. You go over a pothole, get shaken about, the car skitters. However, the extra compliance in the softer springs means that the car will change its attitude more, pitching under braking, rolling more in the corners and sinking more as the downforce comes on with speed. This extra movement of the car upsets the aerodynamics with the downforce, and particularly the distribution of downforce between the front and rear axles, changing more than with a stiffly sprung car. It is all about finding the best compromise for a given car at a given circuit.

Johnny practised with the new springs, felt the suspension was still too stiff and so, with Ralph and Peter oblivious to what I was doing, I went and had a second rummage, found even softer springs and fitted those. And then, just in case Ralph and Peter cottoned on and decided to swap springs on their own cars, I hid the remaining soft ones.

With hindsight, that was a very naughty thing to do. Led astray by the lure of competition, I forgot I was employed by the team, not the driver. But Johnny went on to take pole and win the race, something I will guiltily admit was a hugely satisfying result, given the reflected glow for yours truly, and one that perhaps went some way to repaying Johnny's trust in adopting me.

Towards the end of the year we had three consecutive races in Italy; in Mugello, northern Italy, then Enna in Sicily and finally back up to Misano, which is on the Adriatic Coast. Flying wasn't so common in those days; we, the mechanics and I, just drove from race to race, and for three weeks we enjoyed a fabulous tour of Italy. Prior to that I'd never travelled further than Scotland; now here I was taking in the Mediterranean sights. We stayed in Rome one night; we took the ferry across to Sicily. It was fabulous.

The Enna race was stinking hot. We all ate watermelon – and all went down with the squits. The theory was that it had been grown in sewage. All I knew was that the whole team was in an awful state for race day, particularly those of us who were working on Johnny's car – to the point that we managed to get him started and then ran off to sit on the loo for the whole race. If he'd had a problem, he would have had to sort it out himself, because there was nobody in the pits any more!

But apart from that, it was a fabulous season. What's more, I was learning on the job and proving myself as a race engineer, as the battle between Johnny and his teammate, Corrado, was hard-fought and went right to the wire. And though Corrado won, Johnny's second place in the championship earned him a spot in Formula One for the following season.

With all that going on, I was also having fun at the drawing board during the week.

CHAPTER 11

My weekday job was on the design side. First, I designed a dry sump for a Chevrolet engine to go in the back of the March sports car, after which I was asked to strengthen the gearbox, which meant spending a week with Hewland in Maidenhead, who made the gearboxes.

Next I was told to draw the bodywork for the 1983 March Can-Am series car, a new design based on an old March Formula One chassis, with a Chevrolet engine in the back and bodywork designed by Max Sardou.

Now, Max Sardou was a 'name'. A French aerodynamicist of some repute, he'd been commissioned by March to come up with the bodywork shape. He was an eccentric character, with a pallid complexion and long black greasy hair. He always wore a trench coat, even in the middle of summer, and he drove a Citroen DS with the wing mirrors folded flat to reduce drag.

Sardou's shape for the Can-Am was big and bulbous and apparently designed to ram air into the diffuser. He claimed that the air would flow so fast under the diffuser that it would go sonic and that there would therefore be a sonic boom at the end of the straights! I took one look at it and knew it wouldn't work. You can't ram air until you're supersonic. At Southampton, one of our lab experiments had been on a ramjet, in which we learnt that they do not really work below about mach three.

I went to see Dave Reeves, the production manager at March, scratching my new beard as I outlined the reasons why I didn't think the design would work.

He looked at me as though I were mad. This was Max Sardou we were talking about. Along with Lotus, Sardou was one of the pioneers of ground effect and fresh from designing an eye-catching underbody for the Lola T600 the previous year.

And I was . . . well, who was I? Some kid who had worked for Fittipaldi.

So Reeves told me to button it and get on with the draughting, a job that involved taking Sardou's quarter-scale wind tunnel model shape and blowing it up to full size, as well as working out how to split the shape into separate pieces of bodywork that could be fitted onto the March Formula One chassis.

I must have had brain failure, because I got one of the dimensions wrong – 1in out, I was – but the car was so big that the pattern makers didn't even notice the mistake. What eventually emerged was something so large and ugly it was nicknamed HMS Budweiser (after the team's sponsor).

Still, as far as I was concerned it was good experience in how to design bodywork as components, as opposed to aerodynamic shapes. What's more, it kept me busy until the end of the year, by which time I was wondering, *What am I going to be given next?*

Rather than be stuck with another Sardou-style monster, I decided to be proactive and find something useful to do myself. The 82G, a sports car for which I had designed the sump as my first task at March, had competed at Le Mans that summer (June 1982) but not done well (DNF, 'did not finish'). I spent some time looking over it in the evenings and decided there was a lot wrong with it that could be improved, particularly on the aerodynamic side (it, too, was a Max Sardou design).

Mindful of Dave Reeves' dismissal of my opinion on the Can-Am car, I decided to be brave and go straight to the top with my ideas, so I approached Robin Herd, the incredibly brainy boss of March, one day in the factory. 'What are your plans for the sports car?' I asked him.

He frowned and crinkled his eyes. 'What do you have in mind?'

I said, 'I've had a bit of a look at it and, um, I don't know if you know, but I did my final-year project on ground-effect aerodynamics applied to a sports car, and based on my findings from that project, I think I could do something with it.'

He said, 'Okay, well, I'll tell you what. You have a go at it. But I haven't got any draughtsmen that can help you modify it and there's no budget for wind tunnel testing.'

That final caveat was a bit of a drag, no pun intended. It meant I'd have to reshape much of the car by eye. Which is what I did. I changed the rear wing, reshaped the nose and added an extension to the underwing at the front. In addition, I redrew the whole lower surface and diffuser – the ground-effect bit, in other words – before I set about taking weight out of it.

The nose supports were heavy, but that's because they were made from aluminium plates. So I redesigned them in a sandwich structure with aluminium honeycomb between very thin, 0.7mm-thick sheets of aluminium, to make it light but stiff. I lost another kilogram by allowing a little more pressure drop through the water pipes, enabling me to reduce the water-pipe diameter, and I redesigned the heavy, complicated steering column, yielding further savings. And finally I worked with the bodywork laminators to get the bodywork weight down.

In all, I managed to get about 40-odd kilos out of the car, a significant amount, enough to make it about one second faster, while, by redesigning the aerodynamics, I got a lot more downforce out of it. Not only that, but the fact that the downforce was generated centrally – thanks to the redesign of the underwing – meant it would be better balanced, so if the car pitched nose down under braking, or nose up under acceleration, the distribution between the front axle and the rear axle remained more constant. That underwing earned it the nickname 'lobster claw', thanks to its distinctive shape. But it did the job.

And that's what kept me busy throughout most of Christmas 1982 until, one viciously cold January morning in 1983, we took it for a shakedown test at Donington, with Tiff Needell (who later went on to present *Top Gear* and *Fifth Gear*) driving.

By now, time was of the essence. The car had been rechristened the 83G for the 1983 season and Robin had sold it to an American, Ken Murray, who as well as owning one of those awful Ferrari Testarossas that Magnum PI used to drive, fancied himself as a bit of a racing driver. Ken had hired three drivers: Randy Lanier, Terry Wolters and Marty Hinze, and entered the team in the 24 Hours of Daytona race, due to take place in early February, less than a month away.

We got to Donington, just me, Tiff and a couple of mechanics, and started running the car, but it was so cold that we couldn't get an accurate idea of its performance, compounded by the fact that the fan belt on the Chevy engine then broke.

One of the mechanics borrowed Tiff's car, an Austin Allegro, went and bought a fan belt, came back, and left his car keys in the back of the truck. We carried on, and at least got some valuable miles done. At the end of the day as we were packing up, and saying our goodbyes, I got in my car, a Morris Marina, tried to turn the key but it wouldn't turn. I gave it a bit more force. Snapped it. Turned out I'd picked up Tiff's Allegro key.

Double whammy. Neither of us could get home. Luckily, one of the mechanics had a dodgy mate who lived in Derby. He arrived, hotwired both cars, and two hours later we were on our way back down the M1.

But that was it for testing. The car was shipped off to Daytona, and as part of the deal that Robin had struck with Ken, I went too, beginning what was to be a very interesting period in the US.

CHAPTER 12

And so to Daytona, a gruelling 24-hour race, held at the International Speedway in Daytona Beach, Florida. The curtain-opener for the US motor racing season. A legendary meet.

Which on the one hand was great. But on the other, the car wasn't ready for such a test of endurance. A single shakedown test at Donington does not a finished car make. Not only that, but arriving in the US and linking up with the team, Motorsports Marketing, I soon learnt several slightly dismaying things, none of which gave me any confidence that we were even going to finish Daytona, let alone be competitive.

First, Randy Lanier was an excellent driver. Better, I'm afraid to say, than his co-drivers Terry Wolters, who wore thick Benny Hill glasses that gave him a somewhat comical effect, Marty Hinze, a resident of Daytona Beach whose permanently dilated pupils hinted at a misspent youth that might well have carried on into adulthood, and Ken Murray, who could barely change gear – a wealthy novice who had been allowed to enter himself in the most prestigious sports car race of all after Le Mans.

Second, Motorsports Marketing badly needed a team manager.

Thus my first task was to have a sit-down with Ken after his first practice drive in the car and persuade him that he'd have a far better, more enjoyable and less stressful time leaving the driving to others. Also, that I should be his team manager.

He agreed on both counts and thus, at the grand old age of 24, I was running the car as well as making tactical decisions for the team.

The American mechanics weren't great but I had Ray Eades and another mechanic from March along with me, and we got to work on the car, hoping to get some reliability into it, but with no great expectations for its performance.

Sure enough, we kept breaking down in practice, the work list getting longer far faster than we could tick items off. We stayed up all night getting it ready for qualifying, but still with various problems we qualified an underwhelming fifteenth. We worked through a second night, meaning that by the time the race began we had already been up for the best part of 48 hours – not ideal preparation for a 24-hour race, but we didn't expect the car to run for too long.

It began. Now, in those days, you didn't have a televised timing system. Instead the teams relied on wives and girlfriends to write down car numbers as they passed the pits and hence keep a lap check. The good ones were amazing. Unfortunately, the girls we had weren't the good ones, and by an hour into the race we had no idea of our standing.

Not that I was too worried. My goal was simply to keep running for as long as possible at a pace that didn't massively stress the engine, gearbox, brakes and so forth, to keep Randy Lanier in it as much as possible and Terry Wolters out of it during the night, because he couldn't see.

I'd never done anything like it before. Of course I'd race engineered for Johnny, but I hadn't run a car to the extent that I was making all the strategy decisions in a long race. Formula Two races were short sprint events. Add to that the fact that I was *really* tired.

About four hours in, I was helping Randy get out of the car and Terry get in. Because Randy was shorter, he had a seat insert that I yanked out of the car ready for Terry. I yanked it too hard, it left my grasp, took off like a Frisbee and landed on the roof of the pit building. I spent about 10 minutes after the pit-stop clambering up rather precariously to retrieve the spacer and get it ready for Marty, who was up next.

Later, around midnight, with the car running well, I staggered exhaustedly to the loo. Daytona, like Indianapolis, has a vertical tower showing all the car positions, and as I passed on my way to the toilet block, I glanced up to see that P1 was car 88.

It didn't sink in at first. I was swaying in front of the urinal when suddenly it hit me: *88 – shit, that's us. We're leading.*

Hot-footing it back to the pit lane I found I wasn't mistaken. We had taken the lead at around the 12-hour mark. All the other cars were having problems, but we'd just kept pounding around, and it was only with about an hour to go that the heavens opened and our engine started misfiring, which cost us time. Without that we might have won, but as it was we finished second – second in the 1983 24 Hours of Daytona race. Quite a result.

I nearly lost my chance to celebrate the result. Absolutely knackered, but elated, we finally left the circuit in the hire car, which was a Chevy of some description. Ray, the mechanic, was driving and we headed back to the hotel with me asleep in the front and the other Englishman asleep in the back. But, like Chevy Chase in *National Lampoon's Vacation*, Ray fell asleep too. We were at the traffic lights. His foot must have come off the brake in drive, resulting in the car rolling forward into the middle of the intersection where it was T-boned by another car. As awakenings go it was scary, the car spinning, glass flying everywhere.

We lived. No broken bones. And it was certainly a memorable weekend. The result did not go unnoticed by Robin Herd, who immediately saw the sales potential, leading him to giving me a budget to develop it further.

Enter Al Holbert. An American driver who'd had a lot of success in minor categories, Al was connected with Porsche, and what he wanted was a Porsche engine in the March chassis instead of the Chevy.

In the meantime, Al wanted to compete at the second race of the IMSA season, the Grand Prix of Miami on 27 February and less than a month away. So as a stopgap while we started work on the Porsche installation, he ordered a second Chevy-engined car from Robin.

By now we had funds for wind tunnel research and were able to take a suitably updated version of Sardous' original 25 per cent scale model to the Southampton tunnel in order to develop a high-downforce kit for the car (where I was pleased to see that my original 'aero-by-eye' approach did not feature any howling mistakes). With those changes made, Al Holbert took the modified car and won easily at Miami.

Meantime, we were working at installing the Porsche engine, which was no easy task. The March chassis was not designed to accept a turbocharged engine and was conceived around a normally aspirated V8 Chevrolet. We now had to put a flat six turbocharged Porsche engine complete with gear-box into it. The difference is that a normally aspirated engine draws air from the surrounding atmosphere without any additional pressurisation of that incoming air. The vast majority of petrol-engine road cars are normally aspirated. A turbocharged engine, on the other hand, uses a device to compress the air coming into the engine, making it denser. This denser air is then mixed with a correspondingly increased amount of fuel to give more chemical energy to the charge in the combustion chamber when the spark plug ignites it. For instance, if the turbocharger boosts the charge air to two times atmospheric pressure then the engine will give approximately twice the power of a normally aspirated engine.

So, I went over to Porsche to discuss the installation, but they were very unhelpful and wouldn't give us any drawings or advice – nothing. Al got an engine and gearbox unit sent to March, so we carefully measured it up and created our own drawings of it, then redesigned the back of the chassis and the rear suspension to suit.

By May it was ready and flown straight to Charlotte, a racetrack in North Carolina for two days of testing, and then its first race. I flew out with it and met Al and his team for the first time.

Charlotte in the summer is a hot dustbowl of a place and initial testing immediately revealed an Achilles' heel in the installation: the charge air cooler, which cools the very hot air exiting the turbo compressor, was not doing its job. The ducting I had designed was clearly not working, with the result that the charge air entering the engine was way above Porsche's limit, causing concerns over reliability and costing us power.

For qualifying, Al turned up the boost for one lap and took a gratifying pole, but we all knew the race would expose us. In the event, Al drove brilliantly, keeping the boost as low as he could while maintaining just enough pace to lead from flag to flag.

Post-race, Al invited me back to stay at his house and use his workshops (next to his Porsche dealership in Philadelphia) in order to find a solution.

During the wind tunnel tests we had done a run with the model painted in Flow Vis paint. This is a solution made from a fluorescent powder (originally used to track water flow in sewers) mixed into a witch's brew of paraffin and oil. When the wind blows over this, it forms streaks, with the paraffin evaporating to reveal patterns that indicate the direction and strength of the air flow over the body surface. Fortunately I had brought with me the photographs from the test and, looking carefully again, I noticed that the flow on the sides of the body (where I had positioned the duct inlet) looked weak while that on the top of the engine cover behind the roof looked strong.

So, working with Al's mechanics, we cut out the back of the roof and engine cover and created a new set of ducting to feed the cooler from above (instead of below). It was a little risky, as the time to the next race, at Lime Rock, was short, and we had no spare roof of the original design, so it was a one-way ticket as far as the next race was concerned.

Lime Rock is a tight, bumpy little track set in picturesque woodlands in Connecticut, not quite as hot as Charlotte but the slow tight nature would make it every bit as demanding on charge air cooling requirements. So it was quite some relief that not only were we straightaway the pacesetters in first practice but also the charge temperature was now well within Porsche's limits. The car ran like clockwork all weekend and Al duly took pole.

Al went on to win every remaining race of the season and hence the championship, an amazing year from a humble start.

Our championship win drew to a close that chapter of my career, as Al moved to IndyCar for the following season. However, a tragic postscript is that he died in 1988. He was piloting his Piper aircraft in Ohio and had just taken off when a door came open and the plane started behaving erratically. Rather heroically, Al managed to steer the Piper away from some houses, no doubt saving many lives before it crashed, killing him instantly. He was just 41.

I was devastated to hear of it. Al was a good friend and a great driver, and to live that month in America as his guest and travel the country with him was a tremendous experience. For that, and for his being so good to me, I'm eternally grateful.

It's funny. I had difficulty making myself understood in America. My Midlands accent, developed at college, would get in the way of simple things like ordering breakfast. Those tiny things aside, I was aware how fortunate I was to be gathering so much experience at such an early age: Europe with Formula Two and the United States with IMSA (International Motor

Sports Association). I was seeing the world and I loved that aspect of the job.

On my return from the States, I was given various design tasks on March's Formula Two and Indy cars for 1984, which took me through summer into autumn. With those completed, Robin told me his plans. Or should I say, he told me *my* plans: I was to join an IndyCar team called Truesports, in order to race engineer their driver Bobby Rahal in the March 84C. Back in the USA.

HOW TO BUILD A MARCH 86C

CHAPTER 13

In 1981, my friend Dave McRobert introduced me to a new pastime: hang-gliding. Dave was going out with a nurse from Bath Hospital, and through her I met another nurse, Amanda.

Throughout 1982 I saw her whenever I could. From Bath, where she lived, to Bicester, a town to the north of Oxford where March was based, was a bit of a slog. I used to travel up and down on my Ducati and stay with her at weekends. In the spring of 1983 we bought a cottage in Pickwick, a little village near Chippenham in Wiltshire.

In the summer of 1983 we were married. My dad gave me his yellow Lotus Elan (GWD 214K) as a wedding present, and we took it on our honeymoon in the South of France before beginning life as a married couple in our Pickwick cottage. Between my dad and I, we did 170,000 miles in that car.

All was great until 1984, when Robin sent me to join Truesports to race engineer for Bobby Rahal in the States. The idea was for Amanda to accompany me. She was a nurse and was officially allowed to work in the States, but when we got there we found that there were no jobs available. The team owner, Jim Trueman, also owned a chain of budget hotels, Red Roof Inns, and he promised to give her a job, which he did, in sales.

I left for Columbus in February. Amanda resigned and joined me around March or April time. But she didn't make any friends at Red Roof, our rented condo was soulless and she was homesick. Amanda had two very delineated modes: when she was in a good mood – 'up' – she was great fun. But when she was down she could be hard work, and I suppose you'd have to say that America brought out that latter side. She was back in Blighty by July.

I consoled myself with the racing, which I enjoyed – especially as I had a lot to learn. I came billed by Robin as 'a promising young engineer', replacing their previous, highly experienced engineer, Lee Dykstra. And while

I now had some race-engineering experience from Formula Two and GTP, I had no experience of the oval tracks that make up much of the IndyCar circuit.

The 'ovals' are more like a rounded rectangle, all four corners often very similar in speed. So if the driver says the car's understeering (i.e. that it's tending to under-rotate and carry straight on, what the Americans call 'push') then there are all sorts of things you can do to try to solve that: you might add more front wing to increase front downforce; you might soften the front anti-roll bar, so there's not as much weight transfer across the front tyres; you might change what the Americans call the 'stagger', the difference in diameter between the inside rear tyre and the outside rear tyre; you might alter the cross-weight, which is how weight is carried diagonally across the car, analogous to a wobbly bar table. You have all these and more variables, many of them not present on a standard road-racing car, because an oval-track car only has to turn left.

This was a big challenge to get my head round, but we were a close-knit team. Bobby, the team manager Steve Horne and chief mechanic Jimmy Prescott were patient with me as I learnt the ropes and we got to know each other well during the season.

Internal air travel wasn't common in the States back then, so we'd all jump into one of these vans they called Starcraft, effectively minibuses pimped-out with lots of red velvet. We would travel through the night to the circuits, taking it in turns to drive. You know those old movies where drivers do big steering movements all the time? That's how you had to drive these Starcraft, because they wouldn't go in a straight line; as part of the pimping process, they had been fitted with tyres that were far too wide for the rim. Dreadful things but comfortable, which is what you need when you're driving from track to track across America, although I do feel calling them Starcraft was a bit of an oversell. Those long trips were great fun – apart from the time we drifted into the side of an 18-wheeler truck when one of the guys fell asleep at the wheel.

It helped that I was forging a close relationship with Bobby. I've been fortunate enough to develop strong bonds with a few drivers over the years, but it was Bobby who first taught me how valuable that close relationship between race engineer and driver can be. He was able to describe what the car was doing in a language I could then translate into set-up changes.

Truesports had a drawing office, or more accurately a tiny office with an old drawing board, where I'd draw parts to improve the performance of the 84C and then work with Bobby at the racetrack to fine-tune the set-up. At race weekends we'd go out for dinner in the evening and talk about the car. I'd have a think about it overnight and come up with changes ready for the following morning's session.

So for me it was a nice meeting of the skills in aerodynamics and mechanical design that I'd learnt over previous years, with race engineering, and throughout the season I made some decent changes. The car had an angled engine, specified by its designer, Ralph Bellamy, to help the aerodynamics, but I wasn't convinced so we changed that to reduce the centre-of-gravity height, while redesigning the rear suspension to improve the aero. It was quite a heavy car, so we put a lot into weight saving.

By the end of the season we were able to give Mario Andretti's Lola, which had been the class car of the field, a good run for its money, winning a few races in the process. At the same time, my 83G design had gone on to win the 1984 IMSA championship. So with that, and with us having turned this rather clumsy 84 IndyCar into something that was able to rival and beat the Lola, Robin Herd promoted me to chief designer on next year's IndyCar. I was the grand old age of 25.

CHAPTER 14

It was all change at March. Ralph Bellamy had moved across to work on Formula 3000, designing the March 85B for my old friend Christian Danner (a good car, too. Christian won that debut Formula 3000 season in it). Meanwhile, I started work on the March 85C, which was to be sold to US teams to compete in the 1985 IndyCar season, the first race of which was in April 1985. It was to be my first car designed from scratch.

Now it goes without saying that there are a million and one factors to consider when you're designing a racing car. Here are just three that cropped up in this instance.

THE TASK

Your job as the chassis designer is to take all the elements – the engine; turbocharger; the radiators for the water, engine oil and gearbox oil; driver; fuel tank; suspension; gearbox; and find an elegant package solution for them – so that you can design the externals into the right aerodynamic shape while having a structurally sound, lightweight solution.

A VISION

As a result of that experience at Fittipaldi and March, I'm one of the few designers with a degree of knowledge in different departments who can move between them. What it gives me is the insight to approach a design from a holistic point of view, avoiding the situation where you see a car where clearly the aerodynamicist and the chief designer were having a row, since you've either got nasty mechanical bits sticking out of what was otherwise a clean aerodynamic surface (the structural guys obviously won the battle) or an aerodynamically elegant-looking car that performs poorly because it has the stiffness of a rubber band.

You might see other cars where it looks as if one person's designed the front end of the car and somebody else did the back end. If there's one thing I hope to be remembered for it's that the cars I've been overall responsible for look cohesive.

THE DRIVER

Despite the fact that March planned to sell the 85C to whichever team wanted it – indeed, there were well over a dozen of them competing in the 1985 IndyCar championship – it was Bobby for whom the car was tailored and his input that set the handling targets. And what Bobby wanted, mainly, was for the car to be balanced.

Why? Well, if you watch 1970s motor racing you'll see some drivers driving them like rally cars. Fans and journalists love to see that because it looks dramatic, as though you're witnessing a tense and skilful struggle between man and machine. Gilles Villeneuve, for example, was a master of the controlled slide – 'power slides' they're sometimes called – and could drive sideways all day. He won the adoration of fans as a result.

What he didn't win, however, was the championship. And who knows: maybe his propensity for exuberant driving was partially to blame because the problem is that this style puts an enormous amount of energy into the tyres, which are prone to overheating, as well as reducing the effectiveness of the aerodynamics and hence downforce. Or put another way, when you're going sideways you're not going forwards. Compare Gilles to Niki Lauda who never let the car get ragged. It was always moving forward. His results speak for themselves.

What all drivers want is a car that stays under control throughout all phases of the corner. You want the car to rotate when you turn the wheel at the entry phase of the corner, but not so much that the car tries to swap ends on you. And then at the exit phase of the corner, you want a car that can put down its power without spinning up the rear tyres or snapping sideways. Give them that and the delicate driver will explore the grip of the car to its limit without allowing it to get out of shape.

Bobby was no exception. IndyCars are heavy, which means they can be lazy when it comes to changing direction in corners. What's more, the circuits differ greatly and can be very bumpy, so we needed a car that would maintain its balance over a range of ride-heights. If we could achieve this then Bobby's delicate style would result in a very fast package. On the flipside, Bobby would struggle to extract time from a poorly balanced car that required a more flamboyant style.

We granted his wishes by working on the suspension, and on making the aerodynamics deliver in order to keep the car stable. We also designed the cockpit around his size, because he's a tall guy. When you consider that we were working in the days before data recorders or simulation packages, the driver's input was essential. After all, other than driver feedback all you had in those days was your own experience, instinct and . . .

THE WIND TUNNEL

My old friend the wind tunnel. I used the one at Southampton right up until 1990, which means that including student years I spent about 13 years in that wind tunnel. That's almost a quarter of my life used in five-day periods of stooping, squatting and kneeling over in a 7ft-wide, 5ft-high tube.

Our models were quarter-scale, made out of wood and aluminium, with moving suspension to allow the wheels to go up and down, but no springs or dampers and no internals. The floor of the tunnel was a conveyor belt. But although the tyres touched the ground, the model didn't rest on them. It was in fact hung from a strut on the ceiling. We used a turn buckle to vary the ride-height, and having done that we'd do a run, blow air over the model, about 10 minutes' worth of that, then stop the run, go into the tunnel, stoop over, take a set of spanners, adjust the ride-height and do another one. During the run we would measure the downforce, drag and the 'pitching moment', which allows us to calculate how the load is distributed between the front and rear axles.

LEAD TIMES

Typically, what takes longest is the central monocoque and gearbox casing – everything hangs off those two components. The rear suspension hangs off the gearbox casing, while the nose, front suspension, radiators and most of the bodywork hang off the monocoque, which itself contains the driver and fuel tank. So you need to have a pretty good idea of what the whole car will look like by the time you release the drawings for the monocoque and the transmission casing. Because they are the components that take the longest to make, to establish their release dates you simply work back from when the car is first scheduled to run.

You can keep working on the details after you've done that, so you might finish the front wing sometime later. Something like the driver's mirrors get released a few days before D-Day, because they don't take long to make.

At March, most of the car was made in-house, which for a production company where profit is important was crucial. The gearbox casing was made to our design, sent out to a foundry to cast and then machined by another company, but the monocoque, for instance, was made in-house, as well as all the suspension.

Because all the components were drawn by hand, it was difficult to check every last thing to make sure the components were going to assemble correctly, and we had occasional disasters when the first prototype car was being built: something wouldn't fit, for example, or a suspension member would go through a piece of bodywork. Nowadays, with everything drawn on computer, it is easy to fully assemble the car in the virtual world and check for such howlers before anything is actually made.

Work on the 85C began in August 1984, when I was pulling double-duty, wearing one hat as race engineer for Bobby in the States, and another doing design and wind tunnel work on the 85C in the UK. As a result it had a compressed aero programme and design time. Never good.

THE CHOICE

There's always a trade-off between making something strong and making it aerodynamic. For instance, to make the chassis stiff, you want a wide rim to the cockpit where the driver sits, and so I made the rim width 2in, which on the one hand gave a stiff chassis, but on the other presented a large and not very aerodynamically sympathetic opening to the top of the cockpit. Research 12 months later for its successor, the 86C, showed this to be a much bigger penalty than I had expected: with the compressed design time, I'd had to make a judgement without the time to evaluate it in the tunnel. It was the wrong call.

BRAINWAVES

I was lucky enough to fly business class as I began the commute in August between the US racetracks and March in Bicester, but the seats were upholstered in that squeaky leather that's supposed to be the height of luxury but is in fact slippery and uncomfortable, so for the return night flights I'd down a couple of whiskey and sodas and then wander through to economy.

God knows how airlines like Pan Am and TWA made any money in those days. Half the time you'd have the flight almost to yourself. Sure enough, I'd find three or four seats together and lie across those.

I remember one particular flight over the Irish Sea and the pilot announcing that there was a technical problem. We were going to have to circle over the sea, dump our fuel, then return to Heathrow. Of course that meant a delay back at Heathrow, the bottom line being that by the time we did eventually touch down at JFK in New York it was almost midnight.

There I had to bribe the hire company 20 dollars to stay open ('We're closed.' 'Says here you close at midnight.' 'We're closed.') and give me a car, and then I set off, map balanced on my lap, aiming to get to New Jersey across the Washington Bridge. Except, of course, I got hopelessly lost and ended up in the Bronx.

The Bronx in 1985 wasn't at all how it was portrayed in the films of the period like *Death Wish 3* and *The Exterminator*. Oh no. It was much, much worse. In fact, I'd go as far as to say that anybody needing to film post-apocalyptic scenes in 1985 needed only to set up shop in the Bronx. The ingredients were all there, burnt-out – and still-burning – cars, roaming gangs of sinister-looking miscreants, derelict buildings, shuttered-up shops and shadowy alleyways.

For a lost Englishman, one who but a few hours ago was secretly bemoaning the slippery leather in business class, it was quite a culture shock. So you can imagine my relief when I spotted a cop car pulled over at the side of the road. I drew to a halt, got out and went to ask for assistance.

As I did so, however, I registered what I'd missed before. The cop car had pulled in behind another car, its boot open. The driver of that car stood with his legs splayed and hands across the roof, being frisked.

The cop heard me approach and whether he came to the conclusion that I was the guy's accomplice or not, I don't know. What I do know is that he span round, pulled his gun, dropped to one knee and yelled, 'Freeze'.

I did as I was told, swallowing jagged glass at the same time. On the one hand there was a certain novelty at being in such a cinematic situation. On the other, I was scared shitless.

I mustered my very best English-gentleman voice. 'I'm so sorry to bother you, I can see that you're busy. But I was just wondering if you might be able to direct me to New Jersey.'

His answer? 'Beat it, pal.'

Once again, I did as I was told, cursing myself for having got lost and then making the mistake of stopping. But mistakes happen when you're as exhausted as I was at that time. As I've said, I was on a fairly unremitting schedule.

Even so, I did a lot of work on flights. Being on a plane has the distinct advantage of freeing you from distractions and pressure. I look back at my ideas now and I can pinpoint which ones I did over the Atlantic.

And what of the March 85C? Well, the great news for me as a designer is that it won the championship that year. Possibly the competition was a little weak, but it was still the first car for which I had been totally responsible, and despite the compressed design cycle, it had won!

The sad news for me as a race engineer was that it was won by a team called Penske, not Bobby, the very driver around whom I had designed the car.

The other highlight of the year was that, as well as the championship, it won the Indy 500.

And the Indy 500 of that year was a humdinger.

CHAPTER 15

The Indy 500 is the centrepiece of the championship and a gargantuan sporting event in its own right. Taking place at the legendary 2½-mile Super Speedway oval track at Indianapolis, in economic terms it's bigger than the Super Bowl, which is partly a result of the huge numbers that attend on the race day itself, and partly because it takes place over three weeks of practice, testing and qualifying before the race itself. 'The Month of May', they call it.

As an engineer, you come up with a shopping list of things you'd like to try in terms of Indy 500 set-up. A common mistake was to set up the car with too much understeer, so the driver would go through the corner flat-out without lifting the throttle but he'd lose too much speed because the front tyres would scrub across the track and that action would create drag and slow it down.

Equally, if the car was too nervous at the rear the driver would have to lift the throttle or risk losing the rear and so, again, you'd end up losing speed.

So trying to get the balance of the car just right was crucial at Indy, and a difficult thing to keep right throughout the month. Often in the early days of testing building up to qualifying week, you'd find some teams and drivers starting with very quick times but slowing down as the track rubbered in and the weather warmed up.

There were so many variables. So many different things to try on the car that I'd come up with a list of the key things and then attempt to work through them each day. But despite the track being open from 10am to 6pm, productivity in testing was frustratingly slow. For example:

10.00: First run of the day. Installation run, go out, do two warm-up laps, engine cover off, check for oil leaks, etc.

10.20: First proper run of four timed laps on new tyres. Come in.

Bobby complaining of poor car balance. Check the all-important stagger (difference in diameter of the rear tyres), find it is wrong and adjust it.

11.00: Run again for four timed laps. Come in. Bobby now happy that car balance is as expected based on previous day. Car now low on fuel. Hitch car up to quad bike and tow car to 'Gasoline Alley' to refuel (we were not allowed to refuel in the pit lane for safety reasons); sit in queue at fuel station. Get car back in pit lane and make the set-up change I had prepared on my list for the day.

12.20: Go out, full course yellow thrown because a car has broken down and dropped oil before Bobby has done a lap.

13.10: Finally get out and do four timed lap runs to try to evaluate change. But by now ambient and track temperatures have increased considerably, so we are not sure if it is better or worse. Decide to revert to start-of-day set-up to check; what is known as an A-B-A test.

13.50: Run again on base set-up.

So, at a little after 2pm, four hours after the track opened, we have evaluated precisely one change.

I couldn't get over just how big Indy 500 was, and not just on the day itself, but the build-up to it as well. The grandstand alone has a capacity of upwards of a quarter of a million, with in-field seating raising the attendance to about 400,000 on race day – making it the most-attended single day of sport anywhere on earth. But even knowing that fact doesn't quite prepare you for the size. It is huge. *Vast.* They had a campsite called the Snake Pit, which was rammed for the entire three weeks, and going in there one night was almost as much of an eye-opener as getting lost in the Bronx. Hard rock blasting out. Motorbikes revving. Massive, ZZ Top-looking blokes wandering around with a beer in one hand and a girl in the other. I remember seeing a girl standing on top of a VW camper van advertising blowjobs for $5, and nobody – well, nobody but me – batting an eyelid. I overheard a TV crew interviewing one of the campers, a rather grizzled, lived-in guy in an oily denim jacket. 'How long have you been coming?' they asked him.

'I've been coming here for the last twenty years; haven't missed one yet,' he said proudly.

'Oh, that's fantastic, and what do you think of it?'

'Well it's just the best goddamn event in the whole of the USA.'

'What do you think of the cars then?'

He paused, thinking. 'You know,' he said, 'that's the damnedest thing. Twenty years, I ain't seen one yet.'

He was just there to party.

Race day was quite something. We had to get up early in order to steal a march on the quarter of a million people also trying to get into the circuit. At 7am a cannon went off to signal the gates at the two opposite ends of the oval opening and punters began flooding in. Watching it, we saw two cars collide as they met in the middle. It was pandemonium.

Everybody took their seats. I remember our team manager, Steve Horne, tripping over the low wall, falling flat on his face in the pits and earning a standing ovation from the grandstand, a reminder of just how much attention was focused on us. And, of course, with it being one of the biggest sporting events in the world, there was all the American pomp and cere-mony that goes with it. Jets flying past, pom-pom girls, the 'Star-Spangled Banner'.

That particular year, it looked as though the March 85C was a little quicker than the Lola, which was its nearest rival.

As the race developed it became a tight battle between the two cars. Mario Andretti in the Lola had the lead but Danny Sullivan in the Penske-run March had a performance advantage.

Danny got up to second and was on Mario's tail, but couldn't find a way to overtake. Finally he tried to get past on the inside, but Mario, being the experienced old fox that he is, wasn't making it easy.

The apron is where the banking angle changes, so you get this change in camber of the track, which unbalances the car as it crosses. What Mario did was force Danny down onto the apron, which was aggressive but legiti-mate. Danny was halfway past Mario when the camber changed and he lost the rear and spun – ending up directly in front of Mario. Mario managed to brake and avoid him, and for a moment you could see Danny spinning in a cloud of tyre smoke with Mario just behind him, no doubt grinning in his helmet.

But Danny held on. The car didn't hit anything, and when the spin was complete, he was pointing in the right direction. The engine stalled but Danny put the car in gear, the engine fired and he was able to continue. Later, Danny would say that it was half skill and half 'dumb luck' that he was unhurt and able to continue.

The stewards flew the yellow flag for the pace car while the smoke cleared. Danny continued with heavily flat-spotted tyres, screaming in the radio, 'I've spun, I've spun!' Both drivers came into the pits for a fast tyre change and then went back out. There was a new race order now, but it soon reverted back to Mario in the lead, Danny second. And this time Danny managed a clean overtake to win the race.

The 'spin and win', it's called. It's one of the most dramatic moments in IndyCar history and well worth seeking out on YouTube when you have a chance.

CHAPTER 16

Truesport's team principal was Steve Horne, a gruff Kiwi who liked to run a tight ship. That was fine, nothing wrong with that – up to a point. The trouble was, his style was very autocratic. For example, after qualifying at Indy, he decided that rather than continue with testing the following week leading up to the race, as is the norm, he would get the cars sent back to the race shop in Columbus for three days of prep back there. A questionable decision, but worse, the first thing Bobby and I knew of it was when we drove into the circuit on the Monday to see the Truesport truck heading out!

At the same time, Robin Herd brokered a deal for me to join Kraco, another March customer. On the table was an increased development budget, bigger salary and Michael Andretti, the talented son of Mario, as driver. I'd be moving there on the race-engineering side for 1986, while remaining as chief designer on the Indycar at March. What's more, while Truesports was based in Columbus, Ohio, not the most exciting place to live, Kraco was in LA, which sounded a lot more appealing.

And so, after two years' race engineering at Truesports, and having forged a wonderful relationship with Bobby, I decided to bid them a reluctant farewell and join Kraco for the race-engineering side of things.

I was still pulling double-duty, though, from July flying regularly back to the UK between races to begin research for the 86C.

Knowing that I would be in charge of design for the 1986 car allowed me to put in place a much more thorough wind tunnel and research programme than had been the case for the 1985 car's rushed schedule. The chassis was quite a bit narrower and more elegant. But the big step forward was at the rear. By regulation, IndyCars have a single turbo, and it was a big unit. I had the idea of rotating it through 90 degrees, so instead of sitting across the car, it would sit longitudinally along the axis with the exhaust facing forwards rather than backwards. That way we could split the exhaust into two tailpipes, one to the left, one to the right, with each tailpipe looping around in a 180° bend, then transitioning into a fantail that could blow the back end of the diffuser.

We started developing that in the wind tunnel, using compressed air fed down through the mounting arm of the model, into the model and out through the exhaust, and it looked promising. I then redesigned the rear suspension completely to package it, which wasn't easy because you now had a longitudinal turbocharger with the exhausts and waste gates all trying to vie for the same space with the rear suspension, particularly the spring/damper units.

We rearranged the rear dampers so they sat longitudinally beside the gearbox and above the exit from the exhaust. To prevent people from putting the exhausts into the diffuser – a practice that had become commonplace in Formula One during the 1984 season – IndyCar rules stated that the diffuser must not have holes in it. However, the spring/damper units would need a heat shield to prevent them from being burnt by the exhaust

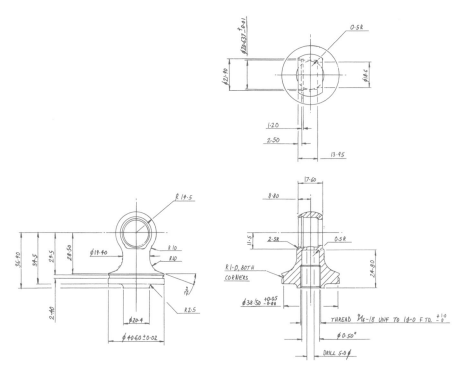

Figure 6a: Technical drawing of the rear damper top of the March 86C.

gas, so I positioned the units in such a way that the heat shield would be naturally tail up, creating a 'coanda effect' downforce-producing extension to the tailpipe. Not legal if considered part of the diffuser, but legal if considered as being there for the primary purpose of protecting the mechanical parts. This arrangement created a very high velocity/low pressure at the back of the main diffuser, drawing much more air through it. The overall package looked a powerful step forward in the tunnel.

Over the Atlantic was where I came up with the idea for the exhaust system and rear suspension. Not only that, but I very clearly remember sketching out the roll hoop layout on the plane.

The new roll hoop was made out of aluminium honeycomb instead of the traditional steel roll hoop, making it lighter and more aerodynamic, with a little titanium capping piece on top. It satisfied the regulations and I felt it was quite safe, because the problem with the steel roll hoop is that

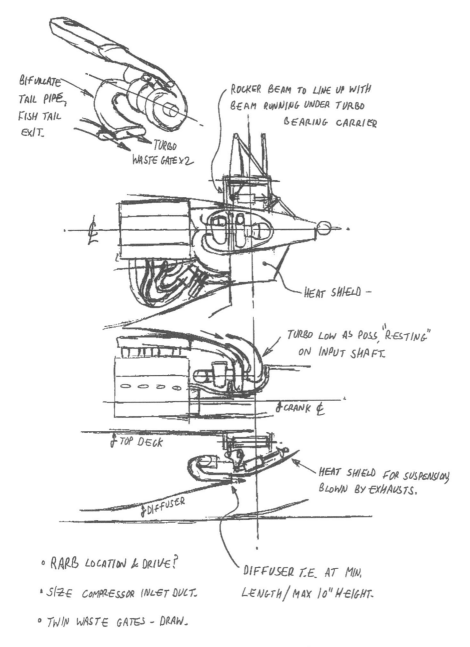

BIFURCATE
TAIL PIPE,
FISH TAIL
EXIT.

TURBO
WASTE GATE×2

ROCKER BEAM TO LINE UP WITH
BEAM RUNNING UNDER TURBO
BEARING CARRIER

HEAT SHIELD –

TURBO LOW AS POSS, "RESTING"
ON INPUT SHAFT

₵ CRANK ₵

₵ TOP DECK

HEAT SHIELD FOR SUSPENSION
BLOWN BY EXHAUSTS.

₵ DIFFUSER

○ RARB LOCATION & DRIVE?

· SIZE COMPRESSOR INLET DUCT.

○ TWIN WASTE GATES - DRAW.

DIFFUSER T.E. AT MIN.
LENGTH / MAX 10" HEIGHT.

Figure 6b: Sketch of the split-exhaust and longitudinal turbocharger
layout of the March 86C.

you've got four tubes going into a composite structure and you need to try to spread that load out so that the tubes don't just punch a hole straight through the structure. It's not easy and there have been plenty of instances where the roll hoop itself has stood an accident okay, but it's punched straight through the chassis and therefore been pretty useless.

It turned out to be a bit controversial. One thing I hadn't really taken into account was that if you went upside down on grass or in gravel, because it was a very pointed structure, it would just plough a furrow and therefore wouldn't properly protect the driver in the way a more rounded hoop would. But we raced with it and, fortunately, there was no such accident.

Which brings me on to an important philosophical point – one that we all struggled with in those days.

CHAPTER 17

I remember being in Italy in May 1982, peering through the window of a TV shop and watching the accident that killed Gilles Villeneuve at the Belgian Grand Prix. Italian TV had no compunction about broadcasting the accident in all its horrible detail, and we were treated over and over again to images of Gilles lying in the middle of the track, his car having literally snapped in two.

I can only speculate how it must feel for other drivers seeing something like that. I've seen drivers on whom it has weighed heavily. Damon Hill, for example, whose own father, Graham Hill, died in a related accident, would probably admit that the risk began to affect his driving. Drivers get older, they have kids. It changes them.

As for the designer? The Ferrari in which Gilles died was one of Harvey Postlethwaite's cars. He'd moved to Ferrari from Fittipaldi, and I recall thinking that it must have been pretty bad for him.

Tragically I was to learn how it felt the hard way. I've had one driver die in a car I've designed. Ayrton. That fact weighs heavily upon me, and while I've got many issues with the FIA and the way they have governed the sport over the years, I give them great credit for their contribution to improving safety in the sport.

The chassis constructor is responsible for two aspects of safety, first, trying to avoid a car component failure. Clearly if a suspension member breaks or a wing falls off at the wrong point of the circuit, the car's going to have an accident, and if that happens it is because somebody on the team has made a mistake. It could be in the design, manufacturing, lack of inspection; it could be a mechanic forgetting to do a bolt up. There is a clause in the FIA regulations warning against unsafe construction design, but the onus is on the teams to do everything we can to put systems in place to eliminate the possibility of human error.

The second aspect of safety is what happens once the accident starts and the car hits whatever it hits; usually a wall, barrier or another car. How does it withstand the impact?

That's the bit that *is* covered by regulations nowadays and it's where the FIA has governed and legislated well, particularly as a result of the work done by the late Sid Watkins, who was the Chief Medical Officer at the FIA.

Sid was a good friend, a very good man. He started his work just after the war when motorcyclists tended not to wear helmets and would often suffer terrible head trauma in the event of an accident.

Sid understood that the best thing for injuries of this kind was to minimise swelling by keeping the body cold. His early work consisted of laying patients on a block of fish ice to keep the body temperature as low as possible. He became a brain surgeon but, after being recruited into Formula One by Bernie Ecclestone, he contributed hugely to making cars safer through his research into how to absorb energy with headrest foams, nose, side and rear-impact structures, and so on.

Back in 1986, in IndyCar, there were barely any safety regulations. You had to show your roll hoop was strong enough by calculation only, and the fuel tank bladder had to be made out of certain material and positioned between the seatback and front of the engine, but that was about it.

So the designer of the car was faced with a choice: if you come up with a design which is faster but less safe, what do you do? For instance, the driver's feet are at the front of the car, so if the nose box isn't robust he's likely to badly break or even lose his legs. But a stronger nose box will be heavier.

Ultimately it was down to the designer to decide how strong to make the car versus how heavy to make it. If you did it in consultation with the drivers they would almost invariably say, 'Make it heavier,' and I do remember Bobby having a go at me when he felt that I hadn't made the front-impact structure strong enough. The problem we have as a designer, of course, is that nobody thanks you for a slow, safe car. Back then I think I took the view that I had to try to make a sensible compromise; not do anything blatantly dangerous, but err towards performance over safety.

It's a horrible position to be in. Taking that decision away from the designer is one of the best things to happen to the sport.

CHAPTER 18

It was January 1986 when I set off for Los Angeles to join Kraco and prepare for the start of the season in March.

Arriving, I distinctly remember that moment of thinking, *Bloody hell, I'm a bloke from Stratford who went to the local tech college, and now I'm living – living – in LA.* From the window of the Hermosa Beach condo that I was to share from March with my draughting assistant, Peter, I could see down to the boardwalk and, beyond that, the glittering ocean. We dumped our stuff and hurried down for a closer look, hoping, nay *expecting,* to see bikini-clad roller-skating beach babes, weight-lifters, the works. All we got was an old guy walking his dog. It turned out it was the day of the Super Bowl, and in America everything else stops for that day.

I liked LA. I never quite got the superficiality – all that 'have a nice day' stuff felt a touch hollow to me – and despite the odd attempt I never got into surfing either. But Los Angeles is a lovely city with a temperament I found appealing, and Kraco was a good team with a great bunch of mechanics.

The race shop was in Compton, a city south of LA whose reputation for gang violence was soon to be immortalised by gangsta rap. I was advised to get hold of a car that was reliable enough that I wouldn't break down while driving through it, but not so decent I ran the risk of being carjacked. It was that kind of place. On one particular Saturday afternoon, Peter and I were working in the little drawing office behind the main workshop when we heard a lot of noise and shouting. Walking through to investigate, we found a load of Mexicans helping themselves to the mechanics' tool boxes. The flash of a knife from one of them sent us running back to the office.

Our driver was Michael Andretti, the son of the legendary Mario and already a championship-winning driver in his own right, but still relatively young and inexperienced. As a result he was open to pretty much anything I suggested and we quickly developed a good rapport.

Unfortunately, our main rivals, Penske and Lola, had clocked what we were doing with the exhaust of our car, and began lobbying the governing body, suggesting our heat shield was illegal. Fortunately my argument, that it was simply a necessary heat shield, prevailed.

There was another problem. The twin waste gates were tightly packaged in the bundle of primary pipes that emerge from the engine and they kept overheating, requiring a lot of pre-season development

Other than that, the car was quick, reliable and relatively easy to set up. Indeed it was significantly quicker than the Lola or the Penske. Very gratifying as a designer. Meanwhile, as a race engineer, our main rival as the season developed turned out to be my old team Truesports. A few days before the Indy 500, Jim Trueman, the owner of Truesports and a good man with a great passion for his race team, lost his battle with cancer. Very fittingly, Bobby went on to win the 500.

In July, a chap called Teddy Mayer approached me. Teddy had been running the Texaco Star Indy team with Tom Sneva as the driver, but had now moved into Formula One with a Lola-built car and Beatrice as sponsor.

Because Teddy knew me well and respected what I'd achieved in IndyCar, he asked me to join as technical director at Beatrice. I was very keen to move into Formula One – or back into it – so I agreed.

Robin Herd knew how I felt and was very good about it. The only stipulation was that I should fulfil my race-engineering obligations to Michael Andretti, which meant flying to the States every fortnight for a race and then back again. It would be a punishing schedule, further compounded by the fact that I now lived close to Bicester, where March was based, but the new design and manufacturing place was in Colnbrook, just by Heathrow. As well as all that, Amanda was pregnant and I was away every other weekend, not to mention the four weeks of Indy 500 and Milwaukee 200. Hardly an ideal situation.

Charlotte was born on 28 August 1986. I'm not sure I've ever told her this – I suppose this is as good a time as any – but she's named after that first win at Charlotte in 1983. Like that win, Charlotte was a joyful breath of fresh air. A baby adds to your responsibility, but with her it was as though a weight had been lifted. Things had been up and down with Amanda – more of which later – but as any parent knows, nothing can dim the joy of a child's birth, and with Charlotte in our lives all other considerations become secondary.

Meanwhile, I got stuck into researching what would have been the Beatrice 1987 car. I should have been enjoying the work, relishing the challenge and being eager to make an impression in Formula One, but I soon discovered that the atmosphere at Beatrice wasn't what it had been at March, with the pub visits and camaraderie replaced by glowering office politics.

The chief designer was Neil Oatley, a very good designer and a lovely, completely straightforward person, while Ross Brawn was head of aerodynamics. The problem was that Teddy did not explain our roles; his style was very much to throw everybody in and let the strongest prevail.

I struggled for inspiration. Initially I concerned myself with trying to find some aerodynamic gains on the existing car but none of my ideas were successful. I just couldn't 'click' somehow.

In the meantime, I'd been given yet another job to do. Understandably, Teddy wanted me to gain experience of Formula One, so I was given the task of race engineering Patrick Tambay, one of the two drivers.

So now I was – deep breath – race engineering Michael Andretti for the IndyCar races, flying back, driving to Heathrow to do the research and design for the 1987 car and going to the Formula One races to race engineer Patrick Tambay. As well as doing my best to keep my marriage together and be a good first-time father.

It was all a bit ambitious really. *Too* ambitious in retrospect, and it contributed to what was my first – and, touch wood, only – creative block. I just couldn't seem to come up with creative solutions on the Formula One car.

I was starting to feel as if I was out of my depth, as though I was about to be rumbled for not being as good as everybody thought I was; a big fish in the smaller pond of Indy, but a minnow in the piranha tank of Formula One.

CHAPTER 19

At Red Bull I've introduced what I call the 24-hour rule, which is that we sit on an idea for a day or so, throw it around and talk about it, but don't do anything concrete until it has been critiqued. Does it still stand up after 24 hours? If the answer's no then we chuck it in the bin.

After that comes developing the idea. In my own case this usually means first a sketch and then the drawing board. In the 1980s, if the drawings were for aerodynamic components they would be passed to the model-makers to make a model by hand. Nowadays almost all manufacturing is by computer-controlled machines; my hand drawings are scanned and then turned into 3D surfaces on our computer system.

Then you go to the wind tunnel, test the parts, and the results will determine whether your ideas are any good or not.

At Beatrice, however, I just wasn't coming up with any brainwaves at all, good or bad. And for me, this was a disaster. I'm accustomed to having ideas all the time. On planes, in the loo, in the dead of night. They come thick and fast, sometimes at inopportune moments. And even if they're not great, especially those dead-of-night ones where you wake up thinking you've cracked it and scribble something down that by morning looks absolute rubbish, the point is that at least you're generating ideas, which is the first step in the process.

Looking back, there were two reasons for this: first, the change of culture moving from March to Beatrice; second, I was exhausted. Often I find I am at my most creative when the pressure is on: pressure can, if managed, kick the old grey matter into a more creative and productive state. Sadly, the extra step to exhaustion has the opposite effect.

In early November, it was suddenly announced that Beatrice was pulling the plug and that the team would be wound up. I'd been there a grand total of four months.

On the one hand, well, at least it wrapped up what wasn't a happy period. On the other, the design cycle of any car needs to start in June, early August at the very latest, after which it's too late to research and design a new car. So, I was in the position now where I couldn't be responsible for the design of a car for the following season. It was just way too late.

Enter Bernie Ecclestone, a cameo role.

CHAPTER 20

The seeds of Bernard Charles Ecclestone's rise were planted in the 1960s, when Formula One was split into two distinct camps. In one was the 'grandee' teams, who built both the chassis and the engine. The likes of BRM, Matra, Alfa Romeo, Maserati, Honda and so on. Biggest of them all – the very grandest of the *grandi costruttori* – was Ferrari. Indeed, it was

Enzo Ferrari who in the 1950s had coined the rather sniffy name for the second camp. He called them *garagisti*. They became known as 'garagistes'.

Typically, British teams, the garagistes, had from 1968 onwards all used the Ford Cosworth DFV, a competitive engine that was relatively cheap to buy and easy to bolt in the back of a car. What the garagistes lacked in funding and engine innovation they made up for in creativity and ingenuity.

Money was tight. In those days, teams negotiated with the individual circuits for start money and prize money. There was no championship money as such. So let's say you were Brabham. You'd go along to Spa and said, 'I want £1,000 start money,' and they might say, 'Well we're only prepared to give you £500; take it or leave it.' That would leave Brabham in a weak position, because nobody was turning up specifically to see them in the way they were for, say, Ferrari.

What the circuits tended to do was pay the grandee teams a lot, and give the crumbs to the garagistes.

Along with Frank Williams, Max Mosley and Colin Chapman, Bernie started the Formula One Constructors' Association. FOCA. It was originally called F1CA but that changed when it dawned on them that F1CA looked a bit like 'fica', which means something rude in Latin languages. ('Pussy', to save you looking it up.)

What FOCA did was create a syndicate of the garagistes, which forced circuits to pay them collectively or none of them would turn up.

It worked. The playing field was levelled and the British teams were pleased. At the same time, Bernie, as representative of the teams, was negotiating with various broadcasting companies. He was generating huge income by selling the sport to the TV companies and then distributing funds back to the teams, replacing the start money with an even bigger purse. Again, the British teams were pleased.

The teams stopped being pleased when it transpired that there was no 'we' of a collective, there was just an 'I' of Bernie. By controlling the TV rights, Bernie basically controlled the entire sport, and of course it has made him a very, very wealthy man, worth £4.2 billion at the last count.

I guess you could argue about the ethics of it, but Bernie and Max Mosley, who was his legal advisor, hadn't done anything illegal; they'd simply seen the loopholes and quietly got on with exploiting them. As someone who makes his living doing something similar, I'd be flirting with hypocrisy if I were to stand in judgement.

Besides, as Lord Hesketh said later, the teams were all too busy fiddling with cars to notice what Bernie was doing. In 1993 they tried to challenge him, but by then the FIA had been formed out of the old FISA, and who was in charge of the FIA? Max Mosley. You can guess how that turned out.

I like Bernie. I liked him then and I like him still. A straightforward bloke, he doesn't talk a lot, but you need to listen to what he does say. As for his impact on the sport, he took it from being a junior league category watched by a few enthusiasts to the major league sport it is today. Yes, of course he's made enemies along the way. There are people who don't like what he's done. But overall, there's no doubt he's been good for the sport.

When I first met him in November 1986, he was still on his way up and combining his involvement with FOCA with his ownership of the Brabham team. He got in touch with me on the back of the Beatrice news. Would I meet regarding a position? We dined at his favourite London restaurant, although for the life of me I can't remember the name of it. Just that it was where Bernie held court. We had two meetings. The first was what you might call a sounding-out exercise. He wanted to get the measure of me, gauge my interest, that kind of thing. The second meeting . . .

'I need a new technical director at Brabham,' he told me.

I knew full well that Gordon Murray was technical director at Brabham. He was a guy I'd always respected, the person who, years before, had responded so thoughtfully to my suggestion for a new suspension system when I was at university, and I was nervous about treading on his toes, dethroning him, whatever you want to call it.

'Gordon is leaving,' said Bernie. 'Nothing to do with you. He's just leaving. We need a new technical director. Whether it's you or not is up to you.'

He produced a contract. 'You don't have to make a decision now,' he said. 'I can recommend you a lawyer if you like.'

The financial offer was good, and I was out of work, so the chances are I would have signed there and then if he'd pushed me. But he didn't, and

I sat on the contract for a couple of days, being about to add my signature when the phone rang again.

It was Bernie. 'I'm selling the team. I've found a buyer, all set up, and if you want to still join, that's up to you, but please be aware that I won't be involved any more.'

That gave me some thinking to do. After all, Bernie was one of the main attractions. With Bernie on board I knew the team would be well funded and run. Without him I might be staring down the barrel of another Beatrice situation.

I decided to err on the side of caution and declined the offer in light of the new development. Once bitten, twice shy and all that. But I remain grateful to Bernie for his honesty and transparency.

That left me at a loose end once again. Fortunately I then heard from Carl Haas, who since 1983 had been partnered with the actor Paul Newman as Newman/Haas Racing. Carl wanted me to join as Mario Andretti's race engineer. Not only that, but he offered me what was an enormous sum of money: $400,000 a year. To give you an idea of just what a rise that was, I'd been earning about $60,000 a year with March/Kraco. Needless to say, I accepted.

Now, it might sound slightly odd that Carl planned to make me the world's highest-paid race engineer (I imagine that must still be the record) when thus far I hadn't actually crossed anyone's palm with the drivers' championship silverware – not Bobby and not Michael Andretti.

But Carl is a shrewd businessman. Carl was the Lola importer for North America and March were Lola's only serious rival at the time. At the risk of sounding arrogant, I guess he figured that if he could stop me returning to March to work on their 1987 IndyCar, and instead contribute to the development of Lola's 1987 car, then he would weaken the enemy and hence strengthen his sales. As a designer, my stock in IndyCar was high. After all, my cars had won the Indy 500 twice: the March 85C in 1985, the 86C the following year. In USA sporting terms, that's a bit like coaching two successive Super Bowl-winning teams.

And then there was Carl. He was a real character, always, but *always* with a huge cigar clamped between his lips. I'm not sure how often it was lit, but it was certainly a permanent fixture, to the extent that on the odd occasion he removed it, you could see where it had left a permanent indent.

He was very superstitious. I remember in Mid-Ohio in 1985, Bobby was on pole, Mario second. Carl always had this thing where he'd make a big performance of blessing his car on the grid – so he'd come up to it and walk around it, touching it while muttering Hebrew under his breath.

That day, he'd gone through the whole rigmarole before he realised he was blessing the wrong car. He was blessing Bobby's car, not Mario's. So great was his indignation that he removed the cigar, actually took it out of his mouth, and tossed it in fury across the track. He marched to Mario's car for a hurried blessing.

It didn't work. Or, you might say, it did work. Because Bobby dominated.

Carl was a likeable guy though. The team was based in Chicago and the first time he picked me up from the airport ready for the first test – early 1987 – we walked back to the car park, got in his car, a brand new BMW, and it wouldn't start.

'This goddamned car,' he growled, 'it's got a security code.' But he'd forgotten it. We tried every significant combination of numbers he could think of – his birthday, his mother's birthday, etc. – until at last I said, 'How about 0000? Isn't that the factory setting?' And that was it.

Carl always had lots of change in his pocket. I can't remember how it happened, but he fell over outside a restaurant one day, and all his quarters and nickels and dimes rolled off down the street. Being so superstitious he assumed it was an omen of bad luck and we had to help him pick up every single dime.

He and his wife, Bernie, both looked after me. The Lola T87 had been designed for the Cosworth DFX engine, which every IndyCar team used up until that point, but my first job was to install a new Chevrolet engine made by Ilmor, a company based in Brixworth, Northamptonshire, and run by their chief designer, Mario Illien and his business partner, Paul Morgan. It marked the beginning of an ongoing and very fruitful relationship with Ilmor.

It also meant I had to design a new front end to the gearbox and a new oil tank for the Lola, so I got stuck in.

Meanwhile there was the job of forging a relationship with another Mario – Andretti – for whom I was to be race engineer. I'd met him previously during my three seasons in IndyCar, but only briefly, so the opening test of the season at Laguna was the first time I was properly introduced to him.

We took seats in a little restaurant in Monterey. The waiter brought the menus and I watched as Mario looked at his, squinted a bit and then stretched his arm right out, trying to find a bit of light from the table lamp to read it.

I thought, *What have I done? This guy needs reading glasses!*

Thankfully my fears would turn out to be groundless. As with many people, his eyesight had started to deteriorate in his mid-forties (I've been extremely lucky in that regard, so far), but while Mario sometimes found it difficult to focus in low light, he was fine in daylight.

I wondered whether he'd asked Michael about me. Or whether Michael had volunteered his opinion. It was by no means certain either way. They had a very strange relationship. On one occasion I remember being with Mario at his house in snowy Pennsylvania. He'd ploughed a circuit for snowmobiles, the idea being that he and Michael would take it in turns to see who could clock the fastest time.

As we stood and watched, Michael went first but tried too hard and ran out of talent. His snowmobile flew up in the air, huge clouds of white temporarily obscuring our view until they cleared to reveal Michael lying winded on his side. Most parents would be concerned for their child's well-being after such a big accident, but not Mario, who simply rolled his eyes and muttered, 'Stupid kid'. They were always very competitive with each other. There was more than one incident on the track in which they took each other out, and I bet Mario rolled his eyes and said, 'Stupid kid', each time.

Anyway, back to that first meeting. We had a pleasant enough dinner, chatting about the usual stuff. I already respected Mario enormously as a driver. It was good to discover that we seemed to get on.

The next morning we began testing the Lola, which ran well. Because everything had been done in such a rush, we hadn't had time to install a radio in the car. In hindsight that was a huge mistake, because towards the end of the day, with testing almost over, we stood in the pit lane watching as the car came round the track and were horrified to see the rear wing tilted over to one side.

Mario wasn't aware of it, and without a radio we couldn't warn him to slow down. He disappeared off through turn one and two, a pair of flat-out left-hand corners at Laguna, and then we heard this huge *boom boom boom*.

It was a sickening sound. We scrambled into the hire cars, me knowing full well that the crash was partly my mistake. I should have insisted we put a radio in the car before we started testing.

The first thing we spotted was some bodywork. Then we got to the complete back end, gearbox and rear wheels lying in the middle of the track. Finally we arrived at the tub, the chassis. It lay on its side where rain had washed away the banking to form a ditch. One wheel was still attached. It was like a light aircraft crash, wreckage everywhere, and there, standing among it all, was Mario, looking in puzzlement at his watch.

'Are you okay?' we said breathlessly.

He tapped at his watch. 'Goddamned watch has stopped,' he said.

That was Mario. A brilliant driver and a real tough cookie.

CHAPTER 21

By the time we got to the first race of the season at Long Beach, we were about three weeks behind schedule. Even so, Mario dominated the race and won. I remember it with some fondness. Not just because we won, but because Amanda brought Charlotte along, who by then was six or seven months old. We were having dinner with Paul Newman that night, and there was a great picture – since lost, sadly – of Paul bouncing Charlotte on his knee.

It was nice to get to know Paul. In addition to our end-of-term concert at Repton, we had end-of-term films, and though most of them were pretty boring, two stood out: *If . . .* starring Malcolm McDowell – memorable for reasons that will be obvious if you've seen the film – and *Butch Cassidy and the Sundance Kid*, which of course starred Paul.

Paul turned out to be a lovely chap, and we often spoke about films and motor racing. I'm strangely immune to celebrities, perhaps in part because motor racing attracts many musicians and actors to race days, often as guests of the teams. In my experience they tend to fall into two distinct categories: those who remain unaffected by their fame, and those who think that being famous entitles them to act like a prima donna. Paul was in the former camp. Down-to-earth, charming and pragmatic to the point that he'd take the stairs rather than a lift, claiming that the exercise helped him cut down on gym fees.

He didn't like being interrupted by fans when he was eating, which having also experienced I can fully understand, and he used to charge people for an autograph, which tended to take people aback until they discovered he wanted them to donate the money to the Scott Newman Centre in remembrance of his son, Scott, who had died of a drug overdose in 1978.

The next race was Phoenix, where Mario put it on pole. However, as the race went on, the car became progressively more 'loose', which is an American way of saying that it was oversteering. We had a radio in the car by now, and Mario was reporting horrendous amounts of oversteer. It wasn't until later that we discovered the car had a broken engine mount.

Thanks to Mario's commitment and skill, we somehow came third, despite a back end that was flexing all over the place. For me, that has to be one of the greatest unsung drives ever, because the car must have been truly evil to drive.

Meanwhile, the team was still getting to grips with some of the modifications we'd made to the car. We'd also developed a new system for pit-stops. Nowadays, in Formula One, mechanics use jacks at the front and rear when the car comes in for a pit-stop, but in IndyCar we had pneumatically powered air jacks on board.

Race engineering Mario with my clipboard, '87.

We also had a relatively small fuel tank, so needed to refuel several times each race. At the pit-stops you could then change tyres, depending on your strategy. There would be a low wall in the pit lane, and behind that was kept the fuel rig, wheels for the next pit-stop and whatever other bits might be needed.

Only five people were allowed on the pit side of the low wall. Two of those were for refuelling, one on the filling pipe and one on the ventilation pipe. The ventilation-pipe guy would also operate the air jacks.

The reason the IndyCars have jacks on board is because of this limitation on how many people are allowed in the pit lane. A front and rear jack man would mean two extra people.

So, at a pit-stop, you'd have all five people waiting for the car to arrive. Your refuelling and jack man would start refuelling and lifting the car.

Typically, you'd have two people, one to change each rear wheel, after which you had a choice of what to do with your front wheels. If you wanted to change both of them, the front-wheel guy had to change the outside front wheel, then run across the front of the car and change the inside front wheel. Three wheels could be changed in the time it took to refuel, but to change all four would add an extra 4sec or so to the pit-stop time.

As race engineer I would make the call on whether we would change that extra tyre and also on what we should adjust on the set-up of the car to keep it balanced for the remainder of the race. It was up to the driver to adjust the car's balance using the anti-roll bars front and rear. Some drivers knew what to do for themselves; others would prefer to radio in, tell you what the car was doing and wait for adjustment advice. The car tends towards over-steer as the race goes on because it loses more rear grip than it does front grip – not always the case, it depends on factors like the ambient tempera-ture, the track temperature, the layout of the circuit, the characteristics of the tyres and so on – but as a rule of thumb, it loses more rear grip as the tyres degrade, so the driver would typically soften the rear bar and stiffen the front bar to maintain balance as the tyres degraded through a stint.

During pit-stops was the time to make additional changes. We could change the front-wing angle, for example, to adjust the aerodynamic balance. In order to adjust the drag and total downforce of the car, I'd also added a little trim tab, between 3mm and 10mm in height, called a Gurney flap, to the car, the idea being that the left-rear-tyre man, who was usually finished before fuelling had finished, could raise a little flap in the rear-wing endplate, pull out the old Gurney flap and replace it with a new one. So, if wind conditions changed, for instance, or ambient temperature rose, or if we just felt we needed a bit more straight line speed halfway through the race, we could change this Gurney flap and adjust drag and downforce.

The other mod we introduced in 1987 was what we called the cross-weight adjuster. On the oval tracks you wouldn't necessarily set the car up to have the same weight on the inside and outside front wheels. To make the car more stable, you'd put more weight onto the outside front tyre, making it work harder and, more importantly, relieving the outside rear.

It was an important set-up parameter and if we could adjust that difference in weight between the two front wheels during the race, that would be an extra way for the driver to keep the car in tune as the balance changed as a result of the fuel load burn, or the wind changing.

So we fitted a simple little hydraulic adjuster in the pushrod of the rear suspension of the Lola, with a master cylinder in the cockpit so that Mario could adjust the cross-weight throughout the race.

We tried to keep it hidden as long as we could, but eventually, of course, people started to spot it and copy it. This is something we'd developed in the pre-season, but we'd kept our powder dry before introducing it for the third race: the Indianopolis 500.

We couldn't have picked a better time. Qualifying at Indianapolis is different to Formula One, where you're tested over a single lap. At Indianapolis, you have to maintain the highest speed you can over four laps, a total of 10 miles – a reasonable distance over which the balance of the car will change. By putting this cross-weight adjuster in the cockpit, Mario had an extra tool to keep the car in balance through his four-lap run. He did so, and it contributed to him qualifying on pole by some margin.

The big problem we had was the oil tank. We kept having oil-pressure dropouts, typically halfway between turn one and turn two. It was clear that if we didn't get on top of it, we wouldn't last the 500 miles.

So I kept redesigning the oil tank. I'd sit down with Mario Illien of Ilmor over dinner in the evening, try and understand what was going on, do a new drawing. The guys would take the oil tank out, weld some different baffles in and try again.

This went on for a while before we realised the problem was air trapped under the baffles in the oil tank. The rotation of turn one would set up a tumble motion inside the tank, moving the trapped air onto the pickup tube, where it would be sucked into the engine. God, it took us ages to work that out. Our final crack at solving the problem came on the morning of qualifying. Shattered, as was always the case at Indianapolis, I'd asked the guys to start the engine while I held a torch over the top of the open oil tank to observe the oil returning into it. There I was, peering in, when the metal top fell off my pen and plopped into the tank.

I gulped, knowing full well that we didn't have time to take the engine out, remove the bottom of the oil tank and then reassemble it before qualifying.

There was a coarse filter in the bottom of the oil tank, so we decided to risk running the car, praying that the lid would stay in the tank. Off went car and pencil top.

It was nerve-wracking. If the filter in the bottom hadn't protected the car, the pencil top would have been sucked into the pumps and destroyed them, and the engine would have been history. But the filter held out and my pen top did the first 220mph-average run in Indianapolis history.

Just as importantly, we stopped getting the oil-pressure dropouts and, come race day, Mario appeared to be unbeatable. By halfway through the race, we were more than one lap in the lead.

The car had a five-speed gearbox with fourth and fifth gears very close to one another. There was only 300 to 400rpm between them in terms of gearing, but if you needed every bit of performance, or conditions were slow, you'd select fourth for higher rpm, meaning more power from the engine. If you wanted to conserve the engine, you'd select fifth, lower rpm, less power but better reliability and fuel consumption.

Because of our level of dominance, Mario selected fifth gear. Unfortunately, that put the engine into a resonance area and 50 miles before the end it dropped a valve. Mario came into the pits running on seven cylinders and that was that, retired, which was absolutely soul-destroying. We'd been so dominant, done everything right, but 50 miles from the end of a 500-mile race, more than a lap ahead of the car in second place, we dropped out. It still makes me cross now, and it's considered one of the great upsets in Indy 500 history.

A week after Indianapolis we went to Milwaukee. A funny track, it used to have grass growing between the cracks in the concrete.

Indy cars in those days used to have a warm-up procedure. They'd go slowly for a couple of laps, warming the engine before the driver would 'get on it' and take it up to full speed. The first time you witness a car coming past you at 225mph, you think, *Wow, God that is fast*. It's a breathtaking thing to be so close to a car going at that speed.

It's strange how quickly you adapt. After three weeks of practice, qualifying and then racing, 225mph doesn't seem fast at all. You then get to Milwaukee, where the cars are doing a mere 170mph or so, and you think, *For goodness sake, when are you going to stop warming up and actually get on it.* It's a very surreal thing after the speed of Indy.

Anyway, Milwaukee was a galling weekend. I took responsibility for the fact that the wing mounting failed, the wing came off and Mario had an accident, breaking a rib, which meant that, despite the painkillers, the padding we added and modifications we made to the seat, he was driving in a lot of pain at Mid-Ohio, the next race. Despite this, he put the car on pole, dominated throughout and won the race – like I said, a tough cookie.

He had an accident at Pocono. There wasn't much left of the car afterwards, but one thing we did find was a load of silver paint down by the gear lever on the inside of the chassis. There was only one thing painted silver in the car and that was his helmet. Somehow in that accident, his helmet had ended up by the gear lever, but he was unhurt. Remarkable.

If you know motor racing, you'll know that there's a lot of talk about the 'Andretti curse'. Indeed, Mario certainly seemed to have more than his fair share of bad luck, and there were plenty of times when he was leading Indy only to break down through no fault of his own. What's more, Michael and even his nephew and grandson seem to have inherited his luck.

I wouldn't know about that. I can't say I believe in 'curses'. What I would say is that he had amazing courage and resilience to keep getting back in the car when he was suffering shunt after shunt, never losing his nerve.

At the Road America circuit in Elkhart Lake we had to deal with the problem of falling leaves – and then the weather. Mario was on pole but it started raining during the race, so he came in and fitted wet tyres. The rain stopped, and as others had pitted again to go back to slicks, in order for us to stay in the lead we needed it to start raining again.

'You need to do a rain dance,' I told Carl, joking.

Carl said, 'Okay,' and started dancing round in circles, chanting in Hebrew. It started raining again and Mario went on to win the race! As you can imagine, that only increased Carl's faith in all that kind of hocus-pocus.

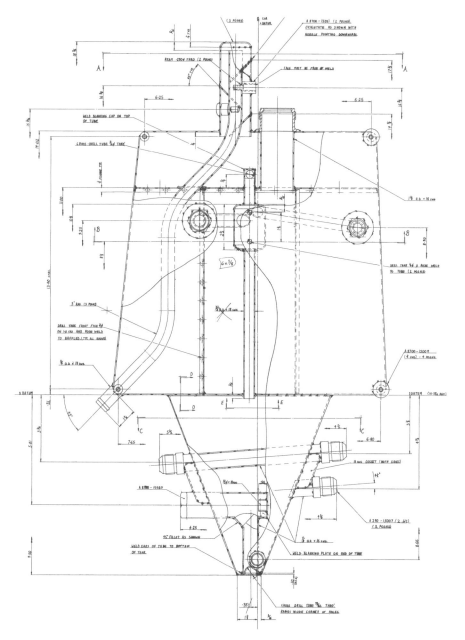

Figure 7: Technical drawing of the problematic oil tank in the Chevrolet-engined Lola.

Elkhart Lake is an old-fashioned American family holiday resort area – think of Butlin's. That night, I put a dollar in the vibrating bed of my room, but instead of the expected massage, it began shaking violently, followed by a huge bang, sparks and smoke. I ended up dragging the mattress onto the floor in order to get a good night's sleep. Oh the glamour!

I was enjoying the season, but by June I had to think about my options for the following year. Carl wanted me to get involved in the design of next year's car but I'd always been upfront with him about my desire to return to Formula One, and I felt I'd done my years in IndyCar. Despite Mario's rocky season in 1987, in particular the Indy 500 upset – which still hurts – my year-old 86C had done well. Penske's own car had proved a flop, and after recording very poor times in the first week of practice for Indy, Roger Penske took the brave decision to scrap the programme and wheel out his March 86C from the previous year. Remarkably, Al Unser (driving for Penske) went on to win after Mario's breakdown, giving me the consolation of having three Indy 500 winners.

Turn Three

HOW TO BUILD
AN 881

CHAPTER 22

During my time commuting to the States, Robin Herd of March was hard at work securing a financier for March's return to Formula One. The fellow he found was an entrepreneur called Akira Akagi.

Akagi was Korean, although he tended to keep that fact quiet, letting people think he was Japanese for ingrained status reasons I don't fully understand. His fortune had been made in Tokyo property, which in the mid- to late 1980s was going through the roof, and he also owned Tokyo's largest department store, Leyton House, which he'd named in honour of the London suburb of Leyton, where he had lived when he was younger.

Why did he – why does anyone – want to invest in an F1 team? Well, when you consider that in the years between 2000 and 2014, Red Bull gained an estimated £1.6 billion in advertising simply by being involved in F1, then it's a bloody good promotional tool. It can also help to pave the way into new markets. For instance, when cans of Red Bull started selling in China, the Chinese were shocked to discover that the Formula One team also made an energy drink. The Japanese, as a nation, are very proud of their engineering prowess and also keen followers of Formula One. Even to this day, over 25 years later, when I go to the Japanese Grand Prix at Suzuka several fans will ask me to sign models of the Leyton House Formula One car from back then.

Thanks to Akagi, March once more had the means to compete in Formula One, and for the 1987 season what they did was take a Formula 3000 car, bolt an F1 engine into the back and fit regulation tyres. With Ivan Capelli driving, they raced it as a Formula One car. On the upside, a low-budget way into Formula One for March and for Leyton House but, on the downside, the car was uncompetitive and performed accordingly, scoring just one point the whole season.

Just as Robin anticipated, however, the experience was intoxicating enough to whet Akagi's appetite, and with Robin suggesting that maybe with a bit more money we could see a genuine improvement in the team's fortunes, it was agreed a proper car would be designed from scratch for the 1988 season. Leyton House Racing, as it was now called, would go from a one-car team to a two-car team, with a second driver alongside Ivan Capelli.

So, on that basis, and feeling that now they had a properly backed effort, Robin approached me in the summer of 1987, when I was race engineering Mario Andretti at Newman Haas, and asked whether I'd be interested in being technical director.

For me, at 28, this was a chance to have another shot at Formula One, but this time in an environment and working with people that I knew and felt comfortable with. True, I was taking a big drop in salary from $400,000 to £140,000 plus a percentage of any prize money, which meant a likely income of less than half when you take the exchange rate into consideration, but for me this was a secondary consideration compared to the chance of pursuing my Formula One dream.

I spoke to Carl, who was very understanding. He insisted I stay on to finish the season with Mario, which was fair enough, and he was keen I didn't get involved in any of March's IndyCar projects, which again I was happy with, so we shook hands and went our separate ways. Carl was one of the big personalities in the sport and we remained friends over the years. His passing in 2016, after a period of illness, was a great loss.

Thus from late July began yet another exhausting phase of double-duty. Once again I was commuting to the States to race engineer Mario, while at home I was working on the Formula One car at March.

Things had changed since I was last a part of the set-up. Still in Bicester, Leyton House were now in separate premises from the rest of March in a little factory unit about half a mile from the production facility. When I'd started with March in 1982, six of us plus drawing boards were crammed into the tiny design office, starved of natural light in the bowels of the factory, right next to the machine shop, and God help us if there was a fire. Now we were in a much more spacious office upstairs with room for eight people (though there were only six to start with) and workshops downstairs.

In the meantime, my return to Formula One coincided with an era when the governing body of the FIA allowed the existing turbocharged 1.5-litre

V6s to race alongside a new formula for normally aspirated 3.5-litre engines. The idea was that 1988 would be a transition year; the turbocharged engines would then be outlawed for 1989 and beyond on the grounds that they were far too expensive for the teams (sound familiar?). That was going to make things very difficult for us, because the V6s were much more powerful than the 3.5-litre V8 engine made by a small private company, Judd, that we were to use. Accordingly, our expectations of getting good results were low. Robin worked out that in order to finish in the top six (i.e. in the points) we would have to be the fastest of the normally aspirated cars. That was my job, he told me. Design that car.

Sure, I told him. But what I *really* wanted to achieve, what became my guiding philosophy as I began design work on the car, was for our normally aspirated car to be in there among the turbos. Even attempting this was ambitious to the point of arrogance, but what the hell: I was young and keen to make my mark in Formula One.

I thought we could do it too, thanks to a rule change in our favour. Up until that year, turbocharged cars hadn't been using traditional petrol, they'd been using toluene, which is a chemical most closely related to piano black, of all things, and a complete health hazard. With engines constantly belching out highly carcinogenic smoke, the FIA insisted teams go back to normal fuel, or at least something closer to it. On top of that, the boost from the turbocharger was to be limited. So while in 1986 they'd been producing something like 1,300 horsepower in qualifying, they were now were restricted to around 900.

Our normally aspirated V8 was giving us 580 horsepower, so we were still a long way behind. However, the design of turbocharged cars had become clumsy. Complacent teams seemed to have settled for simply bolting ever-bigger front and rear wings onto the car, happy with the downforce and content that they had enough power to pull all that drag. Aerodynamically, the cars were quite dull and, in my opinion, less sophisticated than the Indy cars in this respect. On top of this, the turbo engines tend to be heavy installations, so teams were unable to get down to the weight limit.

My feeling was that if we came up with something lighter and way more aerodynamically efficient, we could be competitive. There was no point in running a big wing, because although we'd have lots of downforce in the corners, we would be way too slow on the straight. Just as in IndyCars, where the trick was to achieve a high top speed while maintaining good downforce, my plan was to develop the aero package around a moderate-sized rear wing.

The car would be the Leyton House 881. In terms of providing a template for future designs, it was probably the most important of my career.

CHAPTER 23

Work on the 881 began in July of 1987, with a deadline of February the following year for the first test. Under normal circumstances that's a tight but fairly standard turnaround, but this one would be slightly special, requiring even longer man hours from a very small team, for the simple reason that it was a start-from-scratch project – a clean-sheet-of-paper car (my favourite sort).

It was built around our lead driver, Ivan Capelli. Ivan was a fairly small guy, and I wished to take advantage of this by making the cockpit small. We built a mock-up of the cockpit for him to sit in, then started bringing the pedals back towards him, so that his legs were bent as far as he felt comfortable with. Having determined that envelope of space, we designed the chassis, the idea being to wrap it as tightly as possible around him. I realised that because the driver sits with his heels closer together than the balls of his feet – i.e. heels in, toes out – we could make the chassis V-shaped in cross-section and create a narrower underside to it. Things began to take shape.

The regulations at the time called for all bodywork visible from beneath the car to be flat between the rear edge of the front tyre and the front edge of the rear tyre. The pedals by regulation were positioned on the centre line of the front tyre, roughly 330mm forwards of this flat area, so, to improve the air flow underneath, we raised and sculpted the underside of the chassis and nose, meaning that it was only at the start of that area that the car was flat. It was something that had been done to a small extent before, but we went much further, raising the driver's feet in the process.

We then took that raised sweep and ran it all the way through to the underside of the front wing, so the nose now only existed above the front wing rather than below it as well. What that gave us was an underside to the front-wing profile that was continuous all the way across the car instead of being interrupted by the nose – the first car to have this. Because it's the underside of the wing that is critical, making the front wing continuous across the car gave us more efficient front downforce. The middle of the wing was now working where it hadn't been before, because it had been divided by the nose.

Taken together, the combination of the very narrow V-shaped chassis, the raised pedals and this continuous shape from the underside of the front wing through to the start of the flat bottom area at the back edge of the front wheel made for a much more efficient front end, and our overall aerodynamics took a big step forward. Structurally, we also took advantage of this by making the wing one continuous piece, rather than the traditional left and right halves with a relatively floppy tube passing through the nose to join them.

Next we needed to package the front suspension and driver's feet in this new raised position inside the monocoque. In order to do that, we raised the top of the chassis at the centre line of the front wheels, which was in itself an aerodynamic improvement.

We also sculpted the front-wing endplates. Until that time, everybody had flat front-wing endplates, which stopped just ahead of the front tyre in order that the driver could steer without the wheel hitting the endplate.

The problem with that was that the act of steering created a varying gap between the endplate and the tyre, so you didn't get a nice continuous shape as you steered. What I wanted to do was change the shape of the endplates to give us a continuous shape irrespective of the tyre position, so we sculpted the endplates, extending and bringing them inboard beside the tyre while allowing enough clearance for steering lock. This also seemed to work well, and gave some good gains.

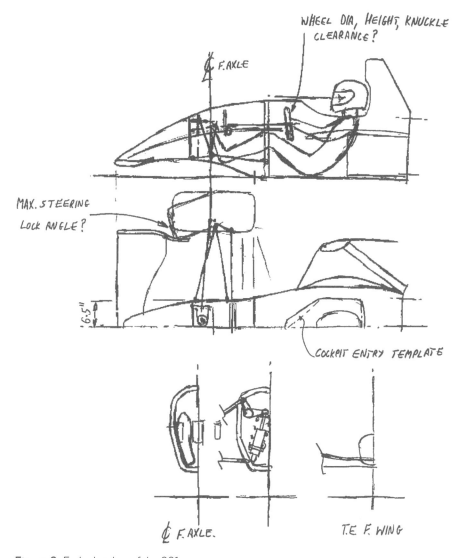

WHEEL DIA, HEIGHT, KNUCKLE CLEARANCE?

₵ F. AXLE

MAX. STEERING LOCK ANGLE?

6.5"

COCKPIT ENTRY TEMPLATE

₵ F. AXLE.

T.E. F. WING

Figure 8: Early sketches of the 881.

We reduced the cockpit aperture size down to the legal minimum size by bringing the chassis over the top of the steering wheel. You get turbulent dirty air in the cavity formed by the cockpit aperture, so by bringing it back and making it more like a closed car with a helmet sticking out of the top we minimised that, resulting in better-quality flow travelling rearwards onto the lower element of the biplane rear-wing arrangement. Following on from that, we redesigned the engine cover. Being a 90-degree V8 engine, the intake trumpets on the Judd were widely spaced, which would force us to have a bulbous engine cover, which would in turn further disrupt the flow to the lower of the two rear-wing sets. The idea was to remake the inlet trumpets to an oval shape and bend them towards the car centre line, get everything narrower, and hence have a narrower engine cover. And because the better-quality air flow was helping the lower wing to work more effectively, the lower pressure generated by it in turn helped to extract flow from the diffuser more efficiently, hence loading up the diffuser.

Talking of which, we narrowed the back of the car and came up with a diffuser that was divided into two arched tunnels per side.

The bottom line of all this work was that while the previous year's car had a downforce-to-drag ratio of about two to one – i.e. two units of downforce for one unit of drag – the 881 had just over three to one, more than 50 per cent more downforce for the same drag. In terms of creating a package, we had taken a huge step forward.

The whole time I was still flying back and forth to the States. One of the great things about flying, as I've mentioned before, is that for eight hours you have nothing else to do, so if you feel as though you're doodling or being inefficient with your time, it doesn't matter. I found that liberating. I had lots of ideas for the 881 on those plane trips: how to package the front suspension, for example, because having adopted the new shape, it wasn't easy to get all the suspension inside this relatively small monocoque. That was sketched out on the plane.

Meanwhile I added other modifications of what I'd learnt on IndyCars. The roll hoop, for instance, was a direct descendant of the aluminium honeycomb roll hoop of the 1986 March. (It seemed obvious to apply that roll bar to the 881, though it had never occurred to me to do the same for the aborted 1987 Beatrice car, when I was suffering from my creative block.)

When it came to developing the aerodynamics, I tended to draw all the aerodynamic parts at the scale of the model, which at that point was one-third (another step on from the quarter-scale wind tunnel models I'd been working with) so that my paper drawings could be easily cut out to form templates for the model-makers. Components were usually made of wood built onto an aluminium spine, although some of the finer bits such as the front wing were made out of carbon fibre.

The model-makers were very good. They quickly made the parts and we rattled through a programme. We were using the Southampton wind tunnel, the 7ft × 5ft working-section tunnel that I'd first encountered as a student. Here I was, eight years later, still there, my familiarity with the surroundings no doubt helping to make this one of those development programmes that just seemed to work.

Not everything, of course. It wasn't as though every drawing resulted in a component, but we had a pretty good hit rate.

By the time the car was complete, it was very tidy. Since it was our first year, we didn't really know our targets, but looking at the car I was proud of it because it looked different, much smaller and more sculpted than its rivals, and I felt it had good engineering practice behind it. How competitive it was going to be, we didn't know.

CHAPTER 24

Imola, northern Italy, was the site of the first test, and once again I felt the elemental sensory assault of Formula One as the teams assembled: the smell of fuel and the sweet scent of hot rubber; the squeal of high-power impact wrenches; the constant, almost addictive drone of engines. House-hold-name drivers like Ayrton Senna and Alain Prost in the McLarens, Nigel Mansell in a Williams, Gerhard Berger in the Ferrari, the reigning world champion Nelson Piquet in the Lotus. It hit me that I was back. This was where I wanted to be.

We set up shop in our garage in the pit lane, exchanging the usual friendly-but-guarded pleasantries with guys from other teams. There's always interest in competitors' cars. Garage doors are often at half-mast, and you get a lot of folk who 'just happen' to be walking by, surreptitiously trying to peer inside your garage.

I might have imagined it, but our garage seemed to attract more walk-bys than usual, maybe because the 881 looked so different.

We played up to our new-kid-on-the-block status. Much the same as Red Bull later, Leyton House became the jokers of the pit lane. One night, one of our mechanics emptied what must have been a gallon of washing-up liquid into the fountains at the entrance to the circuit. We returned the next day to a scene out of the movies. There were soap suds everywhere. Huge, shifting mountains of washing-up bubbles, like some kind of blob-like monster attempting to consume Imola. I'm not exaggerating; it was so big they had to close the road. Police were called. They knew that one of the teams was behind the washing-up-liquid monster, but never got to the bottom of it. I guess this is me admitting it on behalf of Leyton House. Coming clean, you might say.

We started running and there were two immediate problems. The first was that we hadn't left enough room in the cockpit for Ivan to change gear. In those days, of course, it was a stick shift, not the paddles on the steering wheel we have now, and it was mounted on the right just by the steering wheel. Bit of an oversight.

The second and even more worrying problem was the gearbox running way too hot. The 1987 Formula 3000-based car had had a problem with the reliability of the driveshaft CV joints, and we had hoped to solve it by installing a hypoid drive. But when we stripped down the gearbox that evening we found lots of fretting marks. These occur when two bits of metal rub on each other at very high contact pressure, resulting in local welding of the two materials before they then break apart again. As that local welding forms and then breaks, it creates little pits, which eventually create a crack right through the gear tooth; this subsequently falls off, typically followed shortly afterwards by the car grinding to a halt in a haze of gearbox oil. A serious problem.

So, the gear lever. I remember that night well. We cut a hole in the side of the monocoque, got Ivan to sit inside and expanded the hole until he was happy he had enough room to change gear. With that done, I got hold of some wax and moulded it over his knuckles, turfed him out of the car and reinforced the wax by putting temporary fibreglass on the inside, followed by a thin scrim of fibreglass and filler on the outside to create a smooth shape.

Once that was nice and smooth I removed the mould. By this time it was about two in the morning, so I sent everyone home while I made a new blister out of carbon fibre, using all that knowledge and experience I'd accrued working on my models and on my dad's Lotus, not to mention a summer job I once had making fibreglass fishponds in Southampton.

The sun was coming up over Bologna by the time I'd bonded the new blister onto the side of the tub, given it a lick of paint, Miami blue, and stood back to admire my work. When the mechanics returned in the morning, they were quietly complimentary, which from Formula One mechanics is a big compliment!

I guess I'm probably the only technical director in recent history who has made a component overnight for the car.

More importantly, it worked. Ivan could change gear properly. On to problem two: our gearbox temperature stickers indicating that the gearbox was way too hot. Sure enough, when we stripped it down again that night, we found that we were about to lose teeth. The bit of fretting we'd noticed previously was pretty much terminal.

At the same time, interest in our garage was reaching a kind of fever pitch. As we stood there trying to sort out our gearbox problem, I heard a noise from the door behind us and turned to see the unmistakeable form of Harvey Postlethwaite, my mentor at Fittipaldi who had since gone to Ferrari. Here he was crawling under our garage door on his hands and knees.

'Well, well, what have we here, Adrian?' he bellowed. And for reasons that bemuse me still, a mixture of fatigue and politeness kicking in, I greeted him and let him get on with having a nose around our car. Of course what I should have done was tell him to mind his own business. But secretly I was flattered.

It was a four-day test, and although the ongoing gearbox problem stopped us getting as much running done as we would have liked, we were able to establish one very important point: the car was quick, easily the quickest of the normally aspirated cars, which was enough to earn it cover-girl status on the following week's *Autosport*.

That cover. Being at the sharp end of the timesheets. Attracting press attention. It felt like all our hard work – and there was an awful lot of hard work on that car – was paying off.

Question was: how would it race?

CHAPTER 25

Brazil. First race of the 1988 season. We had three days of testing followed by a break of a week before the race, so we had plenty of time to become experts at our new sport of 'flameouts'. Brazilian cars ran on fuel called Alcool, a distilled sugar beet also used for alcoholic drinks. It's quite sweet. They had to put a foul-tasting chemical in the fuel version to prevent people drinking it directly from the pumps.

We soon worked out that if you put your foot down in a hired VW Beetle and turned off the ignition, the alcohol would collect in the exhaust, and then switching the ignition back on would ignite it, causing a huge flame-thrower effect that would light up the long, downhill tunnels that lined the route from Rio to the track.

It was spectacular. We spent many a journey trying to beat each other to the longest flame, often with the rusting silencer box left lying in the road.

The competition continued as we neared the circuit. Gaining access to the track meant a tricky manoeuvre off the dual carriageway, so we were all trying to do our most spectacular U-turns.

On one occasion the Lotus team, who were in a campervan (memo to Lotus, not the best vehicle for handbrake U-turns), lost control and ended up in the central grass area. It goes without saying that the rest of us took great pleasure from their discomfort and sailed past, waving and giving other hand signals on our way into the circuit. Last I heard of them they'd got wind of the fact that the grassy area was infested by snakes and ended up standing on the roof of the van waving their arms for help like castaways.

Meanwhile, the heat was playing havoc with our car, its cooling system not up to the very high ambient temperatures. We qualified mid-field then retired during the race, our lack of experience all too obvious. It was all very dispiriting apart from one thing: an engineer from Williams, James Robinson, introduced himself and took me to one side. He suggested I contact a company called David Brown Gears about our gearbox problem. Very gracious of him, and we became good friends; it turned out that he lived in the next village to us. What's more, his advice proved sound. When we returned to the UK, David Brown were able to fix our gearbox problem.

Back to Imola for the second race of the season, the San Marino Grand Prix, and once again we were plagued by mechanical problems. The downforce caused our nose to collapse: poor detail design but easy to fix.

At Monaco we were paid the first of two visits that season by our sponsor, Akagi. I remember it well because he'd arranged for a boat to sit in the harbour as a team base, only the boat hit a storm in the English Channel, was damaged and didn't arrive until Saturday evening.

Okay, I thought. Monaco. Now here's a circuit; much less power-sensitive – that should be perfect for us. It didn't work out that way. Monaco is a street track that requires a very different kind of set-up. Moreover, that weekend was blighted by changeable weather, the long and short of it being that we never really nailed the set-up.

During the race our second driver, Maurício Gugelmin, retired and Ivan came tenth. And while tenth was by no means a disaster, it was still nowhere near where we wanted to be. More to the point, it showed we weren't getting the performance out of the car that pre-season testing had indicated we should.

That night a party was held on Akagi's boat. A typical Formula One affair; things soon got out of control. Because of the difficulty in getting around in Monaco we had rented some small scooters off a local hire company. They were pretty old and worn out, but that evening, having had way too much to drink, I took up a dare from the mechanics and rode it into the harbour.

It wasn't the smartest move. First, the water was bloody cold; second, I'm not a very strong swimmer, particularly when I'm fully clothed and three sheets to the wind.

Upshot: one red face. Not to mention one destroyed scooter. Mind you, we were pretty reckless with vehicles back in those days. Dare I say it, there wasn't quite the accountability you have nowadays. We were forever trashing hire cars while racing each other or other teams. In those days the track rivalry was intense but teams were much smaller and so was the paddock, and off-track there existed a kind of shared camaraderie. We all ate in the same 'roach coach' rather than sticking to our own 'team centres' as we do now. The competitive spirit was just as pronounced but it was a bit more fun; the term 'politically correct' had not yet been coined.

One trick was to make balloon bombs by filling a dustbin bag with acetylene and then poking it with a lit match. Overnight you'd hear the bang of acetylene bombs going off, followed by cheers along the paddock. Spotting somebody wandering along, half asleep, not aware of what was going on around them, you'd let off an acetylene bomb and watch them jump three feet in the air in shock. Cue: cheers.

I remember a chap, Karl Heinz Zimmerman, who ran the Williams motorhome. He had a cannon that he'd fire if Williams won a race, a proper cannon that he filled with gunpowder. God knows how he managed to get it through customs, but he'd wheel it into the middle of the paddock and set it off. It became a bit of an event. People would gather round. Pit crew, journalists, photographers. One day, a photographer stood too close, got a bit of gunpowder in his eye, threatened to sue and the practice stopped. Bah. Mind you, it took Bernie's interim intervention to stop the litigation, by pointing out that such an action would result in the loss of said journalist's paddock pass. Bernie liked to look after the characters in the pit lanes.

Meanwhile the FIA have since decided that it's too dangerous to let pit crews work overnight, so we have all these hours when the car is impounded, apart from four jokers per year when you're allowed to work overnight. Health-and-safety has its place, of course. The FIA are right, and fair enough, it probably *is* a bad idea to let off a cannon in the paddock. The problem is that you lose something in the process, and it hasn't been replaced.

Anyway, moving on, and by Mexico we were putting the gearbox problems behind us thanks to our David Brown hypoid. This allowed me to go back to concentrating on performance: our drivers were complaining of understeer in the middle of the corners, so we designed a bigger front wing for more front downforce, as well as modifying the front suspension in order to put more rising rate into the geometry. This meant we could run softly sprung at low speed but stiffly at high speed, and that allowed us to run a lower front ride-height, which was better for the aerodynamics of the car. Slowly but surely we were putting our reliability problems behind us and learning how to set up the car.

Next race was Canada. We were nothing special in qualifying, with quite a few normally aspirated cars in front of us. However, we ran better in the race and though Maurício retired, Ivan finished fifth.

You might think I'd have been happy about that. I remember driving back to the airport with the team principal Ian Phillips and our chief designer Tim Holloway, both of whom were delighted that we'd finally scored our first two points. Personally I was disgruntled because we still weren't properly competitive compared to where I felt we should be. I still thought our car should be performing better than it was.

As I've said, the main problem the drivers were reporting was understeer. I reckoned that if we could get over that, we could unlock the car's potential.

We went from Montreal straight to Detroit, a street track, perfect for a normally aspirated car. Or so you'd think.

In fact, it was a disaster. Ivan had an accident in practice, took the front corner off the chassis and broke his foot, so he was a DNS, while Maurício didn't finish. Yet another frustrating result.

By this stage I was seriously puzzled. The rest of the team were okay, even Ivan and Maurício didn't complain – it was Maurício's first year in

Formula One and Ivan had been racing an even less competitive car the previous season, so I guess it was still an improvement for them – but I was not happy. Looking at the other normally aspirated cars on the grid, the AGS, the Minardi, the Dallara, even the Williams, I was convinced our car should be faster, doing better than this. The other cars were, I felt, aerodynamically inferior to us. What were we failing to understand?

I suspected that we had not got the suspension geometry and race-engineering set-up of the car well matched to the aero characteristics. Ivan felt that even at the initial entry to the corner, where the driver is still braking but begins to turn the wheel, the car was understeering. The front suspension geometry had 50 per cent anti-dive, which means that under braking the natural compression of the front suspension is halved due to weight transfer onto the front. The benefit of this is that the car pitches less; the downside is that the suspension is less compliant in this state and therefore the ride suffers and the front wheels are more prone to lock up. Since we were lacking front grip in this braking-and-entry phase of turns, the implication was we could allow the front to pitch down more to improve the ride and give a more forward aero balance. So for the French Grand Prix we made modifications to the chassis to allow a reduction to 15 per cent anti-dive. It was an improvement, which, combined with the bigger front wing and increased rising rate suspension, meant the understeer was reduced and the drivers could start to use the aerodynamics to push the car harder.

By Hockenheim in Germany we were running well. We were up to equal sixth in the constructors' championship and Ivan was eleventh in the drivers'. We introduced a longer nose and a new front wing in Hungary, which is a maximum downforce circuit anyway, and although we had an engine problem that retired Ivan, Maurício finished fifth.

At Monza, Ivan was banging wheels with Riccardo Patrese in a Williams for fifth place. Ivan's a ballsy driver, and it just so happened that he chose the right race for that particular display, because when I showed the damage to Akagi, making the second of his two visits that season, he was most impressed with Ivan's determination to get past Patrese on his way to that fifth place.

Mind you, Mr Akagi was caught out that weekend. In all our dealings with him we had gone through his translator, Akagi always sitting impassively while he waited for our points to be translated. Our Leyton House motorhome was tiny, with seating for six people: the two drivers and their race engineers, Tim Holloway and Andy Brown; Ian Phillips, the team principal; and myself. That weekend Ian stood in order to give Akagi a seat, which he remained in after the rest of us left to get ready for the start of the race. Enter a very pretty Italian journalist who asked for an interview. Looks can obviously go a long way, because he gave it in apparently perfect English.

At sixth in the championship and now routinely scoring points, I stood on the pit wall at Portugal, watching the last corner during practice. Ivan came round and then, behind him, Prost, who was going really slowly.

That was odd, I thought. It turned out Prost had seen Ivan go into the long, fast right-hand corner at a speed he thought was suicidal. He was so convinced there was going to be an accident that he lifted right off.

'I cannot believe that car,' is what I'm told he said on the radio. It was quite something for the great Alain Prost to think our car couldn't possibly take the corner that fast, especially bearing in mind that, because we lacked the horsepower, we had to run a much smaller rear wing than his turbocharged McLaren.

In qualifying we arrived third on the grid but I couldn't stay. I had to work on the 1989 car – what would be the CG891 – and flew home.

Amanda picked me up from the airport and as we drove from Heathrow back home we listened to radio coverage of the race. I was nervous. It had been our strongest showing yet in qualifying. During the race, Ivan kept on Senna's tail but just couldn't get past him.

And then, finally, about two-thirds of the way through the race, Ivan realised what he had to do, which was hang back slightly going into the last corner, pull into Senna's slipstream and then duck out of it at the last moment.

It worked. Ivan overtook Ayrton Senna.

I can clearly remember the sheer euphoria of that moment. This tiny team with limited resources and a normally aspirated engine had just overtaken a McLaren driven by Ayrton Senna. To put this into context, McLaren with their Honda power units had been in a league of their own; if a McLaren was overtaken it was only by its sister car. For a normally aspirated engine to do it? *Fantastic.*

What's more, Ivan went on to finish second behind Prost; we'd got our first podium and the car was finally showing its potential. It was a magical race.

Spain was an unremarkable race by the standards of that very remarkable season. But then came Japan, where to the great delight of our sponsor, Ivan managed a fourth on the grid behind Gerhard Berger (the front row being locked out by Senna and Prost in the McLarens for the eleventh time that season). I wasn't there for the race, still hard at work on the 891. But I was watching, of course, and what I saw was one of the most exciting things to happen that season.

The race began. Senna stalled on the grid and then spent most of the race trying to make up places. It would turn out to be a remarkable drive from Senna, but I was focused on Ivan, who was also having an outstanding race, hounding the front runners and overtaking Berger to put himself in second place behind Prost.

And then – tucked up behind Prost exiting the last chicane, Ivan got the power down well to be just ahead of Prost by the start/finish line. Unfortunately, as the main straight continued on down to turn one, the Honda power meant Alain retook the lead, but on the scoreboard Ivan was registered as race leader for that lap.

It was the first time a normally aspirated car had taken the lead in a Formula One race since 1983. Our hearts in our mouths, we watched as Ivan kept trying to find another way past Prost; he'd done it once, perhaps he could manage it again. Except . . .

Ivan stopped.

Ground to a halt.

Later on, Ron Dennis, owner of McLaren, put it about that we had short-fuelled the car in order to take the lead, and that was why we stopped. It was complete rubbish of course, but the mystery remained: why had our car suddenly stopped and forced Ivan to retire? When we got it back to the pits it fired up and ran perfectly.

Answer? The jury's out. We never quite got to the bottom of it. The engine control unit, the initial suspect, was returned to the supplier, but they found nothing wrong. Several months later Ivan admitted that what *might* have happened – it was possible, he said, sheepishly – is that in adjusting the stiffness of the rear anti-roll bar using a lever positioned under his left arm, he could have knocked the ignition switch, a toggle switch positioned 4in further forwards from the roll bar lever. In truth it's an easy mistake for a driver to make and an example of how you can go through thousands of miles of testing and racing, only to be tripped up by a driver, in the heat of battle, doing something slightly different to what he has done before.

Meanwhile, Senna was driving like a demon. He had fought his way up the placing to put himself second behind Prost, who was having issues with his gearbox.

Senna overtook Prost, drove a succession of fast laps (breaking Ivan's lap record in the process), won the race and settled the championship, his first. But for us it was a real what-might-have-been race. As history now shows, Leyton House only came close to winning a race one other time. To this day it still hurts that of those 'oh so close' two occasions, Japan 1988 and France 1990, neither converted and Leyton House resides among that long list of winless constructors.

CHAPTER 26

A Porsche 911 is a horrible car from a vehicle dynamics point of view. It's all to do with the fact that the engine is hung out the back behind the rear axle. Owners who take early models on tracks often spin them. Once that heavy rear starts coming round, it's like having a sack of coal in the boot: when it starts moving, it's difficult to stop it. You have to make much bigger steering corrections.

Which brings me on to the 1989 car.

We had ended the 1988 season tied with Williams and Arrows in fifth place, Ivan seventh in the drivers' championship. For a little team, it was a phenomenal result and one that launched my name in Formula One. I'd had success in America, but up until then I'd been unknown in the UK. Now I was the hot new kid on the block and in demand for magazine and newspaper interviews – very flattering, of course; we all have egos.

I worked on shifting the weight of the 891, aiming to carry as much weight between the front and rear axles as possible. This allows the car to change direction more easily: picture a 2kg dumbbell with its weight concentrated at the ends; it is much more difficult to rotate this with your wrist than a 2kg bar of the same length but with the weight distributed evenly. Since about 1986, teams had been moving the gear cluster from behind the axle to just in front for this very reason, so we followed suit, as well as developing the aero, narrowing the chassis, making it even more V-shaped and bringing the driver's heels closer together, to the point that they were touching each other.

Ivan and Maurício were fine with that, their one request being that we lengthen the cockpit so they didn't have to drive with such bent knees. On paper the car looked good and in the wind tunnel it showed a good gain in downforce.

In practice, it turned out to be an utter nightmare.

CHAPTER 27

It was July 1989 when I returned to my home in Marsh Gibbon, only to find it empty. Just a note from Amanda. A 'Dear Adrian' letter telling me that she'd gone to her parents' house in Devon.

She was leaving me.

In hindsight I'd rushed into marrying Amanda. She was very pretty and great fun, and frankly I'd considered myself lucky to even be going out with her. Why not marry?

Cracks appeared when we moved to the US and she hadn't settled. In retrospect I should have done more: I should have found a better condo and ensured that her job at Red Roof was more inspiring, but equally her reaction to a little adversity had been to run back home. To make matters worse, we'd sold our cute little Pickwick cottage, so when she returned to the sanctuary of the UK after the Red Roof debacle she had nowhere to live except with her parents. When I returned in August we rush-bought a house in Piddington in Oxfordshire that we never really liked and then found a slightly dilapidated cottage in the next village along, Marsh Gibbon, both of them close to the March works in Bicester.

Thanks to a bridging loan we kept up both houses for a while and with help from various family members I set about restoring the Marsh Gibbon property. My first job was to get the nursery ready for Charlotte.

Things seemed to improve when we moved in. Amanda made friends through Charlotte's nursery. We had another lovely little girl, Hannah, born in February 1989.

I was prepared to try and work it out. I wanted the marriage to work. Amanda didn't feel the same way, hence the letter. She'd taken Hannah and Charlotte with her to her parents' place.

Her moving out marked the beginning of a very difficult period. I was having to juggle attempts at reconciliation with fatherhood and my job, which involved an awful lot of driving down to Devon, a lot of hotel stays, and a crash course in mobile parenting. (My tip: don't try to entertain the kids with a hotel room as your base. Take them home, where they have access to their toys and home comforts, even if it does involve a lot more time in the car.)

For a while I thought there might be hope for Amanda and me. But it turned out I was in denial. It took a particularly foul New Year's Eve bust-up for me to realise that things were terminal.

Work was my respite. Or should have been. But while I was pleased with the design of the 891 on paper, we were again plagued by reliability issues.

It turned out the gearbox-casing design was flawed. Relocating the gears to in front of the axle means either splitting the case into a front and back to allow access to the gears, or making the case continuous and putting a smaller access hatch in the middle. We'd chosen the former route and it was the wrong one. It was the heavier solution and we had problems with cracks around the casing.

In addition, the new engine from Judd wasn't producing the power we'd been promised. Plus we had a silly problem where we'd packaged the fuel pump on the rear bulkhead, directly driven by the exhaust camshaft. However, with the bulkhead flexing as a result of the loads from the engine mount, it caused the pump to seize.

As a result we didn't get the 1989 car ready for the beginning of the season and were forced to use the 881 for Brazil and San Marino.

In the end the 891 made its debut at Monaco and didn't go particularly well. At Mexico, a fourth-place qualifying position indicated potential but we had a complete disaster on race day. For aerodynamic reasons, we didn't have brake pipes in the airstream. They were threaded through the wishbone. As Ivan lined up on the dummy grid for the parade lap, we saw a puddle of brake fluid beneath the wishbone and had to pull the car. On investigation we found that a weld inside the wishbone had left a pip that had pierced the brake pipe.

But at least the car had shown some performance in qualifying. That was one positive takeaway from the experience.

Little did we know that qualifying fourth at Mexico would be the only time the car showed any real performance all season. We just could not find a sweet spot. It was inconsistent and difficult to drive; the drivers were complaining about balance, and never knew what it was going to do next, which is disastrous for a driver. If they can't be certain how a car will react, they can't push their driving to the limit and it creates a vicious circle. The driver loses confidence, he drives more slowly, the performance is even worse.

The bottom line was, we just didn't understand what was going wrong. We carried out deflection tests. Torsion tests. Everything looked fine. The weight distribution was what we expected, the suspension geometry was similar to the 881. It performed as it should in the wind tunnel.

You'll forgive me, then, if I don't go over the events of 1989 in any great detail. It boils down to a series of retirements and slow-running performances, and with each passing race my star dwindled from the hot new kid on the block to a one-hit wonder, yesterday's man. The press like to sensationalise; this was perfect for the 'build you up then knock you down' routine. Some of the press articles were quite hurtful. Since then, and as a result of that year, I have tried to keep a low profile in the media; after all, the safest way to avoid negative press coverage is not to have any at all.

On a professional and personal level, 1989 was a year to forget, an *annus horribilis*. But what to do for the 1990 season? By the end of 1989 we were finally starting to get the car more reliable, but from a performance viewpoint we didn't understand it, didn't understand why it wasn't performing. And, just to rub salt in the wound, many other teams had copied features from the 881, especially the raised nose and V-shaped monocoque, and were now beating us.

CHAPTER 28

Wind tunnels have changed over the years. These days we have resources and computing power to carry out correlation techniques comparing how the car performs in the wind tunnel to how it performs on the track. The car has sensors allocated to measuring aerodynamic loads as well as the cars ride-height, yaw, roll, steering angle, wind direction and so forth. We have transducers to measure pressure on the various aerodynamic surfaces of the car to see if any of them are misbehaving or behaving differently to their cousins on the wind tunnel model. This allows you to build up a detailed picture of whether the car is performing the same on track as it does in the wind tunnel. It's sophisticated, and the difference between results in the wind tunnel and those on the track are generally small. A dedicated team is tasked with identifying the remaining differences, understanding them and attempting, where physics allows, to eliminate them in the future.

Back then, though, things were different. For a start, the model was smaller (one-third scale instead of 60 per cent today), and much more basic. An aluminium frame, it was clad with a nose, chassis and engine cover made of wood, the floor aluminium, the diffuser carbon fibre. Wings were typically wood with aluminium endplates.

The important thing was that it was the right shape, but of course wood isn't that stable, so the stability of the aerodynamic components on the wind tunnel model and the quality of surface finish wasn't that good. Plus the wooden and composite components were made by hand, with all the associated errors, whereas today they are made by computer-controlled machines.

We didn't have proper representation of tyres either. The tyres were made out of nylon with a bit of foam taped around the outside, so they didn't deform in the same way as a proper pneumatic tyre would. Since 2005, Pirelli supply all the teams with pneumatic wind tunnel tyres, exactly the same shape as the actual tyre but 60 per cent scale and constructed in a way that means they deform when loaded by the model in a similar way to the real tyre.

It was these discrepancies between the wind tunnel and what you might call real life – the size of the model, the various simplifications and differences between the tunnel model and the real thing that we had back then – that I felt was the problem with our car.

There was lots of discussion about what to do. Should we go back to the drawing board and hope we struck lucky with another new car? Or should we try to try to understand what was up with the existing one?

Personally, I just didn't see the point of going to work on another car until we understood the problems. It was a bit of a controversial decision at the time, but I elected to stick with our unloved 1989 car and try to understand what was wrong. If we could understand it, we had a chance of fixing it.

Having been so poor at Monaco two years in a row, coupled with a general feeling that we were performing better on smoother tracks, I wondered if we'd made the car too aerodynamically sensitive to ride-height change. I felt that if it could be made less sensitive, there was a better chance the car would behave on track as the wind tunnel said it should.

So in the wind tunnel we worked on the ride-height sensitivity. I tried to revise the front wing and the diffuser into something I hoped would be less sensitive, even if it meant giving away a bit of downforce. I tried to simplify the aerodynamics of the tip of the front wing and the area around the rear wheel on the diffuser.

And that was the 1990 car: the chassis, engine, gearbox and suspension were the same; the principal changes were aerodynamic. In essence the 1990 car was intended to be a desensitised 1989 car.

As the season loomed, I briefed the race engineers. We took the car for its first test at Jerez in Andalusia, Spain, and . . .

It was no better. A whole winter's work, and we were stuck with exactly the same problems as before.

I was at work on my drawing board, puzzling over the car, when one of the model-makers asked for a word. A good guy who I'd known since

IndyCar days, and who, like quite a few of the team, had become a friend, he'd come to see me to question a drawing. I'd left a line too long.

'Ah,' he said. 'You wouldn't have made that mistake a couple of years ago.'

Which about summed it up for me. The team was obviously beginning to lose confidence in me. Added to this, maybe my friendship with so many members of our tiny team was backfiring – familiarity breeds contempt. More to the point, maybe he was right? Maybe I was slipping. Making mistakes. Perhaps the split with Amanda, not to mention a torrid 12 months of trying and mainly failing to get the car to work, was finally taking its toll on me. Maybe the 881 was my pinnacle. Within the Formula One pond maybe I was only capable of being a one-hit wonder.

CHAPTER 29

Events moved fast in those early months of 1990.

First of all, we made arrangements to use a new wind tunnel. What had happened was that teams had become fed up with having to share the country's two moving ground wind tunnels, one at Southampton and one at Imperial College in London, and had started to build their own, rightly figuring that the initial capital expenditure would be compensated for by the long-term savings, not to mention the benefit of being able to use the tunnel seven days a week if they wished rather than for a five-day-week session once a month.

By 1990 Leyton House was the only team still using the wind tunnel at Southampton. Just us and the students.

Meanwhile, Robin Herd, who had sold out to Akagi in 1989, was branching out into new business ventures, one of which was building a wind tunnel, which he did in Brackley, not far from the Leyton House base in Bicester.

The person Robin consulted for the general specification of the tunnel was me, and one of my specifications was for a model movement system which would allow the ride-height of the model to be changed automatically while the tunnel was running. Not only that but it was a bigger tunnel, so we could go to a 40 per cent model, plus of course we could use it for as long as we liked.

That tunnel, the Comtec Tunnel in Brackley, was opened in early 1990, at which point we started to transfer our operation across from Southampton, so for a short period of time we were conducting tests in both tunnels.

There was a big difference in results: the 40 per cent model in the Comtec tunnel was aerodynamically unstable with a very large loss of rear downforce below a certain combination of front and rear ride-height. We went back to the Southampton tunnel, where the model had not shown this stall characteristic. So, for the first time, rather than looking at our model and seeking the answer to our problem on the car itself, we looked at the wind tunnel. As with all good motor-racing-orientated wind tunnels it had a moving conveyor belt, a bit like you get at the supermarket. The reason for this is frame of reference. In real life a car passes through and over stationary air and ground. In the wind tunnel the model is held stationary, so to replicate reality properly both the air and the ground must move at the same speed past the model. Below the conveyor belt was a plate perforated with lots of small holes, with the underside of the plate connected to a suction box. The purpose of this was to stop the low pressure generated under the model from sucking the belt upwards away from the plate. At Southampton this plate was aluminium but, unbeknown to us, beneath that were planks of oak bolted to the plate, through which the suction holes had been drilled. Over time the wood had bowed, creating a bi-material strip. The net result was that the ground plane, instead of being flat, was now gently concave along its length. This shape had naturally unloaded the diffuser, leading us to develop a more aggressive shape that could not cope in reality. And, in another twist, one of the things that had allowed us to develop the more aggressive shape was the move of the gear cluster from behind the axle on the 881 to in front for the 891/901.

It wasn't a euphoric moment because we hadn't yet got a solution, but it was a huge relief. Finally, after 12 months of confusion, pressure, depression and self-doubt, we had a plausible explanation for our problem child. And, as often seemed to be the way back then, at exactly the same time of March 1990, my home life was taking a much happier turn: I had started playing squash with a girl, Marigold, who I'd known through friends since my early twenties. We very much enjoyed each other's company.

However, other problems were brewing on the managerial front at Leyton House. Akagi was evidently in financial trouble and had begun tightening the purse strings. Rather, I should say he appointed someone else to tighten the purse strings on his behalf, and that person was a new financial director by the name of Simon Keeble.

Not long after that we had a dreadful … I was about to say 'race' in Brazil, but the reality was that we didn't get that far. We failed to qualify, returning home with our tails firmly between our legs.

One of us came back with more than just a red face. Post-Brazil, team principal Ian Phillips began complaining of headaches. Blinding headaches that at first he attributed to migraine. In fact it turned out he'd contracted meningitis, which meant he had to spend the next six months in a darkened room recovering, during which time Simon Keeble appointed himself as acting team principal.

Now, if there's one thing a financial director should never ever do, it's be allowed to run a race team, because bean counters, love them or hate them, by and large tend to have a short-term, blinkered approach to the bigger picture. When you've got a car performing badly the answer is to increase not reduce your research expenditure and hope to develop your way out of it. But of course he had his remit from Akagi, so reduce the expenditure is what he did, his reasoning being that we were throwing good money after bad.

I tried to ignore the internal politics and concentrate on using the Comtec wind tunnel (albeit with its associated costs) to understand and overcome the problems with the car. We put the model into the ride-height area, where it exhibited a large loss in rear downforce and sprayed the underside with Flow Vis fluid. This showed, as we'd suspected after the initial Comtec test, that the diffuser was heavily separated at this height, analogous to the stall an aircraft suffers if it flies too nose up. The Flow Vis also showed areas of separation underneath the front wing that had not been present at Southampton.

Armed with that inspiration, I went back to the drawing board to work on new shapes, going through the usual cycle of draw, manufacture, wind tunnel test, analyse results, next cycle – until such time as we had a solution, a new front wing (actually an old one that we re-used) and a completely new diffuser.

Even so, by the time we got through that cycle, Simon Keeble was making no bones about the fact that he was approaching other designers, even putting it about the workforce that he thought he could attract Harvey Postlethwaite to replace me. He and I were at permanent loggerheads by now, constantly getting into shouting matches. I was certain the diffuser we were developing was going to be a good step forwards. He was doubtful, but I did manage to persuade him to spend the money to make it.

With that in the background, I was approached by Jackie Oliver, the boss of Arrows, to see if I would be interested in going there as technical director, while at the same time I was approached by Patrick Head, the technical director at Williams, to see if I'd be interested in joining them as head of research and development.

Arrows was a more senior position and was offering more money. But I'd lost self-confidence around this period and thought that working for a big team like Williams would give me experience of how a championship-winning team operates, how they use their resources and tackle problems, the management structure and so forth. Plus I thought it might be a good thing not to be the guy in charge, with all the attendant pressure. Whereas if I went to Arrows, I might be going from the frying pan into the fire.

I took a look at my situation. I'm not by nature a quitter. I didn't *want* to walk out on Leyton House, the team I had been so centrally involved with from almost the start, especially now I could see light at the end of the (wind) tunnel.

But on the other hand it was obvious the team was financially and managerially in trouble. We had lost our sage-like overall background leadership when Robin sold out to Akagi, and Ian was still very poorly and confined to his darkened house. I was tired of battling with Keeble. Perhaps most worrying of all, rumour had it that the loans associated with Akagi's Tokyo property empire were in trouble with the banks and that the only reason he kept the team going was because closing it might be a warning flare to the banks to start looking a little more carefully.

So, with a heavy heart, the weekend before the French Grand Prix, I rang Patrick Head and said that I'd like to accept his offer and join Williams. On Monday I walked into work and was asked into Simon Keeble's office. He informed me that he had hired Chris Murphy, a designer from Lola, as technical director, with Akagi's blessing (so it was claimed). I was therefore free either to accept a lesser role within the team and 'carry on fiddling in the wind tunnel' or to leave. Effectively I was sacked.

I felt relieved in a way, but it was a strange feeling returning to the design office to inform my colleagues, many of whom had become friends, that I was leaving. I packed my books and drawing instruments, said my good-byes and left. The 3-mile drive back from work to home that Monday morning felt very surreal.

That weekend I settled down to watch the French Grand Prix, which was to be the first one using my new diffuser.

CHAPTER 30

I wish I could have been there. Ivan and Maurício had qualified seventh and tenth respectively, which was pretty decent considering we hadn't even made the grid in Mexico, the previous race.

Clearly, I thought, from the comfort of my sofa, the new diffuser offered the step forward that the Comtec wind tunnel indicated there should be.

Then the race. Now, the difference between our car and the other top 10 runners was the fact that our lower horsepower engine was not so hard on the tyres. As a result, one of our race engineers, Gustav Brunner, elected to run the cars without a mid-race pit-stop. All the other teams decided that they needed to stop once for fresh tyres, otherwise they wouldn't make it to the end of the race, but Gustav, to his everlasting credit, realised that there was a chance for our cars to run non-stop, and that's what they did.

Ivan and Maurício made progress through the first part of the race and were up to third and fourth by the time the other cars began stopping for fresh tyres. Our drivers raced on, and as a result they then ran first and second for most of the race.

A reliability problem forced Maurício to retire while in third, but Ivan was still leading the French Grand Prix. From not qualifying in the previous race, he had gone to now leading most of the next one, probably the biggest transformation in performance in Formula One history.

However, with around three laps to go, he picked up an oil-pressure problem in the high-speed corners and was forced to back off to try to save the engine and reach the finish line. In the process, he was overtaken by Alain Prost and finished second.

A photo from the podium says it all. Ayrton, in third, hands behind his back, wears an enigmatic smile. He was fortunate to come in third, following Maurício's retirement. Alain, in first, was wearing an even more wintry smile, and no doubt also counting himself lucky to have scored what that year's *Autocourse* described as a 'shrewd victory'. And Ivan, punching the air with jubilation, euphoria written all over his face. He had led the race for 45 laps. He had scored the first points of the season for Leyton House and signalled to the world that he and Leyton House were back from the doldrums.

As for me, I took pride in the result and pleasure from proof that I'd resolved a problem that had come close to breaking my spirit.

Meanwhile, I was having what you might call a 'what if' moment. Had I not verbally accepted Patrick's offer and had Keeble not fired me, what then? Politically it would have given me the upper hand over Keeble, but the fact was Keeble was there because Akagi was in financial trouble. Having been through it with Fittipaldi and Beatrice Haas, I had learnt how to read the signals . . .

As a sad footnote to all this, Leyton House lumbered through an uncompetitive 1991 season, at the end of which they were liquidated. Akagi was arrested, having been implicated in a scandal involving the Fuji Bank, and his associate, Ken Marrable, took over. The team was sold to a consortium made up of Marrable, Gustav Brunner and others. With the Leyton House name somewhat tainted, they returned to being called March Formula One for 1992 and raced for the whole of that season, albeit with a bit of a revolving-door policy concerning drivers, until eventually folding in early 1993.

Turn Four

HOW TO BUILD
AN FW14

CHAPTER 31

Williams, based in Didcot, Oxfordshire – a 35min trip from my home in Marsh Gibbon – was roughly triple the size of Leyton House and could boast a history to match.

Their story begins with Frank Williams. An ex-driver, engineer and travelling grocery salesman, he had launched Frank Williams Racing Cars in 1966, and then moved into Formula One in 1969, making a mark right away.

In 1976 Frank fell out with his business partner and left the team, taking engineer Patrick Head, with whom he founded Williams Grand Prix Engineering, overseeing its rise as a major force in Formula One. In 1986 Frank was involved in a car accident that left him in a wheelchair but he continued in Formula One, undaunted. In 1999 he was knighted.

So, as you can imagine, he was quite a character. Frank had showed incredible tenacity in starting Williams Grand Prix, but his masterstroke was teaming up with Patrick, a brilliant engineer. Theirs was a partnership that had already won many championships prior to my arrival.

It was a tight partnership too. What I found on joining was that the team was run as Frank and Patrick's hobby shop, with the pair of them making decisions over lunch.

Still, that was fine, at first, and I fitted right in; Patrick and I complemented each other well. A pragmatic engineer, he'd graduated in mechanical engineering but had seen the aerodynamic potential we demonstrated at Leyton House and recognised that by hiring me he could concentrate on the engineering side while leaving me to concentrate on the performance design. He was particularly good at forcing me to chase reliability, which in those days was not my forte. When I first joined, he said to me, 'Why on earth didn't you fix that flipping fuel pump at Leyton House?' and I remember thinking how right he was, because even though at the time I believed we were doing all we could to address the problem, the bottom line was that we didn't put enough proper research or design effort into fixing it. We should have done more, and ultimately I take responsibility for that.

On my first day, Monday 16 July, the day after the British Grand Prix, he called me into his office in order to boom at me. Son of a rear admiral, he boomed at everybody, not just me. 'I've been impressed with the way your cars went in France and Silverstone,' went the boom. (Ivan's second-place finish in France was no fluke, and the car had notched up overall fastest lap at Silverstone.) 'I think you should be chief designer, not head of research and development. Would you prefer that position?'

I'd been excited about R&D, but chief designer was more my skillset, as well as a chance to have a more profound impact on the performance of the car. True, Williams had lost their way in recent years, but they were still a successful and respected team. Patrick believed the engine side of the car was good. He surmised that if they got the aero right then maybe Williams could be competitive again. Needless to say, I accepted the offer.

My brief was to take a look at the current car before getting stuck into design work for the following season. I drew up a diffuser based on my memory of the one I'd just designed for Leyton House. It was somewhat compromised by the gearbox shape on the Williams, which was bulky, but even so I felt it would be an improvement on their current incarnation.

Straightaway the difference between Williams and Leyton House became clear. Leyton House had employed outside contractors and the lead times were glacial; at Williams, everything was made in-house, and they manufactured that new diffuser in half the time. It went on the car in Hungary and gave us about half a second in increased performance, which even in those days was a decent amount (in today's money, a *huge* amount). Within the team it was an important vindication for me: my arrival had put a few noses out of joint; there were some who thought Leyton House's success in 1988 had been a lucky fluke, that the FW13 was a good car and that there was no need to bring in an outsider from another team. After that I set about my main task: to design the 1991 FW14.

CHAPTER 32

The two drivers of the FW14 were to be Nigel Mansell and Riccardo Patrese. Of the two, the higher-profile name was Nigel. He hadn't yet won a championship, but he was an established frontrunner and had his eyes on the prize. The 1991 season would mark his return to Williams after a two-year stint at Ferrari.

Our first issue was the wind tunnel. On the plus side, we had a tunnel on-site at Didcot but it was an old, slow, quarter-scale tunnel bought from a company called Specialised Mouldings and then adapted in-house, a significant step backwards from the Comtec tunnel and one, given my recent experience, that I was very nervous of relying upon.

However, in a fortuitous bit of timing, my old tutor and senior academic at Southampton University, Ken Burgin, had persuaded the university to invest in purchasing an unwanted tunnel from the Ministry of Defence, transported it from Farnborough to Southampton and then rebuilt it. It was 11ft wide by 8ft high, which would allow us to go up to 40 per cent scale, just as we had done in the Comtec tunnel. What's more, it ran faster than either Comtec or the old one-third scale tunnel at Southampton, and the moving ground plate was all aluminium, so there was no chance of it distorting with age. On the downside, we could only use it for one week a month, whereas our on-site tunnel was available 24/7.

With all that in mind, I proposed to Patrick that we should use the Williams tunnel for the less sensitive areas of the car, i.e. the surfaces you see from above – the top body, radiators and ducts, and the upper shape of the chassis – but develop the more critical surfaces, the front wing and the underside of the car, including the diffuser, at Southampton.

Not an easy solution. In fact a logistical nightmare, because it meant we had to build two different models, one at 25 per cent and the other 40 per cent, and ensure that they were constantly updated with developments from one added to the other. But Patrick agreed it was probably the best way to approach our particular problem.

Now to design the car.

In truth the development route I took and hence the car layout I drew is the one I would have drawn if I'd stayed at Leyton House. Sit a 1990 Leyton House alongside a Williams FW14 and you'll see there's a strong family similarity: the V-shaped chassis, the enclosed steering wheel underneath the small cockpit opening, the shape of the engine cover, front wing and endplates – all of it developed from the 901. My logic was simple: the 901 had finally proved itself to be a decent package to develop from and I knew that its wind tunnel numbers were significantly better than those of the FW13.

However, while the French Grand Prix diffuser had been a big step forward, it was apparent that the 901 was still too aerodynamically ride-height sensitive, the result being it was super-competitive on smooth circuits but average on bumpy ones.

Work at Southampton on the 40 per cent FW14 model indicated that a contributor to this ride sensitivity was likely the front wing. Flow Vis showed the wing to be separating in the middle, so we began developing a more three-dimensional shape to the wing section, with the central section raised and backed off, until the Flow Vis remained clean even at the lowest heights. In addition, we increased the severity of the V-shape on the chassis, particularly around the driver's hips, ensuring that area stayed as high and narrow as possible around the thighs, only at the last moment cutting down to a vertical keel to divide the air left and right, just in front of the driver's bottom.

Next, the front-wing endplates. This was something born at the wind tunnel at Southampton when I asked them to run it at a low speed of about 15 or 20mph. Then, with the rolling road at the same speed, and in complete contravention of common sense and health-and-safety regulations, I made my way along the narrow walkway with a 4in-long tuft of wool attached to the end of a wand in order to observe the flow round the car.

The tuft flapped and eventually tied itself in a knot, a clear indication of an area of dirty, low energy and disordered air.

The front tyre has no bodywork around it so, when it rotates in freestream, the air close to the tyre rotates with it down into the contact patch where the tyre meets the ground, at which point it has nowhere to go except sideways, i.e. it gets squirted out sideways on both the inside and the outside of the tyre.

The outside's not too much of a problem, but that lateral squirt of dirty air inwards across the car causes a lot of damage to the aerodynamics of the floor and diffuser downstream of it. It was this squirt of dirty air that I had witnessed in the tunnel when the wool tuft tied itself in a knot. If I could stop or deflect that squirt, it would be very beneficial.

Then came one of those eureka moments. An idea that pops into your head in the shower or on the journey to work: *Ah, there might be a loophole in*

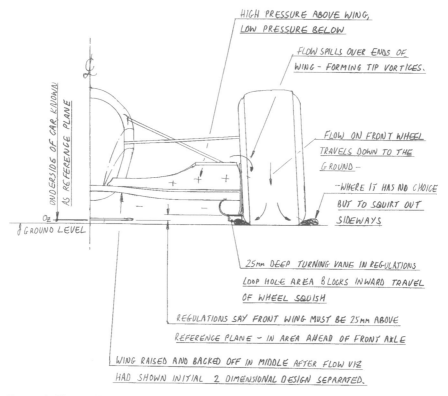

Figure 9: The problematic lateral squirt of dirty air that compromises the aerodynamics of an F1 car.

the rules that can help here. I consulted the rulebook and, sure enough, there it was: the regulations stipulated that forwards of the centre line of the front axle, any bodywork including the front wing and its endplates had to be 25mm above the bottom of the car.

The rules also stipulated that behind the rear edge of the front wheel, any bodywork facing the ground had to be flat and lie on a single plane. That left this little loophole area between the centre line of the front wheel and the back edge of the front wheel where you could do what you want, as long as it didn't go below the bottom of the car.

So what we did was extend the endplate footplate rearwards to the back edge of the front tyre and then attach a little vertical turning vane 25mm deep to the bottom of it. It was very, very effective at stopping that inward squirt, giving us a good chunk of extra downforce.

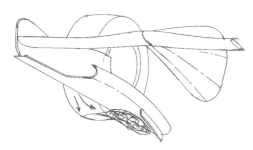

Figure 10: Modifications made to the endplate footplate.

Moments like that are very rewarding and give you quite an inner glow.

Both cars have to be the same size, so you must base your chassis size around the larger of the two drivers, which in this case was Nigel, who was of a powerful build, had big thighs and wide buttocks. Maybe still does.

I was anxious not to make same the same mistake I had at Leyton House, where Capelli had been comfy in a mock-up only to struggle once he sat in the real thing, so I was careful to make sure Nigel was properly accommodated. However, that narrowing of the chassis around the driver's hips and thighs was, with every successive iteration, showing good gains in the tunnel. I measured Nigel carefully and effectively wrapped the lower part of the chassis around him. Patrick only found out about that final step after the chassis mould had been made, and he gave me a bit of a roasting for going too far. So, when Nigel sat in the finished car for the first time, it was me who was having the squeaky bum moment – luckily Nigel pronounced it snug but acceptable.

One feature of the FW13 did make good sense. The radiators. At Leyton House we'd carried them vertically and inclined forwards, whereas the 1990 Williams did the opposite: vertical but inclined rearwards. What it gave was a nice long inlet duct allowing the flow to diffuse properly along the length of the duct, as well as allowing us to bulge the fuel tank out wider. The latter was a great bonus, because being a more powerful V10 instead of the V8 of the Leyton House, the Renault engine used more fuel, which meant it needed a bigger tank. By swinging the radiators rearwards, we could accommodate that extra fuel capacity without having to lengthen the chassis.

Then there was the gearbox. Patrick loved the mechanical challenge of gearbox design and elected to draw the FW14 gearbox himself, casing, internals, everything. So while I got on with the aerodynamics, the layout of the chassis and suspension, followed by the details of the chassis design such as how the front suspension should be attached, Patrick got on with the gearbox, redesigning it to suit the aerodynamics and the diffuser. It was still a transverse gearbox but he managed to narrow the package a fair bit, so it didn't compromise the diffuser and rear-end aerodynamics in the same way that the 1990 Williams had done.

The other big change for 1991 compared to 1990 was going from an H-pattern manual gear change with a good old-fashioned gear lever to what's known as a semi-automatic, or flappy-paddle gear change, mounted on the steering wheel. To change up, you pull the lever on the right; to change down, you pull the lever on the left.

The paddle was something that had been introduced by John Barnard of Ferrari in 1989 and was clearly a step forwards, for two reasons: first, it gave a much quicker gear change, and second, it removed the need for the driver to take his hands off the wheel. One of the most dramatic pieces of on-board footage ever is Ayrton Senna's qualifying lap in a McLaren Honda at Monaco in 1990. Watch it and you'll see that he hardly ever has both hands on the steering wheel. He's constantly changing up and down while manhandling the car with his left arm.

And that was FW14 in a nutshell. As I say, very much an evolution of the Leyton House car in many respects but using the experience and resources of a team that, under Patrick's guidance, was much more developed and structured than we had achieved at Leyton House. It was also the first example of a philosophy I've since tried to continue with throughout my career: if you can come up with a decent concept then develop it year after year until either the regulations change or you realise that it was the wrong route. That, for me, is the most fruitful way to work.

Conversely, you do see cars where there seems to be no continuity. The shape is different from the year before, and different again the year after. The team is confused and doesn't properly understand the car. A good example of that was the 2011 McLaren, which was a decent car. Then they changed it completely for 2012. It went okay but nothing spectacular. But instead of trying to work out how to develop it, they changed it *again* the following year, and got completely lost.

To me it looked as though, with the 2012 car, they had simply tried to be different but not necessarily for good engineering reasons. Then, for 2013, they just tried to copy various features from along the pit lane: the front end of a Red Bull mated to the middle of a Renault to the back of a Ferrari – a camel. Needless to say, it ran badly. The problem was that they kept changing it without every fully understanding what they actually had. Darwin was not wrong. Evolution is often the key once the spark of a good direction has been set.

CHAPTER 33

Nigel and Riccardo both liked the car, performance in testing was decent, if not earth-shattering, and we embarked on the season unsure where we were compared to our main rivals, McLaren and Ferrari.

Qualifying at Phoenix – what was to be the last Formula One race in the

States for a decade – went well. During the race, however, both cars had to retire with gearbox problems. Not a great start.

Meanwhile, if you recall the little skirt we had under the front-wing endplate, it had a rubbing strip at the bottom. At high speeds, downforce lowers the car and the skirt rubs on the ground, so we'd bolted a steel plate to it for wear resistance.

The skirt sparked, and this was visible on the TV coverage. Ferrari and McLaren both worked themselves into a lather about how it must be illegal.

Under pressure to take it off, I said to Patrick, 'Well, it's in the rulebook, it's legal, let them protest.' We'd found a loophole, fair and square, and while it was not the intention of the rule-makers, the FIA, to allow body-work in this area, there was no clause stating the intention of the rules; there was only what they say. Moreover, the only way the rules can change during a season is for reasons of safety, and the sparking was so minimal that nobody could justify it on those grounds.

Patrick agreed; we stuck to our guns and kept our skirt. In the event, the loophole was closed for 1993, by which time every other team had copied us anyway, reducing the advantage.

The highlight of the weekend was Nigel's reaction. After qualifying, he'd climbed out of the car and declared it as good as anything out there, which was a great boost, a declaration of confidence from a driver of Nigel's stature.

I liked Nigel. He's a bit of a Marmite character, for sure, with a repu-tation as being a bore that was far from the truth. To be honest, the important tasks for a driver from my car-focused perspective are that he (a) gives good feedback on the car, and (b) drives it very fast around a series of tracks without making mistakes. And on both counts Nigel delivered. During pre-season testing, he'd given us valuable feedback on the car's strengths and weaknesses, and I knew that by and large, when he was driving, he gave it everything. Other drivers, Alain Prost for example, would build up slowly, particularly in testing, never really stretching them-selves or the car, so by the end of the day you'd be fretting, thinking, *Oh God, this thing's slow*, when it was just that Alain wasn't really extending himself. I guess in many ways that shows great self-confidence on Alain's part, but for the team it was disconcerting.

Nigel wasn't like that. He was an attack dog in the car. When he drove it, you knew it was being bullied into submission. You knew he was giving his best when he was out in it.

We still had our gearbox problems at Interlagos for the second race of the season, the Brazilian Grand Prix. The problem was the so-called gear-dogs, which are the parts that take the drive from the shaft to the gear itself. In those days, it was a six-speed gearbox and it was the sixth gear-dogs that were getting most badly damaged. Above a certain level of damage, the dogs will no longer transmit drive; instead the car jumps out of gear, feeling to the driver like he has selected neutral.

Nobody understood why this new gearbox with its narrow width to suit the aerodynamics and semi-automatic gear-shift operation was giving us this reliability problem.

So for Brazil we elected to run it as a five-speed box. We wouldn't use sixth gear at all, accepting the performance deficit. You're going just as fast at the end of the straight, but you've got bigger rev drops between each gear, which means you come more off the power band on each gear change. We disabled it from a software point of view, so the driver couldn't use it, but the dog ring and the gear were still physically there.

It didn't help. Riccardo came in second behind Senna, though many felt his drive was conservative and that he could have won. However, much to his displeasure, Nigel was a DNF. Gearbox.

That evening we stripped it down and, despite sixth gear being disabled, discovered that the sixth gear-dogs were badly damaged. All along we'd suspected that the semi-automatic engagement was causing the damage. Evidently not.

It was Patrick who realised that we hadn't got proper longitudinal support of the shafts; they were moving lengthwise, which meant you could end up with the dogs engaging even though they weren't supposed to be.

Once we knew that, it was a very simple fix – a case of better end control through the bearings to make sure the shafts didn't float longitudinally.

★   ★   ★

Montreal I remember clearly. Particularly the satisfaction of producing a car that had qualified on pole for the first time in my Formula One career. We went into the race hopeful that we'd got on top of the gearbox problems, and Nigel dominated, to the point that he was almost a lap in the lead by the end of the race.

As he came down to the hairpin, which was probably half a mile from the finish, he started waving to the crowd and, in the process, forgot to change down. The rpm of the engine dropped too low and, through a quirk of the engine control, it stalled. And that was it. He broke down at the hairpin.

I was on the pit wall, watching the race on monitors, and seeing this happen sent my heart to the pit of my stomach. To have been so dominant, only for that to happen. At Leyton House we had twice threatened to win a race; now, in my fourth season of Formula One, it looked like it might finally happen, only for it to be snatched away 20 seconds from the end. It was absolutely soul-destroying.

Nigel was upset, too, of course. He was aware he'd made a big mistake. Never lose concentration until you can see the finish line. And there was that quirk in the software which had caused the engine to shut down at a low rpm; the trouble was, neither he nor Riccardo had ever driven that way before so it had gone undiscovered. But as ever in situations like that, there was no point in playing the blame game. Just as I hate it when drivers forget that they are an employee and start blaming the team when things go wrong, the reverse is also true: you're a team. You stick together.

That incident, in which a driver did something different from what he's ever done before, is by no means isolated. Probably it happened when Ivan caught the ignition switch in Japan. It was to occur many more times in my career and, as I was to learn, the Finnish drivers such as Häkkinen and Räikkönen are specialists at it.

On to Mexico – Mexico City, to be exact, which is an odd place. It's very high, about 16,000ft, and the air's thin. Arriving, you get an acrid burning smell of pollution in your nostrils that never goes away the whole time you're there. Most of the time you can become accustomed to a smell, even the bad ones, but this one not. I always felt a slight tingle and burn in my nose.

My abiding memory of Mexico City is of that smell and the VW Beetles that everybody drove in those days. We were also the victim of a police shakedown. We knew it was happening when a cop started fingering his gun and insisting that we'd gone through red lights, even though we'd done nothing of the sort. Fine payable on the spot, cash handed over below the side window and hence out of sight please.

At the track, Senna and McLaren looked the dominant force. Even so, I believed we had the potential to beat them if (big if) we could just get some reliability into the car. The circuit, a good but bumpy track, has a fast, banked corner leading into the pit straight, which was great because it afforded us the rare opportunity of actually seeing the cars cornering at speed. So often on the pit wall all you can see is the car flashing past you on the straight, and even then from behind a piece of protective glass. Mexico was an exception to that. You could see the cars coming through the dramatic bumpy banked last corner and off down the pit straight, and you could see how they were behaving.

Riccardo picked up a severe case of Mexican belly on Friday night and was too weak to drive at all on Saturday morning. In the end he did just two flying laps all day, but they were good enough for pole, a stunning effort. I liked Riccardo. In the past he'd been branded the 'bad boy' of Formula One, and was held responsible by some for causing the 1978 accident that led to the tragic loss of Ronnie Peterson, who died of an embolism after-wards. However, by the time I started working with Riccardo in 1991 he had become a highly respected driver with a few good results to his credit. He had a lovely Italian charm about him and was passionate about his somewhat unlikely hobby: collecting toy trains.

Nigel finished second in qualifying to give us the front row. During the race itself, Riccardo and Nigel got off in the lead, but then I don't know what happened to Nigel. He had one of his occasional lapses that meant he dropped back to third behind Senna, the two of them tussling behind Riccardo, who built up a 15sec lead.

Nigel finally woke up, got past Senna and closed on Riccardo, eventu-ally finishing about 2 seconds behind him for a Williams one–two.

And that was it. After coming close a few times, finally that first elusive

Grand Prix victory. It was a very special day. I can still remember the feeling of elation walking through the airport to board the plane home.

CHAPTER 34

That year's French Grand Prix was held at the new Magny-Cours circuit. There, a local motorcycle dealer had had the bright idea of lending our drivers two powerful Suzuki GS1100s for the weekend. Patrick and I decided that was far too dangerous for them, and commandeered the bikes for ourselves.

It was a good 20-mile drive along country roads from Magny-Cours to our little hotel, so we had a great ride speeding along sun-dappled country roads. The paddock at Magny-Cours – square in shape and a short walk from the main garages/pit lane – is a friendly one. The various teams' motorhomes are parked around the periphery of the square: in one corner was the Williams motorhome, on another the motorhome of our main sponsor, Camel, while in the middle was what was known as the 'roach coach', the catering marquee for mechanics, each team reserving a mealtime for its boys.

On the third corner was a place to refuel. Finding myself in need of gas on Saturday evening and also feeling rather pleased with myself (we had again qualified first and second) I hopped on the Suzuki and, with all our boys hanging around in the roach coach, decided to put on a bit of a show on my way past.

I popped a wheelie. It was a good wheelie. But the Camel motorhome was coming up very quickly.

Eyes wide open, I made a schoolboy mistake: I got on the front brake before the front wheel was back down. As the locked front wheel dropped and made contact with the lightly gravel-strewn tarmac, it slid out, dumping bike and me on the deck.

With a spray of gravel and noise, we both ploughed into the awning of the Camel motorhome.

There was a moment of silence in the aftermath of the accident. I scrambled to my feet, the bike well buried in the plastic sheet that draped from the awning handrail. To my huge surprise, the tables seemed empty. I could have sworn it was full of guests having supper. Slowly, said guests appeared from under the tables, the ladies looking somewhat dishevelled with their elegant dresses covered in red wine. Simultaneously, I heard a cheer from our mechanics at the roach coach and then turned to see Nigel standing beside Frank Williams, whose wheelchair was articulated into its standing position.

Nigel tells the story that as they witnessed the series of events, Frank flapped his arms and asked, 'Is that one of our boys?'

Nigel replied in his dry, Brummie drawl, 'Yes, Frank. It was Adrian.'

Frank said to his nurse, 'Robin, make sure Adrian receives a bill for a new team uniform, would you?'

Dressed in the Williams team kit of short-sleeve shirt and cotton trousers, I was badly scraped along my left arm and leg. Robin tended to me, spraying on a plastic skin that was supposed to seal the wound, then bandaging it. Needless to say, I felt a complete numpty for making such a silly mistake, not to mention the fact that I was kept awake by the pain for a number of nights.

The race was very good for us, Nigel winning comfortably to give us two wins on the trot. That Sunday night I arrived back in Marsh Gibbon, looking forward to seeing Marigold. It was a lovely balmy summer evening, but to cover the bandages I was wearing a bomber jacket. After a celebratory drink I went for a bath to soak off the bloodstained bandaging. Marigold came in and exclaimed, 'Oh my God, what happened?'

'Didn't you watch the race?' I said.

'No!'

'It was horrific; there was a huge accident at the start/finish line and a car came over the pit wall.'

She started to smile as she squinted at my wounds. 'Those are scrape marks.'

Difficult to pull the wool over Marigold's eyes, even though I was only teasing her.

Worse still, when we peeled off the plastic skin a week later, the wound underneath was festering. It looked like strawberry jam and clotted cream. What's more, I had septicaemia.

However, Mexico and France gave us a bit of momentum to take to the next race at Silverstone, where we hoped that the high-speed corners that were the hallmark of the circuit in that period would suit the down-force-generating characteristics of our car.

Nigel was comfortably on pole, and though Riccardo had to retire after an accident, he went on to win the race in dominant fashion. Renault had a big poster made, titled 'Un deux trois': hat-trick.

Senna ran out of fuel close to the end of the race and was classified fourth. He thumbed a lift from Nigel during the victory lap, waving to spectators as he sat on the sidepod with one leg in the cockpit for the journey back to the pits.

Nigel, in our internal post-race debrief, said he didn't know what to do. 'Did I just drive nicely, or accelerate and get rid of him?' A joke of course, but then again a little broken leg would have been quite nice at that point in the season. Little did I know that is exactly what would happen to our main rival at Silverstone eight years hence.

Either way, we at Williams were buoyant. To win at Silverstone, our home race, which apart from Monaco is the one date in the F1 calendar you really want to win, was a massive boost, particularly because so many of the factory-based workers, the unsung heroes of the sport, who only normally see the fruit of their labours on TV, were there to see it in person.

Our season then started to hiccup a bit. One of Frank's few personal indulgences was to have his own personal aircraft, which was not only an enormous benefit for him, being wheelchair-bound, but meant that for the European races we could fly in and out without having to go commercial, a significant travel time benefit.

Prior to the race at Hungary we arrived at the private terminal at the same time as McLaren, and what should we see but their plane absolutely stuffed with bits of bodywork in bubble wrap.

Clearly they'd been busy. Their reply to our performance advantage was lots of new bits for their car, including a diffuser and other lightweight parts. This, combined perhaps with the lower speed and nature of the Hungaroring circuit, gave them the edge, and Senna won.

The circus moved on to Spa in Belgium. Back to a circuit characterised by lots of medium- and high-speed corners, we were strong, leading the race until we had an engine control unit problem, an unusual failure that we'd not had before or since, but very frustrating because Nigel had been on course for an easy victory.

The bottom line was that for the rest of the season our tight battle with McLaren ebbed and flowed, depending on the nature of the circuit. By the time we got to Suzuka in Japan, the penultimate race, Nigel needed to win for us to have a chance of staying in the championship.

We didn't do it. Senna qualified on pole, Nigel second. During the race, Senna held Nigel up. Eventually Nigel made a mistake trying to get past him, went off and that was that, our championship bid over.

It was disappointing. On balance through the season we had the slightly quicker car, but had been undone by reliability problems. Nevertheless we took from it some positives: in one season we'd gone from being a team that hadn't been truly front-running since 1987, to slogging it out with McLaren for the championship.

But we needed to find more performance for 1992; McLaren finished the season with a quicker package. Which brings me onto something called 'active suspension'.

CHAPTER 35

A BEGINNER'S GUIDE TO ACTIVE SUSPENSION

The faster you go, the more downforce the car generates, which presses the car into the ground and compresses the suspension. This is why you see the cars sparking as the skid plates rub the ground at the end of straights, but not in slow-speed corners, where they're sitting much higher; the reduced downforce generated in a slow-speed corner means that it does not compress the suspension as much.

Aerodynamics work most effectively – in the sense that they offer the most downforce for a given speed – over a very specific and narrow range of ride-heights. They tend to be at their optimum at a particular combination of front and rear ride-height. When you brake, the front goes down, the rear comes up and that changes the aerodynamics. When you accelerate, the opposite happens: when you corner, the car rolls. And, as we said, as the car's speed and hence downforce changes, the ride-height changes.

All those events are deviations from whatever happens to be the optimum ride-height for your particular car. They change the downforce. Not only that but they change the balance of the car.

I think most of us are familiar with the concept of centre of gravity. If you hold a 12in ruler and balance it on your thumb, the balance point will be at 6in: that's the centre of gravity.

It's the same with aerodynamics. You have a balance – known as the centre of pressure – between the downforce on the front and rear axles, and that balance point changes as the car pitches, rolls and changes its ride-heights with speed.

That change in balance, of course, alters the handling of the car, so when you brake the centre pressure moves forwards and you put more downforce on the front tyres relative to the rear, which can mean you have too much front grip when you first turn into the corner. This is why you often see drivers correcting the steering at corner entry. The rear's now sliding too much and they have to undo the lock to correct for that rear over-rotation.

'Active suspension' is something that allows you to lengthen and shorten the suspension struts in such a way that the platform of the car, in other words its ride-height, stays much more constant relative to the ground, irrespective of what the car is doing. In principle, if your control system is good enough, the only fluctuation in ride-height will be due to the need to have some suspension movement in order to absorb bumps in the track surface.

The principle of active suspension is to use an oil pump attached to the engine to generate hydraulic pressure. The hydraulic pressure is used to extend or shorten actuators at each wheel depending on what they need to do to achieve the desired ride-height. So if you brake hard, the front dives but the actuators at the front lengthen to compensate, and vice versa at the rear. It's the same type of technology you see on the arm of a JCB digger.

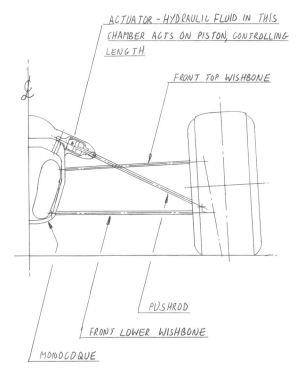

Figure 11: Some of the components involved in active suspension.

Lotus had tried an active system years before, but didn't get it right and eventually gave up. Theirs was a complicated 'full-active' system, which means you throw away all the springs and dampers and try to make the system absorb the bumps as well as controlling the aerodynamic platform of the car. The input from a bump can be in the order of a few milliseconds, so the response rate of the system needs to operate at a high frequency to work properly. This is difficult to achieve and requires a lot of power.

Because of the obvious theoretical potential, other teams tried too, including Williams. What they had come up with was a much slower-acting system, a little bit like old Citroens, whose suspension was designed to stop the rear sagging if you added a caravan or heaved a sack of coal in the boot.

This meant that the system was much simpler in control terms than that of Lotus, because it kept springs and dampers for ride control (absorbing the bumps) and just used the suspension to keep the aerodynamic platform as level as possible.

Even so, Williams had, thus far, made a bit of a hash of active suspension and ended up taking it off the car after false starts in 1986 and again in 1988.

Part of the problem with these earlier efforts had been poor electronic control. So Patrick had acquired two bright young engineers: Steve Wise to design an in-house-manufactured electronic control unit with combined data-recording capability, and Paddy Lowe to write the control algorithms.

They had done their work to the point that they needed a car to go testing with by autumn 1991, so my contribution to the project was to work out how to install the active struts, spring canisters and so forth on the existing FW14a chassis. My slightly inelegant-looking solution was to throw away the front and rear rockers that normally serve to take the load from the suspension pushrods to the spring/damper units, and instead fit the actuators directly on the ends of the pushrods. At the front, this gave rise to bulbous pods on each side of the chassis, meaning that the active car (christened FW14b) is easily distinguished from the passive 14a.

The hydraulic layout was the same as the Williams engineers had used in 1988. It ran the risk of compromise to both ride and response-to-steering inputs, because we were still mixing the platform-control with the ride-control system, but we felt the aerodynamic gains from the platform-control should easily make up the deficit.

During testing in the autumn of 1991, we concentrated on using our test drivers, Damon Hill and Mark Blundell, to do the initial debugging and development work. Once the season finished, we involved Nigel and Riccardo in testing the car. That's where we hit a snag. Both reported that it felt rather uncommunicative and didn't give them much feedback in the first entry part of the corner; they almost had to *trust* it had the grip, rather than knowing.

In addition, Nigel was worried about the safety of the system. He had been at Lotus when they developed their system and had encountered hydraulic failures that dumped the car on the ground, turning it into a high-speed sledge that could easily be heading straight for the barrier. He was so worried, in fact, that he requested a meeting, folding his arms and telling me and Patrick, 'I don't want to race this car. I want to race the passive car.'

At this juncture, I should point out that I had been hard at work on a new car, the FW15. The car was designed to be an active car: the mechanical packaging was rearranged to carry the active components more elegantly while the aerodynamics had been developed to work over the much narrower ride-height band that active suspension allows, meaning that they would probably work poorly over the wide range of passive car. The research on the car had started late because we did not want to commit to this route until we were confident that autumn testing showed everything to be working well. Consequently, the FW15a was to be introduced for the start of the European season in May, with the FW14b carrying us through the first 'flyaway' intercontinental races. To deviate from the plan now (December 1991) and stay with passive suspension would have meant restricting ourselves to the FW14a for the bulk of the 1992 season. Given that McLaren had out-developed us at the tail end of 1991, it seemed highly unlikely we would be able to mount a credible championship campaign with such a strategy. So my response to Nigel's plea was, 'Nigel, the new car's designed around it being active. It won't work well as a passive car. To revert now to passive is dooming ourselves to not winning the championship; we have to commit to active, get it to work and get it reliable.'

Patrick agreed. Nigel was overruled.

If a driver feels at risk, you've got to listen. It was our job as engineers to make sure the car was safe. It's all about trust and trust is a two-way street.

Winter is always an uneasy period. As a team it is just as intense as during the season because we will be busy completing the design of the following season's challenger. From wind tunnel tests and simulation programmes coupled with dyno results from our engine partner (Renault) we will have a good idea of how much faster we expect the new car to be, but we have no idea whether other teams have found more speed.

Pre-season testing, after everybody has launched their new car and started to converge for common tests, usually at Barcelona, is where each team starts to get a broad idea of how competitive they are relative to their rivals. At these tests in February it became apparent that our rivals had not made a big step forward over the winter, whereas with the 14B we had. Indeed, we appeared to have such a big competitive margin that our problem was not, *Will it be quick enough?* The problem was, *Will it be reliable?*

In May 1992 Marigold and I moved into the Old Vicarage next to the church, a bigger house than my little cottage in Marsh Gibbon or Marigold's lodge house in Stow, and one that had a really nice feel to it. In August we were married. Hannah and Charlotte were bridesmaids although Charlotte had a broken arm in plaster, so it was covered in material matching the dress.

I've found that personal life and work life seem to echo each other. If one goes sour, the other goes sour, and if one's going well, the other goes well. So it had proved . . .

CHAPTER 36

The first race of the 1992 season was South Africa, Kyalami, and we set off convinced we had the performance to win but freighted with concerns that our car was unreliable. Fresh in our minds were a couple of scares that pre-season testing had thrown up, so there was much chewing of fingernails and biting of lips.

But the weekend was a dream, an absolute dream. We qualified on pole by a huge amount, locked out the front row and then dominated the race, first and second, no problems at all as far as the active suspension was concerned; a brilliant weekend.

Of course, most of the credit for the success of the active suspension is down to Patrick. Paddy and Steve had got the control side of things working properly; my task was a simple installation job and later to optimise the aerodynamics. The one thing I did do from a control point of view was suggest cockpit adjusters, so drivers could fine-tune the system on the go. To that end we installed three knobs in the cockpit. One for the target front ride-height you're trying to achieve in a low-speed corner, another for high-speed front ride-height and a single knob for rear ride-height. This allowed the drivers to tune the balance of the car 'on the move'; important, as their normal in-cockpit tuning devices, the adjustable front and rear anti-roll bar levers, were deleted as a result of the system layout.

The other thing I noticed from the wind tunnel results was that at very low ride-height the resulting stall of the diffuser reduced the drag of the car (due to reduction of what is known as 'induced drag', which is proportional to the lift or downforce of the vehicle). So we added a button to the steering wheel which, when pressed and held down, dropped the rear ride-height. The drivers used this in areas where they were power- rather than grip-limited (generally in the straights, but also, in Nigel's case, for very fast corners such as Blanchimont at Spa, where, with sufficient courage, the car could still be held flat with no lift of the throttle even with the reduction of rear downforce). Effectively it was an early version of DRS.

After Kyalami it was all about continuing to focus on reliability, so we decided to postpone the planned introduction of the FW15 for the European season and concentrate on making the FW14b as reliable as we could.

From a racing aspect, that was how we spent the remainder of 1992 – making sure the car finished. And generally it did, with not a single active-suspension-related DNF. We messed up Montreal with the wrong set-up, but most of the races were easy victories. Simply put, we dominated.

Despite his initial reservations, the car was made for Nigel. He had tremendous confidence in his car control and could cope with the fact that it moved around a bit on corner entry before the active system caught up with the transient demand of the steering input, because he knew the grip was there; he just had to ignore what he called 'the funny sensations' it gave him and trust that the more speed he carried into the corner the more downforce and thus more grip he'd have.

In the end – actually, very quickly – Nigel was able to develop trust in the car and his ability to control it.

Riccardo, on the other hand, never quite got there. He would turn into the corner, have this funny floating feeling and either back off or delay getting on the throttle until he felt it settle; then, because that experience had failed to inspire any confidence in him, he wouldn't attempt to go any faster at the same corner on the next lap, whereas Nigel thought, *Right, I got through fine on that lap; next lap I'll try a bit quicker.*

The other advantage Nigel had over Riccardo was his tremendous upper body strength. With extra downforce comes heavier steering and the 1992 car did not have power steering. In a fast corner, if the driver is marginal in terms of his strength relative to the steering weight, he will often have to choose his steering position and then almost lock his arms in that position. If the car subsequently steps out at the rear he can correct it, because correction involves a reduction in steering load, but he will struggle to reapply the lock and often runs out of road at the corner exit. Confidence-sapping at the very least.

For a driver, it's all about confidence. Nigel knew that if the car did something unexpected, he'd sort it out, whereas Riccardo didn't have that same level of confidence – at least not with that particular car.

What also helped to destroy Riccardo that season were Nigel's little wind-ups. For example, at the start of the season, the FIA announced that they would be weighing drivers. In contrast to Riccardo, who trained hard, Nigel never took exercise or diet seriously. Case in point, when we were testing at Paul Ricard, we all went out to a swanky fish restaurant and Nigel asked for ketchup to go with his sole.

The waiter cast him a sideways look. 'Ah, Monsieur, you're so funny.'

'Well thank you very much,' said Nigel, and then, as the waiter turned to go, he added, 'but where's my tomato ketchup.'

'Monsieur, seriously?'

'Yeah, seriously.'

The waiter span on his heel and stormed into the kitchen. It was like the Monty Python sketch: all we heard from the kitchen were indignant Gallic voices.

The kitchen door swung open and the chef marched out, bearing a huge catering-sized bottle of tomato ketchup which he upended over Nigel's plate, dowsing the sole in ketchup, a red-faced look of total disdain on his face.

'Thank you very much,' beamed Nigel in his usual Brummie drawl.

And that was pretty much his attitude to diet in a ketchup-drenched nutshell. As a result he knew full well that Riccardo would 'beat' him when it came to the weigh-in, especially as Riccardo had been working particularly hard in the gym all winter.

It's worth noting at this point that if the competition in Formula One is fierce, nowhere is it fiercer than between two teammates. With both of them driving the same car, it's the only contest on the grid that comes down to pure driving skill, and never was that more pronounced than between Nigel and Riccardo in 1992. Coming out of pre-season, both were aware that we had a very competitive car, with a good chance therefore that one of them would be world champion.

So to score an immediate psychological win over Riccardo, Nigel was determined to come in lighter. He stripped all the lining from a spare helmet and then from his shoes. He dehydrated and starved himself for a day and, come the weigh-in, was about ½kg lighter than Riccardo.

It's funny how drivers get inside each other's heads. That really blew Riccardo's mind. He was so proud of the fact that he'd lost weight over the winter and was super-fit. To be beaten by burger-chomping Nigel was a huge psychological blow.

Nigel had another tactic that didn't become apparent until later. Then and now, all teams stage a post-session/race debrief involving both drivers and all the engineers. The drivers talk about how the car has handled. Race engineers will report back on the set-up of the car. This gives feedback to the team concerning how the car is handling and what set-ups best suit the car – valuable information that is used to develop the car further.

Except, what Nigel and his race engineer David Brown did was have two debriefs. In the official one, Nigel would say whatever he thought would send Riccardo's team in the wrong direction, and then later he and David would have the real debrief.

Same with his ride-height knobs. Their positions weren't recorded in the data recorder, so when Nigel finished a run and came into the pit lane he'd change them. Now, if one driver within the team is quicker than the other, it is common practice for the slower side of the garage simply to adopt the same set-up as the quicker car. Since Riccardo was often the slower one, he and his engineer would adopt Nigel's ride-height settings – except, of course, they were incorrect! Because we had such a performance advantage, you could argue it was acceptable, but it caught Nigel out at Montreal where he ran the ride-height too low, making the car unstable in the bumpy braking areas – the danger of running solo and hence excluding the expertise of the rest of the team.

The other funny incident was at Monza. 'Nigel, how is it you're so much quicker than Riccardo through the chicane?' Patrick demanded.

'Well, it's very easy really,' grinned Nigel. 'What I do is, as I'm approaching the kerb, I jam my hands against the rim of the chassis, so the steering wheel can't kick back, and that keeps a much more consistent line.'

Armed with this information, Patrick went to Riccardo's garage.

'Riccardo, what you need to do to keep a better, tighter line through the chicane is jam your knuckles against the cockpit.'

Willing to try anything, Riccardo duly gave it a go – only to return three laps later with blood oozing through the knuckles of his gloves where he'd skinned them on the cockpit. Just another of Nigel's wind-ups.

It was his dry Brummie drawl – that was Nigel's secret weapon. He had such a deadpan way about him. If he was in the lead he'd start singing nursery rhymes over the radio. 'Humpty Dumpty sat on a wall ...' Just amusing himself.

On one occasion he was ahead, singing his nursery rhymes to himself, when suddenly he went quiet.

Finally the radio crackled back into life. 'I'm going to lose.'

'Why?'

'The mirror's fallen off. That's a really bad omen, a broken mirror.'

He was very superstitious like that. I'm glad to say it was mis-founded. He went on to win.

Silverstone, our home race, was especially sweet for the second year in a row, with Nigel enjoying a 50sec lead at the end over third-placed Martin Brundle and Riccardo taking the runner-up spot. In truth it must have been a pretty boring race to watch but the partisan crowd of 'Our Nige' supporters were ecstatic, with hundreds of them clambering over the barriers to invade the track. Nigel was forced to stop and abandon the car on his slowing-down lap, having run over a spectator at very slow speed. We had a letter the next day from said spectator saying that he had broken his foot in the tumble but felt that he was very privileged to suffer such an injury from Nigel.

Monaco was painful. Nigel qualified on pole and dominated the race until about 10 laps from the end when one of the rear wheels came loose. He pitted and the wheel was replaced, but the length of the stop gave Senna a narrow lead as Nigel re-emerged. Nigel was probably 3sec faster than Senna, but despite some flamboyant driving, making his car look big in Senna's mirrors, Senna was far too wise and kept his McLaren tidy to win.

During the post-mortem we discovered why the wheel nut had come loose. A mechanic had trapped one of the cords that keep the tyre blanket in place between the wheel and the hub. When they gunned the wheel nut on, it had sliced the cord, but the remnants of the cord were stuck between the wheel and the axle. Over the course of the race, the cord had slowly worn away, the wheel nut had come loose and that was that. There are so many silly little things that can trip you up; unfortunately this was a classic example.

Massive shame. In my six seasons at Williams we didn't win Monaco once. Ultimately the championship is the prize but, as I've said, Monaco is *the* prestige event. It's the most glamorous, it has the highest TV figures, it's the one all the sponsors attend . . . and it always eluded us.

Otherwise, we dominated the season, with Nigel securing the drivers' championship in Hungary and us the constructors' in Belgium.

It felt very, very good indeed. I didn't then and still don't think of it as 'glory', but no doubt about it, knowing you're performing at a world-class level in the most prestigious engineering-based sport, to come away with victory or even better, of course, the championship, is very satisfying. Tight championship battles are extremely stressful and exhausting, but this one was not one of those. It gave me a very warm glow inside.

Even now, it's funny how early success always stands out. I clearly remember walking through the airport in Mexico after that first win with Riccardo. I put that achievement right up there with my children being born. That's a bit naughty of me, I suppose, but in my defence it was something my whole life had been leading up to, from the kid sketching on bits of paper, making models, right up to becoming the person responsible for the design of a racing car that's won a Formula One championship.

I remember thinking, *This is one of the best days of my life*.

CHAPTER 37

For me, racing has been all-consuming and there are times when it's been *all* I've thought about, day and night. Frank Williams once commented that I am the most competitive person he knew. That competitiveness crept up on me in my early career – I wasn't that way in my youth and certainly not in sport. But perhaps the dismissive attitude from school teachers and the struggle to get through university gave me a determination to prove I can succeed. Put that determination into the sporting arena and it becomes competitiveness.

Marigold said I was the most selfish person she knew. Two failed marriages – the one to her included – suggest she may have a point. It's true that you can become so immersed in what you're trying to achieve as a competitor that you risk tunnel vision, becoming thoughtless as a result and failing to consider the little things that make the people in your life happy and family life smoother. Even so, I prefer to think of myself as 'absorbed' rather than selfish. After all, I'm not thinking about myself, I'm thinking about product.

Issues of focus and absorption were very much uppermost in our minds at the end of the 1992 season when, much to the surprise of the watching world, Williams and Nigel Mansell parted company.

What emerged was that, during the 1991 season, Frank had decided to try and woo a driver of greater perceived standing than Nigel, held secret talks with Alain Prost and, with the seats for 1992 already contracted, signed a contract with him to drive for Williams in 1993.

It was a questionable decision, made even more so in light of the fact that Nigel had then gone on to win the drivers' championship. To be fair to Frank, he was doing his thinking in 1991, when he had no idea that Nigel would be so well suited to the active car, or that he was about to reach a late peak as a driver. It's easy to look back now and wince at the idea of that change because apparently one of Alain's contractual conditions was that he would not accept Nigel as his teammate. They had been teammates at Ferrari in 1990 and had not enjoyed the best of relationships – to put it mildly.

So Alain it was. If it had been him and Nigel in 1993, that would have been a hell of a battle.

The British press were in uproar. Nigel was the working-class boy made good in a sport that can often, and unfortunately increasingly, be accused of being elitist, with only the children of wealthy fathers succeeding. The tabloids idolised him; 'Il Leone', they called him – a title he had gained from the Italian paparazzi during his Ferrari days. The *Sun* launched a 'Save Our Nige' campaign and we had protesters with placards outside the Williams factory for about a week waiting to vent their fury when Frank was driven in. I think the best riposte was from somebody who posted a set of marbles in an envelope with an accompanying note: 'For Frank, as he has clearly lost his!'

So, we now had Alain coming out of retirement, a great driver who had won two championships already, but a bit of a gamble because when a driver comes back you never quite know what you're going to get. For example, Niki Lauda came back after a retirement to win the championship again. He still had that focus. On the other, Michael Schumacher returned but never looked the driver he had been prior to his retirement.

Alain had gained the nickname 'the professor' for his very analytical approach to the sport, particularly his attention to detail in achieving a set-up that suited his ultra-smooth driving style. He was the opposite of the swashbuckling image of a racing driver, always very reserved and thoughtful, but quite nervy – often worrying at his fingernails, which were always bitten down to the quick. Unlike Nigel, who used to 'bully' the car, you never saw Alain's car slide or step out of line. His progress seemed almost stately. You could be forgiven for thinking he was slow until you looked at the stopwatch to see that he'd recorded yet another great time. History tells us that he hadn't lost any of that focus, which became evident at the first race.

In the meantime came a debate over who should take second seat. There was a camp led by Frank calling for the continuity of Riccardo, whereas another lot, led by the engineers including myself, thought that Riccardo, while clearly a great competitor, was rarely on Nigel's pace and wouldn't challenge Alain. We proposed an alternative, Damon Hill. As well as driving for Brabham, Damon had been testing for us, was quick and had given us feedback that was invaluable in developing the active suspension for the 1992 car. He knew it inside out.

The downside again lay in doubts about his mental readiness. Throughout 1992 Damon had been racing in an uncompetitive car, often failing to qualify, which meant that he lacked race experience and therefore was something of a gamble, the opposite to Riccardo, who was a very experienced driver but now, in truth, past his peak.

Meanwhile, with the active car being so dominant, our rivals realised they had to get their own versions to work. So, McLaren, Ferrari and Benetton all launched their cars with active suspension for the start of the 1993 season.

As it turned out, McLaren's system, while neat, was somewhat hobbled by their lack of power as was Benetton's, while Ferrari couldn't get their system to work at all, so they weren't a threat.

Meanwhile, we had been working on the FW15, the car we had been intending to race from the start of the European season in 1992. Eventually we had started testing the car in the autumn of 1992, Damon helping in the development work. The upside of this was that by the start of the 1993 season, it had racked up a lot of test mileage, always very useful when it comes to trying to get reliability out of the car. The downside was that it was a nine-month-old design, in contrast to its new rivals.

The car had evolved over that time though. Rule changes to slow the cars down had been introduced, with a reduction to both overall car width and rear-tyre width. Also, in reaction to our elaborate front-wing endplate, with skirts on the underneath, the FIA had introduced regulations that limited the endplates to a simple shape. Little did we know it at the time, but this was one of the first examples of what has, in my opinion, become a creeping regulatory disease in our sport: ever-more regulations that prescribe in great detail exactly where you cannot have bodywork, where you must have bodywork, even in some areas exactly what shape it must be. A soapbox subject I'll return to later.

The rule changes meant mechanical and aerodynamic changes and development to suit. In addition, we developed electronically controlled power steering, electronically controlled power-assisted braking and a four-channel ABS system. All of the above essentially used the same technology as the active suspension, different from road car systems of the day: power for the assistance came from a high-pressure hydraulic pump (a pump normally used on helicopters) with control from the on-board computer to what is known as a proportional valve, or Moog valve, Moog having a virtual monopoly in the aircraft and helicopter industry in this area. The power steering, in particular, was essential for Alain, who lacked Nigel's upper body strength, and thus needed the extra assistance to cope with the heavy steering created by the massive downforce.

So, yes, despite a few hiccups, particularly in wet races, we dominated the season and won. My second championship, with what is still probably the most technologically advanced car ever to race in Formula 1. A rather sweet year.

I wish I could say the same for 1994.

HOW TO BUILD
AN FW16

CHAPTER 38

In 1993, Ayrton Senna was fed up. Having won the drivers' championship in 1991, he'd spent the next two seasons staring at the rear of a Williams. When Frank asked if he was interested in joining a team that had every intention of winning the next championship as well, who could blame him for wanting to make the switch? So it was that, arguably, the world's best driver signed for the reigning world champions.

Suddenly the question of whether to persuade Alain to stay for another year was moot. He and Ayrton were not the best of friends. Neither was prepared to drive with the other, and if it came down to a choice between Ayrton, who was driving at his peak, and Alain, who was brilliant but had probably crested, you'd choose Ayrton.

Frank idolised him, and with good reason: not only was he one of the all-time special drivers but he had a certain aura about him. And if that sounds a bit corny, fair enough, but I can only say it made perfect sense when you were with him. You felt as though you were with somebody special. How much of that was due to his reputation is impossible to quantify, but you felt it.

Prior to him joining Williams, I'd never had a proper conversation with Ayrton. He had been our main rival in 1991 and the only credible challenger to Alain in 1993. Back to that competitiveness thing, he was our nemesis. To now have him on our side was going to be amazing. I clearly remember the first day he came to the Williams factory at Didcot in the autumn of 1993. I was introduced to him and instructed to give him a tour, so I showed him round the drawing office and factory, introducing him to staff, all the time being impressed by his interest in detail, his inquisitiveness and his obvious enthusiasm.

I took him over to the wind tunnel to show him the model of the 1994 car and he was straight into the minutiae, down on his hands and knees, looking under the diffuser, listening closely as I pointed out key features.

He wasn't an engineer, but he wanted to absorb as much as he could about the design and philosophy of the car. He was of the now slightly old-school approach that the more one can understand technically about a car, the more it will help one understand how to drive and feed back on it to the engineers, which is such a key attribute for any driver. He had a boyish enthusiasm. A desire to learn. It was definitely one of the qualities that made him so great.

Then, of course, there was his driving. As a driver, he seemed to be able to make the car do things others simply couldn't. He first got noticed in Formula One in 1983 during the turbo era, when he developed a very special driving technique in which he would be on the throttle and the brake at the same time. This was in the days before the flappy paddle, of course. You still had a conventional clutch pedal and gear lever. Ayrton's technique was to be on and off both throttle and brake throughout the corner in order to keep the turbo spooled up, so when he needed the power at the corner exit the turbo was already producing the requisite boost.

There was a theory that when the turbocharged engines were banned at the end of the 1988 season he would lose his competitive advantage, because that driving technique wouldn't be relevant any more. Of course he proved them wrong because another of his great talents was the ability to adapt his driving to suit the characteristics of the car. So yes, that particular skill was taken away from him, but he had so many others up his sleeve it didn't matter. His car control and commitment was phenomenal. He had total self-belief in his own ability not to lose control of the car, and that allowed him to put it in places and in attitudes that other drivers wouldn't consider, because they felt it was too dangerous. To him it wasn't a risk, since he had utter faith in his ability to control the car.

What a driver. The thought of working with him was tremendously exciting.

CHAPTER 39

At the end of 1993, Patrick Head and I were returning from testing the FW15 at Paul Ricard (see the Prologue), on our way to Nice airport in a hire car.

I was driving, Patrick in the passenger seat, as we sped along the same twisting mountainous roads on which Frank Williams had had the accident that left him in a wheelchair. Frank had been running late, just as we were that evening, when he lost control of his hire car and rolled down the mountainside, the roof collapsing and fracturing his spine.

We rounded a corner. About half a mile away was a car coming in the opposite direction. Not a problem. There was room to pass.

Except this guy was on the wrong side of the road.

My initial reaction was to assume that, as a foreign visitor, I was the one on the wrong side of the road, but I double-checked and no, I wasn't. He was.

The closing speed was fast. Both cars were going quickly. Mine was an instinctive reaction. I did what most people would have done in that situation. I moved over to the other side of the road.

The car speeding towards us did the same.

Now *I* was the one on the wrong side of the road. And what flashed through my mind was that if we were all killed, the investigation would say I caused the accident by being on the wrong side of the road.

The other thing that flashed through my mind was to cross back over to the correct side of the road. But then if the car speeding towards us did the same thing there would be no time to correct the error a third time.

Thankfully there was a little extra width on my side, a gravelly path beside the road, so I pulled harder over to the left, not necessarily to avoid the guy, more to say, I'm staying on this side. Thank God, he got the message, stayed put and we passed each other safely.

We drove on. The close shave was like an extra passenger in the car.

After a brief moment of stunned silence, Patrick cleared his throat. 'That was a good bit of driving, Adrian,' he croaked.

'Thank you, Patrick,' I squeaked.

Imogen was born on 30 August 1993. She proved to be the ideal baby. She rarely even cried. She slept on a sheepskin, so we'd always take one with us when we went out to a pub or party where she would drift off quite happily through any noise. I remember we had a jukebox, a replica Wurlitzer, in the hall at Fyfield and she was absolutely fascinated by its changing-colour lights and rising bubbles. She used to sit in her nappy holding her milk and watch it quite happily for half an hour or so before she'd get bored and wander off.

During Marigold's pregnancy I took delivery of a 1938 Jaguar SS100 that I'd had rebuilt, having bought it in its stripped-down state in the States. A lovely car. My friend Dave McRobert had a model SS100 on his mantelpiece and that may well be where the fascination first arose.

It was renovated by an enthusiast named Terry Rowing. I'd approached Terry to ask if he would rebuild it in exchange for being allowed to copy the pattern for future replicas. He agreed and five years later we had a finished car. All the replica SS100s you now see around are actually based on my car.

It's something of a tradition to name my cars (yes, there are a few) and I called this one Reginald (a family tradition inherited from my parents – always boys' names on the basis of reliability, one of my dad's little jokes). The day Terry delivered him, I took it for a spin around the Williams car park.

On one particularly beautiful summer's day, I packed the children into Reginald and went for a drive. At the traffic lights, I turned to the girls, who were perched on a sort of luggage shelf in the back. 'What do you think?' I grinned.

Hannah looked excited. 'It's wonderful, Dad; it's like Chitty Chitty Bang Bang.'

Charlotte was less impressed. 'Is that the last one they had left at the garage, Daddy?'

So many very happy memories. I had my family safe and well around me. Ayrton would be racing for us. Life was very, very good.

CHAPTER 40

The FW16 could and should have been a great car for 1994. One of the tricks we had up our sleeve was 'launch control', a system aimed at improving start times. The driver dumps the clutch and the electronic control system does the rest in terms of getting the car off the starting line as quickly as possible.

Another trick – Patrick's baby, not mine – was what's called a CVT, a Continuously Variable Transmission system.

Those of us who are getting on a bit may remember a thing called a DAF Variomatic, a little fibreglass Dutch car with a small engine and, in place of a conventional gearbox, a belt and pulley system that shifted the gear ratio. What that meant was that the engine could sit at a near-constant rpm and all the speed control would be done not by the revs, but by changing the gear ratio.

For a racing engine, that's a benefit. It meant that our engine designer, Renault, could optimise the engine performance for a single rpm and then we would do the rest of the control by changing the ratio of the pulleys.

True, as a gearbox, it's somewhat less efficient because of the greater friction associated with it. But from an engine point of view, being able to tune your inlet and exhaust lengths, as well as your valve timing, to a single rpm means you can generate a lot more power than you can for an engine that has to deliver power over a wide range of rpm.

I have to say it would have sounded hideous to spectators, and would probably have been bad news for the sport, because the sound of an engine lapping at near-constant rpm is horrible compared to that generated by the gear changes and rising and falling rpm that we're used to. I know from experience. We tested our CVT at Silverstone. Yes, it sounded horrible, but it's not our job to ensure that the car sounds nice or smells good or looks pretty. We're shark-like in our purity of purpose. We exist only to make the car go faster; the stopwatch is our master.

In an alternative universe, perhaps, we used the CVT, the other teams cottoned on, and that beloved noise of Formula One, something that drew many of us to the sport in the first place, changed irrevocably, at least for a while.

In reality, however, Ferrari heard of our plans and complained.

Ferrari complaining was to become a recurring theme over the ensuing years. If Ferrari didn't like something (usually because they couldn't get it to work for themselves), they complained to the FIA. Whether or not they were assured of a sympathetic ear is up for debate. I'm sure Max and Bernie would strenuously deny Ferrari were ever showed favouritism. Suffice to say, however, that it was around this time that those in the pit lane began to refer to the FIA as Ferrari International Aid. (It was years later, in 2015, that it emerged that Ferrari did indeed have a secret contract with the FIA that allowed them to veto any regulation changes – galling confirmation of a 'special relationship' that we always suspected but until then had never had confirmed.)

Ferrari didn't know exactly what we were up to, of course, but like us and every other team on the grid they were working on various electronically controlled enhancements. In particular they could not get active suspension to work, with Gerhard Berger being lucky to escape serious injury when their car dumped itself on the ground at the exit of the pit lane in Barcelona. But Max Mosley, it would appear, wanted both to help Ferrari and to slap down Williams/McLaren. So what he did was invoke Article 3.15.

Article 3.15 first became a feature of the regulations sometime after 1968, which was when cars began sprouting those ungainly looking aerodynamically adjustable wings mounted on huge struts at the top of the suspension uprights. The wings had caused a series of accidents – cars were literally taking off – so the FIA introduced Article 3.15, which said, 'Bodywork must be rigidly attached to the entirely sprung part of the car and must remain immobile in relation to the sprung parts of the car.'

Now, in my opinion, the 'must remain immobile' part of this sentence was interpreted somewhat loosely, because what the FIA contended was that the pistons in our active suspension system were not remaining immobile relative to the sprung part of the car. But wait a minute: those pistons cannot be considered bodywork. No matter, it's our bat and ball and we are telling you it is illegal.

That was it. Out went our active suspension. Not just that, but what followed was a series of regulation changes that effectively outlawed everything that we and others had been developing as well. Out went CVT, traction control, launch control, servo-assisted braking, four-channel ABS, rear-wheel steering, electronically controlled power steering. Technology was evil and had no place in F1 seemed the summary. It was also declared that the weight limit was now to be 575kg, including the driver, meaning that a very light driver such as Alain would no longer have a built-in advantage. In-race refuelling was to be reintroduced, something that had been banned at the end of 1984 over concerns it could lead to a major fire . . .

There was no way of challenging these decisions. All you could do was stomp and sulk, go home and be irritable with the family, then go back to work and start again. Only, this time, we were starting again behind our competitors. We were not as far down the electronic control route as them. All our eggs had been in the active-suspension basket for two seasons.

Why, you might ask, did Max take this course of action?

My theory is twofold. First, because the British garagiste teams of Williams, McLaren and Tyrell were beginning to ask questions regarding the ownership of FOCA, and needed showing who was boss, second, because Ferrari threatened to leave the sport, which is something they do every now and then. Rightly or wrongly, there's a feeling that the sport needs Ferrari, and that its credibility partly rests on their involvement. Ferrari hadn't won the World Championship since 1978 and I'm sure Bernie was of the opinion that a Ferrari World Championship would be good for viewing figures. More viewing means more TV money. And more TV money means more income to, well, Mr B. Ecclestone.

Bernie had gone from leading the small British teams against the might of the grandees led by Ferrari, to being desperate to keep them in the sport and ensure they were successful. And, at the same time, to teach the British teams a lesson. Anybody read *Animal Farm*?

CHAPTER 41

The FW16, then, was an evolution of the FW15. Just as I always have and always will, I worked on the basis that if you have a car that seems to be a good concept, try to evolve that concept – don't try to come up with a totally new one unless there is a very good reason.

Once again, if you were to take the FW16 of 1994 and stand it alongside a Leyton House 881, you'd see strong similarities: the shape of the monocoque, the suspension layout, the shape of the sidepods, the rear-wing endplate, the philosophy behind the front wing and the front-wing endplate – all of those evolved from the 881 principle.

Had we become too complacent/conservative? Possibly. With the regulation change from active back to passive suspension we should probably have made more changes in order to develop a car more aerodynamically suited to a large range of ride-heights. You could probably argue that we didn't adapt to what was effectively a major regulation change – the banning of active suspension – as well as we could and should have done, and that I didn't put enough thought and work into this area.

In the end, my main focus in designing the 1994 car was to try to tidy the flow to the beam wing (the lower of the two rear wings) as much as possible. The beam wing serves two purposes: one is to generate downforce in its own right and the other, more powerful purpose, is to generate low pressure above the trailing edge of the diffuser, helping to draw flow through it.

One of the things limiting how low you could mount the beam wing was dirty air coming off the rear top wishbone. One way to improve that was to move the top wishbone, so what I did was lower it about 120mm to the point that it enclosed the driveshaft. In those days, suspension wishbones were made almost universally out of steel tubes welded together, but such a construction would not suit a shape that enclosed the driveshaft. So instead we made it out of carbon fibre as a large 'monocoque' construction that did not have traditional individual legs, the driveshaft passing down the centre of its hollow core. It gave us much cleaner flow on to the mid and tip areas of the beam wing.

The regulations called for a rain light: a square light about 100mm × 100mm. It's used in wet races, when cars throw up a rooster tail of water behind the car.

The rain light aims to cut through that ball of spray so that the following driver can at least see the light in the middle. Sometimes in really heavy weather even that rain light wasn't enough, but as LEDs have become more and more effective, they're now at the stage where they're powerful enough to do the job – blinding, actually, if you stand close behind the car in the garage.

The light usually sat beneath the beam wing. The trouble was that it damaged the flow where the beam wing should have been at its most efficient. The very bit of the wing you want to work best was destroyed by the presence of the rain light.

Getting that wishbone out of the way allowed a much lower profile to the top of the gearbox, which in turn gave the space to put the rain light above the gearbox and forward of the rear axle centre line. It was such a long way forward that it became part of the engine cover, faired in using a polycarbonate transparent cover.

We made the wing anhedral-shaped so that it sat lower at its tips than on the car centre line. So the flow across the wing was now very tidy on the centre line (not disrupted by the rain light) and at the tips (not disrupted by the top wishbone).

Mind you, the FIA didn't like the position of the rain light. They said you had to be directly behind the car to see it, otherwise it was obscured by the pylons that held the wing in place. In fairness to them they were probably right, but it was within the letter of the regulations so they couldn't do anything about it. Rules are rules.

Pre-season testing commenced and straightaway it became apparent that we were going to have serious competition from Benetton who, with Michael Schumacher driving, seemed to have produced a quick car.

Adding to our concern were issues of our own. Ayrton didn't like the seating position, with the low-mounted smallish-diameter steering wheel,

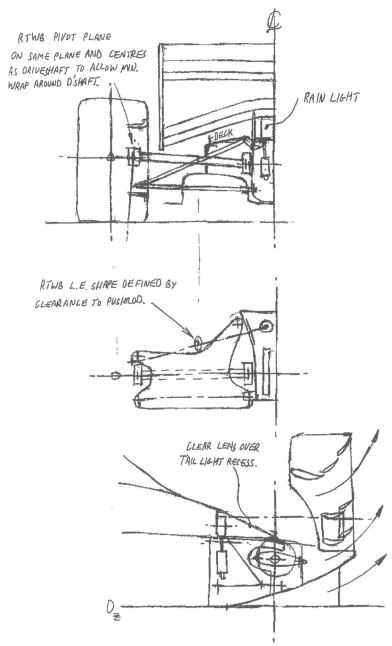

RTWB PIVOT PLANE
ON SAME PLANE AND CENTRES
AS DRIVESHAFT TO ALLOW MIN.
WRAP AROUND D'SHAFT.

RAIN LIGHT

DECK

RTWB L.E. SHAPE DEFINED BY
CLEARANCE TO PUSHROD.

CLEAR LENS OVER
TAIL LIGHT RECESS.

Figure 12: Early sketches of the layout for the FW16,
focusing on improving flow to the rear wing.

but it was far too late to be able to do much about it. Worse, once testing commenced, both he and Damon were finding the car unpredictable, particularly on an uneven surface.

Thankfully we had Damon in the cockpit, who had driven the 1993 car, and that was useful because it made us realise how much we'd lost through the ban on active suspension. It wasn't that we'd produced a bad car as such. It was that we hadn't produced a car that was well suited to passive suspension.

We were casting anxious glances at Benetton. Their car seemed to be very competitive; it looked like they were going to be our prime rival.

Concerned, we left for the first race in Brazil, home turf for Ayrton, who had recently celebrated his thirty-fourth birthday. He had just over a month to live.

CHAPTER 42

Brazil is a colourful place bursting with enthusiasm and joy of life, but like some of the smaller and poorer countries in Africa, it's a country where you have pockets of extreme wealth amid huge numbers of very poor people where life has little value.

They are, of course, mad about Formula One in Brazil, and back then they were nuts about Ayrton Senna. This year he was Team Williams, and no longer our nemesis. What a relief we didn't have to worry about a repeat of the previous year, when Ayrton was driving for McLaren and there had been a chance of him winning the Grand Prix against Alain and Damon in the Williams.

Driving into the circuit in our VW minibus the previous year had meant negotiating a gauntlet of Brazilian fans chanting, blowing horns and waving flags. Being an English team we gulped and smiled wanly, pretending nothing was amiss as our bus inched through a sea of yellow to the circuit gates. Somebody in the crowd spotted our uniforms, our *Williams* uniforms, and pointed us out before starting to hurl abuse. We were the team most likely to prevent Ayrton from winning. It was viral. More abuse came our way.

We gulped harder and smiled a little more wanly, painfully aware that a crowd can so easily become a mob. A surge of something passed through the fans, and the next thing we knew, something hit a window. Then they were rocking the bus, and one of them had even scrambled onto the roof and was jumping up and down.

It went on for several hours. Well, it certainly felt like several hours, but may in fact have been only about 45 seconds before our bus reached the gates and police broke up the crowd with their batons.

At least things would be safer this year, I told myself, arriving with Sheridan Thynne, the head of marketing at Williams. We had Ayrton on our side. São Paulo was his home town. We were late, and Sheridan and

I flagged a taxi to get from São Paulo airport on the outskirts to the hotel. We settled back, hoping for the best as we drew out into the madness of the city morning rush hour.

As we crawled along it became apparent that our driver, possibly having had a heavy night, was nodding off, chin resting on his chest, the works. After about the fourth time of finding ourselves at a standstill and having to rouse him from his slumber, we decided to put a bit of fire in his belly by showing him our Williams travel shirts. 'Ayrton Senna!' we said, 'Ayrton Senna!' indicating onward, onward.

It was one of those 'careful what you wish for' moments. Our actions had the desired effect. Our driver was suddenly wide awake and making haste to our destination. The problem was that he began driving like a lunatic, weaving in and out of the traffic, heedless of the horns blaring around him and oblivious to our abject terror as he attempted to prove that he too, could drive like Ayrton Senna. We got there in one piece, thank God, but exited the car on legs of jelly. It was probably the most frightening drive of my whole life.

The disconcertingly low value placed on life was illustrated not only by the Mercedes stand at the track displaying the latest bullet-proof glass or doors rather than the newest car, but also by an incident I witnessed as I was driving from the circuit to the hotel. A car swerved ahead, and then I saw what looked like a large dog lying in the road. *Oh God*, I thought, *a dog's been killed*, only to realise as I drew closer that, though it was indeed a body, it was human not canine. That's how they dispose of bodies in the favelas, apparently. Just dump them on the highway.

So to qualifying at São Paulo's Interlagos circuit, nestled in the shadow of high-rises that stood like ramparts along the city skyline. Still having problems with the car – especially apparent on a bumpy circuit like Interlagos – Ayrton hung on, and thanks to his phenomenal control and ability managed to put the car on to pole, his starting position very much a measure of his ability rather than of our car's superiority.

On to the race and for the first 21 laps he led ahead of Schumacher, but when they both pitted Schumacher came out ahead. On the pit wall our eyes were glued to the monitors, hearts in mouths, as Ayrton stayed on Schumacher's tail, harrying him. He could take the lead. We knew he could. If anyone could do it, Ayrton could.

But then, on lap 56, coming out of the final corner just behind Schumacher, Ayrton span and stalled – and that was it.

With Ayrton out, there was no reason for the partisan home fans to stay and I watched them empty out of the grandstand, their round-shouldered dejection matching our own. Schumacher came in first, Damon second.

What a great, great shame it was. Even more so in retrospect, when you consider the pressure Ayrton must have been under that day. If he'd won, or at least been second, then perhaps he would have gone on to the next race, the Pacific Grand Prix, and the one after that, Imola, in a different and less intense frame of mind. Perhaps things would have been different. So many 'what ifs' and 'should haves' surrounding his death. So many factors that were individually insignificant but collectively played their part.

In the debrief afterwards Ayrton congratulated Damon on finishing second, held up his hands and said the spin was his mistake and his alone. None of us had it in our hearts to pass judgement. He was driving a difficult car on the limit, and he'd done things with it no other driver could.

Afterwards we were sitting in São Paulo airport lounge, waiting for the flight home, mostly in silence, the way you do when things haven't gone your way, when we received the news that Benetton might be excluded from the Brazilian result.

That perked us up a little. The reason was to do with the bargeboards on their car, the vertical curved boards that sit just in front of the sidepod, their job being to deflect the front wheel wake outwards, diverting it away from the main bodywork and diffuser.

One of the regulations states that all bodywork, viewed from underneath, 'must form a uniform, solid, hard, continuous, impervious surface'. But the bargeboards on the Benetton were mounted with one stay at the front and one at the rear, the combination forming a hole. That's why they were to be excluded, because of this hole. Clearly a hole is not impervious.

Ah, but Benetton said, 'No, actually, it's not a hole, it's a series of stays and a bargeboard,' which is a bit like saying that the bit in the middle of a Polo mint isn't a hole, it's just a place where there happens to be no mint. It seemed a weak argument that wouldn't wash with the FIA.

But it did wash with the FIA. The upshot was that Benetton weren't excluded. And the regulations were altered for 1995 to specifically allow holes in this area!

The next race was a new one: the Pacific Grand Prix held at the Tanaka International Circuit, or IT Circuit, in Aida, Japan.

I didn't go. I stayed behind at Williams. I wanted to work in the wind tunnel in a bid to understand why the car was behaving so badly. Instead I watched on TV as Ayrton once more managed to put his car on pole, knowing that, again, it was down to his ability rather than the car.

In the race he crashed at the first corner. He was lightly bumped by Mika Häkkinen, span, came to rest in the sand track, and that was his race over at the first corner. Another tough result.

All of which meant that by the end of the second race of the season, Ayrton hadn't finished at all and Damon had a single second place. By any measure it was a diabolical start to our year as reigning champs, and as frustrating for us as it was for Ayrton, who must have been cursing his flawed timing: he'd joined a hugely successful team – only to see them lose their competitive edge.

He'd watched the rest of the race from the marshal's hut on the outside of turn one, and I remember that he returned with his suspicions raised. There was something about the sound of the Benetton – Schumacher's Benetton, not his teammate – that sounded wrong to Ayrton. He was convinced they were using traction control.

Still I struggled to understand what was wrong with our own car. Clearly it was an aerodynamic problem. Something was unstable in the aero-dynamics, which meant it had to be related to the ground effect. The two things closest to the ground are the front wing and the floor, so it could be that the diffuser or the front wing was stalling.

We tested at Circuit de Nogaro, a bumpy little circuit in south-western

France. Just a skeleton crew with Damon driving. 'It's jumping around so violently,' he told me, 'I can't see.'

I sent him out again but this time took a scooter to watch the car on the back straight. Just as he'd reported, it was pogoing up and down so much that the front wheels were virtually leaving the track. This at something like 150mph.

No doubt in my mind, something was stalling. For it to be as violent as that, for the front wheels to be almost airborne, there had to be something very unstable about the aerodynamics.

I remember driving back from Nogaro that night. Damon, in his hire car, lights off in 'stealth mode', was bumping me from behind. Little did I know that it was to be a long time before either of us felt like pulling such pranks again.

Back to the wind tunnel I went, trying to understand it. With the wind tunnel model down to the lowest front ride-height, where stall and separation is more likely to occur, we used Flow Vis and it looked fine; nothing in the wind tunnel to indicate the front wing was at fault.

I moved on to the underside of the car, used Flow Vis again, and this time discovered separation underneath the leading edge of the sidepod. The separation was sufficient that the centre of the diffuser was almost completely stalled.

It was a proper *eureka* moment. The issue was a simple geometrical problem requiring a simple geometrical solution. Basically, the sidepod we had on the car was reasonably long, so the front edge of it was close to the front tyres. By making the sidepod long, it has more area to it, so if you can manage to get the same amount of suction along that extra length, you've got more total downforce. But, that extra length also brings it closer to the ground if the front is very low. The resulting constriction was causing very high local velocities in the flow followed by rapid deceleration. This creates a highly adverse pressure gradient and that causes separation – in this case a very violent and catastrophic stall.

It explained what I had seen with my eyes on the straight at France. The bumps were setting up a pitch in the car that put the aerodynamics into an unstable area.

The solution was to go to a much shorter sidepod. It would mean less ultimate-peak downforce but the front of the floor would not get so close to the ground, the diffuser wouldn't stall and we might be back in business.

So, in the period between the Pacific Grand Prix and Imola, I started designing a shorter sidepod, which in the wind tunnel appeared to produce a more stable solution to take to production. It was not a massive change. The mechanical packaging of the car, the radiators and so forth, could stay in the same place, but it still involved a sizeable amount of work because it meant a completely new floor and new bodywork.

With that ongoing, we left for the San Marino GP in Imola – a bumpy circuit that we thought might be bad news for us. We had no idea.

CHAPTER 43

It was sunny and hot at Imola for the San Marino Grand Prix, not at all the kind of weather you associate with the dark events that unfolded right from the moment I arrived at the circuit on Friday morning. The pre-qualifying session was running as I walked in through the car park, and the sight that greeted me was that of a car coming out of the last corner before the final chicane. It wasn't on all four wheels. It was on its side, 20ft in the air, rattling along the wire of the barrier, above the wall, before dropping down and out of sight again.

Christ, I thought, *I hope that guy's all right.*

It was the Brazilian, Rubens Barrichello, in a Jordan. Doing around 140mph, he'd hit a kerb on the corner they call *Variante Bassa* hard enough to launch his car airborne, then into a roll before it came to rest upside down.

Apparently his tongue, as a result of the accident, blocked his airway, and if not for the quick work of Sid Watkins at the trackside he probably would have died. As it was, he was rushed to the medical centre, from where he was airlifted to the Maggiore hospital in Bologna. Back at the circuit the following day, he was reduced to spectator status thanks to a broken nose and arm in plaster.

He was okay. Indeed, Rubens currently holds the record for competing in the most Formula One races. Even so, it was one of those really nasty, what-if crashes. The kind you witness and marvel how anybody could come out of it unhurt. The kind that gives you pause for thought: just what are we doing, running such huge risks?

I wonder if Ayrton thought so too. Later I discovered that he'd been to check on Barrichello, his fellow countryman. Barrichello had recovered consciousness to find Ayrton in tears by his bed, so they say.

With pre-qualifying over, practice started. Ayrton was quick, but as usual the car was difficult over bumps. It was bugging him, same way it bugged us all. We've since discovered that he'd recently had discussions about joining Ferrari, so I guess he had that in the back of his mind as well. There was also the fact that his family apparently disapproved of his new girlfriend, and his suspicion that Schumacher's Benetton was using traction control.

That said, there's no doubt in my mind that his major preoccupation was the fact that he hadn't yet won a race. He wasn't one to apportion blame. If anything, he was too quick to take responsibility for things that weren't his fault. But this was his championship bid and he was yet to score a single point. He knew we were trying to understand the car, and he listened patiently and understandingly as I explained to him what I'd seen at Nogaro, and how I thought the problem was the sidepods, explaining that we were designing new ones, that a solution was in hand.

At the same time, we'd done what we could to address an ongoing issue he had with his seating position, where he felt cramped and was rubbing his knuckles on the inside of the cockpit. Why this was happening I'm still not sure. His hand position on the wheel must have been different from that of his predecessors or teammates. Either way, he wanted the steering wheel lowered slightly to give more knuckle clearance.

The job was to move the steering wheel down by a couple of millimetres, but we had to bear in mind an FIA regulation template, which was an aluminium plate with a width of 200mm and height of 200mm. Officials had to be able to pass it between the driver and the inside of the cockpit, from his upper body down to the pedals. If this wasn't possible, your car was declared illegal and excluded.

If we lowered the steering column, then the template wouldn't pass. The solution was to reduce the diameter of the steering column locally by 4mm, which is what we'd done.

At the track, however, there was still this ride problem to address. More in hope than expectation, we fitted softer springs, but that just meant bigger changes in ride-height, which in turn aggravated the aerodynamic insta-bility. We tried running the front higher, but lost too much downforce. I still had hair then. I was raking my fingers through it, trying to find the answer, knowing in reality that the problem was more profound than anything we could tackle at the track. We were trapped with a bad car. No amount of set-up tuning with springs, dampers or roll bars was ever going to overcome its aerodynamic instability.

There was another incident that day, comparatively minor. The front wing had come off one of the Simtek cars. Driving for Simtek then were Roland Ratzenberger and David Brabham; I'm afraid I don't remember which of them it was who lost their wing that day.

Simtek was run by a guy called Nick Wirth, an aerodynamicist I knew from Leyton House. He was a bright chap, but he'd gained the nickname White Noise because he wouldn't concentrate on one thing. He had a close relationship with Max Mosley and the pair of them had set up Simtek to enter F1 in 1994, making Wirth a very young team owner.

That evening in the paddock I was approached by Charlie Moody, team manager at Simtek, another old Leyton House face and also an old Reptonian – so someone I knew fairly well.

'Adrian,' he said, somewhat sheepishly, 'Nick's told me to fix this front wing. Can you give me some advice?'

I looked at him, knowing he wasn't an engineer and wondering how on earth he'd got roped into sorting out this problem. 'Where's Nick?' I asked.

'He's at a sponsors' dinner.'

'Well look, Charlie, I'm sorry, I'd love to help you, but I don't know anything about the design of your car. I really don't know what to suggest. You need to get Nick back; he's the engineer.'

I watched Charlie leave, worried by our conversation.

Saturday came, and, in qualifying, Roland Ratzenberger, driving his Simtek, came off the track.

He was competing for the final slot on the grid at the time, so instead of pitting to have the car checked over, he continued for another lap. On the straight, the front wing came off altogether, was dragged beneath his car and stopped him cornering. He ploughed into the outside wall at just under 200mph.

Sid Watkins, the chief medical officer, did his best. For the second time that weekend, a driver was airlifted from the Imola circuit to the Maggiore hospital. Roland, sadly, was not as fortunate as Rubens. He was pronounced dead at the hospital.

CHAPTER 44

Ayrton didn't have many close friends within the Formula One paddock, but Roland was one of them. He'd jumped into an official car to take him to the scene of the accident the moment he heard about it. Later, when Roland was pronounced dead, he wept on Sid Watkins' shoulder. The two were great friends, but when Sid asked Ayrton not to race the following day – 'Give it up and let's go fishing,' he'd said – Ayrton could only say that he had to race. He had to go on, no matter how shaken he was. He had to go on.

Ayrton withdrew from qualifying, though his times were enough to put him on pole, which meant that for the third time in a row, it was Ayrton on pole with Schumacher second.

There was much talk of how Roland's accident could have happened.

The mood in the paddock was muted at best. Death in motor racing up until the 1970s had been all too common, but this was the first time a driver had died at an F1 race since Gilles Villeneuve 12 years earlier. For many in the paddock, including myself, it was a new experience. We were in a state of shock. No doubt everyone felt the same way. *Is it worth it? Is all this worth a man dying?*

On the day of the race I was in the back of the truck, close to the time when the cars leave the pit lane for the grid, collecting together my notes and bits and pieces, when in rushed Ayrton, quickly peeling off his racesuit and changing his Nomex underwear.

He's cutting it fine, I thought. What we now know is that on that morning he'd been talking to Alain Prost about reopening the Grand Prix Drivers' Association with the aim of improving safety. As he pulled his overalls back up, he reiterated what he'd already said in the wake of the Pacific Grand Prix – that he thought Benetton were using traction control. After that Pacific race, Ferrari also had to ride out a stink regarding their own possible use of traction control, with subsequent grumbles about favouritism reaching such a peak that, by Imola, Max was forced to issue a statement categorically stating that the FIA didn't love Ferrari any more or less than it loved other teams.

It wasn't Ferrari traction control rumours that concerned Ayrton, though. It was his concern over Benetton: the feeling that he was battling an illegal driver–car combination.

He went into that race with all that buzzing in his head. But he went in, above all, with a desire to win. Ayrton was one of the fiercest, most passionate competitors the sport has known.

CHAPTER 45

The race began badly. Schumacher's teammate JJ Lehto stalled the Benetton and Pedro Lamy, his view obscured, tail-ended him, sending debris everywhere, including into spectators, injuring a number of them. The carnage of the weekend seemed relentless.

The safety car was called out as marshals cleared the debris. On lap five the race resumed with Ayrton in the lead, Schumacher behind.

Tamburello was where it happened. A fast left-hand corner shortly after the pits, it was typically taken flat-out, although most drivers, including Damon, were taking a slightly wider line in order to avoid the bumpy inside section.

Ayrton, it seems, wasn't doing that. He was taking the inside, a slightly shorter and therefore, he felt, faster line, even though he knew the car was unstable over bumps. Again, he had that belief that he could control the car, whatever the situation.

Meanwhile, of course, one of the effects of circulating slowly behind the safety car for five laps was that the tyres had cooled, tyre pressures fallen and ride-heights become lowered as a result.

So when the race restarted, Ayrton's car was bottoming very heavily, by which I mean the underside of the car was making contact with the track. Much later, when we reviewed footage supplied to us from Schumacher's on-board camera, what we saw were showers of sparks from the back of Ayrton's car, particularly through Tamburello.

First lap after the restart – lap six – he made it through Tamburello, but with massive sparking, his car bottoming like crazy. He was ahead of Schumacher. All he needed to do was stop Schumacher from passing him, just as he'd done to Nigel at Suzuka in 1991. But Ayrton wasn't the type to settle back and keep one eye on the mirror. He was a racer, and that's what he did. His lap six was the third fastest of the race – and that's with an almost full fuel tank and tyres at sub-optimum pressure.

The seventh lap was when the accident happened. By now you'd have expected tyre pressures to be normal, but going by Schumacher's on-board footage Ayrton was bottoming even more, sparks spraying like Roman candles behind him as he took the inside line at Tamburello.

What you see next on the on-board footage is the rear of Ayrton's car step out to the right. For a heartbeat the car is pointing to the left, then suddenly it snaps right and disappears off in that direction, out of the camera's field of view.

At the time we were watching coverage on the pit wall and what we saw was that there had been an accident involving Ayrton. A big accident. Damon, who had raced past the crash site, later said that it never occurred to him that the accident might be fatal, not until the red flags started waving. There on the pit wall we were all on autopilot, as David Brown, Ayrton's race engineer, radioed him again and again, but got no response.

I remember snippets. Ayrton sitting perfectly normally in the car, upright with his head against the headrest – but not moving. I can recall seeing Sid and the medical crew arrive. I remember seeing Ayrton being pulled out of the car, motionless on a stretcher. All this on the monitors, of course. Over the radio, Damon was calling for information: 'What the hell's happened? How is he? What's happened?'

But we didn't know. The only information we had came from what we saw on the screens lining the pit wall. Our driver on a stretcher. No movement. No information.

Another thing I remember, something burnt into my brain, is the noise from the spectators. The horns, klaxons and tambourines. All this excited frenzy of noise that carried on despite the terrible tragedy unfolding at Tamburello. The sound, a trademark of Italian Grands Prix, still to this day sends shivers down my spine.

'We don't know, Damon,' I told him, as the cars were reformed on the grid. From over our heads came the sound of a helicopter. 'We just don't know.'

The race began again and we were forced to refocus. The helicopter took Ayrton to hospital. Schumacher won, Damon finished sixth.

The news came through at the airport. Ayrton was dead.

CHAPTER 46

Frank's aircraft flew us back to Kidlington, north of Oxford. I don't think any of us spoke. I really can't recall. Only that Marigold met me at Kidlington and drove me home, knowing I'd be in no fit state to drive myself.

She'd arranged for the local pub to deliver beer to the house, so I could have a few drinks to unwind. It didn't work, but it was a nice thought. It was a warm evening, I can remember that, although it was only May.

What I felt as I drank my beers and then lay awake in bed that night was an overwhelming sense of loss and, much more than that, *waste*. Even back then you knew Ayrton was destined for great – even greater – things. People had speculated that he might be President of Brazil one day. Was it all worth it, just to watch a bunch of cars racing around a track on a Sunday afternoon? Even now, twenty-something years later, I struggle to talk about it without my voice wavering.

The next day was a Bank Holiday Monday. I went into Williams with other key engineers to see if we could understand what had happened. Was it a design fault that had caused the accident? Tamburello was difficult but flat, the kind of big-balls corner that a driver should be able to take without lifting off the throttle. A driver of Ayrton's ability shouldn't have had a problem with a corner like that.

We reviewed what footage we had, and it was clear that the steering wheel had come off. You could see the wheel and the end of the steering column lying beside the car in the TV footage. The obvious conclusion was that the steering column had snapped and that was the cause of the accident.

Patrick was technical director and therefore had technical charge of the team. I was chief designer and responsible for the overall design of the car. And though neither of us were involved in the design or manufacture of the actual components, as leaders of the ship, we had to assume responsibility.

Put simply, if the steering column snapping was the cause of the accident, it was our fault, since we were responsible for putting in place the systems needed to avoid such a thing happening.

It would take a long time before we identified the missing pieces of the jigsaw. I would spend the following months – as it turned out, years – having to watch the accident over and over again: the pictures from Schumacher's car, the circuit TV feed, the race footage, marrying it to the data, trying to understand what had happened, why Ayrton had died that afternoon.

The FW16 had two on-board computers. One controlled the engine and was supplied by Magneti Marelli, the other was a Williams-built ECU that Steve Wise, the head of electronics at Williams, had developed to control the active suspension system in 1992.

Computers had less of a function after the great regulations purge outlawed our electronically controlled systems; however, they did provide some degree of 'data logging', namely using sensors around the car as a diagnostic feature, monitoring such things as loads on the suspension, the gear change, throttle position, engine rpm, wheel speeds, damper positions – areas that gave us information on what the car was doing around the lap.

The Renault Marelli engine control unit had been largely destroyed in the accident, and the Williams control unit was badly damaged too, but we were able to extract some data from it. Importantly, what we were able to ascertain was throttle position, brake pressure and steering torque, and what we saw appeared to substantiate the theory that it was a steering column failure, because it showed the steering column torque falling to near zero. In other words, there was no steering input during this phase. This could either mean that Ayrton had chosen not to steer, or that he was unable to steer because the steering column had failed.

Our feeling, however, that the steering column had been the main cause of the accident changed, however, when the FIA provided us with the on-board footage from Schumacher's car. This indicated that the rear of Ayrton's car had stepped out, which was the opposite to what would happen if the steering column had failed. Obviously, if the steering fails, you expect the car to carry straight on. But if the rear of the car steps out, that can only be from a loss of rear grip, not from a loss of front grip.

That seemed a bit peculiar. Coming from my oval-racing experience in the States, I knew that drivers in Super Speedway are often faced with this problem of the rear stepping out in high-speed corners. The usual method of trying to correct it is by applying opposite lock, i.e. in a left-hand turn, apply lock to the right. But if the car is stepping out in a snappy and harsh manner, the fear is that the rear will suddenly grip and whip the driver around in the opposite direction, resulting in a nose-first crash into a wall. Super Speedway drivers will often let a spin take place rather than risk this happening.

So, did Ayrton suffer that type of Super Speedway accident where the rear loses and then suddenly regains grip and flings him to the outside wall? It can happen to the most experienced and greatest of the Super Speedway drivers in the States.

Very quickly, the question became two-tiered: what caused Ayrton to leave the track in the first place, and, given that he was such an able driver, why was he unable to control it?

We were able to time-match Schumacher's on-board footage with the data from the on-board computer, and what we established was that at the moment the rear of the car stepped out, Ayrton lifted his foot to about 40 per cent throttle and the steering torque dropped.

Now, if you suddenly lose rear grip, that is exactly the reaction you'd expect a driver to make. He doesn't lift his foot fully off the throttle. What he's doing at that point is trying to maximise the grip of the rear tyres, which means trying to minimise the longitudinal force the rear tyres are trying to transmit, be it acceleration or braking, so that they have the maximum capacity for lateral grip. It looked like that's what Ayrton had done; by reducing steering torque he was effectively applying opposite lock, which, as I've said, is the usual way to correct the rear of a car that is stepping out.

The data showed that Ayrton held that position of 40 per cent throttle and low level of steering torque for half a second, then got very heavily on the brake. All we saw after that was extremely high brake pressure as he left the track. Again then, the sequence of events consistent with the data is that the rear stepped out, Ayrton reacted, doing his best to hold the slide by reducing to 40 per cent throttle and reducing steering torque before realising after half a second that he'd lost control, after which he jumped on the brakes.

The initial stepping out of the car was nothing to do with any steering column failure. There had to be another explanation for that.

The safety car was an Opel Vectra, so the pace would have been very slow after the start/finish prang that showered the track with debris. After all those laps at such a slow pace, the tyres would have cooled and tyre pressures been extremely low at the restart, and that, without doubt, would have aggravated the bottoming that we saw.

But this doesn't fully explain everything. In fact, it may be a red herring. Why, for example, did Ayrton's car spark as much on lap seven as it had on the previous lap, when tyre pressures should have become progressively higher? The suspension components themselves all seemed to be fine, so the obvious conclusion is that the tyres were still under-inflated. But why? Their temperature and therefore pressure should have been back up to near normal after a full, hard racing lap.

There is a photograph in *Autosport* (20 February 1997, page 6) that shows a piece of debris on the track, with Ayrton's car about to pass over it. His right front and right rear tyres were completely destroyed in the accident, so it was impossible to examine them and say for certain, but a piece of debris that size could easily have caused a slow puncture. The puncture would have caused the bottoming we saw, and that in turn would have caused the rear to step out as it lost grip, since you've unloaded the tyres meaning that the weight of the car is now being taken on the skids, which have no lateral grip capability. Not only that, but with the car now flat on the deck the diffuser would be completely stalled, resulting in the rear losing most of its downforce.

For me, that offers an explanation as to why the rear suddenly stepped out, and it obviously caught Ayrton by surprise.

Still, that bring us to the second question. Why, after the car had stepped out, did Ayrton fail to control it? Of all the drivers on the grid, he was the one most able to recover that situation. There are two possibilities here. One is that the steering column failed at this point. The other is that as the car came off the back side of the hump pointing left, but with the front wheels still pointing straight ahead, the rear suddenly gripped and threw it sharply right.

What we could see once we were allowed to inspect the steering column was that it did have a fatigue crack present, so it was going to fail sooner or later. It had fatigued roughly a third of the way around the circumference and the rest had snapped, either in the impact or from the pressure Ayrton exerted while trying to control the car after the rear stepped out. Where the steering column failed was where it had been locally reduced by 4mm in diameter.

This led to the further question: would the remaining two-thirds of the column that had not fatigued have had enough strength to transmit the torque required to maintain normal driving? So we built a test rig consisting of the complete car steering system, and, with a saw, cut one-third of the way through the new column to represent the fatigued area. We then got a 'driver' to turn the steering wheel in order to achieve the highest pressure shown by the data recorder. The result was that, yes, even in this damaged state, the column had enough strength left in it. Following that result we conducted various tests, trying to marry data recovered from the ECU for pressure transducers across the steering rack and the steering column data with measurements on the rig. When the car left the edge of the circuit, it travelled across a very uneven boundary from circuit to apron, which put large pressure spikes across the rack with corresponding spikes in the column torque. The only way we could achieve the column torques on the rig was with the column still reasonably intact and thus able to transmit torque due to the rotational inertia of the steering wheel – put simply, a completely broken column could not be made to register any steering column torque readings.

Now, I am responsible for following that request of Ayrton's to lower the steering wheel slightly to avoid him rubbing his knuckles on the inside of the chassis. I am responsible for giving the drawing office the instruction to lower it by 2mm, and when they came back to me to say that it would then interfere with the FIA cockpit template, I instructed them to reduce the steering column diameter locally by 4mm.

What I didn't do was look at the detailed drawing myself or have a proper checking system in place to make sure that it had been done in a safe manner. It's a simple, well-known law of engineering that to maintain stiffness and strength you have to increase wall thickness, but that wasn't done. The wall thickness was not increased.

It's also a simple, well-known law of engineering that if you have a very sharp corner in a component, that causes an area of very high stress; and because of that stress, the component will eventually crack and fatigue; and that fatigue crack will propagate eventually around the whole component and cause failure.

So there were two very bad pieces of engineering in that diameter reduction. Ultimately, Patrick and I were responsible for that.

You question yourself. If you don't, you're a fool. The first thing you ask yourself is: *Do I want to be involved in something where somebody can be killed as a result of a decision I have made?* If you answer yes to that one, the second is: *Do I accept that one of the design team for which I am responsible may make a mistake in the design of the car and the result of that mistake is that somebody may be killed?* Prior to Imola, stupid as this may sound, I had never asked myself those questions.

If you want to continue in motor racing, you have to square that with yourself. You have to be prepared to offer an affirmative to both of those questions because, try as you might, you can never ever guarantee that a mistake will not be made. Designing a racing car means pushing the boundaries of design. If you don't, it won't be competitive. Then there's the decision-making during the race. If a car is carrying damage for some reason, you have to make the decision: *Do I tell a driver to retire the car or let him continue?* If you call it too conservatively, you simply retire the car for no good reason. If you've been too bullish, the driver could have an accident with unknown consequences. It's never an easy judgement.

People ask me if I feel guilty about Ayrton. I do. I was one of the senior officers in a team that designed a car in which a great man was killed. Regardless of whether that steering column caused the accident or not, there is no escaping the fact that it was a bad piece of design that should never have been allowed to get on the car. The system that Patrick and I had in place was inadequate; that cannot be disputed. Our lack of a safety-checking system within the design office was exposed.

So, in the immediate aftermath, Patrick and I discussed that and agreed we would have to go to a category system in which the safety-critical components, including the steering system, braking system, suspension parts and key aerodynamic components such as the front wing and rear wing – all the things that, if they failed, could cause an accident – should be submitted to an experienced stress engineer who would look at the drawings, make sure they were structurally sound and then countersign the drawing.

What I feel the most guilt about, though, is not the possibility that steering column failure may have caused the accident, because I don't think it did, but the fact that I screwed up the aerodynamics of the car. I messed up the transition from active suspension back to passive and designed a car that was aerodynamically unstable, in which Ayrton attempted to do things the car was not capable of doing. Whether he did or didn't get a puncture, his taking the inside, faster-but-bumpier line in a car that was aerodynamically unstable would have made the car difficult to control, even for him.

I think now, *If only we'd had more time.* By Imola, I understood the problem. I just needed time to develop the wind tunnel model and then the parts to go on the car, to give Ayrton a car that was worthy of him. Time denied us all that chance.

CHAPTER 47

There's no such thing as accidental death in Italy. If somebody dies and it's not suicide, then somebody must be held responsible.

So after the death at Imola of Roland and Ayrton, a prosecuting magistrate was assigned by the local Bologna Prosecutor's Office. Two and a half years after the accident, Maurizio Passarini, Bologna's federal prosecutor, decided there was no case against the Simtek team after the death of Roland Ratzenberger, but concluded that Williams team executives and circuit administrators should face a manslaughter charge.

Charged from Williams were Frank, Patrick and me, while Federico Bendinelli, head of Sagis, the firm who administer the Imola circuit, was charged with failing to modify a well-known dangerous corner. Giorgio Poggi, the track official director, and Roland Bruynseraede, the race director from FIA, were charged with being co-responsible for not making safety modifications in the wake of Roland Ratzenberger's death.

The whole thing was something of a travesty as far as I was concerned. I will always feel a degree of responsibility for Ayrton's death but not culpability. The guilt I felt was for me to work out for myself, not in the forum of an Italian court, presided over by a judge who was operating in direct contravention of the family's wishes. The fact that the Ratzenberger case had been so easily swept under the carpet left me suspicious that Passarini's principal motivation might be personal glory and notoriety.

Fast-forwarding, I went on gardening leave from Williams (more of which later) at the end of the 1996 season, and spent most of that period consumed with establishing my defence to the case. The trial began in the summer of 1997. By that time I'd left Williams, but I'd had the foresight to ensure that my contract with McLaren included coverage of my legal fees with respect to the ongoing manslaughter charge. Patrick had made it clear, even when I was still at Williams, that because we were being charged individually, we'd have to defend ourselves individually, which I thought was a slightly strange stance.

Eventually, on the evening before the commencement of the trial, Patrick came up to me and said, 'Just to let you know that as far as I'm concerned, you were the chief designer and responsible for the design of the car and therefore, I believe, you have to take responsibility for this.'

I was dumbfounded. I didn't expect that from Patrick. In my book, as one of the senior officers of the ship you take responsibility. Below me in the organisation was the head of the design office, below him the detail designer who actually drew the component. So, if you want to get into that game, I could say, 'Well actually, you shouldn't be charging me, you should be charging the head of the design office and the design draughtsman over here; it's nothing to do with me. I never saw the design.' Needless to say, I just don't think that's the way one should work. Their names were kept out of the proceedings.

I've mellowed since. Two decades on, looking back, I think Patrick was under pressure and didn't handle it as well as he might have done. Also, to be fair to him, he never repeated that suggestion of his at any point in the trial.

It was a rather different affair to your typical English trial. More like an Italian wedding where random people get to their feet, shout for a while and then sit down again.

The prosecution had appointed as their technical expert a formidable engineer called Mauro Forghieri, Ferrari's technical director in the 1960s and 70s, and without doubt the last of that breed of designer able to design both the chassis and the engine itself. I respected him a great deal, so for him in retirement to come forward and attempt to get us found guilty of manslaughter was a real disappointment. His evidence was focused on the steering column – it was the thrust of the whole case against us. A terrible design that had no place on a racing car, was what he said. Though he was right, that didn't mean it had caused the accident.

We tried our best to make that point, but the judge had absolutely zero technical understanding. Hard though we tried to explain the link between the data and the on-board footage, the concept of the rear stepping out into oversteer, the action of counter-steer, the action of lifting to half throttle, why the driver would do that and how it affect the dynamics of the car, it was clear he had no idea what we were talking about, no matter how many times we said it or how we put it, to the point that our own barrister became frustrated. He and my lawyer, both laymen themselves, completely understood it.

So, it was a complete mess of a trial, and one that seemed to drag on forever, until finally in December 1997 all defendants were cleared of manslaughter charges. Well, the charges were 'not proven', which left the door open and, sure enough, three years later came a retrial, a shorter affair, no fresh evidence offered, same verdict. There was a third one, same verdict, and Italian law says that if there's no fresh evidence and 10 years have passed then that's it.

The car was eventually returned to the UK and crushed, the only right thing to do with it. It sickens me when I hear of cars in which the driver has died being 'found' and rebuilt for personal gain, despite the team having supposedly disposed of them.

CHAPTER 48

Back to 1994, and in the aftermath of Ayrton's death we at Williams were zombified. I can't describe it. You feel as though your lips are moving and your legs are taking you places, but you're not particularly conscious of the words that are coming out of your mouth, or why you've gone from A to B. Life is viewed as if through a screen.

We won the championship that season. Rather, I should say we won the constructors' championship. With Imola always in the back of our minds it was a bittersweet victory.

The fact, however, that it was Benetton we beat to the constructors' title did give us a measure of satisfaction. In my opinion, Ayrton had been right about Benetton. They were not playing with a straight bat all season.

The next race after Imola was always going to be something of an endurance test, and so it proved. Damon became the number one driver, with David Coulthard – 'DC', our test driver, – due to take the second seat, though not for this race.

How Damon felt I'm not sure, but I do think it speaks volumes about his strength of character. He had lost his father, Graham, to a racing-related accident; now he was being promoted to team leader as a result of the death of his teammate. Rather than being intimidated or haunted, he became one of the major motivating forces of the team.

Damon was the only driver we entered for Monaco, a race that was made even more challenging and emotionally draining by yet another horrific accident: Karl Wendlinger in the Sauber lost control exiting the tunnel, hit the barrier at the chicane, rolled and was knocked unconscious. He was in a coma for some time afterwards, and though he eventually regained consciousness and made a full recovery he wasn't able to drive for the rest of the year.

The next day, as drivers stood on the grid immediately before the race, observing a minute's silence in honour of Roland and Ayrton, I thought how hard it must be to stand there remembering your fallen colleagues and then get in your car moments later and carry on. The newspaper reporters must have thought much the same. As news reached us that Wendlinger was in a coma, Max Mosley found himself fielding media scrutiny about safety in the sport. Two fatalities at Imola, and now the horrific TV images of Wendlinger slumped in the cockpit would prove to be the straw that broke the camel's back as far as the world's media was concerned. Suddenly we looked like a house that couldn't keep itself in order. It didn't matter that cars were in fact slower than they had been in recent years, having lost active suspension among other things. 'Killer Machine'-style headlines were beginning to appear; columnists were asking out loud the same question I had asked myself after Imola: *Is it really worth people dying in the name of sport?*

Under huge public pressure Max felt that action had to be taken, and quite rightly. At Monaco it was announced that for the next race, Barcelona, diffusers would be shortened and the complexity of the front-wing endplate reduced – all of which were measures aimed at reducing down-force. Cars would also have to have what was to become known as 'a plank' underneath them, which would be the first thing that touched the ground rather than the floor of the chassis. The plank had to be 10mm thick, effectively raising the whole car 10mm. It reduced the ground effect, further cutting downforce.

Schumacher won from pole, his teammate JJ Lehto was seventh (note the disparity). Damon was a DNF, after a collision with Häkkinen.

For Spain, we had two weeks' notice to implement the new regulations, as well as to continue research on the short sidepod project we'd started just before Imola.

Ironically, the required plank underneath the car helped to counter our aerodynamic instability, by forcing the car to run higher. Although we lost downforce, it made the problems we'd been wrestling with – with the front being very low, the rear high and the front of the sidepod coming too close to the ground and causing aerodynamic stall – less of a problem, because the sidepod was now 10mm higher than it had been before.

In that sense, for once, the regulation changes helped us slightly, at least in the short term.

So, we went to Barcelona with these modified cars, featuring chopped-down diffusers and planks underneath. During the race, Schumacher shot out of sight, leaving Damon in a fairly lonely second. Fortune winked at us about halfway through, though, when Schumacher radioed in to say that he was stuck in gear – fifth I think. Suddenly his lap times dropped away, and Damon was able to sweep past him. The result was an emotional, morale-boosting victory for Damon ahead of Schumacher.

Damon was second in Canada behind Schumacher. In France, Nigel returned for us, which was a big story. Shame he spun off, while Damon hung on for another second behind Schumacher.

Then, like a thread pulled from one of their own designer sweaters, Benetton's season began to unravel at Silverstone. Schumacher ignored a black flag and was disqualified while Damon won and, after that, the season was to and fro, with Damon and Schumacher vying for the lead, and Nigel's return provided some welcome colour. At Hockenheim it emerged that the FIA had been flicking through Schumacher's engine maps – the software loaded into the ECU that controls engine parameters – only to discover one that suggested launch control (for standing starts off the grid) was still active.

Benetton, of course, gasped in horror and claimed it was a mistake, a hangover from 1993 that had never been used this season. Why, the very thought. Unable or unwilling to prove that Benetton had used the system, the FIA dropped the charges.

Circumstantially, though, what was hugely suspicious was the performance difference between Schumacher and his teammates, Lehto and now Jos Verstappen. There is no doubt that Schumacher's a great driver, but this sort of disparity between professional teammates in F1 was unprecedented. Neither had it been apparent to the same extent the previous season, when Martin Brundle was his teammate. It begged the question – was something different about his car? And of course, the thing that you can change – if you're prepared to go down that route – is the electronics. History supports this observation – Schumacher beat his future teammates at Ferrari, but not by anything like the same margin.

During the race at Silverstone, Verstappen's car caught fire during a pit-stop and two Benetton mechanics were hurt in the ensuing conflagration. By some miracle, Jos himself escaped injury, even though his visor was slightly open at the time.

During the week after, FIA reps visited the Benetton factory to examine the refuelling rig used on Verstappen's car. In a statement afterwards, they said, 'The fuel spillage was caused by the fuel valve failing to close properly.

'The valve was slow to close due to the presence of a foreign body.

'The foreign body is believed to have reached the valve because a filter designed to eliminate the risk had been deliberately removed.'

Was the fuel filter left out was because it's a source of pressure drop that slows the fuel flow rate, and leaving it out allowed Benetton faster pit-stops? I know the answer the majority of the pit lane personnel would give you.

The (frankly staggering) decision was handed down that they would escape punishment for the refuelling fire. At which time, the Benetton team were already embroiled in another regulations controversy.

In Belgium, Schumacher's car was found to have an illegal plank. The plank, you'll remember, was the safety measure introduced after Monaco. Benetton's was below the allowed minimum thickness, and though they tried to argue that it had been worn away when Schumacher span over a kerb, they were excluded from the race. They appealed against the decision but lost, and Damon took first. More toing and froing, and by Spain Schumacher had started baiting Damon in the press. He came back from his two-race disqualification, put his car on pole and won the race, meaning that he and Benetton were in the lead.

Japan was probably the race of Damon's life. Run in atrocious conditions it was decided on aggregate. Damon drove perfectly. He couldn't see his rival, Schumacher; he just had to race against the clock and hope that that was good enough to beat him, and it was.

All of which meant that heading into the last round in Adelaide, Australia, Williams were leading the constructors' championship by five points and Damon was just one point behind Schumacher, so it was everything to play for. Assuming they both finished, whoever took the highest position would win the drivers' championship.

I wasn't there at Adelaide. When Max announced regulation changes at Monaco, some of those, such as the plank, had to be introduced straightaway, but many others were intended for the following season. With these on the horizon, I was heavily into the design of the following year's car, so I elected to stay behind and get on with that rather than go to Adelaide.

It's a decision I regret, first because I spent the whole time wondering what was going on rather than working on the car, so I wasn't able to concentrate on my work anyway, and second, because I might have been able to make a difference to the outcome. Yes, we won the constructors' championship, but I think I could have helped Damon in the drivers'.

Nigel stuck his car on pole, which was a remarkable effort. He still had it, that's for sure. Trouble was, he then fluffed the start, so it was Schumacher leading Damon.

The race went on and Damon was doing a good job keeping up with Schumacher, who was only a few seconds ahead. Under pressure, the two of them traded fastest laps as the race went on, both pushing to the absolute edge, knowing there was everything to play for.

On lap 35, Schumacher slid wide in the first left-hander of a left/right corner sequence, clipped the outside barrier and damaged his right rear suspension in the process. Unfortunately for Damon, it was just out of his view, so he didn't see what happened; otherwise he would have known to hang back and pick Schumacher off later. As it was, he saw an opportunity to overtake, braking down the inside on the following right-hander, trying to pull past.

As Damon did that, Schumacher must have realised his suspension was damaged and that he wasn't going to be able to defend the corner, so his only way now was to take Damon out. Given that he was one point in the lead, this would secure the championship for him.

In most people's opinion in the pit lane that's exactly what he did. Schumacher just turned in on Damon and took himself out, but he managed to damage the left front of Damon's car in the process. Damon limped on but with a bent left front suspension: the front top wishbone rear leg was buckled from the impact with Schumacher's car.

Now this is where I kick myself, because bear in mind that all Damon needed to do was come home fifth and score the two points to get himself one point ahead of Schumacher for the championship.

When you look at the results, fifth place was actually one lap down, so he could have afforded to lose a lap and still come home fifth. It might have been possible for him to continue. The leg would be unlikely to fail in tension, and the only place it would see compression would have been in left-hand corners, of which there are only four at Adelaide, so if he had been instructed to brake a bit early for safety and take it easy in the left-hand turns, I think there's a chance the car could have finished. On the other hand, there was undoubtedly a risk involved: the suspension might still have failed, causing an accident of unknown consequences. Maybe, given the year we had just had, it's just as well I wasn't there.

Either way, he didn't finish. He retired, Nigel won the race, Schumacher won the drivers' championship after what was generally considered to be a professional foul, and we won the constructors'. As *Autocourse* said, Damon had 'fought magnificently, lost gallantly and taken his defeat on the chin, just as his father would have done'.

Ultimately, only Michael can ever know for sure. He now finds himself in a coma, everybody in motor racing feeling dreadfully for his wife, Corinna, and their children. His son, Mick, raced against my son, Harri, in German Formula Four and the Asian-based MRF Series in 2015 and 2016. Harri got to know Mick well; he's a super lad and a credit to his parents.

And that was it. Damon found dignity in what was otherwise an undignified end to a dreadful year. No, it's not a year of happy memories, and the FW16 is not a car I look back on with a great deal of fondness. Though it's over two decades later, it's not the tactics of Benetton or the gamesmanship of Michael Schumacher I dwell on when I think about 1994; it's what happened at Imola.

The sadness and sense of waste.

Turn Six

HOW TO BUILD
AN FW18

CHAPTER 49

The 1995 season was a bitty and bad-tempered affair. Damon entered into a war of words with Schumacher, neither he nor DC drove especially well, Patrick and I disagreed about the layout of the gearbox for the 1995 car and Benetton got themselves a more powerful Renault engine.

Upshot: although we had, on balance, the quickest car in the field, a combination of unreliability and driver mistakes lost us the constructors' championship to Benetton, their first and only win, while Schumacher bagged a second victory in the drivers' and then signed for Ferrari.

Meanwhile, my contract with Williams was coming up for renewal.

At that point I wanted two things out of them. One was a bit more money. I'd taken a salary drop when I joined from Leyton House, and given that my design contribution had been key in three championship wins, I felt it was only right that there should be some financial recognition. I've never done the job for the money; I do it for the passion. Even so, we all have an ego, and one way of measuring your success is by how much you're paid. If you can command decent money, then why not?

Even more important was my second request. Coming after the Nigel debacle, I wanted to be involved in the major policy-making decisions of Williams: engine choice, driver choice, battles with the FIA and so on. No more decisions made over lunch for me to learn about them much later. I wanted to be consulted.

At the same time, I was being courted by McLaren and Ferrari.

McLaren, of course, is the fiefdom of Ron Dennis, who enjoyed something of a mixed reputation on the circuit. The only words I'd ever spoken to him were in 1989 in Monaco. In those days the cars were kept by the harbour, about a quarter of a mile from the pit lane. You reached it via a narrow walkway that everybody had to take, so you couldn't avoid people if they were walking in the opposite direction, and even Ron, who was an expert at walking past people, couldn't avoid me as we happened to be crossing paths one afternoon.

He stopped. We passed the time of day. And then he complimented me on my work at Leyton House.

'If you ever want to join McLaren there's a place for you,' he concluded, before adding, as we were about to go our separate ways, 'but please be aware we don't pay superstar salaries.'

I was flattered that he'd noticed what I'd been up to at Leyton House and that he liked it but, on the other hand, the 'superstar salary' comment was odd. Years later, he told me that he remembered the encounter and admitted that he'd been a bit embarrassed afterwards about the comment, wishing he hadn't said it.

Either way, it wasn't Ron I was dealing with. My clandestine meetings were with the managing director, Martin Whitmarsh. McLaren were offering me the job of technical director.

Ferrari were also in contact. Jean Todt had moved from running the Peugeot world rally team to Maranello, to become their new sporting director. For the second time, I went for a clandestine visit to Ferrari, the first having been in 1985 when they made an offer for me to become chief designer on a new Ferrari Indycar project that they were considering.

This time round Marigold came too and we were collected from Bologna airport and whisked over to Jean's farmhouse, where Gerhard Berger was also waiting to meet us. Jean was looking for a new technical director and the terms he was offering were very attractive. He asked what I thought of Michael Schumacher, as they were trying to attract him for the 1996 season. To be honest, I had very mixed feelings about that; Schumacher was clearly a fearsome competitor and the best current driver, but Imola and that conversation with Ayrton, when he was convinced that Michael was using traction control, was still very raw in my mind; I would have found it almost disrespectful to work with Michael so soon afterwards.

So there we were, with a big choice to make: joining Ferrari would involve moving to Italy, and although Marigold said she would be happy to relocate there with Imogen, I did not want a move to jeopardise our marriage in the way that my move to America had done with Amanda in 1984. On top of this, seeing Charlotte and Hannah was hard enough as it was; it would be even more difficult if I was living in Italy and Marigold and I had worked hard to create a happy home for the family.

My other option was to join McLaren, geographically a simple move down the M4.

In the end, both Frank and Patrick assured me that, yes, I would be properly involved in all future policy decisions. My salary was also increased. So I signed for a further three years in June 1995.

Meanwhile, in the wake of what had been a disappointing championship, Frank, with a certain amount of justification since they'd both made mistakes that season, panicked about the capability of our drivers.

Who should go? The decision was taken out of his hands when McLaren offered DC a drive, and no doubt sensing that the writing was on the wall at Williams, he took them up on it.

Not long after, we were approached by representatives of Jacques Villeneuve, son of the late, great Gilles. Frank and Patrick decided to give Jacques a test at Silverstone in late July, early August. Having booked a holiday, I couldn't be there, but we agreed that if Jacques was within one second of Damon's benchmark time at Silverstone then we'd consider giving him another test.

In the event, he was about 2sec off, so I assumed that was it and we wouldn't bother evaluating him further. We didn't. We signed him up. Or, should I say, Frank and Patrick signed him.

On my return from holiday I called a meeting, wondering aloud why the hell we'd decided to sign Jacques when he was 2sec shy of Damon's benchmark time; more to the point, I reminded them that we'd signed a new contract stating I was to be consulted on major policy decisions, with driver choice specifically named as being part of this.

'You were in Barbados,' they said, somewhat lamely.

'But there are telephones. And faxes,' I pointed out.

They were sorry, Frank said. It was born out of a habit 25 years in the forming. But it wouldn't happen again.

★ ★ ★

On to the design, which was very much an evolution of 1995's FW17. For that I'd decided to re-evaluate the seating position, particularly in light of Ayrton's concerns about the steering position, and we'd fashioned a new, longer cockpit opening in which the driver, Damon, sat more reclined, the philosophy being to get his head lower, pedals higher, and with a higher steering wheel – a seating position which is a bit like sitting reclined in the bath with your feet on the taps. Because his lower legs were towards horizontal, we had to adjust the angle of the pedals. Having done that, Damon was much more comfortable with that position than with driving positions he'd experienced in previous cars. This way, I felt that there would be aerodynamic benefit in terms of cleanliness of flow into the engine air intake, which sits just behind the driver's head. Also, by getting his helmet lower, you could get tidy flow onto the rear wing and at the same time lower the centre-of-gravity height. It worked and we came up with what became the definitive seating position that goes on to this day.

Not that it was easy, mind you. Damon's a tall chap, and he has size 11 feet, which were a problem. On the FW14 through to the FW16, the spring damper unit had been situated above the driver's feet, but now with

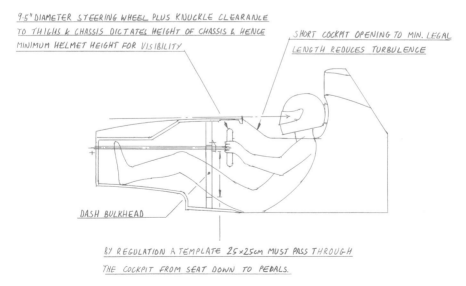

Figure 13a: The seating position in the FW16, with the low-mounted steering wheel.

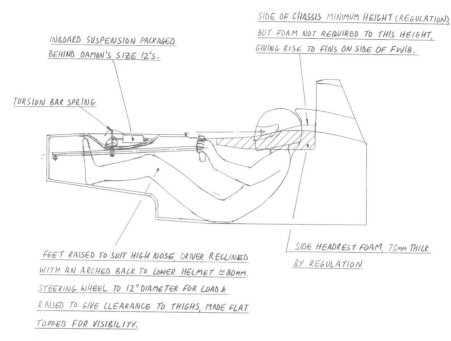

INBOARD SUSPENSION PACKAGED
BEHIND DAMON'S SIZE 12's.

SIDE OF CHASSIS MINIMUM HEIGHT (REGULATION),
BUT FOAM NOT REQUIRED TO THIS HEIGHT,
GIVING RISE TO FINS ON SIDE OF FW18.

TORSION BAR SPRING

FEET RAISED TO SUIT HIGH NOSE, DRIVER RECLINED
WITH AN ARCHED BACK TO LOWER HELMET ≃ 80MM.
STEERING WHEEL TO 12" DIAMETER FOR LOAD &
RAISED TO GIVE CLEARANCE TO THIGHS, MADE FLAT
TOPPED FOR VISIBILITY.

SIDE HEADREST FOAM, 75MM THICK
BY REGULATION

Figure 13b: The seating position in the FW17, with higher pedals and steering wheel, which improved air flow onto the rear wing and lowered the centre-of-gravity height.

the driver's heels raised even further, there was no space to do that, because Damon's plates of meat were in the way.

To solve that I moved the inboard suspension rockers further rearwards, swept the push rods rearwards and then went to a torsion bar spring, as opposed to a coil spring that wraps around the damper. Now, there's nothing new about torsion bars; they've been used on both road cars and racing cars for aeons. But the benefit of them over a coil spring is that the coil spring around the damper inevitably puts bending load into the damper, and that causes friction. Friction is something you fight hard to keep out of a suspension system. Again, we had a problem in getting this torsion bar in above Damon's shins, bearing in mind the dreaded FIA template that has to pass through from the driver's torso to his feet – the one that had caused all the problems with the steering column.

It was a tricky packaging exercise, but we got it all in, with Damon's feet now sitting ahead of the suspension, and the top of the chassis dropping down behind his feet to underneath the suspension, then rising back up again in front of the steering wheel.

The combination of clearing everything out and having a high steering column meant that the driver could now brake with his left foot if he wished: the steering column wasn't in the way if he wanted to move his foot across from left to right to press the brake pedal. Neither Damon nor DC had taken advantage of that during 1995, but Jacques did in 1996 and as the layout caught on, other drivers started left-foot braking too. There's an advantage to it: you eliminate the slight time delay between the driver's right foot coming off the accelerator and onto the brake. Should you want to slow the car slightly without coming off the throttle, the other thing you can do as a driver, commonplace in karting, is to brush the brake lightly to scrub a tiny bit of speed without losing engine response. Or brush the throttle lightly under braking to stop the rear wheels locking at a particular corner.

There was also a regulation change to cope with for 1996. By now the cars themselves were robust. Carbon fibre monocoques were able to withstand huge accidents while protecting the driver. The remaining issue, however, was how to prevent internal injuries caused by the huge G-forces to which the driver was subjected in these big impacts.

Sid Watkins championed two approaches, both for energy absorption. One was to have front-impact structures that would progressively crush in the event of an impact and therefore absorb the energy without putting huge spikes of energy into the monocoque and therefore the driver. Thus, for 1996, further changes were required to the front-impact structure; a rear-impact structure was introduced for 1997 and side-impact structures were introduced after that, to absorb energy if the car went sideways into the barrier.

The other problem Sid identified was that if a driver had damaged his spinal column, or broken his back in an accident, then further spinal column damage could easily occur in the process of extracting the driver from the car.

To prevent this, Sid proposed that the cockpit opening should be widened, allowing the seat, with the driver still sitting in it, to be lifted out complete from the car. The seat also had a receptacle, allowing the driver's head to be secured during the process.

Sid had also done research that showed that the chances of a head injury in a big side or rear impact were significantly reduced by making the rear and side headrests out of a special memory foam called Confor, 75mm thick and covered with a thin layer of Kevlar. This was also introduced for the 1996 season.

As ever, I took a careful look at these new regulations, hoping to spot a loophole, and found one. The new rules called for a minimum height to the chassis beside the head to support these new side headrests, but they did not explicitly say that the 75mm-thick headrests had to be that height, only that they had to have a minimum area. So I measured Damon's shoulder height and then, while maintaining the area, lowered them until they just cleared the top of his shoulders.

True, it wasn't what the regulation intended, but aerodynamically it was a lot cleaner because the chassis only needed to be a thin blade to satisfy the rules. Our rivals did not spot the loophole and got very upset at the first race in Melbourne, but rules are rules and there is no clause about intent of the regulation. Because the chassis is such a long-lead-time component to manufacture, there was no way our rivals could copy it within the season, so we had a sealed-in advantage for 1996. It was widely copied in 1997.

What surprised me most in the evolution of the FW18 was how much extra downforce we were able to extract from it compared to the 17B. We'd shortened the sidepods even further, developed a much longer bargeboard to manage the wake off the back of the front wheels, evolved the front wing, got more out of the second generation of undercut diffuser that we had introduced on the 17B towards the end of the 1995 season, and revised the radiator layout to a forward swept position that allowed for a narrower Coke-bottle profile.

The other philosophical direction I took with the FW18 was to bias the wind tunnel ride-heights towards high rake, i.e. low front/high rear. While this had been the Achilles' heel of the FW16 at the start of 1994, the combination of the plank, 50mm-step bottom and raised front-wing endplates introduced in 1995 as regulatory changes, coupled with our development of much shorter sidepods, meant that the high rake option now looked a good one. Tunnel results were indicating that it could, if the aerodynamics were developed around it, offer much more downforce. Patrick was not keen, because the downside is that you have to pivot the car around the front edge of the plank to avoid it bottoming more and therefore wearing the plank out, and this means you end up raising the centre-of-gravity height. By 1996 we had a simple circuit simulation model that could assess lap-time gain from downforce against lap-time loss due to increased centre-of-gravity height. It indicated a decent lap-time benefit from taking the high rake route, but the tyre models we used in this assessment were crude and did not take into account thermal effects.

So to get a better measure, we conducted the simple experiment of bolting lead to the roll hoop during testing to establish a centre-of-gravity-height-to-lap-time ratio, and to look at how it affected tyre degradation and handling.

We conducted this test at three different tracks, and each one showed downforce to be the dominant term. It is a philosophy that has served me well over the years; to this day Red Bull run more rake than any of their rivals.

In short, the intention of the FIA had been to cut downforce by 30 per cent compared to the start-of-season 1994 cars. With the FW18 we had recovered all of it.

Now, you might say, *But Adrian, by coming up with workarounds for those changes, aren't you deliberately undermining the* FIA's *efforts to improve safety in the sport?* And I would have to agree – but only up to a point. First, that's the name of the game: the FIA are always trying to come up with more restrictive regulations in order to slow the cars down, and our job, as performance designers, is to find ways to claw back that speed. That's an integral part of the essence of Formula One, and if the FIA hadn't come up with those regulation changes, we would have even more downforce. It's an ongoing battle between designer and regulator.

CHAPTER 50

At the end of 1995, Damon's race engineer, David Brown, left for McLaren. We decided to promote internally; a young design engineer, Tim Preston, stepped forward and we promoted him to race engineer for Damon.

The one problem was that Tim had no race-engineering experience, so I decided to oversee the general race engineering of Damon's car while he got up to speed.

I thoroughly enjoyed it. I hadn't been fully involved in race engineering since my final year in IndyCar with Mario Andretti, so to get into it again was an enjoyable trip back in time. As it turned out, Williams had a really big competitive advantage in 1996, with the championship boiling down to a battle between our two drivers, Damon and Jacques, which meant I had the opportunity to try out a few new tricks, taking the odd chance here and there.

Happily, it was a simple and enjoyable year. We started off with a one–two at Melbourne and, as we continued to win races, our performance advantage became clear. Damon and his wife, Georgie, had gone away over the winter, and when he came back in 1996 he was back to where he was prior to the public war of words with Schumacher. He had a spring once more in his step.

Saying that, there was still the odd chink in his armour. The fourth race was Nürburgring; Damon had qualified on pole and was leading, when all of a sudden he came on the radio saying he felt something was wrong with the car.

He was convinced he had a puncture or a suspension problem, but when he arrived in the pits to have it checked out, there was nothing wrong with the car. Something had freaked him that wasn't there. I had a good look around the back of the car and could find nothing wrong, but unfortunately in the process got my radio wire hooked round the rear wing. When

Damon took off I felt a twang as my radio headset was pulled off my head and off down the pit lane. As a result of that stop, he finished fourth when he should have won. We still had a great result for the team, though, with Jacques winning the race. No doubt as a result of Imola and the earlier loss of his father, Damon was always very safety conscious, and occasionally that held him back.

The fifth race was a return to Imola, a track we all found difficult to revisit. Helping me take my mind off it was none other than George Harrison, a good friend of Damon's and a huge racing fan. We spent a lot of time with George, driving him back and forth to the hotel and so on. He'd written a song about Formula One with lines about Bernie Ecclestone, Michael Schumacher and so forth. Unfortunately it could not be released – George would have been sued for libel by many of the F1 paddock figures – but we had a great time playing it in Damon's car, George singing along.

Then to the race. During this period the rule was that you had to race with whatever fuel was left in your tank after qualifying. So you could, if you wanted to, go for a very light fuel load in qualifying and hope to get pole position. The downside was that you'd then have to stop early for fuel, which could potentially cost you very heavily, because if, after your pit-stop, you came out in heavy traffic, you'd be forced to run slowly.

In qualifying, Schumacher, now in a Ferrari, unexpectedly put it on pole with Damon second. I thought about the strategy overnight and decided we should run long, right up to the point that Damon would be about to lap the back markers, which I thought would be about lap 30, and hope that in the meantime Schumacher would have had to stop to refuel and be slowed down by traffic after his pit-stop.

Damon wasn't confident about the strategy. Naturally he wanted to win the race and beat Michael, but with an eye to the championship his main priority was to score more points than Jacques. His reasoning, therefore, was that we should go for a similar strategy to Jacques; better, he believed, than the hero-or-zero strategy I'd dreamt up.

I got my way and I'm relieved to say it worked out well: Damon made good use of the clear track after others pitted and took the flag well clear of Schumacher.

Monaco, our bogey race, should have been an easy win, but yet again it wasn't. An improperly tightened bung on the oil pump worked loose. As soon as it fell out, it pumped all its oil out on lap 40, and that was it, race over from a dominant lead. A real shame.

The Spanish Grand Prix, we made a right mess of, to be honest. The weather was overcast but there was no forecast that said it might rain. Our engineering room was in the back of the truck with no natural light; we were all knee-deep in paperwork ahead of the race and hadn't bothered to look out of the door. By the time we finally saw daylight, it was raining.

This was just before the start, so we weren't prepared for what turned out to be an all-wet race in torrential conditions. Had we been, we would have changed the set-up and made a better job of it. As it was, Damon spun off, Jacques was third, while Schumacher put on a master-class in how to drive in the wet. A salutary lesson for a race engineer that I should have learnt already: always keep your eyes open to what is going on around you.

Montreal saw Damon just edge Jacques out for pole at the circuit named after his father. The debate then began on strategy, with Jacques eventually opting for one stop while I went for two with Damon. Bear in mind this was before the days of computer simulations of how the race should unfold, so I did a simple graph plotting out what lead Damon would need over Jacques by the time he came in for his second stop. I then agreed with Damon that we would not post the actual gap between himself and Jacques on the pit board; we would show the theoretical gap needed for him to emerge ahead after his final stop. And this is where I used my knowledge of Damon's safety consciousness and the fact that he very rarely went off on his own. I built in a bit of a 'factor' to cover for lost time lapping back markers or slow pit-stops. In the event, Damon didn't get held up too much by back markers, and both pit-stops went well, resulting in him exiting the pits with around a 12sec lead, as opposed to the 3sec advertised on the board. After the race, Damon gave me a bit of a dressing down for making him drive so hard – but equally he had to admit he didn't crash.

Another one–two in France, and then back to the home race at Silverstone, where our drivers pulled off another front-row lock-out, with Damon on pole.

He fluffed the start and came round at the end of the first lap in fifth, gradually making his way back up the field until by lap 27 he was third. Approaching his first refuelling stop he had a front-wheel-bearing seize, and that was Damon out of the race.

The consolation for the team was that Jacques won, giving the factory staff something to celebrate. Most of the employees and their families would come to Silverstone as guests of the team, so this was their chance to see the fruits of all their labour actually out and racing.

The day wasn't over, however. After a race is completed, cars are subject to scrutineering checks to ensure they've raced in a legal configuration.

Once those checks are complete, there's an hour of *parc fermé* during which the cars are held in a compound. If a rival team wishes to make a protest during that time, it can do so.

Related to this point, there's a lot of gamesmanship that takes place when cars are held on what we call the dummy grid before a race. Engineers such as myself take the opportunity to have a look at other cars. Mechanics, when they see a senior engineer from an opposing team – e.g. me – in the vicinity, will swarm around their car, attempting to obscure the bit I'm looking at. Ferrari, in particular, are a veritable hive of activity when I wander in their direction.

As a result, what I do is amble towards a section of the car I'm not particularly interested in, thus attracting the mechanics my way, like bees to honey, while one of our photographers snaps away at the bit I really want to see. Ferrari still haven't rumbled that one.

It's all a bit of a game, to be honest. If I really want to look at a car, I need only wait until after the race, when the cars are held in *parc fermé*, where nobody's allowed to touch them for an hour. They're often parked right under your nose, and with all the mechanics busy packing up, you can look at them as much as you like. As I say, that's when the teams can raise a protest if there's something about the car they don't like.

At this particular race, Benetton protested about a detail on our front-wheel endplate. Article 3.4 of the regulations had recently been changed to state that 'in order to prevent tyre damage to other cars, the top and forward edges of the lateral extremities of any bodywork forward of the front wheels must be at least 10mm thick with a radius of at least 5mm'.

I had interpreted 'top and forward edges' to mean exactly that: anything that faces upwards is the top, anything that faces forwards is the front. If something is slanted at greater than 45 degrees from the longitudinal axis of the car, then it's facing sideways more than it is forwards, and therefore it should be considered a sideways edge, not a forward edge. Simple, yes?

I applied this logic to a detail on the bottom edge of the front-wing endplate, known as the footplate, which had a chamfer on it at a greater-than-45-degree angle. It was under 10mm thick, but because it was over 45 degrees I considered it a sideways edge and therefore legal.

Benetton claimed we were in breach of the regulation, so Patrick and I were called to defend ourselves in front of the stewards, with Ross Brawn of Benetton explaining to Charlie Whiting of the FIA why he thought we were illegal, and me, as the designer of the car, answering why I considered it to be within the regulations.

I must admit, as well as being a bit pissed off, I was also really nervous. I'd never been in a position where I'd been called before stewards to justify the legality of my design. With hindsight, I'm not sure whether the champagne I'd drunk was a good or a bad thing. As I said, the whole factory was there celebrating our win and, like everybody else, I had indulged.

So, feeling nervous and slightly tiddly, I stated that the chamfer was sideways facing, not forwards facing, therefore we considered it legal.

Charlie listened to my reasoning and then asked to go with the stewards to view the car. We all trooped down and showed the stewards the car, and Charlie said, 'Well, as you can see, it is chamfered at over 45 degrees.'

He then asked me, with a cheeky glint in his eye, 'Adrian, do you mind if I put a bit of pressure on the footplate?'

I said, 'Of course not,' and watched as he lightly trod on it, snapped it clean off, and then said to the stewards, 'As you can see, even if you don't accept Adian's argument, the footplate clearly isn't strong enough to cause tyre damage.'

The stewards accepted both defences, and dismissed Benetton's protest.

Ross Brawn had been technical director at Benetton in 1994, so I have been cautious of him since that year. We've both been lucky enough to enjoy success as senior engineers within our respective teams, but our style is very different: I enjoy being hands-on in the design of the car and spend at least half my working week with a pencil in my hand. I try to lead by example, doing drawings myself as well as working with other engineers to help develop their ideas.

Ross is different in that respect. He is more of a technical manager and achieves his results by trying to hire the right people – most notably Rory Byrne, for whom I have great respect – and create a structure that allows them to do their job. Different styles but it's interesting to note that one or other of our cars took every single championship from 1992 to 2013 bar four.

Germany was a very hard-fought race. I was interested in trying to improve airflow into the base of the airbox to boost engine power as well as flow onto the rear wing. To that end we manufactured a small fairing for the back of Damon's helmet, and developed the headrest to come over the top of the helmet, with the intention of trying to fashion the helmet and headrest into one aerodynamic form.

It ended up being an own goal. Hockenheim has lots of kerbs and chicanes; like all drivers Damon was jumping kerbs, and that continual bouncing up and down in the cockpit caused his helmet to damage the new, hooked-over headrest so that after about one-third distance it had a big crack in the front, and was lifting on the straight, robbing us of engine power. It was one of those instances where I'd pushed too hard for something. Although it worked, we hadn't evaluated the headrest for long enough in testing to uncover the fact that it would become damaged.

As a result of Damon's car losing performance, Gerhard Berger in the Benetton managed to get past him and looked set to win the race. Then, three laps from the end, Berger's car suffered a massive engine failure. Damon took the win.

Lucky, Adrian; very lucky.

The next race was Hungary, where we, as in Williams, notched up our fifth one–two finish of the season and left as champions: a very satisfying result after the frustrations of the previous year. In the drivers' championship Jacques and Damon had drawn so far ahead of the pack that no one else could possibly catch them.

The next race was the Belgian Grand Prix at Spa. It was after that that I fell out with Williams – the beginning of the end of an era.

CHAPTER 51

Rewind to the German weekend, where a rumour had started to circulate that Frank Williams had signed Heinz-Harald Frentzen to drive for the 1997 season.

I, like Damon and most others in the team, dismissed it as nothing more than paddock gossip and thought little of it. However, it refused to go away.

Back to the current season. After a fairly disastrous Spa (Schumacher won, Jacques came second), I found myself on the plane home from Belgium with Patrick, who'd had a couple of glasses of wine.

'What about all these rumours about Frentzen in 1997?' I asked.

Rather airily, Patrick replied, 'Ah, yes, Adrian, been meaning to tell you. At the start of the year, Frank and I decided to sign Frentzen for 1997 because Damon drove so badly in 1995.'

So there it was, out in the open. The rumours had been correct. Having signed Jacques Villeneuve for two seasons without informing me, it turned out they'd gone and hired Frentzen without telling me too, putting Damon out of a drive and in clear contravention of our agreement, and my contract.

It turned out that they'd had seven months, at the very least, to tell me their thinking and intention. Seven months.

Patrick, with a few glasses of red inside him – the 'red infuriator' he called it – was not likely to be reasonable if I voiced my disgust. We were sitting on a plane. It wasn't like either of us could storm off. So rather than risk things getting ugly I sat there and seethed. Not only was it mystifying from a tactical point of view – Frentzen had shown promise in 1995 but wasn't exceptional – it seemed so obviously wrong and unnecessary; there was absolutely no need for Williams to contract both seats for 1997 before the 1996 season had even started. Damon was about to win the 1996 championship. His reward would be to get the boot. Sound familiar, Nigel fans?

I had no idea why they chose to exclude me from that decision. Still don't. All I knew was I had a choice: suck it up in the full knowledge that this repeat behaviour would keep on happening, or find another team.

What a shame it was to end on such a note. After two years of turmoil we now had a car that was both very quick and reliable. And with me race engineering Damon and us enjoying such an incredible advantage, it had been a low-pressure year that was probably one of the most enjoyable of my career.

So for that to happen . . . drat.

Deciding there was no point in approaching Patrick, I took myself to Frank telling him I needed to review my options, which obviously, as we all know, is code for: *I'm off, mate.*

This got back to Patrick, who commenced his dialogue with all the delicacy and grace of a nightclub bouncer. 'I hear you've told Frank you're going to have to *consider your options*,' he boomed. 'Well, I'm afraid it's not that simple, Adrian, because you must remember you are under contract, and we will not allow you to break your contract.'

'Patrick,' I said, 'it's *you* who has broken the contract.'

As you might imagine, things were pretty terminal.

At this point, McLaren came back into the frame. Despite me turning them down in 1995, Martin Whitmarsh had not given up on me, and had taken to calling me once every couple of months or so, just to see how I was doing. So when it emerged that Damon had lost his drive for 1997 – confirmed by Williams and Damon's lawyer, Michael Breen, shortly after Spa – you can guess who was first on the phone.

We met in a private dining room at the Cliveden Hotel, notorious as the location of the Profumo affair, and began to discuss a future for me at McLaren as technical director, knowing full well that with two years of my Williams contract still to run, any transition was going to be legally messy.

In the meantime, I had a car to design for 1997. As things blew up, and

I found myself at daggers drawn with Patrick, I took solace in my drawing board.

I'd started, of course. Research and design typically begin in June, while the design of the two longest-lead-time components, the monocoque, which is the core chassis, and the transmission housing of the gearbox, has to be completed by mid-September. So I was well into it.

In fact, it was during a holiday that I'd been sitting on an internal flight from Barbados to St Barts, looking out of the window at the shape of the engine intake just underneath the propeller, and thought, *Yes! That's the solution to this airbox problem that had been bugging me throughout the year.* Rather than make the base of the air intake part of the headrest, meaning that you have all the turbulence off the top of the helmet disrupting the flow along the top of the headrest and into the base of the airbox, why not separate it completely, raise the base, and then create a channel between the top of the headrest and the base of the air intake? That was one of the key changes for the FW19, a solution that has subsequently become the norm.

Back to the season, and it was now common knowledge that Damon was to be ousted. The shock of discovering that he was working his notice got to him, and he threw away an easy lead at Monza. At the penultimate race, Portugal, he came in third to Jacques.

And so to Japan, the last race of the season, with Damon nine points ahead of Jacques. All he had to do was secure one point and the championship was his. He just needed to finish in the points. A top-six place.

I really wanted Damon to win now; I felt he thoroughly deserved it. He'd led the team out of the dark days of Imola and become a good friend in the process. Sure enough, the race became Damon's championship when, on lap 37, the wheel nut came off Jacques's car. It must have been a mistake in the pit-stops – the nut couldn't have been tightened properly – and it was a great shame that Jacques's championship challenge ended with a car problem, but Damon was already on course to win the race, which he duly delivered.

It was, for Damon, the perfect way to give the finger to Williams' management: winning the race and bowing out as world champion.

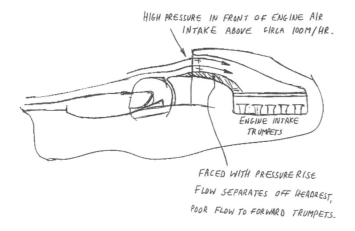

HIGH PRESSURE IN FRONT OF ENGINE AIR
INTAKE ABOVE CIRCA 100M/HR.

ENGINE INTAKE
TRUMPETS

FACED WITH PRESSURE RISE
FLOW SEPARATES OFF HEADREST,
POOR FLOW TO FORWARD TRUMPETS.

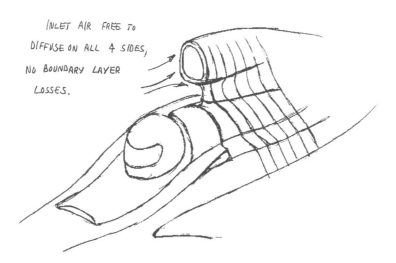

INLET AIR FREE TO
DIFFUSE ON ALL 4 SIDES,
NO BOUNDARY LAYER
LOSSES.

Figure 14: The airbox problem and the solution introduced to the FW19.

Frank, to his credit, said, 'Adrian, you should be on the podium, you've designed the car.' So I went. And no doubt I got champagne sprayed in my eyes, which hurt. (In later years I took to wearing goggles for appearances on the podium. You may laugh, but that champagne *stings*, and Sebastian Vettel, in particular, used to love getting it in my eyes.)

Taking the necessary precautions.

Meanwhile, as winners of the race and the championship, we were given a lovely silver magnum of Moet that's still in my house to this day, a great souvenir of that year.

It was a very emotional moment for all of us, a very drunken evening for Damon, myself and the mechanics in the 'compulsory' karaoke cabins, and perhaps the last day that I truly felt like a Williams employee. Frank was trying very hard to keep me, promising to make amends if I stayed; he put forward a financial proposal that exceeded McLaren's, 'but don't tell Patrick'. And that kind of said it all; it was time to move on. McLaren were ticking my boxes: I liked Martin Whitmarsh; I liked the set-up; I liked the fact that if I joined them I'd be working with DC again; I liked the fact that they were using a Mercedes engine designed and manufactured by my old friend Mario Illien at Ilmor Engines in Brixworth.

On balance the decision was clear: Woking here we come!

Marigold helped with negotiations and McLaren prepared a contract for me to sign. My lawyer, Julian Roskill, advised me not to continue working at Williams, though I hadn't quite finished work on the FW19, which I wanted to. But their advice was that if I stayed, I would effectively be showing I was accepting of Williams breaking my contract. So, 7 November, a Thursday, was my last day at Williams. I never went back.

There are no bad feelings. Not from my side anyway. Frank is Frank; we're still friends and I visit the Williams motorhome every few races for a chat. With Patrick I don't think the two of us will ever go out for dinner *tête-à-tête*, but we'll chat in a social context and still exchange Christmas cards. I respect them both hugely, and I understand that their failure to change wasn't an unwillingness to do so, simply an inability. They were creatures of habit who found they couldn't adapt to a new order. I had loved that about Williams; it was what gave the team its identity, and why I wanted to be part of it. But within that, there just wasn't room for a third person at the table. With hindsight, I should have recognised that in 1995 before I re-signed.

It's a shame because I think we could have gone on to even greater things together. As it is, history tells us that the FW19 proceeded to win the championship. After that, however, Williams fell away somewhat.

Turn Seven

HOW TO BUILD
AN MP4 13

CHAPTER 52

Having left Williams in November 1996, I didn't start with McLaren until 1 August 1997. During that time I was on what is called gardening leave.

Needless to say, after nine years in Formula One with hardly a break, I took the opportunity to do a bit of relaxing. Then came a fair bit of legal work with my lawyer on the Imola manslaughter charge, as well as opposing an injunction that Williams hoped would stop me working anywhere else for the remainder of my contract.

So that was the bad and the ugly. The good? I was going to McLaren, one of the most successful teams in Formula One history, as technical director. At Williams, if the car went badly, it was Patrick and myself who were responsible. At McLaren, the buck would stop with me. I wanted to show that I didn't need Patrick to calm my so-called 'excesses'. On the back of my cramped cockpit at Leyton House, not to mention the reliability problems of the ambitious 1989 design, there had sprung up an enduring paddock myth that I needed somehow 'reining in', and that during my time at Williams, Patrick had stopped me going too far. I didn't feel it was true – or if it was true, then I had learnt my lessons – but as a myth it persisted and so naturally I wanted to prove it untrue. I wanted to show that I was capable of leading the entire engineering side of the company without somebody effectively editing my work.

And so to the car. There was to be a big regulation change for 1998 – one of the biggest during my career – again aimed at improving safety. First of all, we were asked to use a deeper, more boxy chassis, with the intention being to make the chassis even stronger in an impact as well as to inhibit its aero performance, and thus reduce speed.

In addition, the width of the car was to be narrowed for the first time since the early 1970s, and the tyres couldn't be slicks; they had to have grooves in them to reduce the contact patch area of the tyre and hence offer less grip. The intention was to make this new breed of 1998 car significantly slower than the cars of 1997.

I couldn't have meetings with the technical people at McLaren prior to my starting; that would have been in breach of my Williams contract, which was still in litigation. But I got hold of a drawing board, a copy of the new rules and I began sketching at my home in Fyfield and trying to understand what the car should look like to best suit these new rules. It was something of a 'comfort blanket' having it there. I took a kind of solace from it, as I still do. I like to work in silence and I've developed the ability to concentrate fully over the years. Occasionally I might break for a coffee and a biscuit (Hobnob) if I'm stuck and feel I need to walk away and have a break. Just a five-minute break is often enough to spark fresh thoughts. I use a 0.7mm HB propelling pencil for freehand sketching on A4 and a 0.3mm 4H pencil for technical drawing on the board onto transparent film. Roughly 25 per cent of my time at the board is spent on general layout drawings, trying to find solutions for mechanical and aerodynamic conflicts; the rest is spent purely on aerodynamic shapes. The former, done early in the process, is probably what I enjoy the most, whereas the aerodynamic work tends to be more evolutionary.

I always try to draw with passion. In other words, I have to believe that what I'm drawing will be the next step forward. I find that if don't believe in what I'm drawing, it has never worked. However, the nature of it is that probably only around 25 per cent of my drawings end up directly on the car as physical parts. The rest either need further evolution once the CFD (Computational Fluid Dynamics) or wind tunnel results come in, or are quite simply going down the wrong alley and need consigning to the scrap heap. The difficulty is always trying to be honest with yourself, knowing when to stop flogging the proverbial dead horse and move onto something different. Often I see colleagues being much too protective of avenues when it is increasingly obvious that they won't yield results.

The first thing I looked at was the width regulation. A Formula One car has a centre-of-gravity height about 300mm above ground. For example, if a car that has no downforce corners at 1G, and the car is only 600mm wide, 300mm each side from the centre line, then it will be on the point of rolling over. So with our new, narrower cars, it was clear that a very low centre of gravity would be important to reduce the amount of weight transfer.

Now, when a car takes a corner, it will brake in a straight line and then go through a combined phase of turning and braking – what's called 'combined entry' – before getting to the middle of the corner, where it's purely cornering, and then on to the exit of the corner, where it's still cornering but starting to accelerate, which is known as 'combined exit'.

It seemed to me that if you were going to try to reduce the load on the outside front tyre in the critical condition of combined entry, and reduce the load on the outside rear tyre under the critical condition of combined exit – remembering, particularly, that you now had a narrower car – then the way to compensate would be to lengthen the wheelbase.

There were some who said that if the car was being made narrower, you should also make it shorter; that the length-to-width ratio should be preserved. But as I say, my feeling was no: you should do the opposite.

So that was the first thing I started to play around with. I began to draw a car that had a longer wheelbase than the cars of 1997, with everything packaged as low as possible to reduce the centre-of-gravity height.

I also spoke to Mario Illien. We knew each other sufficiently well that I could pick up the phone to him, I guess strictly speaking illegally, during this 'gardening' phase. Indeed, I had the odd dinner with him in order to discuss the engine for 1998 and how our overall package could be developed to suit these new rules. Mario was able to come up with a design that lowered the crankshaft, as well as work on reducing the weight of the cylinder heads.

For the same reason, I wanted the driver low, too. The intention of the rules was that this new box-like chassis had to be a rectangular box in section, but that is not what they said: they simply stated a width-by-depth requirement. It occurred to me that you could lozenge the whole thing and thereby maintain the V-shape, which, as you'll recall, was something I'd been doing since Leyton House days. To comply with the depth-in-section regulation, we had to have two fins on the top side of the chassis. This would have been a problem in terms of restricting the driver's vision, if not

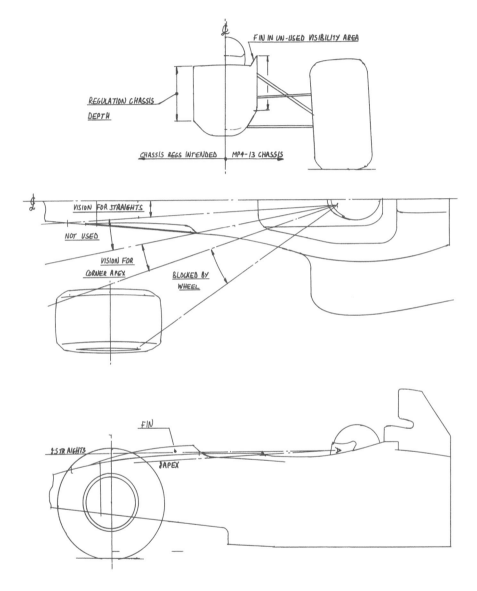

Figure 15: The consequences for the driver's vision of the depth-in-section regulation for the MP4 13.

for the fact that we capitalised on what we knew about a driver's vision during a race, which is that he has almost digital eye movement. He's looking either straight ahead down the straights focusing on the next braking area, or diagonally across at the apex of the corner. That means there's an area he never bothers looking at.

We ended up with fins that came along the side of the car from the front but stopping just short of the cockpit opening. They meant that the driver couldn't see particularly well in that area, but they still allowed him to look straight ahead and diagonally across at the apex.

The regulation changes also meant we had considerably less width between the now wider chassis and the moved inboard (because of the reduced overall width) front wheels. The implication was that stopping the wake off the front tyre from affecting the sidepod and diffuser would be even more of a problem, and that this would need to be a major area of development. The V-shaped chassis should help, but for the other details of front wing, bargeboard and sidepod shapes, wind tunnel testing was needed. For this, all I could do was draw various ideas, but I had nobody to give my drawings to. They just piled up on my desk. But it was an exciting time, a genuine 'clean sheet of paper' design emanating from our spare bedroom!

Meanwhile, Ron did a deal with Frank. I don't know how much was paid, but it was a significant amount in order to have Williams release me from my contract on 1 August. I was quite upset when Ron broke the news, because Julian and I had worked hard on my case and we felt that our contention that Williams had broken my contract would be strong in court. But, with hindsight, Ron did the right thing: all that dirty laundry aired in public would not have been good for any of us. I was now officially to be a McLaren employee.

CHAPTER 53

It was much too far to commute from Fyfield to Woking, where McLaren are based, so Marigold and I looked for a house. This was a time when gazumping was rife; we were stung several times and beginning to lose heart when we decided to take a look around a property in Berkshire, which had caught our eye in *Country Life*. It was bigger than we wanted or indeed could afford, but there was something about it that drew us back.

The house was a grand Georgian home with amazing grounds, owned by a Swedish chap who had been something big in the Abba operation. A nine-car garage filled with vintage Rolls Royces caught my eye, my interest in classic cars having grown in the wake of my enjoyment of the Jaguar SS100, and we liked the fact that the house had a history: apparently there had been a property on the site since the Domesday Book, and it was in the gardens of the current house that Sir Walter Scott wrote his poem, *Marmion*.

We must have looked round the house on three or four occasions, and every time we returned there was less art on the walls and fewer vintage cars, to the point that eventually the walls were bare and the Rolls Royces had disappeared, leaving just one rusty old Jaguar XK120 in the garage. It was very obvious that the Swedish owner was losing all his money.

Predatory as we unashamedly were, we tabled a low offer, were accepted, and on 1 August 1997 we moved in.

Or rather I should say Marigold moved in, for you may recall that 1 August was also my first day at my new job.

There at McLaren I took occupancy of an office that had been used by a predecessor, technical director John Barnard (he had since left to join Ferrari, to be replaced by a committee approach that hadn't quite worked, hence me), with a bunch of drawings under my arm, all dated '1 August 1997', for legal reasons.

I met my new workmates. I would be working once again with Neil

Oatley, who was in charge of the mechanical design of the car, a French-man named Henri Durand, who was in charge of aerodynamics, and Steve Nicholls, a Californian who oversaw the race team. I was shown around. Something niggled at me. Something I couldn't put my finger on at first, before the penny finally dropped: everything in McLaren was grey.

Obviously I knew that McLaren's livery leant towards grey as a colour scheme, but it wasn't until that first day that I realised just how grey-focused it was as a company. It's Ron's favourite 'colour'. Everything in the factory was grey. Everything in the offices was grey. Even the call-sign of his aircraft is GREY.

Everything, that was, apart from my office. John Barnard had left at the end of the 1980s, and the office looked as though it hadn't been touched since then: it was floor-to-ceiling mahogany panelled walls, a black window frame, mahogany desk, dark brown carpet. In the corner was my drawing board from Fyfield, which looked out of place, not being brown. In order to catch up on the very late start of 1 August for the design cycle, I was work-ing crazy hours seven days a week and, after two weeks of this, the office was a seriously depressing place to be, come midnight.

Ron had insisted I attend Hungary for the race on 16 August. To be honest, I wanted to work on the 1998 car, but he was hoping I might have some influence on the 1997 model, offering some advice regarding set-up and so forth. Figuring I would get to see the team and drivers, DC and Mika Häkkinen, in action, and because Ron can be awfully persuasive when he wants to be, I agreed.

Before leaving, I asked the factory manager if he could cheer the office up a bit. Needless to say, we were knee-deep in colour charts at our new home, so I brought a paint chart in and asked for duck-egg blue, as well as a pale-toned carpet and a nicer light-tan chair.

Off we flew to Hungary and I put on my grey uniform for the first time. It felt a bit weird wearing a different-colour uniform, and though I man-aged to stop myself wandering into the wrong garage on that occasion, I must admit I've done it since. You see drivers do it all the time, occasionally even pulling in to the wrong pit box in practice.

Through that Hungarian weekend, I started to get to know Mika and found him receptive to my ideas. I suggested using more softly sprung springs on the car. David was running better than Mika so understandably was reluctant to change, but Mika ran with it. Flying back, I already had a good feeling about that relationship.

My office, now, was a breath of fresh air, too. Everything I'd asked for had been done, the factory manager had done a great job. What was dark and cheerless previously was now duck-egg blue with a tan carpet, a tremendous improvement. Stepping from the monotone of the wider McLaren factory into my office was like that bit in *The Wizard of Oz* when they turn on the technicolour. The long nights would be less depressing from now on.

Ron, however, was less impressed when, on Monday evening, he came round to see how I was getting on. Standing at the doorway, his jaw dropped and he stood gulping like a goldfish for what was probably 30 seconds, but felt like about five minutes, going redder and eventually deep purple, with me thinking, *My God, he's going to have a heart attack*, until, without uttering a single word, he span on his heel and returned to the sanctuary of McLaren grey.

Luckily, it was very much the honeymoon period and I couldn't do anything wrong, so I got away with it, though his wife Lisa recounted years later that he was incandescent with rage when he got home that night. Ron was ... well, let's say he liked to have a firm control on everything around him. Imposing grey upon the world of McLaren was an example of that in action. He didn't like it being challenged.

The other race I attended during 1997 was Jerez, the final round of the championship. It was a good one to attend: going into that round it was a head-to-head between Jacques Villeneuve driving the Williams FW19 – which had been near complete as a design when I left – and Michael Schumacher in the Ferrari.

Obviously, I was now a bystander, but I was hoping Jacques would win because it was a design for which I was responsible. Such was the general dislike of Ferrari along the pit lane that most of the teams wanted Williams to win too, particularly after Villeneuve had been handed a ridiculously harsh penalty by the FIA for a yellow flag incident at the previous race in Japan.

In the event, Schumacher managed to get ahead of Jacques, only apparently to be told by his team that he had a water pressure problem and could not finish the race. He kept going, and when Jacques went to overtake Schumacher turned into him, attempting to take the pair of them out just as he had done with Damon.

Only this time he messed it up. He took himself out but not Jacques, who continued to race, on course to win the championship. All Jacques had to do was score two points by the finish.

At this point, Ron Dennis called in an agreement he'd had with Frank, which was that if the McLarens helped Jacques during the race, then Williams would help McLaren win that particular race.

Frank agreed to this, as there had been occasions during the pit-stops when Jacques had ended up behind David and Mika but had been waved through. Therefore Villeneuve was given the radio instruction to let the McLarens pass, so we now had Mika winning the first race of his career, David second and Villeneuve third, winning the championship.

Like I say, I was a bystander to this particular bit of gamesmanship. For me it was just brilliant that my last Williams car had gone on to win both the drivers' and the constructors' titles. I had designed for seven seasons at Williams and, during that time, we had won the constructors' five times and the drivers' four times.

Still. You move on. With a sigh. I had an MP4 13 to design in my new cheerful non-grey office.

CHAPTER 54

The wind tunnel that McLaren used was a commercial tunnel based close to Twickenham, on an industrial estate. There, the first runs of my gardening-leave design in late August were disappointing, at least 10 per cent or more down on the model that Henri and his team had developed in-house.

That was a bit embarrassing. Just as when I had joined Williams, there were those at McLaren within the engineering offices who felt they were on the way back up and did not need me to arrive and confuse their direction. A step forward with my design in the wind tunnel would quieten the detraction, so this poor result was a double blow – competitively and politically. I must admit that I'd thought it would be an improvement, although in retrospect it was more than a little arrogant to think that a new shape based on my thoughts in the bedroom would outperform what McLaren had spent months developing in the wind tunnel.

However, Peter Prodromou, the Greek aerodynamicist who worked for Henri, thought the model had promise, which was good of him, and pretty soon we were making important strides forward.

The V-shaped chassis and low headrests both seemed to work well, as did the front wing. What Henri and the team had done was show that having a longer sidepod to help push the front wheel wake outboard was a definite improvement. We hybridised the sidepod from their model onto the new one, and worked on how that interacted with the bargeboards, as well as developing the shape of the brake ducts and the diffuser. After a further two weeks of testing, the hybrid design started to move well ahead of where it had been mid-August. Remember: what we were trying to do was claw back performance lost in light of the regulation changes, and in that respect we got good numbers, not a long way down on where their 1997 car had been.

Meanwhile it became apparent that one area in which McLaren were well ahead of Williams was in composites – namely, all the parts of the car manufactured from carbon fibre, which at the time were the chassis, body-work and wings, but now also including the suspension and gearbox casing. Our head of composites at Williams, Brian O'Rourke, was a very conservative fellow and – despite carbon composites being a relatively new and fast-developing field – the composite technology on the car when I joined Williams had not significantly progressed by the time I left six years later. A managerial mistake on the part of Patrick and myself.

In the areas of stress analysis and lightweight composite design, Neil's design office were well ahead. This, combined with Mario Illien's care in reducing the engine weight, meant that the car was very light, needing about 40kg of ballast to meet the minimum weight limit of 580kg. That was a whole new problem. Where would we put it? F1 cars typically use tungsten as a material for their ballast, but 40kg still requires 2.1 litres of ballast, quite a big volume to find space for low down on an F1 car. We came up with a solution by placing a hatch below the fuel tank, where we could interchange 'pizzas' of various weights to suit the ballast requirement on the day.

It was a very compressed design time, and I was working crazy hours. Marigold and the girls hardly saw me because I was hardly home, doing all I could to try to catch up. But there was a great spirit about the place. A real can-do attitude, with the doubters converted. We thought we were on to something, and that translated into a kind of sustained, communal adrenalin rush.

On to the first test at Ricard, and both drivers said the car was tricky to drive, which was worrying. But on the other hand, the word on the grapevine was that all teams had similar issues. Narrower cars meant that dirty air from the front wheel wake was upsetting the aerodynamics in an inconsistent manner. Factor in the new grooved tyres and we were looking at cars that were simply more difficult to drive. (And so it would prove. I've never seen so many cars spin as I did in the pre-season of 1998, and then the first few races of the season.)

A week later, we took the car to Barcelona for the first public test with other teams present as well. It was a four-day test but we'd missed the first two days because we needed a new steel rear top wishbone, the carbon composite one having broken at Ricard. In the event, I was walking into terminal one at Heathrow when head of race engineering, Steve Hallam, rang me to say that Mika had just done a lap time of 1min 21.7.

'That's good,' I said, 'What's everybody else doing?'

'Well, the next quickest is 1min 23.3' came the reply.

We'd just gone well over a second quicker than the cars that had been there for two days. I don't mind admitting, I walked into the airport with a bounce in my step. That sounded promising.

We topped the timesheets at a second Barcelona test the following week and headed off for the first race of the season in Melbourne feeling positive, though you're never quite sure whether others have been sandbagging.

In the meantime, in a similar way to with Damon in 1996, I was to be Mika's de facto race engineer for the year while his new race engineer Mark Slade got up to speed. Mika and I got on well – he was perceptive with his feedback, and I think it gave him confidence that someone, i.e. me, was at last taking the time to try to understand and translate what he was saying with words like 'floaty' and 'can't feel the steering wheel', and what those mean in engineering terms.

Like so many gifted natural drivers, he would adapt his driving to whatever the car was doing and then report what the car was doing once he'd adapted his driving, rather than communicating what the car would do if he drove it the way he wanted to drive it.

We went in as firm favourites for the season, which is always a poisoned chalice: if you win, it's expected, and if you lose, then you fail.

Something starting to brew as a potential issue in the background was that, before I arrived, McLaren had developed what they called brake steer.

There are two ways of steering a vehicle. One is to physically turn the steering wheel, the other is to retard the inside wheel(s). In the case of a tank, you speed up the outside track and slow down the inside track to turn. You can do the same with a car by braking the inside rear wheel.

It's a system used on trials cars, the very small and light cars built for competitions that involve climbing steep hills. Because they're designed to scale hills and have most of their weight on the rear axle, the front wheels are very light and therefore don't have much steering capability. So, when its front wheels are almost in the air, a trials car is steered by what they call fiddle brakes – a pair of handbrakes the driver can operate. If he wants to turn right, he pulls the handbrake on the right-hand side to slow down the right rear wheel, and vice versa if he wants to turn left.

What McLaren had done in early 1997 was to take that trials car principle and apply it to a Formula One car. They put a fourth pedal in the footwell so that when the driver reached the middle of a slow-speed corner, where traditionally a car would understeer (push straight on), he would then press that fourth pedal to apply brake to the inside rear wheel. On the steering wheel was a switch to toggle, depending on whether it was a left-hand or a right-hand corner.

During 1993, Benetton had developed an electronically controlled rear-wheel steering system. However, fearing that this could become a significant driver aid, Max Mosley, as part of the swingeing restrictions introduced for the 1994 season, had Article 10 of the Technical Regulations changed to ban four-wheel steering, the intention being a ban on geometric steering of the rear wheels. As far as McLaren were concerned, however – and the governing body was happy to accept this – steering the car by using a fourth pedal was perfectly legal.

Unfortunately for McLaren, when one of their cars broke down during the Austrian Grand Prix, a sharp-eyed photographer stuck a camera in the cockpit and got a photo of the fourth pedal – the secret was out.

Apparently Ferrari tried the fourth pedal approach and couldn't get it to work, so as normal they complained about it, meaning that the Melbourne weekend was abuzz with controversy surrounding the legality of our system.

Prior to the race, Charlie Whiting of the FIA asked me for a set of drawings for the system, which I gave to him. Qualifying was good: first and second by a reasonable margin, and then came the race.

I was standing on the pit wall as usual. McLaren had seats in their pit, but I really didn't like these, feeling more able to concentrate standing than sitting, so I had my seat removed during my time there. I was slightly concerned that this brake steer system could be overused by the drivers, causing overheating of the inside rear brake disk and hence leading to brake disc failure. I'd briefed both drivers to go easy on the fourth pedal – if we had sufficient pace not to need to use it, then please don't. Unfortunately, going easy on the equipment doesn't seem to translate into Finnish!

Mika charged off and we could see on the telemetry that the inside rear brake disc was getting hot. We sent a coded radio message telling him to lay off the brake, but he was slightly deaf following a horrendous accident in 1995 (the one where Sid Watkins performed an emergency trackside tracheotomy), and somehow he heard the message as 'pit now', which he duly did.

In he came, only to be waved straight through, by which time he was behind DC.

Ron got on the radio to David and said, 'Mika is behind you, due to a team error, therefore please let him past.'

Most drivers would have said, *go stuff yourself*, but David is one of the gentlemen of the circuit. He believed that something must have happened to Mika, and that he should act as per the pre-race agreement, which was that whoever got to the initial corner first would not then be challenged by the other, so he let Mika pass. They finished Mika first and David second.

I had mixed feelings about it. Mika had got to the initial corner first, had driven impeccably, and then come into the pits under a misheard communication. Who in that situation should win the race? Should it be David because he'd inherited the lead or should it be Mika as per the pre-race agreement?

It's a difficult one to argue one way or the other. I was happy to leave that decision with Ron.

Either way, the net result was that my first McLaren had won the race – only for us to be handed a directive saying that the braking system was illegal and we had to take it off for the rest of the season, despite it having been deemed legal the previous season.

That took the edge off our Australian high. After all, Melbourne is one of those atypical circuits where, just because you do well there, it doesn't mean you're going to repeat that elsewhere, the reason being that almost all the corners are slow and medium-speed 90-degree turns. What's more, we were wondering how much of our advantage had been down to the brake steer system. The McLaren personnel who had been instrumental in developing it during the 1997 season estimated it to be worth around three-quarters of a second per lap, which was pretty much what our advantage appeared to be at Melbourne.

However, although I went to Brazil nervous that Australia would be our one-race hit and that we would now be swallowed up by Ferrari and Schumacher, my fears proved unfounded. The car was well balanced even without with the system, Mika again on pole, David second, and they finished that way too. A very satisfying result.

Argentina, not so good. We were using Bridgestone tyres, whereas Williams and Ferrari had been struggling with an understeer problem caused by their Goodyears. Unfortunately (for us), Goodyear sorted out the problem for Argentina by copying Bridgestone's lead and introducing a wider front tyre. Schumacher clawed back a second and won ahead of Mika.

Back to San Marino, where it really came home to me how much I hated returning to Imola. Every year, I borrowed a scooter and drove out to Tamburello on Saturday evening to pay my respects, but inevitably I'd be spotted by spectators, which only added to the discomfort. Even so, it was something I felt the need to do. I must admit, I was always pleased to see the circuit in the rear-view mirror when the weekend was over.

DC bounced back to win in Imola, after Mika retired with a gearbox problem. We dominated in Spain. Next came Monaco, and having never won there, I really wanted to do so. Practice was fraught. Mika was driving at the limit, which in Monaco meant his car was occasionally brushing the wall, bending the rear track rod in the process.

I had a think. Wagging my finger and telling him not to brush the wall wasn't going to work. Instead I decided to double skin the track rod in order to strengthen it, which turned out to be one of my better decisions, because he did indeed make contact with the wall during the race.

What's more, he won. David was a DNF – a reliability worry there – but Mika winning at Monaco was a big, big tick on my bucket list. *At last.*

Schumacher stayed on our tail throughout the season. Whatever you think of him, he had tenacity.

At Spa, the forecast was for dry weather, but Spa sits in the middle of the Ardennes Forest and tends to have its own microclimate. When it's hot the evaporation build into clouds and suddenly you get these huge rainstorms from nowhere. That's exactly what happened on the Sunday. It was throwing it down.

Things started badly when DC lost it on the first lap, helping to cause a 13-car pile-up. Shortly after the restart, DC now in the spare car, Mika span and took himself out, along with Johnny Herbert in a Sauber. It was pandemonium out there – the Bridgestone wets were proving themselves very poor at this circuit. Schumacher gained the lead and on lap 25 came up on DC, who was a back-marker, about to lap him. Through gritted teeth we gave DC instructions to let Schumacher past and, being a gent, DC was about to do just that, except that Schumacher misjudged his closing speed in the spray and went right into the back of him.

Both cars appeared in the pits, David having lost his rear wing, Schumacher his right front wheel. I thought there might be a chance of getting DC back out to salvage points, so I asked the mechanics to set about trying to change the wing.

Next thing we knew, a raging Schumacher appeared in the garage, convinced that DC had taken him out deliberately (pot, kettle) and wanting to have it out with him. We then had the sight of our mechanics forming a wall around DC to stop what would have been a highly embarrassing and undignified set-to.

Still, it did mean that Ferrari were out, so it was a null race for us, and a popular victory for Damon in a Jordan.

The penultimate race was at Nürburgring, where we just didn't have the pace in qualifying, ending up with Mika third and David fifth on the grid, Ferrari locking out the front row.

DC wasn't especially sharp that weekend. It's sometimes difficult for drivers to put their finger on why, when they're fit, well rested and feeling positive, it just doesn't quite work, and this weekend was a good example of that weird racing hex at work. David is a great driver who, on his day, was unbeatable, but he'd occasionally have weak weekends when he wasn't properly competitive or would have a stupid spin or accident.

On to the race, and Ferrari duly employed team orders: the cars got off in grid order with Schumacher leading, Eddie Irvine, in the other Ferrari, second, and Mika third. However, Irvine was instructed by Ferrari to drive as slowly as he could while keeping Mika behind him in order for Schumacher to build up a huge advantage. The first laps were incredibly frustrating as we watched this unfold. It was clear what Ferrari were up to.

And then on lap 13, Mika pulled a blinding overtake, a brilliant out-braking move into the chicane towards the end of the lap to get past Irvine. By then Schumacher was 8½sec up the road, but Mika proceeded to put in a series of what were effectively qualifying laps, driving absolutely ten-tenths. On the limit, in other words.

By lap 24, Mika had closed the gap from 8½sec down to 3½sec behind Schumacher.

Schumacher came in for a pit-stop but we kept Mika out there, figuring our best chance was to stay on old tyres and low fuel and keep him running, hoping to close on Schumacher and then get him at the second stop. In the event, such was Mika's pace and the speed of our boys in the pit-stop, that he came out just ahead after the first stop – and went on to victory. I remember sitting on a packing box behind the garage after the race shaking with emotion; that victory kept us in the hunt.

The result of that penultimate race in Luxembourg meant that Mika was now back in the lead of the championship by 4 points and we were 15 points ahead in the constructors', with everything to play for at the last race, Suzuka.

Qualifying, Schumacher put in a great lap to qualify on pole, 2/10sec ahead of Mika. That was disappointing – I'd expected Suzuka's high-speed corners to flatter our car. Still, we had a four-point lead, so even if Schumacher won, as long as Mika could finish second, we would win the drivers' championship and, as long as we had a decent result, also the constructors'.

In the event, Schumacher stalled on the dummy grid and was forced to start at the back for the race. With my heart in my mouth I watched him make astounding progress through the field, to the point where he was back up to third by lap 22. That was okay if it stayed that way, but the pressure was still on us to get to the finish, so it remained a nail-biting time until, on lap 31, Schumacher's tyre exploded and that was it, he was out. 'We are the champions – of the world.'

What a celebration. Bearing in mind that McLaren had been through some bad years and hadn't won a championship since Ayrton in 1991, it was a big, big deal for them; for me it was huge to win the championship straight off with my new team; and for Mika and Mario, the Ilmor Mercedes engine designer, it was their first Formula One championship. That Queen song was played a lot after the race.

The circuit is on the edge of a leisure park, complete with Ferris wheel, fairground rides and so forth, and it was a proper party that night. We all piled in to karaoke cabins. Norbert Haug, the Sporting Director of Mercedes, who always fancied himself as a bit of a blues singer, did 'Mustang Sally'; Ron did his usual funny/drunken/annoying thing of tearing the back pockets off people's trousers – if you were really unlucky, the whole of the back of your trousers, leading to various pictures of myself and Mario with our trousers held together with duct tape.

The worst point, of course, about those Tokyo races was that you'd roll into bed at about four in the morning and then have to get up for the flight at about five, so you got an hour's sleep before awaking with the saké hangover from hell. One thing I can say for sure, though. It was well worth it.

CHAPTER 55

On 25 July 1998, with that season in full swing, Marigold gave birth to our second – and my fourth – child.

We called him Harrison William Innes Newey. The William was in tribute to my 'Grandfather Bill', killed during the Second World War and about whom my dad used to wax lyrical. The only thing was, when I called Dad to tell him of Harri's birth and his middle name, he said, 'Dear boy, his name wasn't William, it was Wilfred.'

I came off the phone and said, 'Marigold, we've got a bit of a prob-lem . . .'

She said, '*We* haven't got a problem; *you* have a problem.'

I had to phone Dad back and fib that the name had already been registered.

It was a thrilling time, although I'd be telling another fib if I were to say that I'm the sort of chap who falls head over heels in love with their baby the moment they clap eyes on him/her. I'm not a 'baby' person, but as they grow and start to develop a personality, I love them to bits. When Harri, aged eight said, 'Daddy, I'd like to go karting,' I thought, *Well, actually, that's not a bad idea*. One of the things I have noticed over the years is how the drivers I have worked with are generally very bright guys who have developed many skill sets. I think motor racing teaches you a lot of good life skills; it teaches you that if you want to achieve something, you have to work hard at it. Driving a racing car isn't just about strutting about in overalls; it involves mental and physical preparation, training, working with the engineers, learning how to present and market yourself, how to deal with failure and move on from a bad race, and the self-analysis and determination that is vital for success in almost all walks of life.

On that premise I said, 'Okay, great, let's go karting.' I didn't make him work for it in the way my father had done with me, but in my defence he was eight, not fourteen. Years later, Harri told me he was actually thinking of taking up indoor karting as some of his school friends had done. Could have saved me a fortune if he had said that at the time!

I took him along to the local kart track, Blackbush in Camberley, just as my father had taken me all those years before, and we stood and watched karts going round. Harri was keen, so over the next few weeks we bought a second-hand kart and a little trailer for the back of my Land Rover Discovery, and began visiting Blackbush for afternoon practice sessions.

I got on well with the other dads. Many of them knew who I was, but nobody cared, which was great, just as I wanted it. I'd never been into school football matches, where you're watching your kid run up and down while socialising with parents on the touchline; that never really floated my boat. Not surprisingly, this came much more naturally to me.

We started entering Harri in races and his driving improved. I remember one race at Whilton Mill near Milton Keynes, where Mark Webber came along. Mark was kneeling beside the kart talking to Harri, and as I stood nearby I overheard a passing child say to his dad, 'Dad, we've got no chance. I mean, look at that kid; he's got Adrian Newey engineering him and Mark Webber coaching him.'

As Harri continued to improve I began to feel guilty because my work was keeping him away from the kart track. I gave DC a ring. 'Harri needs somebody to run him,' I said. 'I don't have the time to do it.'

'Well, funny you should say that; the guy who ran me through karting, a chap called Dave Boyce, might be available. He may be able to take Harri on as one of his charges.'

Despite living near Glasgow, Dave accepted and has become a very dear family friend, mentor and life coach to Harri. At times Harri has lamented the fact that Dave was running him, because it meant he was effectively a one-kart team, whereas you had these other teams run by big commercial enterprises – with four or five karts – which, by driving (aka hunting) in packs, made themselves very difficult to beat.

Having 'Newey' on his back meant Harri got picked on at times, too. Other karting kids would say, 'Why is your dad so tight? Why doesn't he buy you better gear?' Some of the dads spend an absolute fortune on their kids' karting; stories of them re-mortgaging their house to do so are not uncommon.

In the meantime Marigold and I were firm that Harri's schooling should come first, which put him at something of a disadvantage, for there is definitely a new breed of drivers who do the bare minimum in the way of academics in order to spend all their time at the track. To me that is a very high-risk strategy to adopt with your child: Lewis Hamilton is a shining example of this working, but for every success story associated with that route there are dozens of kids who reach 20 with no career and no education. Not only that, they have lost a normal childhood playing with children of their own age.

It is true that our school-first approach compromised Harri's karting career. Even so, he's gone on to compete in ADAC Formula 4, teammate to Michael Schumacher's son, Mick, and recently won his first major championship, the 2016/17 MRF Challenge Formula 2000 Championship.

Imogen, too, enjoys a challenge. In her gap year, she went to Australia to complete a yacht masters course before travelling, on her own, for three months at the age of 19. She evidently has a taste for adventure, having climbed Kilimanjaro, undertaken a 7-day dog-sledging trip in the Arctic and even spent 7 weeks sleeping in a tent in the Himalayas at over 4,300 meters altitude.

Yet this thirst for action is just one of Imogen's traits. She's always been incredibly creative – a talent and passion that I assume she has inherited from my mother and I. As soon as she could hold a pencil, Imogen loved drawing and colouring. She'd spend many hours watching me draw – her job was to colour in the cars. Over the years, she has developed her artistic skills to an exceptional level and has produced some wonderful pieces. I'm so pleased that she has harnessed this artistic prowess, along with her determination and organisational skills, to pursue a career in interior design.

Hannah's also a very artistic person. In fact, Harri seems to be the only one of my children to have missed out on this gene. She is a loving, kind-natured girl with a quirky sense of humour and a true love of animals. What you see is what you get with Hannah. When she was small, she was always the first to dive in, whether in the school play, a muddy puddle or on the dance floor. Hard working academically, she achieved numerous A*s in her GCSEs and straight-As in her A-levels before briefly spending time studying medicine at Brighton and Sussex Medical School. She loved certain aspects, particularly anatomy, but was less keen on others and realised that being a doctor was not for her. This change in direction has led her to study for a Masters' degree in Medical Illustration at Dundee University, a perfect subject given her love of art and anatomy.

My eldest, Charlotte, studied History of Art at Leeds, and met a chap, Justin Salisbury, while she was there. In her final year at Leeds, Justin's father died unexpectedly of a heart attack and then his mother was run over by a bus, quite literally, a week later. Six or so years later, she's made a full recovery, but at the time all this happened Justin's parents owned a run-down guesthouse in Brighton and a derelict guesthouse in Penzance. Justin dropped out of uni to try and run the one in Brighton.

The place was more like student digs than a guesthouse, every spindle of the staircase, for example, being a different colour of the rainbow. When Charlotte graduated, she went to Brighton to join him, and having decided to focus her final-year thesis on street art, had the idea of calling the place Artist Residence, bringing in street artists and giving them the basement in exchange for them decorating a room, giving each one a unique feel. They did that and she also managed to get the place onto a Channel 4 programme, *Hotel Inspector*, hosted by Alex Polizzi of Trust House Forte, from whom they learnt a great deal. Together they transformed it from a run-down guesthouse into what has been voted the top hotel in Brighton.

Charlotte also lived for a year in Penzance, organising builders and tradesman to resurrect the Penzance building from derelict to their second boutique hotel, another Artist Residence.

By now I was thinking, *Well, this is great and it's fabulous experience for Charlotte, but if they do break up for any reason, Charlotte's going to have no reward for all her hard work.*

They then found a derelict building in Pimlico, which I bought and then we set about renovating. I say 'we'. In truth, Charlotte and Justin did 99 per cent of the work, but I got a bit involved, and was able to bring to the project my experience of travelling the world to make sure they got the key features right. For example, as a business person travelling, there are a few basics you always look for: a comfortable bed, a shower that works, lights and TV that are easy to use, and – particularly for those who are light sleepers – not too much noise. Of all the hotels I've used over the years, the number that don't get those basics right is frightening.

The Pimlico Artist Residence went on to win an award for London's best small hotel and it is going extremely well. Charlotte and Justin have since added a restaurant called Cambridge Street Café. With any family, there are highs and lows, but the kids seem to have weathered it well and I'm really proud of them.

CHAPTER 56

I turned 40 on Boxing Day 1998. Marigold organised a fortieth party for me. Providing the music was a band formed by our friend, Lord Charles Brocket.

Known as Lord Brocket of Brocket Hall, Charlie had built up a big Ferrari collection, but when Brocket Hall found itself in the red Charlie very foolishly decided the way out was to pretend the cars had been stolen and claim insurance. So he cut the cars up – absolute travesty – and buried them, but made such a poor job of it that he was soon caught and sent to prison.

While inside, he formed a band with some of his fellow inmates called The Timelords (clever name) and it was these guys who rolled up to The

My fortieth birthday party with Damon and George, looking rightly shocked by my singing.

Cedars in order to provide the entertainment for my fortieth. What a night.

Perhaps the highlight of the evening was during The Timelords' performance, when first Damon and then George Harrison joined them on stage. For George it was the first time he had sung in 'public' in about five years – since the onset of throat cancer and its ensuing treatment – which made it an especially emotional moment for Olivia, his wife.

He was a lovely man, George, and his passing was a great loss to us. Like Ayrton he was one of those people who had a presence. Did they have it because of who they were and what they had achieved? The answer is probably yes, but it doesn't matter, because it makes them who they are. George was a very generous man, a deep thinker who had a great, dry wit, and I remember, at about two in the morning, standing outside to get a breath of fresh air with George doing the same, it being a beautifully clear starry night. We spent an hour or so shooting the shit. It seemed terribly meaningful at the time, but you know how it is when you've had a few. You can't remember it the following morning, more's the pity.

Looking forward to 1999, and with the regulations pretty stable, I'd been concentrating on understanding the existing car in an attempt to build on what we had. Thus the 1999 car was very much an evolution of the previous year. But the luxury of being able to start wind tunnel testing in May, instead of August, meant we were able to make quite a significant improvement on the aero side compared to the 1998 car.

I guess the main talking point of that season was Schumacher breaking his leg at Silverstone. Mika was leading the drivers' championship, but Ferrari were just ahead in the constructors' when, at the British Grand Prix, Schumacher had brake failure, crashed and broke his leg, putting him out for several races. Him out should have left us with a relatively easy cruise to the championship from what was already a leading position. Did we capitalise on it? No. The team just fell asleep. We kept throwing things away. We lost our focus.

At Nürburgring, third race from the season end, Ferrari introduced new bargeboards. They made a huge show about it, draping covers over them whenever the car was stationary. As a result, I wasn't able to get a good look at them – this was in the days before teams commissioned their own 'spy' photographers.

We went to Malaysia, the penultimate race of the season, for which Schumacher returned. Irvine won, with Schumacher second and Mika third, which put Irvine into the championship lead, four points ahead of Mika, and Ferrari into the constructors' lead, four points ahead of us.

After the race, Ron and I went down to have a look at the cars in *parc fermé*. 'Look,' said Ron, 'the tyres on this Ferrari are illegal. They're slicks. All the grooves have worn out.' I agreed but in the meantime I was getting my first look at the bargeboards, and they *also* looked illegal. Why? The regulations say that the car has to be flat when viewed from underneath, which means that any outlying bodywork has to have a shadow plate underneath it. Looking at these new bargeboards, to me the shadow plate didn't look big enough to do the job.

Off we went to see Charlie Whiting, the FIA technical director. Charlie went down, had a look, came back and said, 'Well, I don't agree on the tyres, I think they're okay. But Adrian, yes, those bargeboards do look illegal.'

The cars were held in *parc fermé* and eventually we heard that Ferrari had been excluded from the race. Reason: illegal bargeboards.

Ross Brawn appeared on TV to accept that the team had made a silly mistake and that yes, the bargeboards were illegal. McLaren left the race with Mika as world champion and also took the constructors' title on the basis that Ferrari had been excluded.

Ferrari then protested. What we now know is that they were encouraged to protest by Max Mosley, the President of the FIA (living up to Ferrari International Aid).

I spoke to Max about this years afterwards and he said that, as far as he was concerned, we, McLaren, had lured Ferrari into a trap, because we knew their bargeboards were illegal and had waited for them to be ahead before we protested about them.

That's complete rubbish. I hadn't managed to have a proper look at them until after the Malaysian race. But even if that were the case, it doesn't alter the fact that Ferrari won using illegal bargeboards.

The ensuing Court of Appeal hearing made the Spanish Inquisition look exemplary, though sadly I cannot go into detail for fear of attracting the attention of m'learned friends. Suffice to say that Charlie Whiting was 'on holiday' and therefore could not state his findings. Anyway, the post-race ruling was overturned, and we went from believing we were champions to suddenly no longer being champions. In truth, it is easy to make silly mistakes such as Ferrari had made; it was the fact that they had been well and truly let off the hook after being publicly excluded that really riled me. I am absolutely sure this would never have happened had it been us who had made a similar mistake. It meant that we went into that final race with jangling nerves, burdened with a sense of injustice but determined to fight on.

During practice Irvine crashed at the hairpin, subsequently qualifying only fifth, with Schumacher on pole and Mika second. That meant Ferrari would be trying to come up with strategies that put Irvine close behind Mika. Irvine had a four-point lead, so he didn't have to finish ahead of Mika, but if they finished in grid order with Mika second and Irvine fifth, then Mika would be champion.

Saturday evening we sat and talked through various scenarios. If Schumacher does this, how should we cover? If Irvine does that, how should we react? Mika was there, too, the lot of us crammed into a tiny whitewashed office above the paddock in Suzuka, an hour or so spent going over and over every permutation we could think of until, at last, Mika stood up and, without a word, left the room. You know what? He was absolutely right to do so. It was getting way too complicated and that's where Mika's inner self-confidence and Finnish nonconformity came in. It's my belief that he simply thought, *Screw this, I'm just going to win the race*. It was a mark of Mika to have that mindset, and it's what made him a great driver: despite the turmoil of having been told he was the champion a few days earlier, only to have that taken away from him, he was able to handle the pressure-cooker of this last race without any signs of cracks. Very few can do that.

I really liked Mika. He was typically Finnish in as much as he used as few words as possible – until he'd had two glasses of 'Finnish white wine' (vodka), at which point he would use the maximum number of words possible. But he was a superb guy to work with. Once you took the time and trouble to understand what he wanted from the car, he would reward that trust in spades. He had the opposite approach to drivers such as Alain Prost or Sebastian Vettel in that, once we had had our debrief over the handling of the car, he would simply walk away and trust us to come up with solutions, and then not turn up until the next session, be it qualifying or race. Sometimes drivers can get lost in the details of poring over the data, and as a result become too mechanical in their driving, like method actors, rather than driving by feel. Look at the results, though: clearly both approaches can work.

Mika won the race. He got the jump on Schumacher at the start and disappeared off into the distance, eventually finishing a full 5sec ahead of him – his second drivers' championship secured – with Irvine a minute and a half behind Schumacher in third. Sadly, DC crashed out from what would have been third.

That meant that Ferrari took the constructors' title, the first time they'd won the championship since 1983, but we were super-happy for Mika. His drive was superb – the true mark of a champion. He dug deep and blitzed Ferrari.

Me? By the end of that season, I'd almost had enough. The bargeboard incident was the low point of a season that had drained me, mentally and physically, not to mention putting a huge strain on my marriage.

In a bid to relax Marigold and I went away, but a week in Dubai did little to help me decompress, after which Ron had organised a trip to Las Vegas to watch Lennox Lewis fight Evander Holyfield. We stayed in an amazing suite in the Bellagio with floor-to-ceiling windows and a panoramic view. We had front-row seats to the fight, and both Marigold and Lisa Dennis were wearing pale dresses. Splattered with blood, Lisa Dennis squealed with delight, in true Californian cowgirl style. Marigold was slightly less amused but the trip was an amazing experience. All told, not a very relaxing break though.

CHAPTER 57

The 2000 car was the third evolution of the 1998 car, and generally very competitive. With two races to go, Mika led the championship by two points from Schumacher, while we led Ferrari by four points in the constructors'. In the end our season was scuppered, primarily by engine-reliability issues, highlighted by Mika retiring from a dominant lead in the penultimate race of the season, the US Grand Prix, with engine failure. Schumacher took his third drivers' championship, with Ferrari scooping the constructors', and thus began a period of Ferrari-Schumacher dominance that lasted for a further four years.

For me the main thing that stands out from the 2000 season is an incident that occurred that August, when Ron invited Marigold, Martin Whitmarsh and his wife Debbie, and myself down to his house in the South of France.

Sitting around the pool there, Ron said to Martin and me, 'Look, long term, I want you two to have the keys to McLaren. I'll step back; you two can run it.'

I said, 'Well that's great . . .' I cleared my throat. 'But when will that be?'

'Well,' he said, 'I'm not prepared to put a timescale on that. But look, I want your commitment. Are you prepared to do that or are you not?'

To my surprise, Martin said yes, and pledged his loyalty. But I'm afraid I was not prepared to do so, and replied, 'Well, no, I'm sorry Ron. Much as I enjoy it, I'm not going to give you my word that I'll sit here indefinitely waiting for you to retire.'

A chill wind blew across the pool area that afternoon in the South of France. Ron has many strengths, but he has some significant weaknesses, and one of those is the expectation of unquestioning, undying loyalty from his staff. When I wasn't prepared to show that, our relationship came off the heat, and from then on was never the same again. Painting my office was one thing. Not dropping to my knees with gratitude at his offer? That was quite another.

We had nine months of that French *froideur*. Then, with the expiry of my initial employment contract approaching, came a set of negotiations, into which I entered with optimism. After all, McLaren had gone from being a team sampling the odd race win here and there, to a multiple-championship-winning outfit.

Ron saw it differently and made an offer that would have seen me earning less than I had over the previous seasons. I'll be honest, I was taken aback. Yes, on the one hand, you might say that with the numbers already so high I should have been happy either way, but it doesn't really work like that. I had helped the company towards a period of prosperity (increased sponsorship, more prize money, greater team revenue across the board), had achieved a 50 per cent win rate over the past 10 seasons, and I was being rewarded for my efforts with . . . a pay cut.

'Take it or leave it,' he said.

'I'm not signing that contract,' I said.

The talks reached an impasse.

It was about that time that I got a call from Bobby Rahal, my old friend from IndyCar, who had been appointed Managing Director of Jaguar Racing in Milton Keynes.

'What would it take for you to join?' he said, when we met.

We talked ambitions, finances. In any situation like that, I need to know how serious is the team. Do they want to be championship contenders? Do they have the necessary resources? Talk turned to salary.

Bobby said, 'We're prepared to offer £X.'

Where 'X' was a huge number compared to what I had been on at McLaren – two and a half times as much. Almost unbelievably big. It was a flat rate, no bonuses, but that's what I wanted because in 2000 we'd lost the championship primarily through engine-reliability woes, which were outside my control.

We agreed to keep talking; the impasse with Ron continued. Bobby and I had a second meeting and along for the ride this time was none other than Niki Lauda.

That threw me somewhat. I didn't know Niki was involved in Jaguar, and while he had reputation as a legendary driver, he also had a name for being cut-throat when it came to business.

Even so, I knew I would have a fabulous working relationship with Bobby, which meant with Ford money behind them they had the ingredients to become competitive (and yes, it was difficult to forget that salary). Marigold was involved in negotiating the package and I was feeling good about the offer. At yet another meeting – this time without Niki – I shook hands with Bobby and signed a letter of intent to say I would join Jaguar.

The next day, I went into Ron's office and said, 'Ron, I'm afraid I've got some news. We don't seem to be getting anywhere with this contract negotiation, so I've decided to join Jaguar.'

He went the colour of his office walls. 'You can't,' he managed.

'Well, I'm afraid I can,' I said.

'I don't want you to.'

I said, 'Well I'm sorry, but you really should have thought about that before you played hard ball on negotiations.'

With that I left his office, took the afternoon off, collected Charlotte and Hannah, and took them to see the film *The Mummy Returns* in Woking.

Like any responsible cinemagoer I turned off my phone as soon as I got settled, so little did I know that as I enjoyed the Ancient Egyptian spectacle of The Mummy returning, all hell was breaking loose in the outside world: knowing I got on well with his wife, Lisa, Ron had sent his plane to the South of France to pick her up and bring her back to formulate a battle plan. His next job was to get on the phone to Marigold, a long conversation that had prompted Marigold to ring and text me, so that by the time I emerged blinking from the cinema my phone was one long list of missed calls, texts and voicemails.

At home, Marigold said, 'Ron's not taking this lying down,' and sure enough, he and Lisa turned up at the gates shortly afterwards. What followed was a lengthy sit-down during which Ron rubbished Jaguar's aspirations, warned me of a power struggle between Niki and Bobby, asked if I wanted to end up working for Niki (which is what would happen if Niki won that particular power struggle), and finally asked me what I wanted from McLaren.

I said, 'Well, long term, I'd like to look at being involved in other things, apart from simply motor racing.'

'Like what?'

'Well,' I said, 'one of the things I love about motor racing is the fact it's a sport that involves man and machine. I enjoy the fact that you're competing against your peers, you're working with the driver, you're involved in all sorts of different aspects, the mechanical design, the aerodynamics, the packaging of the car, the race engineering, so every day is different . . .'

Ron looked at me. 'Yes?'

'And if you take that philosophy of man, machine and competition, and you ask yourself, where else is there big-budget man-and-machine sporting competition outside of the motor racing umbrella? The only other area where several million pounds of research money per year is spent is the America's Cup. I think it would be fascinating to be involved in that.'

Incredibly, Ron agreed to a contract which, roughly speaking, said that if, after two years, I wished to reduce my involvement in Formula One and start building a profile in the America's Cup, he would go about finding the budget for McLaren to enter it. And if he wasn't able to find the budget for that, he would pay me for 50 per cent of my time spent on it. He also matched the financial terms Jaguar had offered.

Lisa waded in. She's very charming. 'You'd be mad to refuse this offer,' she said, assuring me how much I was valued at McLaren.

After four or five hours of charm offensive from this formidable double act, Marigold and I withdrew to the kitchen for talks. It was a very generous offer. Very generous.

We came to the conclusion that, for whatever reason – perhaps the terms of a sponsorship deal – Ron needed to keep me. Why play hard ball in the first place, you might ask? Beats me. Perhaps it was Ron trying to be clever, thinking I had no alternatives. Or maybe he was punishing me for not swearing undying allegiance? But his master stroke was highlighting that a power struggle was going on between Bobby and Niki Lauda – I was interested in Jaguar primarily because of my relationship with Bobby, the relationship between team principal and technical director within a team being key. I did not want to join, only to become a pawn in a Ford-management-backed power struggle within the team. A big career risk. Back to the sitting room we went.

'Okay,' I told Ron, 'I'll stay.'

Of course there was fall-out, and I felt terrible that I'd gone back on my word to Bobby, who was extremely upset. The great thing though is that, a year later, we patched up our differences and we remain very good friends. Ron was right, Bobby did indeed last another two months or so at Jaguar before he was shown the door. The fact that the Jaguar team had a huge senior management turnover during the following years says that it was probably the right decision for me not to join them. Having bought the team off Jackie Stewart, Ford continually interfered with its running – never a recipe for success.

So Ron kept me. But he didn't like it. I suspect he didn't like the fact that one of his employees had become close to being indispensable and had, in his eyes, held him to ransom. Unbeknown to me, he charged Martin with ensuring that this could never happen again.

Martin's solution was to introduce a matrix structure to the engineering departments of McLaren, an unnecessarily complex and wretchedly un-workable system of department heads and 'performance creators' inform-ally known as 'mullahs', after the learned Muslim scholars.

It didn't work. Added to that, we had just moved into a new Norman Foster-designed factory. On the face of it, our new factory should have been good but, to appreciate why to some of us it wasn't, you have to under-stand that one of the best ways to upset Ron Dennis is to sit down in his office, where he'll usually have a few piles of papers neatly stacked on his desk, and just tip one of those piles by a few millimetres, knowing he'll then focus on that pile for ages, because he won't be sure whether you've straightened it or made it crooked.

That's him in a nutshell. He is very, very neat and organised, which of course are positive qualities until such time as they cross the line into becoming overly controlling.

To me the new building was oppressive in its ordered greyness. Reminiscent of something from Fritz Lang's *Metropolis*, it featured rows and rows of desks with nothing out of line. Built by the Empire. Not an environment in which I, among others, found it easy to be creative. When we first moved in, we weren't even allowed glasses of water at our desk, and absolutely no tea or coffee or personal effects. Somebody pointed out that it was probably illegal to deny workers water at their desk, so he had to relent on that, but not on the tea or coffee, and as far as personal effects went, you were allowed one family picture on your desk but it had to be stored in a drawer overnight.

Meanwhile, if you were part of the workforce, you had to enter the building walking down a circular staircase into an underground corridor with a grey floor and white walls; it felt like you were entering some Orwellian film. You'd then walk back up another circular staircase into the middle of the building, to your workstation.

I hated walking through the corridor, so instead I would walk along the grass verge, then cross the inner road and enter through the race bay where the trucks were parked. I was spotted doing this by the constantly watched bank of CCTV monitors in the basement and sent an email warning me that if I did not revert to using the prescribed route into the office I would face 'an internal examination'. Crikey.

CHAPTER 58

As you might imagine, *Metropolis*-McLaren was not an environment in which I flourished. The 2002 car, the first to be produced as a product of this matrix system, was a bit of a clumsy design, certainly not one of my best, so for 2003, feeling that we needed to make big strides to catch up with Ferrari, we embarked on an ambitious design, much more tightly packaged, with very different aerodynamics.

It turned out to be a problem child. Yet again I was stuck with a car that was giving good numbers in the wind tunnel and should have been a huge leap forward from the previous year's model, but that was in fact aerodynamically unstable on the track, giving me unpleasant flashbacks to the 1989 Leyton House design and the start-of-season 1994 Williams that Ayrton battled with.

By this time, Henri Durand, who had been the head of aerodynamics at McLaren when I joined, had moved on, so I'd appointed Peter Prodromou as the new head of aerodynamics. He and I spent a lot of time trying to figure out what had gone wrong. We had a fabulous new on-site wind tunnel, the upside of the new building. We had a car that should have been much quicker than the outgoing MP4 17. Yet it was slower and the drivers were saying it was unstable.

So, while we tried to understand what on earth was wrong with the 18, we carried on through the 2003 season with an updated MP4 17 and actually had a more successful season than I would have expected. David managed to win a few races with it, including Monaco, while Kimi Räikkönen, who had replaced Mika, did a great job of keeping our championship hopes alive, to the extent that by the end of the sixth round in Austria he was actually leading the championship from Schumacher. Kimi was very similar to Mika – almost a young clone, both in demeanour and in his approach to the task at hand. Both had supreme confidence in their ability to drive faster than anybody else, and both drove instinctively by feel, presumably the result of growing up in a country where even the taxi drivers opposite-lock their way around the icy roads.

Then, at Nürburgring, he was leading comfortably when the engine went. The Mercedes engine reliability was really quite desperate. It had lost us the championship in 2000 and it was continuing to be a source of woe.

As I've already said, the Mercedes engine was at that time built by Ilmor, run by Mario with his partner, Paul Morgan. In 1998/99 their engine was the most powerful and the reliability, while not 100 per cent, had been acceptable. Tragically, Paul died in 2001. He was a vintage aircraft enthusiast and had a plane called a Hawker Sea Fury, the fastest piston-engined aircraft of the Second World War. As the name implies, it was a naval aircraft built for take-off and landing on aircraft carriers, and it was renowned for being so powerful that if the front wheels got stuck in a rut – for instance, on a grass runway strip – it was liable to do a forward flip if given full throttle.

That's exactly what happened to Paul. He landed at his local airfield, Sywell, where the front wheels became lodged in an irrigation ditch, and when he revved the engine to pull himself out instead of pulling the aircraft forward it flipped over, killing him. He was just 52.

Not only was it a tragic accident that robbed us of a great person and engineer, but it also left Ilmor compromised. Paul had been the company's managing director, and his death left Mario, the technical director, responsible for running the shop floor and overseeing managerial and procedural matters, all of which left him completely overstretched.

The engines suffered as a result, with our performance slipping below Ferrari's and BMW's. Worse still, reliability became even more of an issue.

Meanwhile, back at the wind tunnel, Peter and I felt we had understood the aerodynamic problem, which was related to the shape of the chassis and front of the sidepod overloading the vortex that forms off a delta wing (think of a Concorde wing shape in miniature) just in front of the sidepod, causing the vortex to be unstable and burst in certain conditions. The problem could be alleviated by trimming the wing, but this lost downforce. The proper solution was to reshape the chassis and sidepod to alleviate the high-pressure stagnant air that was forming above the wing. But this required a new chassis, which is perfectly normal when designing a new car for the following season. However, there was an alternative view, led by Martin and two of the mullahs, Paddy Lowe and Pat Fry, that with development the existing 18 could be made reliable and competitive. The engineering fraternity was divided: should we make significant modifications to the shape of the monocoque and the sidepod to allow the revised aerodynamics which I felt were essential to overcome the stability problems properly, or should we simply sort out the reliability problems and try to improve the performance of the unraced and unloved 18?

Martin called a meeting of the engineering department heads, the mullahs, Neil Oatley (now an executive engineering director) and myself.

Martin chaired the meeting and, after a brief discussion, to my horror asked for a show of hands. It was a rigged result that Martin knew would go against me with the mullahs following Martin and Mike Coughlan (our chief designer) and Peter Prod, the heads, following me. Poor Neil didn't know what to do; it was unfair to ask him to vote. I have to admit I totally lost it, called Martin all the names under the sun and stormed out – not necessarily my proudest moment. Not only did I feel strongly it was the wrong decision, but also my opinion had been squashed by committee – effectively I was no longer technical director. Ron was making me pay for the swimming pool incident and Jaguargate – but to the detriment of his team? And so it was that we started the 2004 season with the MP4 19A (in fact the 18 with a different badge), which was a thoroughly uncompetitive and badly handling car that performed poorly at the start of the 2004 season – far and away the worst start to a season McLaren had had for around a decade.

By the time realisation finally dawned and we got our collective arse into gear, with Ron finally agreeing that actually, yes, we needed a new monocoque, there wasn't time to redo the cooling system, so it still wasn't the car I'd wanted to make the previous September/October. But at least it was a step in the right direction. With a new monocoque, new suspension and new bodywork, that car was finally ready to race at Spa, the fourteenth race of the championship. We went from being uncompetitive to winning that race, first time out – quite a turnaround. It was such a shame. We could have had a decent season if only we'd produced that car in the first place . . .

Turn Eight

HOW TO BUILD
AN MP4 20

CHAPTER 59

The one thing to get my creative juices flowing and keep me motivated in 2004 was the fact that we had quite a big regulation change coming up. In the FIA's continual drive to slow the cars down, they decided to put further aerodynamic restrictions in place for the 2005 season, the main one being to raise the height of the front wing by 50mm.

While that might not sound like a particularly big change, it is, because the aerodynamics of the front wing and the flow structures that come off it very much dictate the aerodynamics of the rest of the car.

If the flow that comes off the front wing is messy and interacts poorly with the front wheel and front suspension, so that you also get a lot of wake coming off those components, then all that poor quality air goes over the rest of the car, which won't work properly as a result.

In fact, if you had to pick the single most important aerodynamic component on the car, you'd say the front wing; it's there to create front downforce and the trick is building a front wing that generates that downforce while creating the minimum amount of disruption to the flow over the rest of the car.

It's not an easy problem and has become ever-more difficult as the regulations have become increasingly restrictive on the front wing itself, which is why, when you look at the cars today, the front wings have become such incredibly complex, intricate pieces. The front wing of a current Formula One car is a work of art really, a very complicated piece that not only creates downforce, but also creates a lot of vortical structures whose aim is to manage the flow around the front wheel and over the rest of the car.

So we started doing studies on this new raised front wing, using CFD as the way to understand the flow mechanisms around the car. CFD (as explained, it stands for computation fluid dynamics) is a mathematical simulation of the aerodynamics of the car. It's numerically intensive, which means that to run it, you need powerful computers. As a design and development tool it was really starting to come of age, and what it showed in those early simulations was that the vortex system coming off the end-plate of the front wing was now going smack into the lower wishbone of the front suspension and creating a huge mess.

At more or less exactly the same time as those simulations came out, I left with the family for our regular 10-day holiday in Barbados and, as has so often been the case, I found that holiday a very creative period.

There on the beach I started to think about the flow structures that were resulting from raising the front wing – not only the lack of front downforce that came from the front wing being further from the ground, but also the fact that the front wing tip vortex was now much higher and crashing into the front lower wishbone.

The solution came to me. And it was blindingly obvious. Raise the front lower wishbone, from what would traditionally be towards the bottom of the front wheel rim, to more or less level with the centre line of the front axle, a raise of around 120mm, and then tie the wishbone mountings in to the bottom corner of the chassis, a naturally very stiff mounting that would go some way to counteract the loss of stiffness caused by the much raised wishbone.

I sent lots of faxes, trying to find solutions to the conflict between aero utopia and the associated packaging and structural challenges. Images came backwards and forwards, and though I was soon spending more time in the hotel room than I was on the beach, it was a very productive period. Faxes would arrive at reception, I'd look at them, mark them up, scribble some notes, fax them back to the factory and the whole process would start again.

Marigold wasn't happy, the kids felt a bit neglected, but in that 10 days we made a huge amount of progress.

After my return, the main issues were the raised lower wishbone suspension and how we should treat what we called the hoop wing, which sprouted out from the side of the chassis and down to the bottom of the bodywork box. Getting this hoop wing and the raised front lower wishbone to work with the bargeboards behind it allowed us to take major steps in

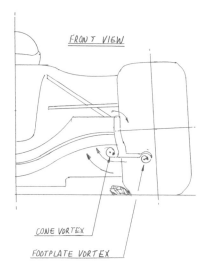

FRONT VIEW

CONE VORTEX

FOOTPLATE VORTEX

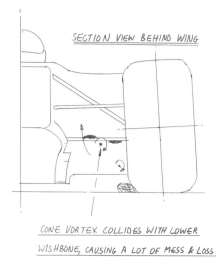

SECTION VIEW BEHIND WING

CONE VORTEX COLLIDES WITH LOWER
WISHBONE, CAUSING A LOT OF MESS & LOSS

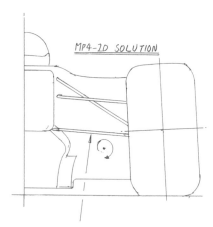

MP4-20 SOLUTION

LOWER WISHBONE RAISED, ALLOWING CONE
VORTEX TO REMAIN COHERENT AND
PASS FREELY. WISHBONE NOW MOUNTS
DIRECTLY ON LOWER CORNER OF CHASSIS

Figure 16: Our solution to the aerodynamic
problems on the front wing of the MP4 20,
which were caused by regulations requiring it
to be raised by 50mm.

recovering the downforce that we had lost from the raising of the front wing in the first place.

We further evolved the philosophy that had gone into the 19B of creating a smooth line from the keel – the vertical splitter that goes from under the driver's thighs around his backside. Normally there would then be a step out to the front of the sidepod, but this was a source of pressure rise, the problem that had flawed the 18A. The 19B reduced the width of the step, and with the 20 we took the obvious extra measure and narrowed the lower part of the sidepod further to give one smooth continuous line from the front of the keel all the way back to the coke at the rear. Importantly, along with the raised front suspension, it was a feature our competitors would be unlikely to copy during the 2005 season, as they would require a new chassis. Sadly, or perhaps flatteringly, our advantage only lasted one season, as both were copied by all the top teams the following year.

The other big performance step involved the gear change system, and here a very clever mathematician, Giles Wood, together with one of the mullahs, Tim Goss, really came up trumps.

All F1 cars of this time used what is known as a dog gearbox, which is to say that the drive between the shaft on which the gears rotate and the individual gears themselves is transmitted between 'dogs' (raised castellations on the sides of the gears) and 'dog rings' (raised castellations on a ring splined to the shaft). A gear change was performed by the on-board computer, on request from the driver's paddle pull, killing the engine torque by cutting the spark and then commanding the hydraulic control system to disengage the current dog ring and, once revs were matched, engage the next one.

The key here is the time involved in waiting for the engine to slow down before engaging the next gear; failure to wait long enough will destroy the dogs. Typically this process took about 0.1sec, during which time the car is not accelerating. Multiply this loss of acceleration by every up-gear change in a lap (typically about 25) and the loss of lap time compared to a 'seamless shift' (one in which there is no loss of torque during a gear change), and you come up with a theoretical lap-time benefit of around 0.35sec per lap – significant.

With this carrot in mind, in 2003 we had started developing a double-clutch gearbox, now known as a DSG, as part of our 'how are we going to beat Ferrari' technology plan. A DSG works by carrying odd gears, 1-3-5-7 on one shaft, and the even gears, 2-4-6 on another. Each shaft has its own clutch. The computer anticipates that, say, the next gear change will be from third to fourth and pre-selects fourth gear. When the driver calls for it, instead of cutting the torque for a long time, it simply engages the clutch on the evens shaft while disengaging the odds. The energy of the engine slowing down is absorbed by the clutches and the car accelerates without interruption across a gear change.

It was this DSG system that we hoped to have ready for the start of the 2004 season, and the lap-time gain that it offered had been used as additional ammunition by Martin and the mullahs as to why a re-badged MP4 18 with this gearbox would be good enough for 2004. But the policy failed on two counts: first, it was not ready and second, it was heavy and bulky. Many top-end sports cars now use DSGs for the smoothness of the shift, but their gearboxes weigh 150kg instead of 90kg as a result.

However, during running on a transient gearbox dyno at Mercedes in Stuttgart with a prototype during the summer of 2004, Giles and Tim realised that with independent control of the odds and evens dog rings and some clever maths predicting where the dogs would be at any moment in time, the separate shafts and clutches were not necessary. Suddenly, with that eureka moment, we had a gearbox that could match the theoretical lap-time benefit of a DSG but with only a minimal weight and bulk increase compared to a conventional gearbox.

During pre-season testing, the car was instantly quick – significantly quicker than anybody else – while the feedback from Kimi was that it was a very nice, well-balanced car to drive. The new gearbox, after a few teething troubles, worked well. An encouraging start.

Beginning the season, cautiously optimistic, we found that although the car showed promise we were struggling to extract the performance from it. We were a lowly sixth and eighth in Australia, fourth and ninth in Malaysia.

Pablo Montoya, who by now was Kimi's teammate, rather disgraced himself by breaking his ankle 'playing tennis' after the second race in Malaysia. He was out for a while, so we used Pedro de la Rosa and then Alex Wurz drove in his place.

By the third race, Bahrain, we were starting to get a bit more on top of the car, to the extent that Pedro, in his stand-in role, set the fastest lap. The potential was starting to unlock through evolving the set-up, but it was taking time.

Come the fourth race, Imola, Kimi qualified on pole but then, at the start of the race, dropped the clutch with far more revs on it that he had ever done before, a huge amount that overloaded the transmission system and failed the driveshaft joint. That was that. The car barely even moved.

Something like that you can view one of two ways. You could say we should have made the car strong enough to take such abuse and, had we known, we would have done. The problem is no other driver had ever done anything like that previously, so the issue had never come up before. It was similar to Nigel stalling at Montreal in 1991.

Nevertheless, from there, things began to turn around.

In the fifth race in Spain, Kimi managed to convert his pole position into the car's first win, which was a very satisfying moment, especially after the political machinations of the previous season. Finally starting to deliver the potential of the car, we got into our stride, qualifying on pole in Monaco and going on to win. Pablo returned but wasn't fully recovered.

And then we got to the United States . . .

CHAPTER 60

The 2005 US Grand Prix at Indianapolis goes down as one of the most controversial in the history of the sport.

On the face of it, Formula One at Indianapolis seems logical. The track has huge seating capacity and a massive domestic and international profile.

Its downside is its suitability. It had only ever been famous as a Super Speedway, and that's the key to what went wrong in 2005.

What distinguishes a super-speedway from a normal road course is the fact that you only have four corners; they're all taken at high speed on a banked track and there's no run-off. So if a driver loses control, either through error or car failure, he's heading for a very hard wall on the outside, hence the huge accidents that so often happen at these super-speedway tracks.

Formula One cars are just not designed for that type of track. You can't simply transplant the F1 circus to a super-speedway track and expect to race; it would be way too dangerous. So what they'd been doing since 2000, when the US Grand Prix fixture was introduced at Indianapolis, was install an infield twisty road section to the circuit so that only two of the corners were the banked corners of the existing track, and the rest were inside the oval, which, to be honest, made it a bit of a fiddly, badly flowing circuit.

So that's the background. We arrived that June, and during initial practice our cars were quick enough to make us think that we were going to have an advantage over our competitors.

Worryingly, however, Ralf Schumacher, Michael's brother, had a huge accident exiting a banked corner. He was unhurt but it was a big crash, and clearly the result of tyre failure.

Michelin investigated and found that the very high loads inflicted by the banked corner were causing a standing wave to be initiated in the side wall of the rear tyre, which in turn was causing the tyre to explode – what happened to Ralf. The standing wave was causing high-frequency distortions of the sidewall, leading the steel cords within the tyre to fail, with catastrophic consequences. It became increasingly evident that just about all the Michelin-shod cars were experiencing this problem after 30 or so laps. The situation was worsened by a hugely unpopular 2005 rule change, which stopped teams changing tyres during the race.

Michelin went away and worked through the night in order to try and understand the problem, to no avail. Their engineers came back to say that the tyre would indeed be good for a certain number of laps, but unsafe for a race distance.

All of which meant that we were cleared to qualify, but if we raced we'd be risking the drivers' lives and potentially those of spectators as well, in as much as there's always a risk of debris going into the crowd. The choices for the Michelin-shod teams were:

(1) Race in an unsafe state, which, of course, none of us wanted to do.
(2) Don't race at all; again, hardly an attractive option.
(3) Persuade the FIA to change the circuit layout.

Collectively we decided to urge number three. Meanwhile Ferrari, on Bridgestone tyres and sniffing the chance to win the race and keep their championship hopes alive, were saying, *No, it's Michelin's problem, it's their team's problem, it's nothing to do with us; we'll just carry on and race.*

It rumbled on overnight until at last the FIA said, *No, we will not sanction any modifications to the circuit. If you race, then it's on your own heads.*

The Michelin teams were all agreed it wasn't safe to race, but at the same time we wanted to put on at least a semblance of a show for the paying spectators. We agreed that we'd all go to the pre-grid, then peel back into the pits at the end of the warm-up lap and not race.

The race began, and I'm sure I wasn't the only one wondering if everybody would abide by our gentleman's agreement. But they did. At the end of the parade lap, all the Michelin-shod cars came into the pits, leaving just the six Bridgestone cars on the grid. Inevitably, of course, the Ferraris had a very easy first and second, followed by the two Jordans, followed by the two Minardis. It was a complete disaster for Formula One, and for Indianapolis in particular, because, as you can imagine the fans were livid, all demanding their money back.

And, of course, for Michelin it was a complete PR disaster, given that their tyres had led to what was effectively the cancellation of the US Grand Prix.

It was a very surreal weekend and a sad day for Formula One. Did we go back there the following year? Yes we did, but, not surprisingly, the spectators voted with their feet and were absent.

Engine problems continued to plague us. I was torn by my loyalty to Mario and my annoyance that his engines kept failing, costing us many points and wins. For a while it was up in the air as to whether it would be Kimi, or Fernando Alonso in the Renault, who won the drivers' championship, but in the end Alonso clinched the title at the Brazilian Grand Prix, the third race from the end of the season – the one silver lining of his victory being that at least it ended the years of Schumacher-Ferrari dominance.

The next race, the Japanese Grand Prix at Suzuka – a race that *Autocourse* called one of the 'greatest of the century' – was to see Kimi's greatest drive.

Things had started badly for him. An engine failure on the Friday had seen him awarded a 10-place grid penalty, but despite starting well down the grid he put together one of the drives of his life to win the race on the last lap – all this despite knowing the drivers' title was beyond his reach. Hats off.

Now we were just two points behind Renault going into the last race in China, which was the first time a Grand Prix had been held in China. Sadly it was not to be. For the first time in that second half of the season Renault were genuinely quicker than us, and having locked out the front row of the grid, they kept us behind them and the race finished in grid order, Renault the champs.

For me it was a sad end to what should have been a championship season. We'd had the quickest car on balance and won 10 of the 17 races, but we didn't win either the drivers' or the constructors' due, primarily, to all those engine failures.

Despite the disappointment of losing both championships though, at least we had proved we could still design a quick car – very important for one's rate card. And that was important for me because I was disillusioned with the way things had gone at McLaren.

The way I had been dealing with it was by concentrating on doing my bit technically, working closely with the engineers I valued – in particular, Peter Prodromou and Mike Coughlan, the chief designer – and not so closely with the mullahs in the matrix system, but even so I knew I was getting to the point where I was losing my mojo. I was having to force myself rather than it coming naturally – never a good sign.

CHAPTER 61

It was during the 2004 season that Red Bull hove into view. Ford got tired of funding the Jaguar team, and at the end of 2004 sold it to the energy drink company, Red Bull.

Dietrich Mateschitz, the boss of Red Bull, took the view that the Formula One paddock was a bit boring and staid, and so set himself the challenge of trying to get it to take itself a bit less seriously, and to inject a bit of fun and glamour back into it. The team came onto the scene with lots of razzmatazz, throwing parties, bringing in models and even launching a *Private Eye*-style newspaper called *The Red Bulletin* that you could pick up as you walked into the paddock.

The established teams thought that the whole thing was a bit of a joke, a good-time Charlie team who'd be there for two or three years tops before they either lost their money or got bored with the whole thing. Don't forget that in 2005, Red Bull was nowhere near the brand it is now. It was still very much a drink promoted by skateboarders and snowboarders, a little bit grungy and left-field. You certainly wouldn't see it on sale in petrol stations and it wouldn't be in the mini-bar of your hotel the way that it is now.

As well as shaking up the paddock, Dietrich felt he needed to appoint a new team principal, and with the help and advice of his long-time confidant, Dr Helmut Marko, the man Dietrich trusts more than any other when it comes to motor racing matters, he began casting around for a suitable candidate.

Based on Helmut's advice, they looked at a guy called Christian Horner.

Christian's history is that he was a driver who rose through the junior ranks of Formula Three and F3000 and, in the process, launched the

Arden team with his father, Garry, expanding it to a two-car team with himself and another driver. Having come to the conclusion that he'd be better off retiring from driving to concentrate on running the team for his Red Bull-sponsored drivers in F3000, he was the perfect guy for Dietrich and Helmut. They hired him.

Next the team chose David Coulthard as their lead driver for 2005. David had been let go by McLaren because he wasn't as quick as Kimi, but he was still one of the best out there, with a wealth of experience, and it was a coup for Red Bull to get him.

With things beginning to fall into place, Christian decided that the Jaguar-inherited technical team needed strengthening and leadership. He knew of my reputation, and with DC in his ear saying, 'If you want to get somewhere, you need to try and get Adrian,' he set out to do just that. His tactic was to build a relationship with me by 'accidentally' bumping into me in the paddock. I'd be walking one way and he'd happen to be going in the other direction. 'Oh, hello, Adrian . . .'

He'd stop and chat – Christian's a very personable and sociable person, somebody who's very easy to talk to – so we got to know each other a bit. He then made a point of making sure that Marigold and I were invited along to the premiere screening of a new *Star Wars* film at Monaco, where we sat with Christian and his girlfriend, Beverley (I must admit, I fell asleep).

Through all these little meetings we got to know each other, and I began to suspect that he was building up to making an approach.

This was ongoing throughout the first half of the 2005 season. At Silverstone that year, I was walking past the line of trucks in the paddock. As I came level with the Red Bull truck, a very austere-looking gentleman in a black leather jacket stepped forwards and in a German-accent, said, 'I am Dr Helmut Marko. I work for Red Bull. You will give me a ring.' Then he gave me his business card, span on his heel and walked away. That was my first meeting with Helmut.

I have to admit I was slightly taken aback by Helmut's directness (I have since learnt it is the Austrian way), but I thought, *There's something interesting here. It's a young start-up team. If the financial stability is there, then this could be an opportunity to be involved with the team from more or less the outset.* That was something that very much appealed to me. In many ways, I think you could call it unfinished business from the Leyton House days – I'd always lamented the fact that we had the rug pulled from under us just when things were getting interesting. I'd gone off and worked for two great teams in Williams and McLaren, but they were teams that had already won races and championships long before I ever joined. I'd brought fresh design input and ideas, but the infrastructure was all there. I didn't have to be involved in growing the team; all I had to do was supply engineering creativity and direction.

This was something new, a fresh challenge.

I phoned Christian and told him of my encounter with Helmut. A week or so later, DC, Christian and I met in a private room at the Bluebird Club to discuss the team and whether I'd be interested in joining it.

I was. By this time I'd come to the conclusion that I needed to be out of McLaren, and the chance to work for this new team became more attractive the more I learnt about them, providing they had the financial security and the motivation to try to win, rather than just throw parties.

Cautious still, I called DC to ensure he wasn't simply putting on the corporate face of Red Bull, doing his bit for the team. 'No, Adrian,' he assured me. 'Believe me, this bunch are for real. They want to get the job done.'

The one thing we hadn't discussed was salaries. Both Christian and I are very British like that – we try not to discuss the dirty subject of money – and the matter had yet to be broached when it was agreed that we would all go over to the Red Bull Headquarters at Salzburg to meet the big man, Dietrich, and discuss terms.

It was a surreal weekend. It was meant to be clandestine, because I was still employed by McLaren and didn't want it known by McLaren that I was being courted. Marigold and I, DC, and Christian and Beverley took a private jet from Luton to Salzburg to see Dietrich's famed 'Hangar 7' – a showpiece museum and meeting venue. It has two parts to it: a hangar to store and maintain some of his aircraft, and then another architecturally interesting showpiece dome also containing a spectacular array of aircraft.

Among several other military planes, he has one of the very few, if not the only, privately owned Apache Attack helicopters in the world.

I was wearing a baseball hat as a token disguise as we were ushered inside – only to be greeted by a Japanese tourist party, who must have been motor racing enthusiasts, because they instantly began photographing me and insisting on autographs. So much for secrecy, and thank God this was before the days social media really took off.

We met Dietrich, shook hands. One rather dizzying passenger ride in a stunt jet later, we were taken out in Salzburg and then, on Sunday morning, flown by an ex-German air force seaplane to a lake about 20 miles away. There we had a lovely lunch before another trip, this time by helicopter, in order to meet Dietrich for a second time.

Up to this point, my salary had still not been discussed. Asking for a salary always seems an awkward thing to do and it certainly is not my prime motivation. But, as I've said previously, a salary is a way of measuring how much you are valued, and that is important to me. Marigold and I agreed she should take the negotiating bit and that I should ask for the same money as I earned at McLaren, which in turn was the same as I'd been offered by Jaguar. I wasn't even part of the discussion when the figure came up, but apparently it wasn't well received. The words 'send him home' were uttered, either by Dietrich or Dr Helmut Marko.

Put it this way, the Austrians took some persuading that I was worth the price tag. Apparently Dietrich rang Gerhard Berger. Gerhard recalls the conversation: 'Gerhard, we have Adrian Newey here in Salzburg, but he is very expensive; what should we do?' Gerhard: 'Well it depends on the value you put on a second lap.' I owe Gerhard a large debt of gratitude.

To his credit, Dietrich is not one to mess about, not one of life's hagglers. If Gerhard Berger said I was worth it then so be it.

It was a deal, and so when we arrived back from the Chinese Grand Prix, I went to see Ron to deliver my news.

Things were very different this time around. Ron knew my mind was made up. Even so, my announcement heralded a little more toing and froing, with Ron wanting me to delay announcing my departure (I am told he was hoping to secure key people with my name as bait) and

Christian keen to make their announcement for pretty much the same reasons.

In the end I was fed up with Ron's games, so I went back and said, 'Sorry Ron, I'm afraid it's going to be announced and I'm not sure I can stop it. Red Bull wish to announce it, that's that.'

What I didn't expect was to return to my desk and be told to leave the building, on the spot. I was allowed to pack my briefcase before being escorted out of the building, a rather sad end to my career at McLaren.

An even sourer footnote is that our car, the MP4 20, won the 'Car of the Year' award at that year's *Autosport* awards, a big end-of-season industry bash held at the Grosvenor House Hotel in London. By now, Marigold and I were guests of Red Bull and sitting at their table, content to watch as Ron collected the award. Would he mention my contribution in his speech, I wondered?

He certainly mentioned me. He told the room how I had left McLaren to join Red Bull because I wanted a quiet, low-pressure job working for a team that would never ever succeed. Oh yes, and how I was doing it all for the money.

Sitting beside me, Christian was indignant on my behalf, but I found myself feeling a little more philosophical. I thought, *Well, at least I know I've made the right decision.* Funnily enough, it reminded me of an incident years before, when I was late to the wedding of Robin Herd. Well, not that late. I arrived before the bride at least. But as I walked in, Max Mosley turned in his seat and said, 'Ah, Leyton House – slow and late again.' And I thought to myself then, as I did now: *Dig deep Adrian, and show them.*

Turn Nine

HOW TO BUILD
AN RB5

CHAPTER 62

Having frog-marched me out of the office, McLaren raised no protest when it came to me joining Red Bull before my contract with them ended. There was to be no gardening leave this time; McLaren didn't view Red Bull as a threat and therefore weren't worried about releasing me early. I was to start on 1 March.

A few weeks beforehand, an informal meeting was called in a pub outside Milton Keynes in order for me to meet Red Bull's senior engineering staff. It was a strange affair. One of the 'old guard' told me: 'Adrian, here at Jaguar (!) we have our procedures and processes and a way of doing things, and we expect you to fit in with them.'

I let the comment pass. But that, in a nutshell, explained why Jaguar had never finished higher than seventh in the constructors' championship. Regardless of my ability, you would think that there would be a recognition by its senior engineers that Jaguar's engineering processes and approach had not brought results; also, that the chance to learn how a championship-winning team approached the challenge would be of great interest, especially given the change of ownership that had now been in place for a year.

It's strange – and apologies if you hail from the area – but it seems to be a Midlands thing, this arrogant assumption that the way *we* do things is best, despite all evidence to the contrary. This is the culture that had brought us such great products as the Morris Marina, Austin Allegro and Norton Commando, and here it was alive and well and flourishing at Red Bull. The fact that certain members of staff were still proudly referring to the team as Jaguar was as big a clue as any that a far-reaching cultural change was in order.

Christian did a deal with Martin Whitmarsh, and my drawing board completed its fourth journey from my bedroom at Fyfield via McLaren's old and new factories to Milton Keynes. And I began work at a desk that

I'd come so close to using four years earlier when I nearly joined Jaguar.

I buried myself in the research and design of what was to be the 2007 car, the RB3. My first job was to lay it out, as well as drawing aerodynamic components for the wind tunnel model – a job that kept me quiet for a good six or seven weeks.

Working long hours, I drew a new car from front to back, using my memory of the McLaren shape as a starting point. Doing this is perfectly acceptable from a legal standpoint, because whatever is in your head is fair game. What you can't do, however, is use materials, drawings, documents and so forth. There have been various examples of industrial espionage in F1, the highest-profile being in 2007 when McLaren were fined $100m and lost all their championship points after it was discovered that they had obtained inside information from a disgruntled Ferrari employee.

Anyway, the car I drew was a better basis than the current 2006 Red Bull car, which overheated, had poor downforce, handled poorly and had an unreliable gearbox. Apart from that it was okay!

I also felt that the team lacked two major research facilities. The first was a transient gearbox dyno – at McLaren we had used the Mercedes facility at Stuttgart, but as a private team using customer Ferrari engines we did not have access to what is quite a specialised piece of equipment. I felt it was essential if we were to develop our own version of the 2005 McLaren quick-shift transmission. An American company, MTS, who supply the rolling road for most teams' wind tunnels, said they could make such a thing but the cost would be around £1m. I presented to Dietrich why I felt we needed to purchase this and he agreed without question.

The next thing I felt we needed was a driver-in-the-loop simulator, which again is something we'd been developing at McLaren – basically an incredibly advanced arcade game that the driver can sit in and drive a simulated lap of a circuit.

The value from an engineering point of view isn't for driver training, it's for testing set-ups on the car. So, for instance, if we want to evaluate a different suspension geometry or a different shape to the aerodynamic map of the car, we can use the simulator as a tool to do that and see if it makes the car handle better or worse, quicker or slower.

In truth, at McLaren it was arguable whether we had got it to the stage where the results could be trusted. But it seemed clear that this was the future – testing was becoming more and more restricted by regulations, while simulation technology, led by the film and gaming industry, was advancing in leaps and bounds.

To do a DIL simulation properly you need a wrap-around 3D screen so that it's representative of what a driver would really see, even in his peripheral vision. That's fairly easy to do – the driver can wear 3D glasses, just like in the cinema. A sound system is also required – the requisite sounds are relatively easy to synthesise and play back through a driver's ear plugs.

The difficult bit is the motion system. In a racing car you brake at about 4G. To put that in a simulator, you'd need a motion platform the size of a football pitch. We couldn't do that, but we split the difference and decided to go up to 1G using a system that had a long travel (in other words, that could move a long way).

The problem was that as the project developed I began to have reservations, first about our own in-house simulation team and second about the company to which they'd given the contract to build the simulator. At the same time, I felt that my aerodynamic ideas were being progressed too slowly, with parts taking a long time to come through. There was a meetings culture and too much cosy talk reporting what we had done, and not enough thought about what we should do next. Additionally, we were wasting time arguing over a flawed and probably unworkable Wheel Motion System for the wind tunnel, when in fact the entire wind tunnel programme was in a mess.

With hindsight, I spent too long designing the 2007 car and not enough time trying to sort out these core problems. I began to feel that there was a sub-culture going on behind my back; people saying yes to my face but then carrying on with their own agenda just as they had in the Jaguar days. I had my suspicions who they were, but pulling them up on it always led to vigorous denials. So to understand it, Christian and I employed Jayne Poole, an old and trusted family friend, as trouble-shooter. Having worked at Crest Hotels, then risen through the ranks at Hogg Robinson, Jayne was perfectly placed to begin with us as a three-day-a-week HR management consultant in the autumn of 2006, though I kept it quiet that we knew each other so that she could gain unguarded feedback from the engineers and other members of the workforce. I also had allies in Christian and Rob Marshall, and from McLaren I poached my old cohort Peter Prodromou, as well as Giles Wood, one of the cleverest people I know. As well as the quick-shift transmission, Giles had contributed a lot to the McLaren driver-in-the-loop simulator, so he was the perfect person to drive the simulator project forward.

In the end, Jayne confirmed my suspicions and I took the decision to undertake three senior sackings. Not a decision that's ever taken lightly, I can assure you. But the change in atmosphere almost overnight was remarkable; the other quasi-militants over whom I had a question mark completely turned around, possibly relieved to be free of a mistaken loyalty to their outgoing bosses. Although F1 is a technical sport, it is, in the end, a people sport. It is all about the employees and creating a working environment that plays to and enhances their individual strengths.

Next on the to-do list was to find an engine supplier. As I mentioned, we were using Ferrari engines, but to a downgraded spec compared to the works team. Christian and I had a meeting with Jean Todt, sporting director at Ferrari, but he made it clear that they would not supply to the same spec as the works team. Mercedes in early 2006, with their V8 engine (new for that year), looked in a terrible mess, but Renault appeared to be strong. So we approached Renault, and Rob White, their technical director on the engine side, agreed to supply us engines to the same specification as the works. To improve communications between the engineering departments, I persuaded Christian to expand the main engineering office out in a mezzanine so that all departments were in one big room instead of spread around the site. I also introduced a culture that meetings should only be deemed a success if a clear set of ideas and actions came from them; they should not be used simply to read out reports that should have already been read prior to the meeting.

The final big-ticket task was driver choice. David had been the lead driver for 2006, while for the second driver they'd operated a funny system in which they used an Austrian, Christian Klien, for a few races and then an

Italian driver, Antonio Liuzzi, for others. Christian was a good driver, but he was never going to be among the elite, while Antonio had been phenomenal in karting and was naturally gifted, but, like so many Italians, he didn't seem able to translate his genetic gift into real speed when it came to Formula One; he continually underperformed.

We looked at Mark Webber. He'd driven for Jaguar before, but had a slightly troubled time and left for Williams. He was a driver I rated highly, so we approached him, discovering to our delight that he liked the idea of working with me. That was the 2007 driving team sorted then.

Also, I'd returned from a visit to the America's Cup in Valencia with an idea. I'd discovered that because yachting teams are smaller and spend so long at the race venue, they effectively decamp and move there, lock, stock and barrel. After a day on the water, the sailing team would sit with factory-based engineers and discuss what they'd learnt, what they felt about the boat, where improvements could be made and so on.

It struck me as a pleasant contrast to what so often happens in motor racing – and Jaguar/Red Bull was a good (i.e. bad) example of this – where there exists a dismissive 'us vs them' situation between the factory-based team and the race team, with race engineers often taking a rather high-handed 'it's our baby now' approach to the car, which in turn infuriates the factory-based engineers.

We started to think about setting up an Operations Room in Building One at Milton Keynes, and having it linked to a control room at the track. Instead of being restricted to five or six engineers at a race, the team could have access to all the expertise of the factory. These rooms would have full video-conferencing capability, so if there was a reliability problem with, say, the gearbox, the race team personnel could call the gearbox experts from the factory and talk about the problems using video communications coupled with a big network pipe, so that all the data we acquire on the car through the various sensors and on-board computer could be wired back to the factory in real time.

That last bit was the important but difficult challenge. We approached AT&T, the American telecoms giant, to ask if it could be done. After some deliberation they came back and said yes, it would be possible.

We now had several building blocks in place, many of which would take two years or more to reach maturity, but there was a buzz of excitement around the factory – of anticipation.

CHAPTER 63

Meanwhile, my classic car enthusiasm had continued to grow. Dave McRobert and I had been competing in long-distance rallies in his dad's Wolseley and my SS100 'Reginald', taking in the Monte Carlo Historic, Mille Miglin and the Liege to Rome rally a couple of times too.

The first Liege trip was quite a drama. We ended up having to make a repair overnight before the rally began, and only just made the start. But make it we did, and it was great: starting in Belgium, we hacked along beautiful and largely empty roads through Germany, France and into Italy.

However, as we came over the Alps, we started to hear a horrible knocking noise from the rear axle. I wasn't sure what the problem was. Arriving in Italy we paid a visit to the Ferrari test track at Fiorano, where a handful of mechanics in red overalls came charging out to look at the car, refilling the oil in the back axle theatrically which was not, as it turned out, the cause. (The problem was the whole back axle was trying to break clear from the rest of the car!)

Next day, one of the national newspapers ran a story along the lines of, 'Ferrari Needed to Fix Newey'. Bloody cheek.

More rallies followed and they were great fun. Many of them were essentially two rallies within the rally. You'd have the regularity section, where over certain sections you had to maintain a certain average speed, which was what I'd been doing with Dave, and then there was the competition section, where you drove as fast as you could against the clock. I thought that looked a bit more fun and what I'd like to have a go at next.

With that in mind I bought a Ford GT40 (registration number VRE 777G), which was a big investment at the time, far more money than I'd ever spent on a car (although, as it turns out, a very good one, because this was in 2003 and classic car prices have since shot up). I thought I'd like to race it at that September's Goodwood Revival, which, along with the Monaco Historic, is probably the best classic car competitive race event in the world. So I rang Lord Charles March, who advised me to ring his competition secretary.

'Yes,' said the competition secretary when I called, 'certainly you can race. Now, if you can just send in your race licence . . .'

I know this sounds ridiculous for somebody who's spent their career in motor racing, but I had no idea you needed a licence for such an event. I don't know what I thought; I suppose I just assumed you could turn up and race.

As it was, shortly afterwards I snapped my Achilles' tendon playing tennis, so I ended up attending the Revival on crutches. However, a friend, Jodie Kidd, was racing and therefore had a racing licence, so I asked her how she went about getting it.

She said, 'Well, a chap called Joe Macari, who lives in my village, gave me lessons and got me a licence. Ring him.'

So I rang Joe, a qualified racing driving instructor, and he said, 'Yeah, absolutely. I can give you lessons,' and that was how I met Joe, who has become a close friend.

Joe was the examiner for my provisional racing licence. But to convert that into a full licence I would need to race the GT40 at, say, Goodwood or another international event – higher-grade races as opposed to small national events. You have to collect six signatures by driving competently in six national races.

To cut a long story short, I got my six signatures, by which time it was May 2004. I managed to get some races during 2004 and 2005, had some good results and notched up quite a few wins in my class.

I really enjoyed driving the GT40, but occasionally it would be very unstable under braking for no obvious reasons.

Now, the person to beat at that time was a chap called Ray Bellm, who'd had a lot of success in sports car racing, one of the most successful amateur drivers ever. In a race at Donington, having matched his lap times, I was starting to get close to him before my engine failed. So, going to Le Mans in July of 2006, I knew he would be my main rival. In the first race I finished second to Ray, which meant I would be second on the grid for the next race.

We got off in grid order and I stayed with Ray through the first half of the lap, off down the Mulsanne Straight. Then, braking for the second chicane on the Mulsanne, the rear snapped out and hit the barrier on the right, and all of a sudden I was on three wheels at close to 200mph.

People say your life flashes before you when you think you might die. But although this was one of those situations where I knew there was going to be a big accident, I can honestly say that all I was thinking was, *How do I slow this down? What's the best thing to hit?* The fact was, I knew I was going to hit something, because the brake pedal had gone to the floor, the right rear wheel was gone and, despite frantically down-changing, the car wasn't slowing down anywhere near fast enough, so I picked the barrier that divides the chicane, hoping it would be the softest thing to hit at huge speed, though I had no idea what the barrier was made of.

I remember the windscreen shattering and thinking, *Oh, bugger, it's broken the windscreen.* Only later, playing the sequence of events back in my mind, did I realise that my seat belts must have stretched so much that my eyes were inches from the screen. I remember also being several feet in the air, and looking down from the passenger side window at Ray while he looked up at me, and me thinking, *Should I wave?*

CHAPTER 64

On autopilot, I pulled myself out of the GT40 and turned to see it badly damaged, all the bodywork off, doors off, wheels off, the whole thing.

I was distraught. And this is something I'd never normally do, but I threw my helmet on the ground in disgust, and damaged that as well. Then I sat down, a bit shaky.

I was lucky to escape unhurt, and it's a testament to the strength of the GT40 that I had. If I'd bought the Porsche 908 that I'd originally intended to buy, and had experienced the same accident, I wouldn't be here today. As it was, my only immediately obvious injury was a cut on my right hand. With time, it became evident I had whiplash, causing me to have a blinding headache and to progressively lose the sight out of my right eye over the next couple of days. DC, ever the thoughtful gent, rang and said I must see a specialist, who diagnosed that my skull was out of shape, stuck his thumb in my mouth and manipulated my pallet. It was painful but afterwards the relief was remarkable and my sight returned.

While the GT40 was being rebuilt, I bought a lightweight Jaguar E-Type (registration number PS1 175) and went back to Goodwood later in the year with that. I went out for the first practice session and, after only two laps of gentle bedding in, had another accident.

I have no idea what went wrong for that one. I just remember waking up in the ambulance convinced I was still at Le Mans, and saying to the nurse, 'I'm feeling car sick; can you let me out please. Stop the ambulance!'

I was probably a bit aggressive. Apparently it's quite normal in concussion cases. She said, 'No, we can't stop the ambulance. How old are you?' I replied, 'Twenty-eight.' And then slipped back into unconsciousness.

I came round again in the hospital at Goodwood to see Dario Franchitti lying in the bed next to me. 'What happened to you?' I asked. 'Had an accident,' Dario replied. At which point we both slipped back into unconsciousness. Apparently this short question-and-answer routine went on in both directions about 10 times over the following six hours as we both slipped in and out of consciousness before we were taken off to our respective rooms for overnight admission.

A few days later I rang the driver, Justin Law, who'd been following me. 'Can you tell me what happened?' I asked him.

He said, 'Well, it was very strange. Going into the kink on the back straight, the rear started progressively sliding and kept sliding until you span and hit the barrier. It was a very odd accident to watch; you do not expect the rear to come round there.'

We'll never truly know the cause, because the right rear tyre was damaged in the accident, but a marshal radioed in from Lavant, the corner onto the back straight, to say that the right rear tyre looked low, so it seems a deflation of that tyre was most likely. The car itself was damaged, but nowhere near as badly as the GT40 had been; a little bit of panel-beating was needed to sort it out.

However, the bottom line was that I'd now had two big accidents in the space of three or four months and had gained a reputation of being a crasher, which I still carry to this day (a tad unfair because I'm hardly the only one to have had accidents).

Towards the end of the year, I competed in a six-hour race with Joe and another friend, Rob Wilson, in a BMW at Misano in Italy. That restored my confidence a bit, with us finishing second overall. Joe, with his many contacts, then got us an entry into the 24-hour race at Le Mans, driving a GT2 Ferrari. The car was owned by Ben Aucott, another amateur driver/ friend, which made us the only all-amateur entry on the grid of 55 cars.

Le Mans is an amazing event. Along with the Monaco GP and the Indy 500, it is considered to be one of the three races in the world that carry the most kudos. To compete as an amateur in such a high-profile event is at once both exhilarating and intimidating. Joe, Ben and I went into it saying that our ambition was to try to finish, which, of course, put pressure on each of us not to let the other two down. I was acutely aware of this after the accidents in the GT40 and E-Type, the extra tension initially causing my driving to be a bit stiff and lacking in rhythm.

Earlier in the day, I'd noticed a 5ft-tall poster promoting the race.

Unwisely, as it proved, I'd jokingly suggested that Joe, as our de facto sporting director for the weekend, had a duty to supply us with one of these posters each as a piece of memorabilia.

The race itself went smoothly enough until, at about 2am, when I was standing, helmet on, waiting to take over from Joe, there was a huge commotion in the garage. Joe, unbeknown to me, had delegated the poster challenge to one of his lads, who took it upon himself, Stanley knife in hand, to commit art theft in the signing-on room, which now served as the marshals' and journalists' sleeping quarters. It appears he rolled the poster up but, in his haste to exit, tripped over a sleeping body and woke the room up. Rolled-up poster in hand, he then ran down the stairs, through our garage and off down the pit lane, pursued by a dozen or so angry officials and marshals!

At 11.30 on Sunday morning I got in for my final stint, three and a half hours from the finish. Then, about one hour in, it started raining, so I came in for wets and a splash of fuel. Back out again, the rain was torrential, visibility appalling, and the car was aquaplaning all over the place, properly scary. People started going off the track, and through the carnage we climbed to twenty-second overall and fourth in our class. My engineer radioed to me: 'Adrian, the Panoz behind you is gaining at 3sec per lap.' I replied, doubtless with my voice raised a couple of octaves, 'I bet he hasn't got a wife and four kids!' At 2.30, half an hour from the finish, they finally brought the safety car out and I came in to hand over to Ben for the safety car cruise to the finish. I had been in the car for three hours and was mentally exhausted from the concentration in the rain. To see Ben cross the finish line brought, for all of us, a tremendous sense of achievement and pride.

In 2009 I returned to the Goodwood TT, competing there for the first time since the accident. I teamed up with Bobby, just as I had done in 2006, but this time there were no mishaps and we won. A very sweet victory.

However, in 2010 I had a third accident, this time in a Ginetta at Snetterton. My head wasn't in the right place at the time, for marital reasons that we'll get to in due course, and I was spun round by a car trying to overtake me and then T-boned by the car behind that, which knocked me out.

The concussion was less severe than the E-Type accident but, even so, I was painfully aware I needed to avoid it happening again. You can only have so many concussions before it causes lasting problems in old age.

I was back at Goodwood in 2012, this time partnering Martin Brundle, and also suffering an attack of nerves. *Should I be here? What am I doing? Why am I putting myself under this pressure?*

Martin had put us on pole, but those nerves got the better of me and I rather stupidly ran wide halfway round the first lap and spun on the grass. By the time I got going again, I was right at the back of the field.

After that I drove what I consider to be the best race of my life. Having spun, the pressure was off and those nerves disappeared. I made my way through the field, so that at about the 30min mark, halfway through the race, I was back up to fourth and had set the record for the fastest lap in a GT car at Goodwood ever, which stood for some years afterwards. When the safety car came out and I was able to peel in and hand over to Martin, he emerged from the pits in second place and only just behind the leader. It was then fairly easy for him to overtake him and we notched our second TT win.

What was interesting was the psychology of that race. I was feeling the pressure and as such was driving badly at the start. But once that pressure was relieved, I was far more competitive. I've seen the same thing in Formula One drivers.

I returned to Goodwood the following year for the GT40-only race, a one-off two-driver race to celebrate the fiftieth anniversary of the GT40. Through Paul and Dean Lanzante, the father and son preparers who ran the GT40 and E-Type, I met Kenny Brack. Kenny is quite a character, a Swede who had won the Indy 500. He takes any racing seriously, including Goodwood, and therefore insisted on doing a fair bit of testing prior to the race. During one of these tests he went off under braking, reporting that the rear suddenly snapped on him.

A careful trawl through the car and Dean noted that the rear calliper bores were worn to the point that the pistons could tip and jam. Is that what caused the Le Mans shunt? I don't know for sure, but with new callipers neither of us have suffered a snap under braking again.

Qualifying was wet, so Kenny the Swede showboated it around – an awesome display of car control but not the quickest way. Check it out on YouTube; I wasn't sure whether to be impressed or to thump him when I saw it!

Regardless, the race was dry and we managed to win, giving me a Goodwood hat-trick of two in the E-Type and one in the GT40.

With that under my belt I decided it was time to give it a rest for a bit. I was conscious of those two concussions, if you'll excuse the pun, as well as being cheesed off with a rumour going around that I was cheating by using the wind tunnel at Red Bull to test the GT40 and E-Type. As if.

Instead I took to motorbiking. In 2014 a group of us including Charley Boorman staged an off-road bike ride from Victoria Falls in Zimbabwe, down through Botswana to Johannesburg, which was a really good crack. We enjoyed it so much we did the same the following year, through Morocco and the Atlas Mountains, and then through Mongolia and the Gobi Desert. Boys behaving badly – on dirt bikes.

Back to cars and I bought a Lotus Gold Leaf 49, my childhood dream car, the first car I'd ever built as a 1:12-scale model. I stripped and rebuilt it myself with the help and guidance of Paul Lanzante and Classic Team Lotus. It was a kind of circle-of-life thing, going from building the model from a kit to the real thing nearly 50 years later. Driving for the first time at the Lotus test track in Norfolk in a car that I had spent all the time I could grab over the last year rebuilding, was a special moment. I then made the rather bold decision, never having raced a single-seater car, to enter it for the high-profile 2016 Monaco Historic.

I hadn't had a lot of time in the car and we had a few teething problems. I got to Monaco, and DC, who lives there, picked me up from the airport.

Late at night you can drive the circuit, and that's what he did, showing me what to look out for. Next day I saw Gerhard Berger, who walked the track with me offering further advice – all of which meant that I'd had pointers from not one but two Monaco winners.

Even so, it was daunting. A feature of the Monaco circuit is its narrow roads and tall barriers. You feel as though you're driving through a tunnel and you're very aware that there's very little room for error.

As a result I probably took it too gently in the first practice session. Rain for the second session meant my overall qualifying was poor, but for the race I had a good start, managed to overtake a couple of cars on the first lap and then had my own bit of space for the rest of the race. It was an absolutely brilliant experience. If my Goodwood drive was my best, then this was my most enjoyable – to be racing an ex-Graham Hill Lotus 49 around Monaco is as good as a fulfilled childhood dream ever gets!

One of the questions I'm often asked is, do I think my extra-curricular driving helps me in my professional job as an engineer? The answer is yes. On a technical level I'm better able to understand what drivers are talking about when they're describing the handling of the car, and what they want out of it.

It also helps me to understand what they go through psychologically. When I get in the driving seat, although it's only at amateur level, I do feel the pressure, particularly at the big televised events such as Le Mans, Goodwood and Monaco, but more to the point it's the pressure I put on myself to do well. A driver does the same. He might say he wants to do well for the team, and of course that's true, but it's more selfish than that. He wants to do the best for himself.

CHAPTER 65

Around 1998 my dad retired from his veterinary practice. A few years later, he and Mum moved to Yorkshire. My mother had grown up there and they often visited for holidays; in particular they liked walking the dogs on the moors, so it made sense that they should end up there. They moved to a small village called Scalby, just north of Scarborough.

I got into the habit of driving up to see them once every two or three months or so, taking Harri. Charlotte, Hannah and Imogen went less often: it was a long journey. But Harri was happy in his car seat, and he enjoyed stopping off at motorway service stations, Hatfield being a perennial favourite as we could have breakfast 'on the road' looking down at the motorway traffic passing below us. They were happy weekends spent walking the dogs on the moors and visiting local attractions. One weekend we all went up as a family. We were having evening drinks in a local hotel when I heard a cockney voice from behind me: 'Adrian, what the bloody hell are you doing here?' I turned to see Barry Sheene with a big smile on his face. Barry and his mate, Steve Parrish, had flown his heli up. In true racing-fraternity lack of respect for regulations and flight plans, he'd almost caused the RAF to scramble before getting lost and landing on an old people's home bowling green – much to the excitement, fascination or anger of the residents. He then recounted the tale of his latest shunt on a motorbike and dropped his trousers in the middle of the bar to show off his bruises, much to my mum's delight. What a legend.

It was during one such visit that my father took me aside. 'Son,' he said, 'I don't know why, but sometimes I feel as if my brain's turning to cotton wool.'

I didn't think too much of it, but a few days later, my mother rang to say that he had suffered a brain haemorrhage and was in hospital.

I rushed up. He'd had a brain bleed. Luckily, it hadn't been too severe, leaving him with slight paralysis similar to the effect of a mild stroke. The doctor's advice was to keep an eye on it but nothing more. What emerged was that he'd probably been having bleeds for quite some time. He was a great fitness fanatic and would take the dogs for a run in the woods. He hadn't admitted it to my mother, but it seems he'd woken up on the ground a couple of times, not knowing how he'd ended up there. He'd obviously had blackouts, probably caused by very small haemorrhages.

About four weeks later, my mother rang to say that it had happened again and this time it was much worse, leaving Dad unable to walk without the aid of sticks. Mentally he was no longer fully there either. Conversations with him became repetitive, a bit random.

I picked up the phone to Sid Watkins, and told him what had happened.

'Look, there's a chap down in London, a specialist,' he said. 'I suggest you bring your father down to him to run some tests.'

So I drove back up to Yorkshire, collected Dad, returned down the M1. In London we turned a corner and saw the Post Office Tower in front of us, and it was as if we'd gone back in time to when he used to take me to racing car shows, me aged about 12 and always being really excited at the sight of that tower, except this time the roles were reversed and it was he who was thrilled to clap eyes on it, saying, 'Look, Adrian, look.'

He was admitted to hospital. However, as the surgeon began examining him, he had yet another haemorrhage. Rushing him into the operating theatre, they saved him. I know it sounds an awful thing to say, but it might have been better for both my parents if they hadn't done, because after that final bleed Dad was in terrible shape, unable to walk or even hold a conversation. He could talk, but what he had to say was generally random and out of context. He'd repeatedly say, 'Oh Adrian, we heard you coming on your motorcycle,' which must have been a reference to my Ducati, the bike I'd had in my twenties.

Through my motor racing connections, we managed to get Dad admitted to a local home run by the Ben charity for people in the automotive trade, and there they did a super job of looking after him.

Unfortunately my mother took it very hard. After all that arguing in my childhood years, they had grown to be as close a couple as you can imagine. They still bickered a bit, but were inseparable. Soul mates. Mum's life revolved around my father, and living on her own in Scalby she found herself feeling lonely.

We found her a cottage in Ascot so that she could be close to Dad and to us, but having spent about five nights there, she decided she hated it because of the traffic noise and returned to Scalby.

Then, after a month or so back in Scalby, my mother passed away, effectively from a broken heart.

I had to tell my dad.

'I'm so sorry, but Mum has passed away.' He looked at me and with perfect lucidity, the first and only time he'd shown that since the big bleed, and said, 'I know.'

It was remarkable how his damaged brain was suddenly able to comprehend; how he even seemed to sense what had happened before I told him. Theirs was, in the end, a true love story.

After that, Harri and I used to visit him regularly in the nursing home. We'd take board games, play a few by the side of his bed, and then leave. That's all we could really do for him; I think it made him happy just to watch us play games. Apparently, he was a Lothario, even then; he used to flirt with the nurses constantly. Initially, he'd made some attempts at recovery, to the point that he could walk with a zimmer frame, but after a few months he gave up. And then, in February 2008, on a cold winter's day, he passed away, peacefully.

It all began with Dad. When I stand at my drawing board, inspired by a love of cars and the constant, ongoing desire to improve them, not just their speed and performance, but ultimately the way in which they move through the world, the impact they have – aesthetic, environmental, sporting enjoyment – it all comes back to him, his workshop and his eccentric love of tinkering with all things mechanical. That and my mum's love of art and painting.

CHAPTER 66

Despite our new driver line-up, new design and Renault engine, our 2007 car generally lacked pace and we finished fifth in the constructors' championship, which, even though it improved on Jaguar's previous seventh, was nowhere near where we wanted to be.

During 2007 there was a lot of criticism that overtaking in F1 was too difficult, resulting in processional races with position changes coming only from pit-stop strategies. An overtaking working group was set up to do proper research on how the aerodynamic regulations could be altered in a way that meant the cars behind would be less compromised by the wake of the leading car.

Apart from the raising of the front wing in 2005, the aero rules had been fairly stable since 1998 and hence the cars were now well evolved, with nobody making big steps forward. Lots of small iterations were the way teams were continuing to improve their cars, which played into the hands of the top established teams with big budgets, experienced and well-organised aero teams and top-level infrastructure.

We were playing catch-up and it was likely that it would take us a while, but a big aero regulation change *could* offer a big opportunity for some fresh thinking. Originally, the regulation change was to be introduced for the 2008 season but I felt that, from a personal, infrastructure and organisational point of view, we would not be ready to capitalise. In the meantime I had had a reshuffle, taking an old colleague from my McLaren days, Paul Monaghan, out of his role as head of race engineering and instead giving him licence to operate in a more maverick role in the company, but with a specific task to be the point of contact with the FIA on all regulatory matters. I asked Paul to see if he could delay the rule change one year to the 2009 season. He managed to argue that the changes were being rushed and that more research was needed, giving the delay I wanted; the rules were eventually published in March 2008.

RB4 was the 2008 model and it was a reasonable car. We still had too many reliability problems, though, and the season got off to a bad start when David had an accident in Melbourne and the car pretty much disintegrated around him. The suspension was too fragile, to the point that, in Malaysia, he clipped a kerb in one of the high-speed corners, the front suspension failed and he lost both front wheels.

Towards the end of 2005 Dietrich had acquired a second team from the bankrupt Minardi operation in Faenza, Italy, which he renamed Scuderia Toro Rosso. This was to serve as a driver-training team for the senior team, Red Bull Racing, as well as promoting Red Bull (the drink) in Italy, where sales were sluggish. Research and design of the cars was to be done by a third company, Red Bull Technology, for whom I work. Hence the Red Bull Racing and Toro Rosso cars were identical designs for the 2007 and

2008 seasons, the only differences being that Toro Rosso used the Ferrari engine that we (RBR) had discarded at the end of 2006.

Thus, for the design team in Milton Keynes, the highlight of the year was when, at a very wet Monza, an exciting young driver, Sebastian Vettel, qualified on pole for STR while Mark was third for us, RBR. The race was also run in torrential rain, and none of us expected this raw young talent to retain his grid position for too long – except that's what he did. Sebastian's performance that day was fearless as he took a dominant first victory to become, at 21 years and 73 days, the youngest race winner in the history of the sport. A quite remarkable drive, it also gave the design team at Milton Keynes their first victory.

However, it was a major source of embarrassment for us, wearing my other hat for Red Bull Racing, as we were getting beaten quite often by the 'junior' team using our unwanted Ferrari engines. At the end-of-season state-of-the-nation meeting in Salzburg, Austria, Dietrich gave us a pretty hard time. There was huge pressure from Austria to improve. Rightly, he expected more. Bravely, or stupidly, I decided, *We're not going to be challenging for the championship; we're unlikely to win a race this year. Our big opportunity is these new regulations.* So once we got back from the second race, I stood back from the development of the 2008 car and got stuck into research and design of the RB5 for 2009.

The 2009 regulations specified a front wing that was the full width of the car, with a neutral section over the central 500mm of the wing, and a delayed diffuser. This meant the front end of the diffuser could not now be positioned forward of the centre of the rear axle. The area around the bargeboards was also heavily restricted, while the various appendages and flicks on the sidepod were effectively banned. The rear wing was also made much narrower but taller, giving the rear end of the car a rather awkward look.

So, aerodynamically, a very different car. The first question was: what do you do with this new front wing? You've now got a front wing sitting directly ahead of the front tyres. As mentioned before, all wings will shed a vortex at their tip – that's a function of the fact that on a racing car you've got high pressure on top of the wing and low pressure underneath, so the air effectively tries to take a short cut round the tip and spin from top surface to bottom surface, creating this vortical structure that sheds off downstream.

There are lots of examples of vortices in nature. Tornados, for example. And if you watch an aircraft take off from Heathrow on a damp day, you'll see a vapour trail spinning from the tip of the wing, which is the wing tip vortex we're talking about. You see it on a racing car, coming off the rear wing on a wet day, when the humidity is such that it causes the flow to condense into a vapour trail.

All wings in Formula One, certainly in the last 30 years, had been only partially in front of the front tyre, so these tip vortices were always shed to the inside of the front tyre. With the wing now so wide, we had the chance actually to manipulate the shape of the endplate to attempt to shed the tip vortex *outside* of the front tyre, and that's aerodynamically a huge difference. That inboard vortex can cause a huge amount of damage to the flow structures downstream, because it interacts with the front wheel wake and pulls the front wheel wake inboard onto the rest of the car. Normally that would then be managed by the bargeboards, but that opportunity was now limited by the regulation restrictions in that area.

The other thing that became evident was that a discontinuity between the neutral section of the front wing in the centre and the conventional wing at 250mm from the car centre line was also shedding a very strong vortex, known as the 250 Vortex because it's shed at 250mm from the car centre line. That vortex is actually very useful because the rotation pushes the lower part of the front wheel wake outboard, away from the rest of the car, which reduces the chances of the front wheel wake being ingested into the diffuser, the sensitive bit of the car.

The downside of it is that, just as its corkscrew action pushes the lower part of the wheel wake outboard, it pulls the upper part of the front wheel wake inboard and onto the rear wing. With all this in mind, the design direction we took was to camber the front-wing endplates to get the tip vortex outside of the front wheel, as well as shaping the inboard end of the front wing to maximise and strengthen the 250 Vortex while keeping it stable.

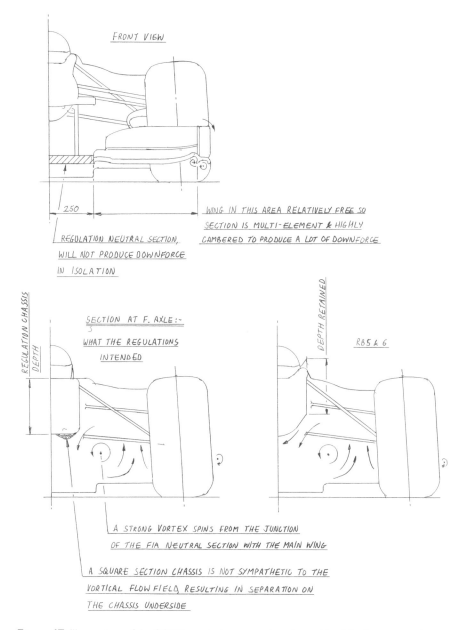

FRONT VIEW

250

REGULATION NEUTRAL SECTION,
WILL NOT PRODUCE DOWNFORCE
IN ISOLATION

WING IN THIS AREA RELATIVELY FREE SO
SECTION IS MULTI-ELEMENT & HIGHLY
CAMBERED TO PRODUCE A LOT OF DOWNFORCE

REGULATION CHASSIS DEPTH

SECTION AT F. AXLE:-

WHAT THE REGULATIONS
INTENDED

DEPTH RETAINED

RB5 & 6

A STRONG VORTEX SPINS FROM THE JUNCTION
OF THE FIA NEUTRAL SECTION WITH THE MAIN WING

A SQUARE SECTION CHASSIS IS NOT SYMPATHETIC TO THE
VORTICAL FLOW FIELD, RESULTING IN SEPARATION ON
THE CHASSIS UNDERSIDE

Figure 17: Illustrations of the 2009 regulations regarding the width of the front wing, the aerodynamic problems they created as a result of the subsequent vortical flow field and our solution on the RB5, with its V-shaped chassis.

Because the 250 Vortex was such a strong vortex it was causing separation of the flow from the bottom corner of the monocoque. Effectively, you've got a square-cross-section chassis sitting in a rotating circular flow, which is not very elegant.

However, I realised while poring over the rules that there was a loophole allowing us to do something similar to what we'd done on the 1998 McLaren, which was to distort the chassis into a V-shape cross-section. Again the rules said that the depth of the chassis had to be a certain prescribed figure which varied along the length, but it was only a depth; it didn't say it had to be rectangular.

So we adopted the same principle as with the 1998 McLaren – albeit now with rounded corners to the fins to satisfy a corner radius regulation – which gave us a side to the chassis that was much more sympathetic to this very strong vortical structure coming off the wing.

The other problem associated with the 250 Vortex was that it sat high, clattering into the front suspension despite the raised wishbone we had carried over from the 2005 McLaren. The solution was to raise the inboard end even further, a compromise for the suspension geometry but overall a net gain for lap time according to the driver-in-the-loop simulator (which was now commissioned and proving a very useful tool).

At the rear of the car, the diffuser shape was critical, particularly the area around the rear tyre. We were struggling early on with the tyre squish, which you may recall from the section on the FW14. This occurs when a tyre rotates the flow that's trapped against the surface of the tyre as it reaches the ground and is only able to squirt sideways, so you get a dirty mess of air emerging laterally.

With the diffuser now not starting until level with the rear axle, that squish was getting ingested into the diffuser at the worst possible point. One way to help manage that was to put wings on the rear brake duct and a fence on the top side of the floor to create vortices that would act in the opposite direction to the tyre squish. That seemed quite effective; we were making big gains.

The other thing that is critical to making a diffuser work well is to have a low-pressure field at the back of the diffuser, helping to draw the flow through. This is the job of the beam wing. Sitting just above the trailing edge of the diffuser, it provides a nice low-pressure area. However, with pushrod rear suspension, the unanimous choice of the pit lane in recent seasons, the pushrod and its associated rocker and inbound suspension corrupt the flow onto the beam wing at the inboard end, hugely reducing its efficiency.

With the diffuser now starting further aft, we realised that there was space to include a pullrod, where the rocker and inboard suspension are carried low and out of the way, tucked in just in front of the gearbox. This gave much lower narrower bodywork and hence much stronger flow onto the beam wing – a further good gain in downforce.

In combination with this, we made the lower rear bodywork very narrow to feed flow to the Gurney flap tab on the back of the diffuser, but then widened the bodywork above this to form a fish-tail platform to pressurise the flow beside the rear wheels and consequently reduce losses off the side of the tyre.

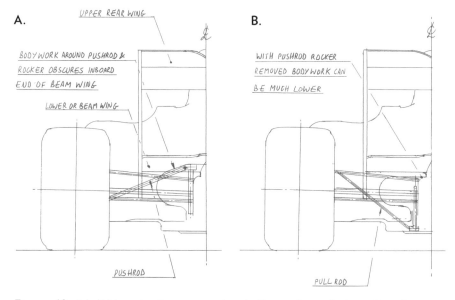

A.

UPPER REAR WING

BODYWORK AROUND PUSHROD &
ROCKER OBSCURES INBOARD
END OF BEAM WING

LOWER OR BEAM WING

PUSHROD

B.

WITH PUSHROD ROCKER
REMOVED BODYWORK CAN
BE MUCH LOWER

PULL ROD

Figures 18a & b: With pushrod rear suspension, the flow quality to the lower (beam) rear wing is compromised (left). The pullrod we introduced on the RB5 hugely improved things (right).

This combination of pullrod suspension, a fence to spin a vortex beside the rear tyres, in combination with wings mounted in the rear brake duct area, and a narrow low/fish-tail wide upper rear bodywork has now become the norm in F1. Unfortunately there are no plagiarism rules!

What we missed was something that had always been there – if you believe it's legal – and that's what came to be known as the double diffuser.

Three teams had it: Williams, Toyota and Ross Brawn's new team, Brawn. Ross had joined Honda about the same time as I joined Red Bull and we'd both suffered a similar lack of success in those intervening years of 2007 and 2008. Honda decided they'd had enough and pulled the plug in November.

Ross had managed to negotiate that Honda pay the bills for the following year, so at least the workforce weren't out on their ears. He also managed to persuade Martin Whitmarsh and McLaren to get Mercedes to give them an engine, which was a little galling when he had just blocked us. It was also, as it turned out, a huge own goal as Mercedes had ambitions to own their own team, and having a Mercedes engine in the back of the Brawn paved the way for that route, demoting McLaren to a customer in the process.

It was while Brawn were still under the aegis of Honda that one of their Japanese engineers had seen the potential for a double diffuser. He'd spotted a loophole in the regulations.

Basically, the rules call for two planes on the car, the reference plane, which is in the middle of the car, and the step planes, which are on each side and have to be 50mm higher than the reference plane in the middle.

The regulations then talk about a vertical transition between the reference plane and the step planes to link this 50mm difference in height. The regulations go on to say that there should be no holes in the step and reference planes.

What a Japanese engineer working at Honda spotted was that the regulations did not preclude a hole in the vertical transition between the reference plane and the step plane.

It was a clever interpretation. Was it legal? It was questionable. When the cars appeared at the start of 2009, three teams had spotted this loophole, which, given that it had been there since 1995, suggests that personnel from those teams had either moved around or been talking to each other.

Either way, the bottom line was that Williams, Toyota and Brawn had this new double diffuser.

As you can imagine, it made us blink hard. We requested clarification from Charlie Whiting, Max Mosley and the FIA. Charlie was noncommittal, but Max was more definitive. He said there's no way these cars are legal, don't worry, they'll be banned, they won't be able to race.

To this day, I'm not sure whether they were legal or not. There's no doubt it was a clever interpretation by the Honda engineer, but in any case the legality was soon reduced to a side issue as we once again became bogged down in FIA politics. At the time, Max was arguing with both McLaren and Ferrari about governance and future directions of the sport. A cynic might observe that it became less about whether or not the double diffuser was legal and more about teaching both teams a lesson. Since neither McLaren nor Ferrari had a double diffuser, it suited Max to say it was legal.

Unfortunately, we got caught up in all that; the fact that we didn't have a double diffuser either was just collateral.

It was a lot of performance. It effectively allowed you to circumvent the diffuser regulation height restriction; instead of having a diffuser at the back of the car that was only 175mm tall, you could effectively make it 300mm tall. Ross Brawn must have known about that for quite some time, because he had been lobbying in the latter stages of the firming up of the regulations to further restrict the diffuser. Instead of being 175mm tall, he wanted it restricted down to 125mm, knowing full well that with the double diffuser above it, it mattered much less how tall the diffuser underneath was.

Was it gamesmanship or simply a case of going a step too far in exploiting a loophole?

Would I have done the same thing? I think not, but it's a good question.

CHAPTER 67

The other thing I should say about the regulations for 2009 is that, way back in 1999, we'd been working on an energy-recovery-and-storage system that was ruled illegal after Ferrari objected. This year, however, came a U-turn of sorts, with teams being given the green light to use a KERS – Kinetic Energy Recovery System.

KERS works on a similar principle to a Prius or other hybrid cars, where the energy normally wasted as heat during braking is instead stored and then used to accelerate the car afterwards.

The trouble was you needed to make sure that your car was at least 35kg underweight, otherwise by the time you put the KERS in it would be overweight, and slower. Nor could you get away from the fact it needed cooling, which meant an aerodynamic hit from the extra radiator required. There was also a problem with weight distribution when it came to packaging the batteries.

Overall I'd say the roughly 0.4sec theoretical benefit was heavily eroded by the aerodynamic penalty and the fact that we couldn't get the weight distribution exactly where we wanted it. Factor in a fire that we had at the factory, caused by the lithium-ion batteries going into thermal runaway, and I took the view that KERS wasn't worth chasing for a team of our size.

Testing at Jerez went well. It became obvious that Brawn had the quickest car, but we looked to be in the thick of the action with Mercedes, Ferrari, BMW and Toyota. Our car certainly drew the most admiring glances along the pit lane.

With DC taking a temporary break from driving and joining the world of TV punditry, Sebastian moved over from Toro Rosso to join the 'senior' team. Sebastian, as I've said, was one of those drivers who likes to look over the data. He did everything on the edge, pushed himself and the car very hard, and he made mistakes, but he's a very, very fast learner and I don't think he's ever made the same mistake twice. He was honest with himself, and if he felt he had underperformed he would really beat himself up about it, but he always came back stronger.

He was very young when he joined us, and though he came with tremendous natural ability but not much experience he's a very bright guy, and he used that to accelerate his learning curve, so his rate of improvement was tremendous. Does he occasionally let the pressure get to him? Yes, is the short answer, and we still occasionally see that in his driving. But you have to understand what a pressure-cooker atmosphere F1 can be. It can be difficult to appreciate as an outsider.

Unfortunately, Mark had a cycling accident during the off-season. He suffered broken ribs, a broken shoulder and, worst of all, a bad break on his lower leg. That happened in November, so his recuperation time to be fit to drive the car for the start of the season was short.

We didn't see him until the car was ready to run in February, and when he tried it for size he was obviously in pain. He has a huge amount of 'Aussie Grit' and determination, and was determined to prove he could drive the car. I think he knew it was going to be a good one, and having put all those years of blood and sweat into less impressive cars in Formula One, he didn't want to miss out on the chance to drive what would hopefully be a competitive ride.

It's a tribute to Mark that he did everything he could to speed his recovery but, even so, the truth was that when he came back in the new year and started testing, his strength wasn't all there. I suspect that affected him in the early races.

In the first race, in Australia, we were the only team who looked like we might give Brawn a hard time. Sebastian qualified third, and then in the race was penalised for a move on Kubica and given a 10-place grid penalty for the next race.

The second race, in Malaysia, was a wet shambles. The weather and Sebastian's penalty meant the race was disappointing. Sebastian span off, Mark was sixth.

During Malaysia the whole double-diffuser issue reached its height when we as Red Bull joined in an unholy alliance with Ferrari and McLaren to protest against Brawn. By the end of Malaysia it was evident the double diffusers were going to be allowed, so I elected not to go to the Chinese Grand Prix, the third race, but instead to stay behind, get my head down and commence research on a double diffuser of our own. It was obvious the performance benefit was significant, and we needed to find a way to get it onto our car, even though the car wasn't designed for it.

In the event, I missed our first race win.

China was again a wet race. Sebastian qualified on pole with Mark third; in the race we had the quickest car. Mark did it the hard way and overtook Button in the Brawn, a bold move on the outside of one of the quick corners that took him to second, and we scored what was not just our first race win, but our first one–two.

In order to get ahead, we needed a double diffuser on the car as quickly as possible and so, in Monaco, we attempted to do that. However, the fit of the parts was poor. We hadn't spent enough time thinking about how to do the split lines in the bodywork, the quality wasn't there and I'd rushed the aerodynamics. So while it was a benefit, it wasn't the big performance boost we might have expected.

In the race, Sebastian crashed out and Button went on to win yet again, with Mark finishing fifth.

We didn't win in Turkey but it was a good, solid performance. For Silverstone, we finally got a more considered version of the double diffuser on the car. It hadn't been easy because the gearbox and rear suspension wasn't designed for it, but nevertheless in the wind tunnel it was a good step forwards. Silverstone's high-speed nature rewarded us handsomely; we qualified on pole, and in the race Sebastian and Mark quite simply disappeared. They dominated and won easily.

We now had a car that was able to beat the Brawns on pace, and that's exactly what we did at Silverstone – a very rewarding weekend at our home track after a lot of long days and nights by all involved to get the new bits designed, manufactured and on the car.

It was after that race that Christian held his after-race party. By now he'd bought an old vicarage in a pretty Oxfordshire village and decided to throw a party on Sunday evening for the race team and other friends and family – about 50 of us.

Also there was my pal Joe Macari, who came in a brand-new Ferrari California. After one or two (three or four) drinks, I decided to celebrate our win by nabbing the keys and then, when everyone was in the marquee listening to the band, doing doughnuts on Christian's lawn.

Mark tells it well. He said that from inside the tent it was like a strobe going off as the Ferrari span around outside: headlights, tail lights, going round and round . . .

Slowly people came out to watch. I'd probably done about 30 doughnuts by the time I finished and got out of the car to a round of applause. And then, I must admit, I simply left Joe's Ferrari there on the lawn.

Well, I say 'lawn'. I was staying over that night, and when I awoke with a rather sore head the next morning and looked out of the window, what I saw was a 'lawn' that was now a series of brown muddy circles. Christian forgave me, of course – about three years later.

CHAPTER 68

Germany, the next race, was another one–two, with Mark taking the win. I was pleased for him that day. Up until then, all the attention had been on Sebastian as the new wonderkid, so for Mark to beat him fair and square in Germany was fantastic.

They were a good pairing from an engineering point of view. Sebastian had a good feel for the tyres. He was always talking to Bridgestone, and subsequently to Pirelli, in order to develop his understanding of the tyres. The balance of the car at corner entry was everything to him. He was also very sensitive to the driveability of the engine, i.e. the way it delivers its power. While Mark was less alive to those things, he was more in tune with the aerodynamics. Be it a high-speed or medium-speed corner, Mark could pick up very small aerodynamic changes that might be needed and report back with great accuracy.

It was a winning combination: Mark reporting on the aero, Sebastian giving feedback on the mechanical aspects of the tyres, the suspension and the driveability of the engine. I must admit that after Mark retired we lost that level of aerodynamic feedback.

So we'd now had three one–twos, with Sebastian winning two and Mark the third. They were competing against each other for race wins, which brought a fresh edge to the competition between the two.

Then there was the nip and tuck between us and Brawn. Could we get that point deficit down to zero before the end of the season? We knew from Andy Cowell's power curve that Brawn's Mercedes' engine had a power advantage, so at races such as Monza, which were very much power-dominated, we probably wouldn't be competitive, and that's how it turned out. The truth was, we couldn't ever quite close the gap. We won more races but we were always a little behind in terms of the championship, to the point that by Brazil, the penultimate race, although Mark won and Sebastian was third, Button was crowned world champion. In the constructors', Brawn had pulled so far ahead they couldn't be caught. We scored more points than Brawn in the second half of the season, but it wasn't enough to close their early lead.

So that was 2009, a season in which, even though we didn't win the championship, we established ourselves as race winners, a team capable of beating the establishment of McLaren and Ferrari. We could hold our heads up, and for all the remaining doubters of the old Jaguar brigade still at Red Bull, we'd proved that the new regime could work. For us, it was the watershed year. Even better was to come.

Turn Ten

HOW TO BUILD
AN RB6

CHAPTER 69

For 2010 the regulations stayed stable, the major change being that KERS was banned. At the same time, the big opportunity for us was now to develop the double diffuser with the freedom to design the gearbox and rear suspension to suit.

So that's what we did. In order to get the most out of a double diffuser, you want it to start as far forward as possible. To this end, we increased the length from the back of the engine to the rear-wheel centre line, giving us a greater area in which to accommodate the upper diffuser inlet. Recall that the regulations say only that surfaces lying on the reference or step planes shall be visible from underneath; slots leading out from the step transition across the step plane were deemed legal provided that interior parts of the car or bodywork could not be seen from underneath through these slots. Crucially, suspension members are not classed as bodywork, so if it's a suspension leg that you see through the slot, that's okay. To take advantage, then, of the long length forwards to the engine I needed to be able to stop the resulting slot being visible from underneath. The solution was to put a very extreme angle on the front leg of the rear lower wishbone suspension member and join it more or less to the back of the engine through a yoke arrangement around the engine to the gearbox studs. This huge inlet to the upper diffuser coupled with a very narrow gearbox allowed a very deep, wide upper profile that was in turn linked in to a forward mounted beam wing, the latter forming a very effective extractor. The resulting exit to the upper diffuser was so big that the mechanics would often warn one of the smaller guys, Bal, not to get too close in case he got sucked in!

The front of the car, we simply refined. We went even more extreme on the V-shape of the chassis, which meant that the eyebrows at the top of the chassis were exaggerated. The other major area of work was developing the front wing, in particular at high ride-heights to improve our slow-speed corner performance, which was RB5's main end-of-season weakness.

One area I had not been happy with over the previous years was the exhaust outlet position. Exiting the exhaust into the diffuser was one of the practices that had been banned to reduce performance after Imola 1994, and since 2001 everybody had converged on top exits through the upper bodywork to blow the beam wing, the lower of the two rear-wing sets. This gave some downforce, but the effect was relatively small.

With the double diffuser, there was the opportunity to exit the exhaust low down into the side of the upper diffuser without it being seen from below and therefore contravening the rules. This was a further big step in the wind tunnel.

On paper, the downforce was immense. Even if you went back to the original sliding-skirt ground-effect cars of the 1970s, the RB6 created more downforce than those; i.e. the most in Formula One history. This meant that Mark could take quick corners, like Copse at Silverstone – corners that previously would involve a change down a gear and a big lift, maybe even a brake – flat-out in top gear. We were up around 5G, the highest G a car's ever pulled.

But it didn't start smoothly. We went to the first test with the car in Jerez in the south of Spain, but it kept destroying the rear tyres, even on quite short runs. Mark said, 'It feels very nervous at the rear; I can't control the back of the car.'

By now, we were starting to put pressure taps on the car and we could see that some of them were dropping out at the points where Mark said he was getting oversteer from the back. Yet again, it was that awful feeling and something of a recurring theme when you realise that, yes, you've produced a car that in the wind tunnel had lots of downforce, but on the track is unstable.

We had our theories, though. Peter Prod was there at the test with me and Peter's very good in situations like that, very methodical, so we sat down and started to think, *Okay, what's causing these instabilities?*

There were a few things we were a bit worried about when we were developing them, in particular a trend copied from other teams of curling up the edges of the floor along the side of the car, which generates local downforce through camber in the same way that a wing does. However,

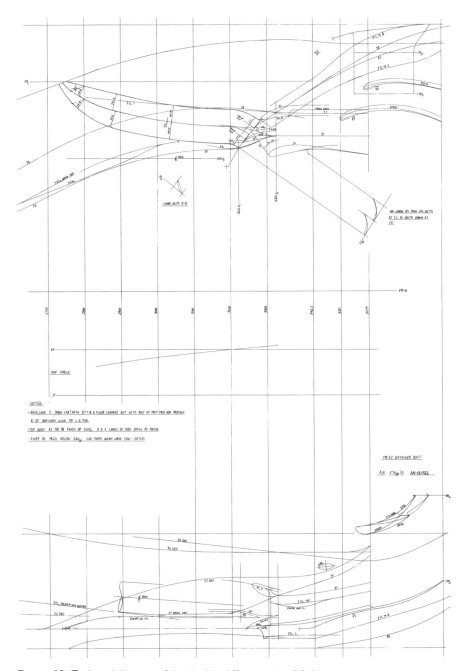

Figure 19: Technical drawing of the double diffuser on the RB6.

that local load comes with associated losses to the total pressure of the air flowing to the rear of the car. We could see in CFD that those losses were ending up in the rear-wheel squish area, potentially destabilising the diffuser.

Over those two days at Jerez we worked through a programme of removing the two curls along the side of the floor and then playing with trims beside the rear tyre. By the end of that second day, the car was behaving as intended: we weren't getting these dropouts on the pressure taps and Mark was reporting that the car now felt like a high-downforce version of the RB5, which is what it was meant to be.

It was a huge relief. I must admit that when we saw the pressure-tap dropouts, it was a head-in-the-hands moment, thinking, *Oh my God, we had this great season last year; we've now overcooked it and we've got a turkey – think 891, FW16, MP4 18.*

However, a good two days of methodical work and we'd managed to solve the problem. The advent of maturity of CFD to the point that we could now use it as a key tool for understanding the complicated flow structures around the car, coupled with the use of pressure taps on the car to understand which areas were misbehaving on the track compared to what our tools – the wind tunnel and CFD – said, was vital in this analytical detective work. Had those clues from the CFD and pressure taps been available for the above-mentioned problem children, then we would have got on top of them much quicker, but in those days the resource and computing power required was not available. Conversely, had they not been available and used hard by us in 2010, then maybe RB6 would have gone down in the history books as another tricky car.

CHAPTER 70

By now, Mercedes had bought out Brawn, so the Brawn cars that had been so dominant the year before were painted silver, in the colour of Mercedes.

However, they didn't look that competitive in pre-season, so we were looking at Ferrari and McLaren as our main rivals and thinking we probably had a pace advantage over them. In fact, our car was competitive to the point that I deliberately chose to run it with a bit of extra ballast and fuel in order to make ourselves look slow. I was worried that the FIA might find a way of restricting us, and I didn't particularly want to attract the extra attention you get with a fast car. If people think you're quick, they'll spend time looking at your car. If you look slow, they walk straight past. In fact to help the disguise, our paint shop, under the management of Dave Quinn, had even painted dummy exhausts onto the top body in the conventional outlet position for the press launch.

The season began in March of that year, 2010. At around the same time, the marriage to Marigold broke down – very sad. Up until that time, I'd always felt that if home life was going badly, work life went badly too. This year, however, proved the exception to that rule. I threw myself even more fully into my work. My drawing board became my safe haven.

Bahrain, meanwhile, the first race of the season, gave us mixed fortunes. I felt quietly confident of the pace of the car, but knew we still had a few rough edges. Sure enough, Sebastian took pole and in the race led until lap 33, when the car started misfiring on seven cylinders with a broken spark plug. From what had been a commanding lead, we finished with Sebastian fourth and Mark eighth, which was pretty galling.

What we noticed through practice in Australia was that wheel nuts were starting to work loose. We didn't have enough bearing area between the brake disk bell and the flange of the wheel itself, so if you overtightened the nuts this would start to collapse the magnesium wheel. We also had problems with drive pegs that were sticking proud of the wheel face. It caught us out in the race. After locking out the front row of the grid in qualifying, the wheel nut worked its way loose during the race and that was that – Sebastian retired, Mark was ninth.

All our own fault. It was a mistake in design; we'd had the warning signs in testing but failed to take appropriate action. It was an example where, yes, we thought we'd fixed it, but we hadn't properly stood back and understood the problem, so it caught us out. We were showing that, while we'd now managed to produce a quick car, we still had much to do in terms of being an all-round great team able to field a car that was reliable and fit for purpose.

Equally, from the pit wall, our strategy wasn't as sharp as it could have been. When you're on the pit wall, you've been doing a thousand and one other things throughout the week; you're now trying to make decisions with very little time, often with limited information in a harsh, noisy environment. As a result, you're prone to error.

What we needed was better tools and better backup to try and make better decisions. First and foremost that meant developing new software tools. To this end we had hired a young gaming expert, Will Courtenay, to write programmes. I think we were one of the first people to start using these tools – Monte Carlo Gaming Theory was one of them – but in 2010, at that stage of the season, they were still in their infancy.

For Malaysia we had a new suspension idea to try: the aerodynamics of a Formula One car with its big front wing close to the ground mean that it is aerodynamically much more sensitive to front ride-height than rear. The closer you can get the front wing to the ground, the more efficient the car becomes, which means running the car as low as possible. But even with the very stiff front suspension that we run, the ride-height in the pit lane would be around 30mm, reducing to 7mm at an end of straight as the plank brushes along the tarmac.

Many years beforehand, while I was still at McLaren, it had occurred to me that if we longitudinally linked the bump side of the rear suspension to the droop side of the front suspension using actuators in series with the central heave springs, then we could have an arrangement where for say every 10mm that the rear went into bump, it would push the front up 3mm, allowing a much lower static front ride-height. We started work on it at McLaren, but it didn't really work because the rear ride-height sensitivity on the 2005 car was still too high.

However, the RB6 had a very benign rear ride-height characteristic, but, thanks to the big front wings allowed by the 2009 regulations, a very steep front characteristic. So I resurrected the idea and our vehicle dynamics team did a super job of modelling it in simulation, then on the driver-in-the-loop simulator.

Now we faced a dilemma. If we declared this system – which later became known as FRIC (front-rear interconnected suspension) – was aimed at improving the aerodynamics, it would be declared illegal in the same way as active suspension was banned. Fortunately, the system also reduced the pitch stiffness of the suspension system, improving the ride. Thus its prime purpose became ride improvement, which the FIA accepted. As a footnote, after many other teams adopted it, it was banned at the end of 2014 because its primary purpose was considered aerodynamic!

Whatever the motive, we got it on the car for Malaysia, which, combined with the natural pace of the car, gave us a front-row lock-out and, at last, a trouble-free run to a 1–2 finish.

In China, again, we qualified first and second. The race itself was wet and we didn't play the conditions well. Result: a pretty poor sixth and eighth. For Spain we had a big update with a new diffuser, new exhausts, new bargeboards, new beam wing and new rear brake duct wings.

The effort from all departments was outstanding, with long shifts seven days a week at the factory and then an all-nighter on Thursday by the mechanics, getting the parts on the car. The wind tunnel results tied in well with the car once it hit the track, Mark rewarding us with pole on a time that was 0.9sec clear of Hamilton in third, Seb being second. In the race, Mark disappeared to claim a dominant victory, with Sebastian earning a very lucky podium place in third. Lucky because, with him lying in third place and with 12 laps to go, a front brake disc disintegrated, chunks of carbon and dust coming out of the wheel, but the failure occurred at a part of the circuit where there was enough run-off to avoid an accident. We brought him in, changed tyres and the mechanics had a quick look at the brake duct 'cake tin', the ducting that covers the brake disc, but could see nothing wrong (the brake disc itself is not really visible with the cake tin in place) so sent him on his way again.

We had no way of knowing from the data what had happened other than that brake pressures and travels looked normal; the left front brake disc infrared temperature sensor showed only ambient temperature. This was one of those horrible safety vs results situations. Do we instruct Seb to retire the car or do we risk safety by continuing to race in the hope of scoring points? In the end, I took the decision that we should continue, Seb necessarily braking early on corners because he had only three working brakes. Ultimately, of course, it was his choice to retire the car if he wished to.

After we got the car back from *parc ferm*é we were able to see that the brake disc had shattered, but luckily a quadrant of disc remained between the pads, preventing the pads and pistons from falling out, with the attendant loss of brake fluid.

We got away with it, but I was mightily relieved when Seb crossed the finish line. As it turned out, those 15 points were vital for the championship ...

Monaco was a much less stressful race. Mark did a superb job in qualifying to stick it on pole, with Sebastian third. In the race, Mark commanded from the front while Sebastian managed to pass Kubica: our first Monaco victory and a one–two at that. As you can imagine, that was a very sweet victory indeed.

For Monaco, Red Bull had decided, in typically OTT fashion, that rather than simply having a motor home they would build a huge floating pontoon, which they'd store in the Alps for most of the year but dock in the harbour for the Monaco weekend. On top of the pontoon went the 'Energy Station', a three-storey structure that required 21 days of build in Imperia in Italy (40 miles up the coast from Monaco) and two days of set-up in Monaco before it was operational. Around 70 people were involved in constructing the platform over three weeks.

It's become a regular sight at Monaco and really is quite spectacular, a great place to entertain guests and sponsors. Does it justify the money?

That's for them to decide, but what it does do is provide us with a big party area, and when you win, as we did that year, then it really *is* a party. To the side of the energy station they have a swimming pool and after that win we all celebrated by jumping in, after which Mark and Sebastian grabbed hold of each other, linked hands and leapt into the harbour, a three-storey drop.

The next race, Istanbul, was a reversal in fortunes. No doubt about it – jumping into the harbour would be the last time Mark and Sebastian held hands.

CHAPTER 71

We were top of the constructors' championship for the first time that year, with Mark leading the drivers' from Sebastian.

At Istanbul, Mark had qualified on pole, with Sebastian third. In the race they got off in grid order, Mark leading, Hamilton in the McLaren behind him and then Sebastian, the three running round nose to tail like a high-speed train.

Sebastian managed to get past Hamilton in the pit-stops and then went for a move on Mark, got a good run on him, was past, and next tried to cut to the outside to get his line for the following left-hand corner.

And the two of them collided.

It was an unnecessary move to the right on Sebastian's part. Some people questioned whether Mark could have missed him. Either way, Seb was out of the race, and while Mark continued he was damaged and ended up finishing third, with McLaren first and second.

Two teammates colliding always brings problems within the team, but it was escalated to near anarchy by Dr Helmut Marko, who, on camera, jumped to the defence of his protégé, Sebastian, saying it was Mark's fault, no debate. The two drivers started blaming each other; a war of words ensued. Christian and I were caught trying to manage the damage behind the scenes, while publicly there is no doubt it was handled very badly.

From then on, Mark and Sebastian's relationship was strained. It also highlighted to Mark the fact that Helmut was pro-Sebastian, and he let that fact rile him. As far as I was concerned, I treated them both equally, but I admit I was not involved in all the operational details of things like engine and parts allocation. For a driver, psychology within the team is important; on the other hand, there's no point wasting energy on things you can't change. Mark, with his partner Ann, perhaps started spending too much time worrying about Helmut and Sebastian; understandable in many ways, but also, potentially, self-harming. To succeed in F1 you need total focus. Leaving unnecessary baggage completely behind you when you get in the car is something very few drivers, if any, can do.

Montreal, I didn't go to. I felt I needed to be putting some time into the development of the RB7. As it was, we made a tactical error by trying to be too clever with our tyre choice in qualifying and rather handed the victory to Hamilton, with Mark and Sebastian second and third respectively.

At Valencia, Helmut, diplomatic as ever, approached Mark in practice and said, 'Mark, you're always shit at Valencia; will this year be any different?' which is not really the best way to motivate a driver.

Indeed, Mark had a bad start. Valencia's a street circuit and, as with Monaco, that makes overtaking difficult, so we decided to call him in for an early first stop in the hope that he could get some clear air, run fast and undercut the cars in front.

He came out just behind Kovalainen in the Lotus. Kovalainen was slow but in no mind to let Mark past. Mark hustled, coming up behind him and expecting him to brake at about the same place that Mark would normally brake. Instead, Kovalainen braked probably 50m earlier, a result of the difference in braking performance between Lotus and our car, and it caught Mark out. If Mark had been following Kovalainen to one side instead of being right behind him, it wouldn't have been a problem – Mark would have overtaken him. But at that point Mark was still slipstreaming, ready to pull out and not expecting Heikki to brake so early.

If the driver in front gets on the brakes in that situation, the closing speed between the two cars is huge. Mark went into the back of Kovalainen, slightly to one side, his front wheel climbed the rear wheel of Kovalainen's car and launched him high into the air.

I didn't see any of this. I had my head down looking at lap times when I felt Christian grab my right arm. I thought, *Christian, that's a bit familiar, what's going on?*

I looked up to see Christian's face ghostly white, and then on the screen saw Mark sliding towards the barrier backwards at high speed. Only afterwards did I see quite how much air he got.

It was a big accident. Luckily Mark was unhurt because the car landed without going off into the crowds, another car or the bridge over the circuit (the latter being quite close). About the only undamaged part left of the car was the steering wheel, and Mark, in a fit of anger and disgust, threw it to the floor, breaking that as well. I guess he had Helmut's words ringing in his ears as he did that.

One trend that had started to emerge during the season was a move among several of our rivals to place the regulation nose cameras between the wing pylons just above the regulation neutral central portion of the front wing. Copying this, we found in CFD and the wind tunnel that it gave a lot of extra downforce from the front wing but this also produced a lot of associated wake, damaging the flow to the floor. CFD and the tunnel disagreed over the impact of this, the former saying the damage outweighed the benefit, the latter the opposite. Since it was a relatively simple manufacturing task to move the cameras from the tip of the nose down to the new position, I elected to make it a test item for the next race, Silverstone.

To this end, two spare nose assemblies were prepared, but a problem with the nose fixing on Seb's car meant that the nose dropped and destroyed his assembly before Seb had completed a single lap with it. Mark tested the other assembly but did not like it in the first practice session, this assembly then being swapped to Seb's car for the second one. Seb was noncommittal, but subsequent analysis back at the factory did show the new assembly to be slightly up in overall aero load.

Keen to gather more data to understand why Mark didn't like it, I asked Ciaron Pilbeam, Mark's race engineer, on Saturday morning whether he intended to use it again that weekend. Ciaron said no, he had no further interest in it, so I asked Rocky, Seb's race engineer, to fit it for qualifying.

In qualifying, Seb edged Mark for pole, a front-row lock-out in the home race. The race brought a reverse of fortunes, Seb, making a poor start from pole, was too aggressive into the first corner trying to defend against Hamilton and got a puncture, which dropped him to the tail of the field. After that, Mark had a relatively easy cruise to victory, with Sebastian recovering through the field to finish a fairly distant seventh.

Unfortunately the sweetness of that second consecutive home race victory was somewhat dulled when Mark came on the radio on his victory lap in reply to Christian's congratulations to say, 'Yeah mate, not bad for a number two driver.' Mark was incensed that Seb had been given 'his' assembly, despite the fact he didn't want it. Possibly I am an insensitive engineer, but for me the interest is in developing and understanding the car, so if one of the drivers doesn't want it – give it to the other. What I didn't anticipate was the snowball effect that would result. The press had a field day with Mark's radio message; things were getting very fractious. It was such a shame, because I have the greatest respect for Mark as a driver, a person and as the guy who had been so important through his feedback for the development of the cars.

The championship was tight, very much a five-horse race between our two guys, the two McLaren drivers and Alonso in the Ferrari. In Germany, Sebastian qualified on pole, Mark fourth. In the race, Ferrari picked up bad PR for deploying team orders in a move that allowed Alonso to win from his teammate Massa but saw them fined $100,000. Sebastian and Mark came in third and sixth respectively.

Hungary, Mark won and Sebastian was third after incurring a silly penalty for dropping too far back from the safety car while leading, which handed Mark the lead in the drivers' championship.

Spa, Mark qualified on pole but had a problem at the start that left him in seventh at the end of the first lap. He recovered well to finish second, while Sebastian made an error of judgement and crashed into Button, eliminating the pair of them. Very frustrating. We had the fastest car but we kept throwing points away.

Monza is all about horsepower along the straights, which was not our strength. Thus, in what was basically a damage-limitation exercise, Sebastian finished fourth, Mark sixth, which was about as good as we could hope for.

The next race was our maiden visit to Singapore – an interesting place. When you drive from the airport to the hotel you get to a gold and glitzy roundabout that has a big sign on it saying, 'The Fountain of Wealth' – the name of the roundabout. They have a culture that appears to openly worship money. The country is very clean, very green, and the fans are extraordinarily enthusiastic.

As for the circuit, it's a bumpy street track, bumpier than Monaco but not dissimilar in as much as cars race between walls with very little margin for error. I must admit, I like the street circuits. I think they have more character than what you might call the 'clean sheet of paper' circuits that have cropped up in recent years. Those all feel very formulaic and lacking in character, but I guess that's what you get when Bernie always uses the same architect to design them.

Sebastian got to grips with this new circuit quickly and was the fastest through practice. We were struggling a bit, though, with the handling on such a bumpy track, and one of the things I realised was that when the car was going too high in rebound over the bumps we were actually losing a lot of downforce because we were going outside the operating window of the car.

Realising that, we ran the rear lower, which stabilised the car, and going into qualifying we were quietly confident of getting pole. In the event, I think maybe we were a bit too complacent, and Alonso managed to put together a remarkable lap to nab pole. From there he won the race, leaving Sebastian and Mark to take second and third, faster than Alonso but unable to overtake.

On to Suzuka, Japan, which is one of the classics, a high-speed track with very challenging corners, a scene of some great battles and one of the circuits I most enjoy visiting, not least because of the passion of the Japanese fans. You'll arrive at the circuit in the morning to see fans already sitting in the grandstand. Long after the race, when our boys are getting the cars ready to be crated for the next race, fans will still be sitting in the grandstand, intently watching the boys pack the cars up.

And yet, funnily, enough, the Japanese have never really provided the sport with great competitors, be it drivers or chassis designers. Why is that, you ask? I think for a Japanese team it's quite difficult, because they're based so far away from the hub of motorsport, which is the UK.

Most Formula One teams are in the UK and that becomes self-feeding, because if the teams are there, all the specialist suppliers tend to grow up around them. In terms of workforce, poaching people from another team becomes easier, because they probably don't even have to move house if they're living around Oxfordshire. It's one of the reasons why Toyota, based in Germany, struggled. Sauber in Switzerland, the same problem. If you've grown up and lived in England, you probably aren't going to want to go and live in Cologne or just outside Zurich.

I think Ferrari get away with it because there's a passion associated with the name and most people think of Italy as being a nice country to live in, even if they're English.

Back to Suzuka, what made it a stressful weekend was the high-speed nature of the circuit and the fact that there are saw-tooth kerbs on the exit of the high-speed corners. As I mentioned earlier, we had pursued a high rake set-up to get the front wing closer to the ground, but here that route meant that the endplates of the front wing and the front-wing structure were getting a huge hammering over the kerbs.

A second factor was aeroelastics. Aeroelastics is a term used to describe how an aerodynamic shape such as a wing deforms under load due to the flexing of the structure that forms it. Look out of the window of a passenger aircraft when you take off or hit turbulence and you will see the wing flexing – the tip of a Boeing 747 wing deflects over 6m at full gust loading.

We had been playing with aeroelastics in various areas of the car through the year, in particular the front wing to get the endplates closer to the ground in high-speed corners, but for Suzuka it was too close.

Paul Monaghan and I spent most of the weekend trying to strengthen and stiffen them to ensure they were safe for the race. The solution was to add carbon cleats, which the boys did a superb job of making in the field, using carbon cloth and resin. For the race, the drivers, having locked out the front row, were under strict instructions to stay off the exit curves of the high-speed corners to give the wings a chance of surviving.

As a result it was one of the more nerve-racking races for me on the pit wall, because I knew we had the performance to win but could we make it to the end of the race without the front wings falling apart? Could we manage the drivers to make sure they didn't start racing each other too much? Both of them had their eye on the championship, so the rivalry was intense. In the event, Mark pushed Seb all the way but, with radio reminders every time we saw one of them go over the exit kerbs in the critical areas, they both behaved. I was mightily relieved when they crossed the line one–two.

Post-race, the steadily rising 'Red Bull must be cheating' movement among our rivals reached a crescendo. People had either not understood or not known about our P Spring system (front-rear interconnected suspension); they simply observed that we were able to run a very low static front ride-height and therefore assumed we must be cheating. And the circuit TV footage of our front wing oscillating wildly over the kerbs in practice had been widely broadcast, so we must be cheating with that as well.

In the end, the FIA measured our front wing again and pronounced it legal (as they had done at every race) and themselves happy with our suspension system.

After Suzuka we were in good spirits. There was no point going straight to Korea, so we spent a couple of days in Tokyo. We ended up going for a big meal with the marketing team and Chaleo Yoovidhya, the 50 per cent Thai owner of Red Bull.

Chaleo hosted the dinner with his wife, Daranee, then we all went off to a whiskey bar. By now, I must admit, I'd had a few too many glasses of saké, and DC was there, always a bad influence. A girl in motorcycle leathers arrived, we got talking and I rather disgraced myself by dipping pineapple chunks into the 1958 glass of Scotch I'd been given (Chaleo had asked the year of my birth and bought the bottle – God knows how much it cost) and feeding them to this girl.

After that, things became hazy. At one point I was in a hotel room with biker girl (though nothing happened, and I later found out she was Chaleo's niece, so that's just as well), when DC turned up with a bottle of champagne, Christian, Martin Brundle and DC who'd all been standing in the corridor, it turned out, with a glass pressed against the door listening to activities!

From there, having drunk the champagne, biker girl and I re-joined the group in a nightclub, after which things got a little hazy – I can't quite remember all the details. What I can recall is waking up the next morning and there being a traffic cone in the room with me. How did it get there? Pass.

The next day, very hung-over, we flew to Korea, so we took the cone, giving it its own seat on the plane. The boys in the garage stickered it, gave it a paddock pass and it became our mascot for the rest of the campaign. Though not a lucky one in Korea.

The track in Korea was new, but being of the formulaic variety was nothing you could get terribly excited about. We were very quick and qualified first and second.

The race itself was wet at the start. It kept being delayed because of just how hard it was raining. It eventually got under way with a safety car and when that peeled in Sebastian started pulling away from Mark, who, in turn, was leaving the rest of the field behind.

To me, this was where Mark's intense rivalry boiled over; he was so determined to try and stay with Sebastian and beat him in the wet that he overdrove the car, lost control and span, hit the barrier, and that was that for him – in fact, he was lucky not to get hurt when Rosberg was unable to avoid him and slammed into the side.

The race was red flagged while they cleared up the mess; they got going again and Sebastian disappeared off into what should have been an easy win until, with about 10 laps to go, we saw lots of flames and smoke coming out of the exhaust. His engine had blown up.

It was a low point. Fernando went on to win and now had an 11-point lead over Mark, with Sebastian trailing in fourth, 25 points behind.

The ifs and buts of motor racing: if Mark hadn't crashed he would have had a 21-point lead, if Seb's engine hadn't blown he would have had a seven-point lead.

Going into Brazil, the penultimate race, there was a lot of politicking going on. Logically, Mark had a better chance of winning the drivers' championship, and therefore Mark's camp felt that team orders should be invoked: e.g. if the order was Sebastian first and Mark second, we should reverse it to allow Mark to win and keep his championship hopes alive, because Sebastian was too far back to be in with a realistic shout at winning it.

Sebastian, of course, had other ideas. He was still in with a mathematical chance of winning and thus wanted to keep racing as competitively as possible. As you might imagine, these background politics rumbled on throughout the race weekend, which wasn't ideal preparation – and, as ever, Christian and I were caught in the middle. In reality we had little choice but to respect Seb's position, therefore our stance was let them race as long as the running order left Seb with a mathematical chance in Abu Dhabi.

Brazil, with its broad mixture of corners, was a circuit well suited to our cars, so it was a matter of going out and doing the best job we could. Fortunately, on the track, the weekend itself was relatively straightforward. The cars were quick, qualified first and second on the grid, and had a clear advantage in the race.

It panned out as we suspected it might, with Sebastian leading, Mark second; team orders were not invoked, so that was how it finished. With hindsight, you can imagine the hammering we would have got and the negative publicity Red Bull would have received had we somehow (illegally) invoked team orders and got them to swap positions.

The exciting news was that, despite the politics between our drivers, we had sealed our first constructors' championship, sweet reward for all the hard work and dedication shown by everybody throughout the team. For me personally it was also quite something. I'd won championships with Williams and McLaren, but to take such a big gamble on a little 'fizzy drinks' company'-owned team, the joke of the pit lane, and help steer it to a constructors' victory was a very, very sweet success indeed.

That said, I probably didn't fully savour it at the time, because having got this close, we wanted to score the double.

We organised an impromptu championship celebration party in a strange country-house-turned-nightclub somewhere in the suburbs of São Paulo, to which Christian and I were late arriving. We couldn't find the entrance, so we wandered around the back and saw our boys behind metal crowd barriers, drinking champagne. As we both climbed over, a bunch of ape-like Brazilian bouncers appeared to stop us getting in.

I said, 'Come on, this is our party, don't be ridiculous,' but you know what bouncers are like; they weren't having any of it. First they picked up Christian around his middle and turfed him back over the metal barrier as a dog would do with its puppy, then they made a move on me. I must have been feeling punchy because I put my fists up, Marquess of Queensbury rules, and said, 'Absolutely not, you're not picking me up', which was probably wasted as I somehow doubt English was their strong point. Luckily for me at that moment, the Renault mechanics arrived behind us, shouted 'Adrian is in trouble' in their heavy French accents and jumped the barrier to surround me. For a moment it looked like it was going to be a re-enactment of the recent riots in Paris until Christian said, 'Come on Adrian, let's go.' We both decided that discretion was the better (or safer) part of valour. I climbed back over the barrier and that was that – a celebration party to which we were denied entry. Our championship celebration was a quiet drink in the lounge at the airport.

From there, Christian and I flew to Dubai, being only an hour's drive from Abu Dhabi, and stayed in a hotel on the beach for a few days – a funny break in which we felt in limbo, awaiting our fate at the last race.

Abu Dhabi is a night race, and one of the quirks of that is that the first and third practice sessions are in the heat of the day and bear little or no resemblance to how the car's going to perform in qualifying or the race. The race starts at dusk and goes into darkness, and with the much cooler track temperatures the tyres behave completely differently. Being a desert circuit, it's dusty and dirty on the first day, but crowd-wise it has an easy-going, party atmosphere.

This time, the politics of the race were simple. For Sebastian to win the championship he needed to win the race with Fernando fifth or lower; for Mark he needed to win the race with Fernando third or lower, etc.

Abu Dhabi is characterised by two very long straights and in practice we'd been suffering a bit on those compared to some of our competitors. In the race itself, Sebastian managed to get away in the lead from pole, with Mark, who'd qualified a relatively poor fifth, maintaining that spot through the early part of the race.

Fernando was in third and, if it stayed that way, he was going to win the championship.

We had to do something. Mark was stuck behind Button and unable to overtake, so we decided to pit him early and put him on a different strategy to see if he could undercut the cars in front.

Ferrari were obsessed by Mark as being their main challenger, and maybe forgetting that Sebastian also had a chance to win the championship, decided to cover our pit-stop with Mark and brought Alonso in, too, to make sure they kept Fernando ahead of Mark.

A huge mistake on their part, I'm happy to say. We only did that out of desperation with Mark and it didn't really work: Mark eventually finished eighth, so in fact our strategy actually lost him places, rather than gaining them. It wasn't deliberate, it wasn't designed to do that, it was just a roll of the dice. There was no point in sitting where we were with Mark – we had to try something.

But Ferrari's slight panic in covering Mark meant that Alonso also went backwards, and so instead of Fernando being in third and winning the championship, he was stuck down in seventh and not going to win as long as Seb kept going in the lead.

In truth, we all thought that, with the long straights, Alonso and Mark would start to make progress back up the field, but Vitaly Petrov in the Renault drove the defensive race of his life and kept Alonso behind him. To our amazement, Alonso got stuck, dropping further and further behind and finding himself powerless to get past Petrov.

Sebastian's race engineer, Rocky, came on the radio as Sebastian crossed the line, saying, 'Congratulations, you've won the race . . .'

And then he counted down as each driver crossed the line: Hamilton second, Button third, Rosberg fourth, Kubica fifth, Petrov sixth . . .

'Sebastian, you are world champion.'

It still makes me feel emotional, even now. It was an against-all-odds final race. Truth be told, though, despite us having easily the fastest car that year, we had made winning the drivers' championship harder work than it should have been through a mixture of reliability mistakes, strategy mistakes and indeed errors on the part of both drivers.

Afterwards came a feeling of disbelief. I remember sitting on one of the packing boxes behind the garage shortly after the race. Kenny, our chief mechanic, who'd been fantastic across the years, invariably displaying a positive can-do attitude, came to find me. I very rarely smoke, but if we've won a race and I'm trying to wind down, then I do, so it was great to see him come round the corner with two cigarettes, one for himself and one for me. We sat there for an hour, feeling slightly emotional and watching the clock tick by to see if we were going to get a protest from Ferrari or not.

We didn't. Instead we staggered back to the hotel, where there was an impromptu party in one of the function rooms. Christian and I were flying to Austria, where they'd made it known that they wanted Christian, me, Helmut and the drivers to take part in a victory parade, so we knew we had to leave the airport about five or six the following morning.

Once again, when Christian and I tried to get into our party, we were turned away by the bouncers on the door only this time we said, 'That's it,' and the pair of us rushed the bouncers, pushed past them and finally got into our own party. The team drink is Jägerbombs, Jägermeister and Red Bull, and I can assure you it results in a stinking hangover.

I felt for Mark on the flight; it must have been awful for him to sit on that private plane, heading back to Austria with the rest of us to celebrate what, for him, was a loss. It's a testament to his sense of duty that he did; I'm not sure I would have.

Anyway, we got to the Abu Dhabi airport, met Sebastian, whose big celebration was to treat himself to a McDonald's – apparently he'd been

The joy and relief of landing the double, with Christian in Abu Dhabi, 2010.

craving one for the whole season, but his training didn't allow it – then flew to Salzburg, back to Hangar 7, to be greeted by a brass band, a red carpet and a very, very happy Dietrich.

Later we were presented with the trophy, which went in our cabinet in the reception area at Milton Keynes.

Therein lies a tale. Initially, we'd put up a set of shelves for the trophies, but Helmut rightly decided that the reception area was looking scruffy and needed revamping. While all that was going on, there was a period of about two months when the area was closed, which meant that late at night, for security reasons, the only way out from my office to the car park was a long walk to the other end of the factory, a good 10-minute trot.

One particular night I walked down to reception, which had all the yellow criss-cross tape across it saying *no entry*, etc.

Being nosy, I ducked past the criss-cross tape, into reception and noticed that they'd installed glass doors.

I thought, *Hm, I'll just see if these sliding doors work.*

Sure enough, they did. From there I could see a vestibule with pieces of wood nailed across it. However, there was a gap in the wood, which I thought I could just about squeeze through. I did that, and was congratulating myself on avoiding the long walk, when . . . *boof* – the piece of hardboard on which I'd been standing collapsed under my weight, sending me plummeting 5ft down into a pit below.

Well, I thought, as I threw my briefcase back over the top, then climbed sheepishly out of the hole, shook myself off and walked to the car, *at least nobody saw*.

Or so I thought. At the Christmas party that year, Christian broadcast the CCTV footage to the entire team.

Served me right for mucking up his lawn.

Turn Eleven

HOW TO BUILD
AN RB8

CHAPTER 72

The FIA now performed a U-turn. They're very good at those. They said that in fact, on second thoughts, now they'd come to think about it double diffusers *do* give too much downforce, so they were going to ban them for 2011.

That was announced in the spring of 2010, and came in the form of stringent new regulations banning the hole in the floor. Now the challenge was how to claw back some of the downforce these regulation restrictions would impose.

How? Well, the side exhaust blowing into the double diffuser on the RB6 had proved effective, and the drivers could feel the extra downforce from the exhaust system when it blew hard on the exit of low-speed corners. Using that seemed a way we might be able to recover some of the lost downforce.

At the same time, we knew that, in theory, increasing the rake of the car, i.e. raising the rear ride-height, would give more downforce as it turns the whole of the flat floor into a gentle diffuser as well as lowering the front wing. The problem is that the tyre-squish area and the loss that the dirty jet of air from it causes, becomes more and more difficult to manage the higher the ride-height.

So I thought if we could arrange the exhaust system in such a way that it was pointing in the rough direction of the tyre squish, that could be a way of trying to manage it by having very high-energy exhaust gas blowing down and back into this low-energy squish area.

The problem is that with the ride-heights we were targeting in low-speed corners, when squish really becomes a problem, the rear of the car is around 100mm above the ground. That means you somehow have to get the exhaust floor to drop that 100mm or so. That became the main focus of our work through the summer and autumn of 2010 researching the RB7. In short, how do we get this exhaust flow down into the contact patch area?

The answer was through lots of detailed work on the shape of the exhaust outlet and careful optimisation of the surrounding bodywork, especially the vortex-creating fence on top of the floor, first introduced on the RB5, together with a much larger nose but highly cambered wings mounted to the brake ducts: all of this was aimed at getting a shallow but wide jet of exhaust gas to be manipulated through a downwash flow field into the squish area. Once we got it working, the downforce gains were absolutely huge, to the point that with the exhaust blowing hard we were back up towards where we'd been with the double diffuser in low-speed corners.

To maximise that effect, what we needed was for the exhaust to be blowing all the time. Normally, of course, as the driver brakes, changes down and enters the corner, he's completely off throttle and there's next to no exhaust flow coming out of the back, which means that in that critical

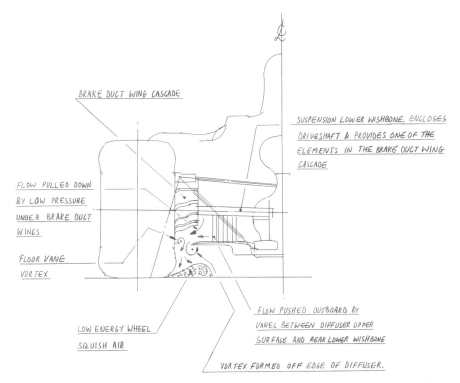

Figure 20: Extensive work on the shape of the exhaust outlet and careful optimisation of the surrounding bodywork provided a good solution to the 2011 ban on double diffusers.

braking-and-entry phase you're not getting effective downforce from the exhaust – when you most need it. What you ideally want is for the exhaust to be working hard, not only on corner exit, which it does naturally, but also on corner entry.

Back in 1994, when I was at Williams and we last had exhausts blowing the diffuser, I had approached Bernard Dudot, technical director at Renault, to ask him whether it would be possible to keep the throttle open around the lap and regulate the power in some other way, e.g. with spark cut to individual cylinders and ignition timing. Bernard's team had started development work on this idea, but when blown diffusers were banned in the aftermath of Imola the project was scrapped.

Seventeen years later, I asked Renault, now under the technical leadership of Rob White, to relaunch the project. While the Renault V8 was less powerful than the Mercedes, in this area they did a superb job of blending cylinder cut, ignition timing and throttle position to give what became known as 'hot-blowing'. It was the key to our success in that 2011 season.

Ferrari put their exhaust in a similar place, just in front of the rear wheel, but didn't appear to get as much out of the system as we did; McLaren had come up with an incredibly complicated exhaust system trying to achieve a similar thing, which, frankly, just didn't work, and having struggled through pre-season testing, they then did a depressingly fast job of simply copying our exhaust and having it on the car for Melbourne, overnight making them very competitive.

The other regulation change for 2011 was to reintroduce KERS.

If you recall, KERS had been allowed in 2009, though very few teams had run it before it was banned altogether in 2010. The FIA performed another of their famous U-turns and decided to legalise it again, the reason being that the whole issue of energy recovery was very big in road cars at the time, and the FIA like to be seen as being in the vanguard of that.

Despite a chequered relationship with KERS in 2009, most of the teams had in the meantime worked out that if you could install it in such a way that it didn't put the car over the weight limit and didn't compromise the aerodynamics or weight distribution, there was a reasonable lap-time benefit to be had.

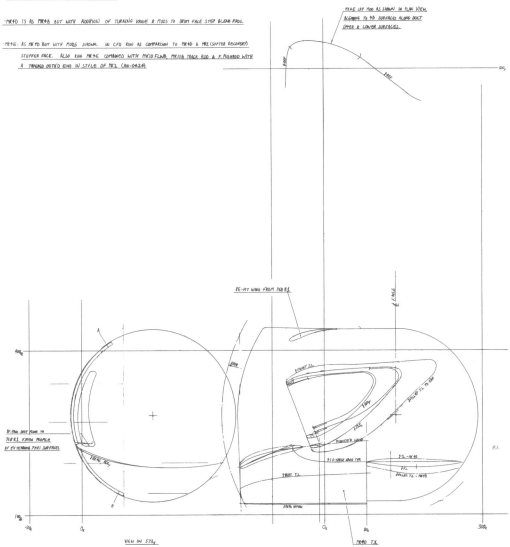

Figure 21: Technical drawing of the brake duct and the associated wing on the RB8.

Not only that, but it could be of strategic benefit in terms of start-line performance, and if you didn't have it, relative to a car that did, you'd probably lose two places off the grid. Also, in the race it could be used strategically to help overtaking.

All those attractions meant that just about every team reintroduced KERS on their cars, including us. We knew we could keep the car just about underweight with it, but we needed to install the batteries in a way that didn't compromise the aerodynamics.

This led to the solution of putting the batteries between the engine and gearbox that I described in Chapter 2, an ambitious challenge but one that offered significant aero performance if we could make it reliable.

It took a while. We got the KERS on the car but it gave us reliability problems in those early races. Often it would start to overheat during the race, or the vibration would give us electrical connection problems. The engineers were cursing me, and everybody along the pit lane knew we were struggling to make it reliable – they could hear us on the radio having to tell our drivers to disable KERS and finish the race without it.

The silver lining was our new exhaust system. The amount of performance it gave us meant that even if we lost KERS during races we had enough of a performance benefit to still win the race. Had we not had that exhaust, it would have been a much more dubious call on my part, but the inherent aerodynamic benefit we got from now having this very narrow rear was around a quarter of a second in itself.

It wasn't initially a runaway season. McLaren, in particular, gave us a hard time, and we also had quite a few issues trying to get the exhaust system reliable and managing the exhaust temperatures – keeping it from cracking and breaking was a challenge. Often, we ran more conservative engine maps in the race than in qualifying to preserve the exhaust pipe life and we got into quite a development programme on our exhaust materials, which are made from Inconel. This is a material originally developed by the US military for the tail wire hooks on naval jet fighters. As an industry we don't tend to be inventors of new materials, but we are very good at using them aggressively, and this was an example of that practice at work. It's funny how things have changed. If you go back to the 1950s and 1960s, things like disc brakes were developed in motorsport and found their way onto road cars. Features such as that do not make the leap from track to road these days. Instead, motorsport is used by big engineering companies, particularly aeronautical ones, as an environment in which we can test their products in a much accelerated timescale compared to that in normal industry.

CHAPTER 73

At Silverstone, Ferrari decided they couldn't get their exhaust to work, so in typical fashion they decided to try to get ours banned.

Their argument to the FIA was that we were using the engine as a downforce-producing device, and because the engine is a movable aerodynamic device, in as much as it has pistons and valves that go up and down, that meant we had movable bodywork, which is illegal.

Now, obviously, a car has to have an engine. That engine has to have moving internals and wherever you put the exhaust it is still going to have an aerodynamic effect on the car. So you get into this grey area, which has become an increasing matter of debate, of primary and secondary purpose. In a conflict such as this, Charlie Whiting of the FIA has to decide whether the exhausts are being used for the primary purpose of creating downforce.

The outcome was that the practice of keeping the throttle open when the driver has taken his foot off the accelerator pedal was banned for Silverstone, then reintroduced for the following race after all sorts of wranglings. With that political hurdle overcome, it was a reasonably straightforward run to a second double championship, proving that we were a team to be taken seriously, not just one-hit wonders. I wouldn't even have bothered mentioning the brouhaha at Silverstone were it not for the fact that it had repercussions. For as we began work on the 2012 car, the RB8, regulations were announced that greatly restricted where the exhaust could be placed. Even worse were new regulations to try to ban hot blowing.

We discussed with Renault what ways round these there might be on the engine-management side of the regulation. At the same time we started to look at where we could position the exhaust to try and get the exhaust gas to flow down into the area by the rear tyre, because it was now a well-understood and clearly very powerful effect. One of the problems was that if we simply bulked the sidepods out at the rear to get the exhaust as close as the regulations allowed to the rear tyre, and then put a ramp linking the exhaust exit to the area beside the rear tyre (to encourage the exhaust flow down into the area), we lost the so-called Coke-bottle effect.

The Coke-bottle shape is something McLaren had first introduced as a response to the regulation changes that banned the sliding-skirt cars back in 1983.

What McLaren realised was that once there wasn't a diffuser blocking the area next to the rear tyres it was best to narrow the bodywork to allow the flow around the rear tyres and onto the lower of the two rear wings. It was this principle that we then took further on the RB5, narrowing it even further low down and widening it into a fish tail higher up.

Back to the present, wind tunnel and CFD tests showed that this solution worked reasonably well 'exhaust on', with some of the exhaust gas ending up down where we wanted it, but it was poor 'exhaust off' (i.e. no flow through the exhaust) because of the loss of the Coke-bottle-shaped bodywork. And with the ban on hot blowing under braking and corner entry, there would now be no significant exhaust flow, so a real problem.

The other development at the rear of the car was the rear suspension. Apart from the exhausts, another way to improve tyre-squish control at high rear ride-height is to make the wings mounted to the rear brake duct bodywork area more powerful by giving the lower wing a very nose-up, long-chord and highly cambered (curved) profile. However, we were now up against a physical limit; the lower suspension members of the wishbone and track rod were getting in the way and disrupting the flow fields. The solution was to revisit what I had done on the 1994 Williams FW16, bring the suspension legs onto the same plane as the driveshaft and then make

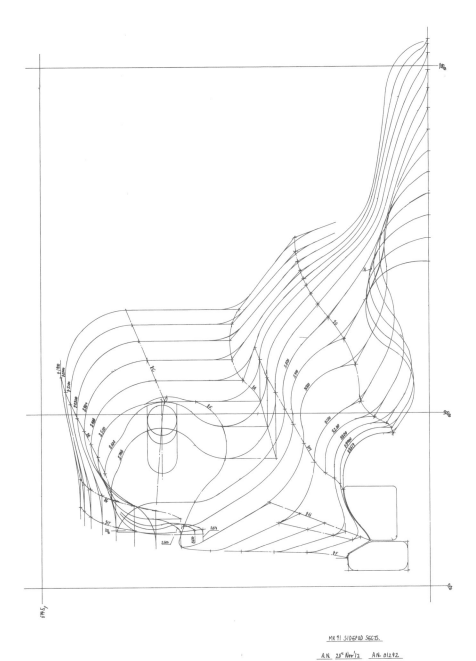

MR 91 SIDEPOD SECTS.

A.N. 20ᵗ Nov'12   A.N. 01292

Figure 22: Technical drawing of the sidepod showing exhaust
outlet and undercut duct inlet and exit on the RB8.

a larger hollow structure that enclosed the driveshaft. This allowed two benefits: it got the suspension legs out of the way and it allowed the resulting 'single' leg to be used as another wing in a Red Baron-style triplane arrangement of wings. It was also another nice baked-in-for-the-season solution that other teams would not be able to copy without making a new gearbox casing.

We decided to launch the RB8 in January with a Coke bottle shape and a benign exhaust position that did little other than blow the beam wing a bit, i.e. a step back to pre-RB10. The plan was to introduce new bodywork for the very last test, this bodywork being much wider with the ramp down to just beside the rear tyres. By then we felt that the reduction in downforce from having this extra blockage around the rear tyres would be outweighed by the extra downforce we'd get 'exhaust on' for traction out of the corners.

Both Sebastian and Mark drove the car for the last two days of the final test before Melbourne using this new bodywork, and Sebastian wasn't convinced – he felt the car was inconsistent. Mark seemed somewhat happier with it, but it was not the step forward we thought it should be and certainly our lap times, compared to our main competitors, McLaren, Ferrari and Mercedes, were somewhat worrying. We knew we'd lost a lot from these regulation changes; we'd been the first to use the exhaust in 2010 and perhaps developed the car around it much more than the others, so – in a scenario reminiscent of when Williams had been on active suspension longer than others – we had more to lose and relearn.

Off we went to Melbourne for the first race of the 2012 season, feeling very apprehensive.

CHAPTER 74

Daniel Ricciardo, a graduate of Helmut Marko's young driver training programme, scored his first-ever championship points at Melbourne. As a team that had now won two championships and was in the hunt for more, we at Red Bull had the pulling power to attract the very best drivers. Talks had been held with Fernando Alonso but there was, shall we say, a clash of personalities between him and Dietrich and so those broke down. During the 2012 season, we got wind of the fact that Lewis Hamilton was unsettled at McLaren. I already knew Lewis from my McLaren days; he was driving in Formula 3000 but was signed to McLaren, and he'd often come to the factory for a go on the simulator. He's a tremendously friendly guy. True, he's gone a bit showbiz in recent years, but he's one of the few drivers who will stop and chat, give people the time of day.

Anyway, he approached us about a possible drive with Red Bull and came to see me at my home, which was quite funny, because my PA at the time was a huge Hamilton fan and I didn't tell her he was coming. I was working away upstairs and the doorbell must have rung, because the next thing I knew Anne-Lise was bursting into my office in a complete red flush, looking very uncool indeed, going, 'Erm, uh, Lewis is at the front door, what do I do? What do I do?'

I said, 'Well, showing him in would be a good start.'

It didn't work out with Lewis though. We were committed to Sebastian and Mark. And besides, Red Bull had invested a huge amount in their driver training programme. Dietrich takes huge pride in developing sportsmen wherever possible. Helmut's baby, the training programme, had already produced Sebastian and was now looking like it had another star graduate in the form of Daniel – it has since given us Max Verstappen. At the time of writing, you would have to say the top drivers in Formula One are Vettel, Ricciardo, Verstappen, Hamilton and Alonso – and three of those are a product of Helmut's scheme, so it's actually turned out to be phenomenally successful. That's really the result of Dietrich's investment in the sport at all levels and Helmut's management of the driver programme.

Ricciardo flourished at Melbourne, but sadly the same couldn't be said for us. Our apprehension proved correct and we just weren't there in qualifying, with Mark placing fifth and Sebastian sixth. Neither was happy with the car and Sebastian struggled more than Mark. Losing the support of the exhaust downforce on corner entry was a big disadvantage given Seb's driving style – he turns the car very late and hard in order to get it rotated, which requires a very stable rear end. Mark didn't suffer as much with his slightly more traditional approach of breaking in a straight line before turning the car progressively and accelerating away.

After Melbourne, Sebastian said he felt more comfortable in the pre-update bodywork, where we had kept the Coke bottle shape and hadn't tried to do anything clever with the exhaust. We needed to find out which was the better route: the pre-season Coke bottle style or the bulkier outboard exhaust and ramp solution. So, for China, we reverted to the Coke bottle RB5-style on Sebastian's car. Mark qualified seventh and Sebastian a lowly eleventh. Reverting the bodywork did help corner entry a little but hurt the corner exit slightly, though both effects were underwhelming compared to what the wind tunnel and driver simulator had suggested. Seb was still very unhappy with the stability on entry. It was an improvement but even so, we were clearly not going to win the championship if we couldn't unlock a bit of performance from this car. As usual, it was a matter of getting our heads down and working hard to try and understand the problem. And this is where a bit of experience comes in, because what you can't do is let the race schedule force you into making poor decisions. You can't panic.

Various teams had come up with different solutions to the problem of the exhaust position, but McLaren's proved the most popular along the pit lane. Other teams, including Ferrari and Mercedes, had copied it. However, it didn't seem like an elegant solution to me because it meant that the exhaust flow was unguided for a significant distance and fighting against the natural flow in the coke.

By now, we had a lot of pressure taps on the key aero surfaces of both the car and the wind tunnel model. Coupled with CFD, which can be integrated for the same pressure information, this allows comparison between the environments: tunnel, CFD and car. As mentioned before, this is incredibly useful, because now when you have a lack of correlation you can pinpoint which areas are misbehaving and understand why.

On the RB8, these taps showed a big discrepancy in the diffuser performance on corner entry compared to results in the tunnels, where it's difficult to distort a model tyre and get it to behave as a car tyre does in cornering. By regulation, the tyres have very tall sidewalls, so the tread at the contact patch can move sideways by as much as 40mm in heavy cornering – you can see this in camera shots from the rear and also slow motion slots from the front when the cars jump kerbs at chicanes. This distortion of the tyre can cause separation of the flow on the inner sidewall and much worse squish losses. On the basis of the pressure taps and total pressure rakes, this looked to be the cause of our problem.

We changed the shape of the tyre in CFD to see what would happen and we started to see very badly behaved flow beside the rear tyre and, consequently, big reductions in downforce. The good news was that this seemed to be a theory in keeping with what Sebastian, in particular, was saying about how the car was behaving – this lack of rear downforce on corner entry. What's more, we'd come to that conclusion reasonably quickly: the problem had become evident really in Melbourne and, within a month, we'd developed our CFD tool in a way that demonstrated the problem.

One of our young aerodynamicists, Alistair Brizell, spotted a way to limit the coke effect underneath the exhaust ramp. The rules say that in cross-section, the bodywork must have a radius of no less than 75mm in the area above 100mm from the bottom of the car. But the floor top surface is carried at around 60mm, allowing a coke profile duct 40mm deep to be cut in below the ramp. In CFD this looked interesting. It benefited straight line driving but, in cornering conditions, the duct became badly separated, therefore compromising the performance of the diffuser gurney flap. Nevertheless, it was a relatively simple modification that we could apply to the existing bodywork. We took this to Bahrain and the results appeared to confirm we were barking up the right tree with our exhaust solution. The challenge now was to develop this undercut duct principle and stop it from separating when the car cornered.

One solution would be to extend the duct to underneath the beam wing, the lower of the two rear wings, so that the duct exit would be in an area of low pressure. This would help to draw air through the duct. We would also need to make the inlet to the duct as long and radiused as possible – a bigger duct would be less likely to separate and would have a much higher flow rate through it, so minimising the blockage caused by the bulky exhaust-orientated bodywork above.

The second problem was how to stop the duct exit flow compromising the gurney. If we could make the exit to the duct tall and narrow, then the bulk of it would be inboard of the gurney but this meant turning the duct

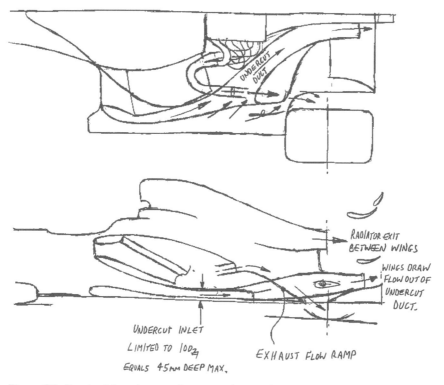

Figure 23: Sketch of the exhaust with its ramp down to the rear squish area, and the undercut duct beneath it.

cross-section from long but shallow in height at the inlet to tall but narrow at the exit. Never an easy problem when you are trying to keep duct losses to a minimum.

With the KERS batteries situated in and around the gearbox (a feature carried over from the RB7 and now working reliably), the engine was positioned so far enough forward that the exhaust pipes were not encroaching into the duct.

It took a while for us to get it to work. In the space of a few weeks, I drew about a dozen variations, working long hours to get those ducts into CFD, look at the results, see where the separations were in the duct, re-draw and go through the loop again. It was a very intense period but the results started to come in and we could see in CFD that this was now giving a much cleaner flow in the crucial area beside the rear tyre.

We arrived in Monaco with the fruits of our labour – the second generation of our first fully ducted undercut principle. Happily, Renault managed to get more flow into the exhaust on entry through careful interpretation of the rules. These two modifications really seemed to bring the car alive and Mark won the race.

While the new bodywork had been a step in the right direction, the exhaust effect on corner exit looked much weaker than the tunnel and CFD suggested it should be. An explanation, proposed by one of our aerodynamicists, Craig Skinner, was that this was due to pulsing in the exhaust. When each cylinder's exhaust valve opens, it creates a shock wave, and when this shock wave reaches the end of the pipe, it creates a doughnut-like ring vortex that travels off downstream. Pulse jets such as the World War II V1 "doodlebugs" have this flow feature. Craig was able to find various papers on the subject and created a transient CFD model and applied it to our bodywork: sure enough, the effect of the ring vortex was to push the flow off the ramp surface such that only a small proportion of the exhaust gas was ending up where we wanted it.

The solution was twofold: reduce the strength of the shock waves, which Renault did by fitting a resonator in the exhaust system to absorb and reflect the shock waves. We created a raised area on each side of the ramp, so that the exhaust pipe end sat in a gulley with only one of the four sides open.

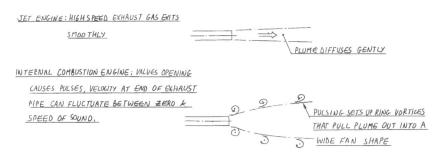

JET ENGINE: HIGH SPEED EXHAUST GAS EXITS
SMOOTHLY

PLUME DIFFUSES GENTLY

INTERNAL COMBUSTION ENGINE; VALVES OPENING
CAUSES PULSES, VELOCITY AT END OF EXHAUST
PIPE CAN FLUCTUATE BETWEEN ZERO &
SPEED OF SOUND.

PULSING SETS UP RING VORTICES
THAT PULL PLUME OUT INTO A
WIDE FAN SHAPE

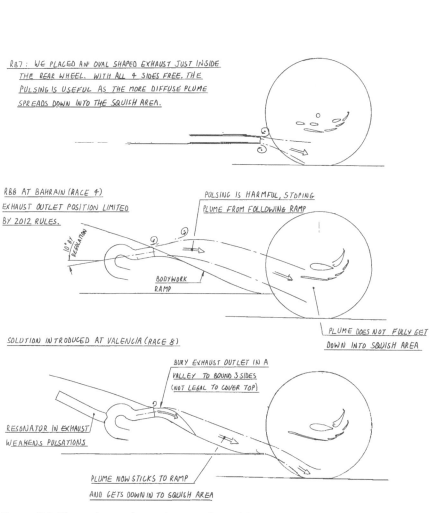

RB7: WE PLACED AN' OVAL SHAPED EXHAUST JUST INSIDE
THE REAR WHEEL, WITH ALL 4 SIDES FREE. THE
PULSING IS USEFUL AS THE MORE DIFFUSE PLUME
SPREADS DOWN INTO THE SQUISH AREA.

RB8 AT BAHRAIN (RACE 4)
EXHAUST OUTLET POSITION LIMITED
BY 2012 RULES.

10° BY REGULATION

BODYWORK
RAMP

PULSING IS HARMFUL, STOPING
PLUME FROM FOLLOWING RAMP

PLUME DOES NOT FULLY GET
DOWN INTO SQUISH AREA

SOLUTION INTRODUCED AT VALENCIA (RACE 8)

BURY EXHAUST OUTLET IN A
VALLEY TO BOUND 3 SIDES
(NOT LEGAL TO COVER TOP)

RESONATOR IN EXHAUST
WEAKENS PULSATIONS

PLUME NOW STICKS TO RAMP
AND GETS DOWN IN TO SQUISH AREA

Figure 24: The evolution of our solution to the problematic pulsing exhaust, introduced to the RB8.

The ring vortex was contained and only formed on that fourth side.

The new bodywork and exhaust were introduced at Valencia and both were good step forwards, with the car now handling much more to both drivers' liking. The improvement in exhaust gas management was even visually obvious – we were now getting heat staining on the bodywork by the rear tyre.

In the race, Sebastian was leading comfortably when he had an alternator failure. This was frustrating because Renault's alternators were made by Magneti Marelli, an Italian supplier, and we'd been having failures through the year. I think that was the first to cause a DNF but Renault and Marelli hadn't put enough work into understanding the problem, and it cost us what would have been an easy win. It especially was painful because it meant that Alonso, who went on to win the race, had gone from being more or less tied with Sebastian to 26 points clear of him, and down to fourth in the drivers'.

The season rumbled on and by the time we got to Singapore, Seb was fourth in the drivers' championship, 39 points behind Fernando, with Mark a further 8 points behind. And while Sebastian dominated Singapore and the following races in Japan, Korea and India, the following race at Abu Dhabi burst the bubble.

We were looking dominant through practice and then fell foul of a stupid fuelling mistake during qualifying. The regulations stipulate that the car must have at least a litre of fuel left in it at the end of qualifying, which the FIA then drain and sample to make sure it complies with the regulations. In this particular case, Sebastian's car had been short-fuelled and so during qualifying it ran out of fuel out on the circuit. Sebastian was excluded from qualifying and had to start from the pit lane. In the race itself, he did a great job of getting the car back through the field and he managed to finish third – a good piece of damage limitation – with Fernando finishing second.

From Abu Dhabi we crossed the Atlantic to a new track in Austin, Texas – our first return to America in some years. The race proved to be remarkably popular, with sell-out grandstands and a great atmosphere. In qualifying, Sebastian managed to get pole a tenth of a second ahead of

Hamilton but come the race itself, the wind changed direction and caught us out on the set-up. It meant that in the very fast sweeping corners around the back of the circuit, a car that had been well-balanced was now over-steering heavily. The wind direction had caused us to lose rear downforce, which is a common and well-known problem. We hadn't been astute enough in looking at the weather predictions. A mistake we wouldn't make again.

The result was a win for Hamilton in the McLaren, with Sebastian coming in second. Mark retired with an alternator problem – again! But more importantly, this was the race at which we secured the constructors' championship, a hat-trick. Going back to 2008, none of us could have dreamt of winning three in a row.

There were plenty of celebrations, but we still had the unfinished business of trying to secure that drivers' title with Sebastian. So off we went to Brazil.

For the weekend of the last race it seemed as though both Sebastian and Alonso were feeling the pressure: in qualifying, Mark out-qualified Sebastian for the first time in several races and, just as unusually, Felipe Massa did better than his teammate Alonso. We ended up with Sebastian starting P4 and Alonso back in P8.

That left us doing our sums. Points-wise, Alonso was three behind, which meant Sebastian needed to finish ahead of Alonso. If they were level on points, then Seb would win it on the count-back of number of race wins.

The forecast was for rain at some point during the race and, indeed, as we lined up on the grid, you could feel the moisture in the air – it was just a matter of when. But it was still dry, so everybody started on slicks.

Straightaway, there was drama. Mark, starting alongside Sebastian on the second row, squeezed him up against the wall on the inside, meaning that in order to prevent his front wing being squashed, Sebastian had to drop down to first gear, losing his position and costing him momentum.

Exiting turn one he was down from fourth to tenth, and trailing Alonso. Then, approaching turn four, Bruno Senna in the Williams made the most ridiculous move on Sebastian, turning straight across him and cannoning into the side of him, spinning Seb around and leaving him stuck in the middle of the track.

On the pit wall our hearts sank. Luckily, the anti-stall had kicked in, so the engine was still running.

But the car had a gaping hole in the sidepod. And it looked for all the world that we were out.

Seb managed to get going again, but it was looking pretty desperate, to say the least. It was also now spitting with rain, which was causing havoc, accidents up and down the field. At the same time, Sebastian got his head down and set about trying to move back up from his position of last at the end of the first lap. Over the next seven laps, he managed to climb back up, overtaking on average two to three cars per lap.

He was doing brilliantly, but on the pit wall we were faced with a difficult decision. Seb's car was damaged. Should we pull him in? Is the car safe? Paul Monaghan, my right-hand man at the race track, got his camera out and took a picture of the car from the pit wall, and it showed that although the bodywork was badly damaged it looked safe.

Much more worrying was the fact that one of the exhaust pipes had clearly taken a lot of the impact and was folded almost flat, squished together, which would have two effects: first of all, of course, you'd be losing power; second, if one of them cracked as a result, the escaping gas would probably set the bodywork on fire and that would be that: race over.

Even so, there was nothing we could do. It wasn't unsafe – if it did catch fire, Sebastian would still have time to get out. There was no remedial action we could take in a pit-stop that wouldn't hugely delay things, so we elected to let him keep running and hope he made it to the end.

On he drove. Pit-stops came and went. It started raining heavily, and inevitably the order was changing as it always does in the rain.

With 13 laps to go, Seb had fought back up to second place and now had Michael Schumacher ahead of him. I must admit, Christian and I were sitting on the wall thinking, *Oh goodness, Michael's going to make his car too wide and difficult for Sebastian to pass.*

This, after all, was Michael Schumacher: the old enemy.

But blow me down, it was the exact opposite. Michael was a gentleman and moved to one side to let Seb past. He clearly did not want to hinder Seb in his championship aspirations.

Meanwhile, at the front of the pack, the most extraordinary thing happened, Nico Hülkenberg in the Force India made an overly ambitious move on Hamilton and took Hamilton and himself out of the race.

The result was that Alonso, sitting in fourth, was suddenly elevated to second, with Button leading. More sums. If we could now finish in order with Sebastian in sixth and Alonso second, that would be enough for Seb to win the championship by three points, but if Button hit a problem, crashed or whatever, then Alonso would win. We watched Button. We watched Alonso. We watched Seb. We kept an eye on that exhaust, praying it would hold together.

It was a very nail-biting countdown of those last few laps. I had never been more relieved to see a car cross the finish line than that one.

So we won it. Well, not the race. Mark came in fourth and Sebastian sixth. But we won the drivers' championship, our third 'double' on the trot.

We were due to fly home that night, and so the celebration consisted of Christian, Jayne and myself sitting in the hotel bar enjoying a caipirinha or four – always my favourite drink in Brazil – before heading to the airport.

I can't begin to describe the feeling. Surreal, I suppose. For Red Bull to have gone from being been a nowhere team to three-time double winners was unbelievable. If you'd showed me that script in 2008 I would have thanked you for your optimism and politely shown you the door, twirling my finger at my temple in your wake.

But here I was in the hotel bar in Brazil with two of my dearest friends, toasting a third – *third* – double. Someone pinch me.

CHAPTER 75

Work was my sanctuary in the period following my split with Marigold. Marigold had moved out; I was rattling around at home on my own during the week, with Imogen and Harri joining me at weekends, and Hannah during holidays from university. Christian was great, as was Beverley, his girlfriend, who took it upon herself to try to find me a new girlfriend.

I did date a girl through the spring and summer of 2011, but we split up in September, meaning that I was once again a single man when I accepted an invitation to a Christmas party later that year.

Also at the party was my good friend and next-door neighbour, Chris Evans – not the one who plays Captain America, the other one – and at around midnight Chris suggested he and I share a cab home. On the way back, however, we decided to stop at a local watering hole.

It was while there that I became embroiled in a rather dull conversation with a man so overbearing that I kept being forced to take a step back. Eventually I'd backed up so far that I ended up on the wrong side of the bar, at which point a young lady approached and asked for a glass of champagne.

'Well, certainly,' I said, 'but I'm afraid I don't actually work here.'

She said, 'Well who do you work for, then?'

'I work for a fizzy drinks company,' I replied.

'Oh, which one?'

'Red Bull.'

She was into marketing and so asked all about the marketing angles of Red Bull – the energy drink company as opposed to the Formula One team – so I gave her a bit of BS, not having the faintest idea what either of us were talking about.

Her name was Amanda, and because she worked for a company organising golfing events she knew Chris, who, unbeknown to us, was doing a little behind-the-scenes matchmaking of his own.

A while later, we all piled back to my house in separate cabs, Amanda sharing with Chris, me with the rest of the group. Because Chris knew the door code and let himself in, Mandy assumed it was his house. After a few further drinks, he did his usual thing of quietly disappearing, as did the others, leaving Mandy and me alone. We carried on chatting until about seven in the morning, at which point she took a taxi home.

The relationship went on from there. We met a couple of times for dinner at local restaurants. I invited her back to the house, at which point she said, 'Oh I didn't realise you live in Chris's house.' We managed to clear up that little misunderstanding.

Meanwhile, I'd mentioned that my job at the fizzy drinks company was actually as an engineer for their Formula One team, though she had no idea what that entailed. This was the end of 2011 and we'd just won our second championship. Milton Keynes was very proud of us. Christian and I had already been to a rather unusual ceremony in which we were given the keys to Milton Keynes, which I believe means we can now herd our sheep through the middle of the town if we wish. There was a parade, with Sebastian and Mark running the cars around the streets. Roads were closed for what was anticipated to be a big civic event.

I said to Mandy, 'Look, we're running the race cars through the streets of Milton Keynes; would you like to come along and watch?'

'Yes, I'd love to,' she said, and so, the morning after our third date, both of us nursing hangovers, I collected her and off we went to Milton Keynes.

I suppose I hadn't really thought about the hoopla involved, but, arriving at the factory, we found assorted media and fans assembled outside. As I got out of the car, a few dozen people descended on me to ask for autographs and photos.

Mandy was pretty shocked. She looked from the media and autograph hunters to me and then back again, evidently seeing me in a new light.

'Adrian,' she said, 'who *are* you?'

She knew little about motor racing. Almost nothing, in fact. When we made it inside the building she recognised David Coulthard, but that was only because a friend of hers had a nodding-head David dashboard ornament.

Celebrating victory at Monaco with Mandy, 2012.

For his part, David knew a hangover when he saw one. 'You look as if you could do with a coffee,' he said to her, twinkly as ever.

Mandy and I were inseparable after that. In the summer of 2012 she moved in. We discovered that we both love seeing the world, and we've been on fascinating trips to Cuba, Nepal, Vietnam and Cambodia, with various other trips planned. Personally, I love seeing more out-of-the-way, off-the-beaten-track destinations and cultures – to see life as it's lived – and Mandy has a similar view on life.

Ahead of the 2016 August break, I went out to the garage and fished out my toolbox, in which was hidden a diamond that I'd bought from a friend years before – an investment that I'd hidden in said toolbox for safe keeping. I had it made up into a lovely ring, and took that with me for the vacation – destination Antigua for a more relaxed holiday.

On the day I planned to propose, we took a cruise around the island on a Boston Whaler. I was paranoid about losing the ring, so I put it on my necklace and hid it under my T-shirt, forgetting, of course, that we would be getting out of the boat and going for the odd swim, hence I was constantly shuffling around, trying to keep the ring safe but out of sight.

Eventually, when it came to popping the question, I asked the skipper if he wouldn't mind hiding behind the wheelhouse while I proposed; then, assuming all went well, if he would take a couple of photographs.

When I started the proposal routine, Mandy burst out laughing. I thought, *Why on earth is she laughing? That's not what I expected!*

But I carried on regardless, asked my question, and, to my joy, she said yes. It was only later that she explained she was laughing because the skipper was bobbing up and down like a meerkat from behind the wheelhouse, awaiting his moment to take the photographs.

Mandy grew up in South Africa, where she was a top-level swimmer, to the point that she won several national gold medals. In her early twenties she moved to Scotland as a coach for Scottish and British Swimming, specialising in coaching open-water swimmers and attending various international events in that capacity. That's what's so good about our relationship: having been a sportswoman herself, she understands competition, understands the sacrifices that are sometimes involved in competing at a high level. She knows that when I'm preoccupied and focused on my work, seemingly blinkered, it's not because I'm being rude and thoughtless it's because, if you're going to compete at the top, you have to be that way sometimes. Well that's my excuse anyway! But I can't tell you how much I value that, and how helpful it is for our relationship.

With the success I've had over the years, and in particular the success that we as Red Bull had in those four consecutive years, comes recognition, so I've been very honoured to receive various awards.

The first came from the K7 club, which was formed by Donald Campbell as a way of thanking those who helped him with his record attempts. After his death, the club created an award, the Bluebird Trophy, for 'those who have contributed most to British endeavour in the realm of high speed on land, water and in the air'. To be awarded it, particularly when I looked at the list of previous recipients engraved on the side, was a huge honour.

It also meant a lot because the 1964 *Bluebird* land-speed record car was an incredibly advanced machine for its day. Designed by aeronautical engineers, it was the first car to properly understand and use ground effect.

The racing car designers of the day could have learnt a lot from *Bluebird*, which is a reminder to try to keep extending one's vision beyond the immediate little bubble in front of one.

The other notable award is the Segrave Trophy presented by the RAC. Awarded for outstanding skill, courage and initiative on land, water and in the air, it's named in honour of British land-speed pioneer Sir Henry Segrave and was first awarded in 1930.

I was awarded it in 2010, and again, looking down the roll call of previous winners made me quite giddy: Amy Johnson, Sir Malcolm Campbell, Geoffrey de Havilland, Donald Campbell, Stirling Moss – the list goes on and on.

Then came a phone call to say that I was to be included in the New Year's Honours List, 2011.

I'm still not exactly sure how the system works, but to be honoured in that way was wonderful; the OBE joins a small display of my grandfather's war medals at home.

I was lucky because the Queen herself was giving out the awards that day, and when I stepped forward to receive mine she said, 'Ah yes, I remember you; you're the man who showed my husband around McLaren when he got stuck in a racing car.'

Which was absolutely correct. For the official opening of the new factory at McLaren, Ron managed to secure the Queen for the ceremony and I had the honour of showing Prince Philip around the factory.

He'd shown great interest in the wind tunnel, and then, when we got to one of the cars, he said, 'Can I sit in it?'

He climbed in, got a bit stuck and must have recounted the story to the Queen, who remembered it. That's a remarkable memory – I doubt it was a briefing.

CHAPTER 76

Winning the hat-trick was amazing but, such is the relentless wheel of Formula One, the focus was now on our next title defender for 2013, the RB9.

The RB9 was very much an evolution of the RB8, so the principles we'd established in terms of getting the exhaust plume to stay attached, the undercut duct, all the architecture of the car, were the same, with various aerodynamic tidy-ups and evolutions.

The start of the season was very much a tight battle between us and Mercedes. As it turned out, the biggest thing that swung our competitiveness were the tyres. Pirelli had changed construction of the tyres for the start of the season. They were a bit more fragile and less able to handle high loads, and that seemed to affect our car more than Mercedes.

At Silverstone, which is one of the highest-load circuits on the calendar, the tyres quite simply weren't up to the job and the weekend was marred by tyres exploding. We were lucky nobody got hurt.

As a result of that, Pirelli took stock, realised their 2013 tyres weren't able to handle the loads, and reverted to the tyres of the previous season. These seemed to suit our car much better, and partly as a result of that change the rest of the season was a complete dream. Sebastian won every single race of the second half, giving him the record for the most number of consecutive wins.

Once we got into the swing of that dominance, the pressure was off, and in the end we cruised to four consecutive doubles which, no matter how many times you say it, is still difficult to believe: we won the double four times in a row!

After which the sport changed – and not for the better in my opinion.

Our purple era abruptly ended post-2013 when an engine regulation change moved us away from the normally aspirated V8s to turbocharged hybrid engines.

It was something that Max, in his last years as FIA President, had pushed for. His logic was that if road car manufacturers involved in the sport were going to be spending hundreds of millions of pounds per year on engine development, it made sense to alter the regulations to make sure the research they're doing is relevant to the general automotive industry, to further the development of the cars that we drive on the road every day and make them more fuel efficient, save the planet and so forth.

Sounds logical? To achieve that aim, an Engine Working Group was set up, from which was born a new set of regulations. They specified that the engine must be a V6 engine of 1.5-litre capacity with a specified bore and stroke. Only one spark plug per cylinder. Only one fuel injector per cylinder. A single turbocharger driving an electric motor to recover heat from the exhaust system. An electric motor linked to the crankshaft, both of those electric motors then linked to a battery and capable of driving or being driven by the battery.

Highly specific regulations for a very specific application. No road car manufacturer, when he's building his road car, is limited to those regulations. So if the road car manufacturer wants to have two fuel injectors per cylinder, he can do so. If he wants to have a completely different bore or stroke, he can do so. And, more importantly, he is developing an engine that is typically driven at very low throttle settings because you're cruising on a motorway or stuck in a traffic jam.

We're now coming into our fourth season with these engine regulations. That means that engine manufacturers have been researching these engines for six years and yet there's no evidence that it's coming through in the showroom yet. Or, put another way, if it has improved the breed, we can look forward to a new generation of Mercedes that will be well ahead of their showroom competitors – time will tell.

I personally think that this move towards road relevance has been a red herring. If you do want to do it, then why not go further and say, 'Okay, here's 100 litres of fuel; you build whatever you want.' That would be a fascinating arms race. But of course the problem then is the very real chance that some teams will come up with a solution that is so much better than the others that they disappear over the horizon – although, ironically, that's exactly what's been happening with Mercedes anyway. So, in my opinion, nobody wins. Not the automotive industry, not the sport, not the spectator.

There's no doubt Mercedes have done an extremely good job on the power unit and they've produced the best engine. They've probably had the biggest budget to do so, but regardless of how they've done it, the bottom line is they've produced a power unit which has been significantly better than Renault's. And that's not a direct criticism of Renault; it's just a reflection of where things are.

At the same time, the chassis regulations have become evermore restricted, so every piece of new technology that teams have developed almost invariably gets banned by the FIA: exhaust blowing, aero elastics, front-rear interconnected suspension, the list goes on and on. It's increasingly difficult to get a significant benefit over your competitors on the chassis. And because of these very restrictive chassis regulations, all the cars look the same. If you took the 2016 Formula One grid and painted all the cars white, you'd have to be quite an expert to know which one's which.

Now, to me, what makes Formula One unique compared to other top-level sports is the fact that it's not just the sportsmen – it's the sportsmen and the car, man and machine, the technology, the battle of the car-cum-sportsman who's driving it. And for that reason I think it's so important that we maintain technical differentiation between the cars, and within the car the engine should not become the dominant differentiator among the top teams.

I also think the sport has lost some of its spectacle. These hybrid engines sound flat, they don't sound exciting. The sound of a normally aspirated V10 made the hair on your skin stand up. People who came to the circuit for the first time tingled with excitement at the noise the cars made. The noise is a very important element that's been lost, to the point that the support GP2 race, for instance, sounds far more exciting than the Formula One race, which is wrong.

You watch the on-board cameras and there's a distinct lack of drama. Contrast a pole lap from Hamilton in 2016 with Ayrton's Monaco qualifying lap from 1988 (check it out, it's worth watching). You watch Ayrton manhandling that car around Monaco; it looks brutal and you think, *That's amazing; I could never in a million years do that*. You watch a qualifying lap now for pole position, and though you'd be mistaken of course, you might well sit there and think, *Yes, with a bit of practice, I could do that*.

In this sense, it's lost its magic. The sportsman is no longer the gladiator, he's just another person. We have muddled up our thinking, gone the wrong way. Is this entertainment or is it a technology-development exercise for the automotive industry? Either way, we're achieving neither.

I guess one of the things about Formula One rules is that anybody who is an enthusiast has an opinion, which is a good thing: it stimulates passion. The bottom line is that the FIA are responsible for these technical and sporting regulations under which we operate. You could argue about the rights and wrongs of Max's stewardship, but at least he made decisions and things changed. Under Jean Todt's presidency, the solution to all problems is to form committees made up of the teams themselves. The problem with that, of course, is that no team in reality votes for what's for the good of the sport; they vote for what will help their team. At the same time, no proper research is being done to ask: what do we want to achieve? Do we want more dramatic-looking cars? Do we want cars that look more difficult to drive, requiring more of a gladiator to handle them? Do we want more overtaking? Do we want to pursue road relevance with the technology, in which case go electric or serial hybrid and be done with it? Do we want more noise, more drama?

There are all these things to consider, and it's not until you've thought about them that you can set about saying, 'Okay, now let's do the research to fit those criteria. What are the best regulations we can come up with?'

The good news about Liberty buying the sport off the previous venture capitalist owners, CVC, is that they understand how to market sport; that's their business. They promise to bring a breath of fresh air and proper research to this conundrum.

CHAPTER 77

The spring of 2014 was a bit of a crunch decision-time. Red Bull seemed to be stuck on the engine front. Renault hadn't produced a particularly good hybrid engine, and while we all make mistakes the important thing is that you recognise it and plan your way out.

Christian, Helmut and I visited Carlos Ghosn, the President of Renault, and didn't come out feeling reassured that there was a real commitment to catching up, which was quite depressing.

Mercedes had strung us along a few times, but were not going to supply us with an engine because they didn't want to risk their car being beaten by a Red Bull with their own engine in it. Exactly the same situation with Ferrari.

We talked about building our own engine, but the money required was, even for Dietrich, just colossal, way too much.

So the spring of 2014 was a depressing time, with no apparent light at the end of the tunnel. I was considering my options, when who should approach me but Niki Lauda from Mercedes. There began a series of talks about me joining Mercedes, Niki paying me a couple of visits at home in order to discuss it. I was tempted, but not *that* much. To move to Mercedes, the team that was clearly going to win the championship that year, 2014, effectively replacing Ross Brawn, just didn't feel right, and I would have felt like a trophy hunter. So I thanked Niki but turned that one down.

I was also approached by one of the LMP1 sports car teams. That was very interesting in principle; to be involved in a team with the aim of winning Le Mans remains on my bucket list. But the team is based in Germany and that bit didn't appeal. Then came a third approach, and it was from Ferrari. I'd been courted by them before, but this time they meant business. I travelled to visit Luca Montezemolo, the President of Ferrari at the time, seeing him at his farmhouse close to Tuscany. We held serious talks and their offer was amazing. Luca wanted to give me the whole Ferrari operation, road and race car. The promise was of an almost film-star life-style and the most ridiculously large financial offer, well over double the already generous salary I was receiving at Red Bull.

I had a very difficult decision to make, and it was one that cost me many nights' sleep as I went over and over the various factors: family, cultural, work differences, the chances of success or failure, the repercussions of either . . .

But in the end I thanked Luca and turned him down.

Why? Good question.

Well, there were of course family matters to consider: the children, all doing different things, and my relationship with Mandy to take into account. All went into the pot when it came to making my decision. But in work terms, what I returned to was this one simple thought: I just didn't want to leave Red Bull.

After all, Red Bull was home. The team I'd joined had been imbued with the 'old' Midlands spirit: that slightly negative, head-in-the-sand, hands-over-our ears attitude. But the team as it is now has fostered a 'new' Midlands spirit, a can-do, work-hard-and-improve attitude. We'd gone from being the paddock joke, the upstart, party-hard fizzy drinks company, to four-time world champions, and we'd done it the old-fashioned way, using principles that to me were in keeping with the true spirit of motor racing. I thought back to the beginning of the 2012 season when we couldn't get the car right, and I remembered with pride that our shoulders hadn't dropped. We'd got our heads down, worked through it and solved the problem. I thought how we'd developed young drivers instead of buying up star names; how we'd helped put Milton Keynes on the map; how through-out it all we'd never stopped working; how we'd always taken the road less travelled, even when it meant facing seemingly insurmountable problems or technical challenges; how we never took the simple option in search of an easy life or sat back on our laurels feeling pleased with ourselves and decided 'that'll do'. We'd always continued innovating.

It's not just my philosophy, of course; this is an ideology shared by Christian, and we had very much moulded the team around ideals we both shared. But speaking for myself, I felt that what I'd achieved at Red

Bull was in many ways a means of giving something back to motor racing after motor racing had given so much to me. We'd introduced a team that was new, that was different, but that could get results. My work there offered fulfilment in a sport I had adored since childhood – a sport I'd loved, not always for what it was, but for what it had the potential to be: the total synchronicity of man and machine, the perfect combination of style, efficiency and speed.

EPILOGUE
(OR 'HOW TO DESIGN AN ASTON MARTIN')

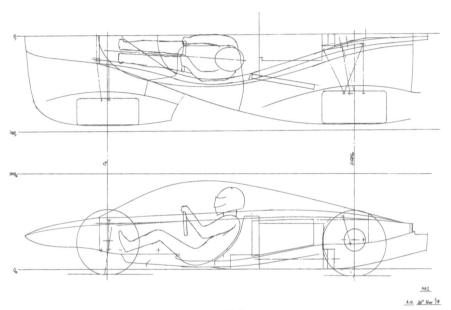

Figure 25: Initial drawing of the Aston Martin Valkyrie.

So, I turned down Ferrari. But given my diminishing passion for the sport as it currently finds itself, I still needed to rethink things at Red Bull. I didn't want to leave; equally, I didn't want to be flogging my guts out trying to find competitiveness in a car that couldn't compete on engine performance. And I wanted a new challenge. Motor racing has been a fantastic career that had absorbed me from the age of 21 at Fittipaldi's in 1980 through to 2014, during which time the number of engineers in a top team has gone from around 5 to well over 200.

So, after lots of discussions with Christian and Jayne, we agreed the best way forward was for me to step back into a less hands-on role. I'm still involved in the design of the cars, and still spend roughly half of my time on the Formula One side of the operation – the car continues to have some features that have come off my drawing board – but most areas are now the responsibility of other senior members of the team, giving them the space to develop and grow. I have also stepped back from doing almost all of the races to doing only a handful; flying to and fro has well and truly lost its novelty!

However, if I was going to do that, what other things could I get involved in? By this time, the middle of 2014, we had something like 750 employees, a huge workforce who all had bills to pay and lives to live, so if anything happens in the future – for instance, if a regulatory cost cap is put in place, forcing the team to shrink – then Christian and I have a responsibility to try to find alternative work for those people, not simply put them out on the street.

So we discussed and subsequently set up a small department, separate to the Formula One team, called Red Bull Advanced Technologies.

It's not a new idea – Enzo Ferrari had done the same way back in the 1950s when he began selling road cars in order to finance his race team. McLaren and Williams have both branched out into automotive and/or selling technology to the general industry.

Around that time the yachtsman Ben Ainslie approached me. He was setting up a new team to challenge for the America's Cup in 2017. Would I be interested in joining? No, I said, but I am interested in working with you, and maybe there's an opportunity here to team up with our new company, Red Bull Advanced Technologies.

After the upset with Ron when I almost left McLaren in 2001, during which time we discussed the idea of entering the America's Cup, I had remained interested in the possibility. In many ways, both sporting and technically, it is similar to motor racing – aerodynamics, hydrodynamics (still aerodynamics but in a dense fluid), lightweight structures, stability and control, etc. Even the course is like a race track, except that corner apexes are replaced by poles and the track is almost infinitely wide between the corners. But there are extra variables that make it a more difficult problem than a race car – the track roughness varies from day to day, and the power source is also highly variable. Plus, with the hydrofoils of the current America's Cup catamaran generation, you have a three-state boat, both hulls in the water, one hull in the water and both hulls in the air on the foils. With so many variables, it seemed clear that in order to evaluate different candidate designs (for regulations that are much more open than F1) we needed a really good simulation package and a sailor in the loop simulator.

Based on this recommendation, Ben's team commissioned RBAT to write a package, which involved 12 months of challenging work for our team but which represented, I believe, a huge step on from what other America's Cup teams have available to them.

Unfortunately, by the time we'd done all that, the money needed for us to be involved in the design of the boat was not available, which was a shame, because I knew enough about it by then to believe we could have come up with some exciting ideas. Unfortunately, Red Bull Advanced Technologies is a commercial entity, so we cannot work for free.

Some years previously, in early 2010, Sony PlayStation had approached me to ask if I would be interested in designing a 'no rules' F1 car for their game. As luck would have it, we went skiing shortly afterwards but the snow that year was poor, so I used the idle moments to come up with ideas, a spec sheet and some sketches. All a bit of fun, but I enjoyed the process and the chance to come up with ideas without the constraints of the regulatory chains that we normally work within.

If you take that thread of being able to come up with a concept that is relatively free of regulatory constraint within the automation sector, the reality is you have to come out of motor racing – and move into road cars.

One of my other ambitions ever since I'd been a boy was to design a road-going sports car, and that had been my final-year project at university. Looking at the high-end road-going sports cars available, I felt there was an opportunity. Cars, including sports cars, have generally become very big, heavy and clumsy, with technology such as four-wheel steer then introduced to attempt to make them feel light again – while adding yet more weight! Hasn't the point been missed?

The first thing you always have to think before you design anything is: what am I trying to achieve here? So I sat and thought: *Okay, if I had the opportunity to design a road-going sports car from a clean sheet of paper, what attributes would I want from it?* And the shortlist I came up with was: it must look beautiful and be a piece of art, so that even if you never drive it you still derive joy from owning it and looking it.

Second, when you do drive it, you must feel a tingle of excitement before you get in; maybe even trepidation that this thing is slightly intimidating, but also the confidence that you can master it as long as you are respectful and have your wits about you.

It must sound great. It must be small, nimble and responsive. It should be the kind of car you can take to a circuit and lap faster than any other road car around, which again means lightweight coupled with high power. It also means that downforce becomes a necessity.

Finally, it needs to be reasonably comfortable to drive and enjoy. In other words, if it simply feels like a racing car on the road – i.e. it's harsh and jerky, it vibrates, it's hot, it shakes over every little pothole – then it's failed. It should be a comfortable drive, and should have a glovebox for your sunglasses and odds and ends, and a degree of luggage space.

So I wanted it to be a car of two characters. One, when stuck in traffic in Oxford Street, provides a reasonably comfortable environment. But if you wanted to take it to the track and drive it at a pace that would beat most categories of racing car, it would be capable of doing that too.

Once you start to lay down the goals, you can start to think, okay, how do I achieve that?

Mandy and I went to the Maldives for a holiday in the August break of 2014, and as I sat there on the beach, I came up with my list and started on some sketches and ideas.

Through that autumn as a weekend hobby project I began to develop the spec; first big decision – the power unit. For the combustion engine, the choice really was twin turbo V6 or naturally aspirated V12. The core engine of the V6 is clearly much smaller and lighter, but to that you have to add the turbos, and the intercoolers to cool the charge air. In the end, I came to the conclusion that a high-revving solid-mounted V12 (that is, the engine also forms the structure, as on a F1 car) would be a similar weight but would require less overall cooling and would, of course, sound much more dramatic, especially if the 12 exhaust pipes were brought together into a single exit.

To keep such a high-revving engine tractable in traffic I felt we needed a small electric motor to work with it, this motor then performing many other functions: starter, alternator, reverse gears. It couples to a new transmission concept that I hope will combine very quick gear changes with a much lighter solution than the current double-clutch gearboxes used by top-end sports cars.

From there I began laying out the car, in effect a two-seater version of the PlayStation X1 car. The seating position is F1 style, very reclined with raised feet, which is actually very comfortable. To minimise the width of the front of the chassis I rotated the occupants by five degrees so that they sit slightly on the squint, a common practice in Le Mans prototype cars.

With the basic scheme in place by Christmas, we then set up a very small team: Ben Butler on the design, Nathan Sykes on CFD and Giles Wood on simulation for my ideas on the transmission and active suspension, along with two surfacers to take my pencil aero shapes and turn them into solid surfaces for CFD. By the autumn of 2015 we had CFD results and performance simulation results.

At that point, we had no partner. Dietrich had made it plain from the start that Red Bull Advanced Technologies must stand on its own feet financially, so we started casting around for backing. Effectively we had two choices: find a private backer or partner with a major car manufacturer.

Christian and I both knew people at Aston Martin and decided they might be an ideal fit: an iconic British brand, famous for its sports cars, located not far away in Gaydon, Warwickshire, and well known for the beauty of its cars – but whose engineering could be, let's say, a bit wanting.

If they could bring their experience of getting a road car through legislation and working with suppliers, contributing to the styling expertise in the process, we believed that could work really well.

So we signed a non-disclosure agreement and did a 'show and tell'. We pitched our ideas for the architecture of the car, the packaging and occupant space, use of a high-revving bespoke V12 engine, active suspension to cope with the downforce, and a small electric motor for round-town smoothness and practicality among other uses.

They showed us a mid-engined hyper-car they had been working on, broadly similar looking but a much bigger, wider car. There was a fair bit of disbelief from them that such a small cabin as we were proposing could comfortably fit two people side by side, so they built a cockpit mock-up and were amazed that it worked. As in F1, it's about having space where you need it but not where you don't. There was a self-winding push-back about the five-degree arrow seating among the Midlanders, but in the end we proved that was not a problem. There was also endless debate about the engine, some favouring a V6 turbo, some a V8 turbo and others using a derivative of their regular V12.

Finally, after endless meetings with lots of people, Andy Palmer, their CEO, Christian and I agreed to go forward, though we put the use of a bespoke Cosworth-designed V12 in the contract.

A full-scale show car model was made, hybridising our aero surfaces with Aston's styling. Initially, this was shown privately in Monaco, then publicly – the green painted surfaces of that model are effectively Aston under the direction of Miles Nurnberger, while the black surfaces of canopy, rear wing and everything below the waistline are ours.

The interest was staggering. We announced production of 150 road cars and 25 track-only variants, and within a very few weeks Aston Martin had taken 150 deposits, had about another 20 people with deposits in the queue and several hundred more people with their name down should one come available beyond that. Internally, the project was given the code name Nebula by the guys – an acronym for Newey, Red Bull and Aston.

The cost? £2m. A shame, of course, because it means that the car can only be owned by a wealthy few. For Aston, it's what's known as a halo car, so it gets people talking about Aston Martin. It's an advertisement for their more mainstream products, and a technology demonstrator. For Red Bull it's our opportunity to show that we can be involved in successful products outside of Formula One; an opportunity to demonstrate that as Advanced Technologies we can take the techniques and methodology we've learnt in Formula One and apply it in other areas. If we can do that successfully, then we can grow Advanced Technologies and hopefully tackle other projects in the future.

For instance, I would love to design a car aimed at the general road user, one that's affordable and economical, by which I mean something that has a genuinely small carbon footprint, unlike the current rash of electric cars, whose use of electricity – electricity mainly created by the burning of fossil fuels – is something of an environmental red herring.

If I can contribute towards reducing the CO_2 footprint of cars from birth to death in the general automotive industry, and at the same time design cars that people enjoy, that is something I would relish as a challenge.

I hope I can do that. I believe I can. After all, I like to think I've shown some aptitude in motor racing. Cars for which I've been responsible have won 10 constructors' titles and 154 races, and in that time I've been lucky enough to move among brilliant and inspirational drivers, visionary money men, movie legends – even a Beatle. I've weathered tragedy and savoured victory, navigated the choppy waters of a sport that first entranced me as a car-obsessed child and subsequently accompanied me into adulthood, when I discovered a talent for turning my mad ideas into reality, and was fortunate enough to find paid work doing it.

Thirty-five years later, I can look back on an eventful, fruitful career – one spent designing cars and asking myself the same series of simple questions. How can we increase performance? How can we improve efficiency? How can we do this differently?

How can I do this better?

GLOSSARY

ACTIVE SUSPENSION

Discussed in depth elsewhere, the short version is that it's an electronically controlled, hydraulically powered system used as a means of maximising downforce by keeping the height of the car constant to the ground.

ACTUATORS

Typically, electronically controlled (but hydraulically powered) pistons that change length in accordance with command signals from the on-board computer. In the active suspension era, these were used as part of the suspension system. Now they are also used for gear selection and DRS flap movement.

AIRBOX

Normally located above and behind the driver's head inside the roll hoop, the airbox ducts air from the roll-hoop intake to the engine-intake trumpets and contains an air filter along its length.

CAMBER

The angle of the tyre relative to the ground when viewed from the front. Typically, racing cars run around four degrees of front camber. This can be seen by the spectator as the tyres 'leaning in' towards the centre of the car.

CASTOR

The angle of the steering axis when viewed from the side. Castor is used to create a change in camber with steering lock and also stability; shopping trolleys, for instance, will often run a lot of castor to keep the wheels straight.

CHARGE AIR COOLER

On a turbo-charged engine, the action of the compressor is to raise its pressure, but, as a consequence, the temperature of the air is increased. The engine loses power as a result of the raised air temperature, so the job of the 'charge air cooler' – effectively a radiator – is to cool the charge down again before it enters the engine.

COMPOSITE STRUCTURE

Strictly speaking, a composite structure is any structure made of more than one material. In motor racing it is commonly used to refer to any large component made out of carbon fibre, often containing inserts of aluminium or titanium.

DAMPER

An undamped spring will continue to oscillate after load input. If you twang the end of a ruler, for example, it will continue to oscillate for some time after the initial finger push. A damper is typically an oil-filled piston within a cylinder, whose job is to 'damp' this oscillation. The damper settings must be tuned to suit the spring rate and response to inputs, such as steering, that the race engineer prescribes.

DIFFUSER

A device that expands and slows air down; a hair dryer, for instance, will often have a diffuser attachment to take the concentrated hot blast of air and diffuse it into a slower-moving but wider flow. In motor racing, a diffuser is fitted to the back of the floor. If a low-pressure region of air is generated at the back of the diffuser, for instance by a rear wing, this creates the slow-moving broad area analogous to that created by the hair-dryer attachment. Because of the contraction ahead of it, the air flowing under the car is forced to travel much faster, thereby creating a low-pressure area underneath the car.

DOWNFORCE

For a full explanation, please see . . . well, the whole book. But put simply, it is the opposite of an aircraft's lift – a means of pushing the car into the ground.

DRAG

The aerodynamic force that arises from the movement of an object through air. It's what you feel when you try to stand upright on a windy day. In motor racing, it absorbs power from the engine and is ultimately what limits the speed of the car.

ECU

Or electronic control unit. Effectively an on-board computer that is used to control items such as the engine and the gearbox in response to the driver's demands. All modern cars have them.

ENDPLATE

The vertical bit on the end of the front and rear wings, used to improve the efficiency of the wing.

EXCLUSION BOX

Areas on the car where the regulations state you cannot have any bodywork.

FREESTREAM

Undisturbed air, which in the real world would be stationary air, that the car passes through. In the wind tunnel, where the model is held still, it is the speed of the air passing through the wind tunnel.

GEARBOX DYNO

A factory-based piece of equipment, it typically contains three powerful and very fast-response electric motors used to replicate the action of the engine and rear wheels around a lap, allowing the actual car gearbox to be developed without having to run the car.

GEAR-DOGS

You can picture a gear-dog if you interlock your fingers and then try to slide your left hand past your right hand. That's exactly what a gear-dog

does. It allows the torque from the shafts within the gearbox to be transmitted through the gears.

HYPOID DRIVE

A bevel drive consists of two cone-shaped gears sitting at right angles to turn the longitudinal gearbox shafts through 90 degrees and off down the drive shafts. A hypoid drive is almost identical, except the shaft centres are offset vertically from each other by a small amount.

KART RACING TWO-STROKE

Normally 100cc for fixed-wheel karts and between 200cc and 250cc for gearbox karts (such as mine). Engines in my youth were always stolen out of motorcycles and re-tuned to suit karting.

KERS

Or Kinetic Energy Recovery System. On a Formula One car, an electric motor is mounted on the end of the crankshaft. Every time the car brakes, some of the braking force is provided by the electric motor performing a charging action, in a similar manner to the little dynamos that people have on their bicycles to operate lights. This electrical energy is stored in the battery and then used on button-request by the driver to augment acceleration down the next straight.

MONOCOQUE
The main structure, the chassis. It contains the driver and the fuel tank, and provides mountings for the front suspension, the engine, and the nose and side-impact structures.

NACA DUCT
Developed by the National Advisory Committee for Aeronautics in the US, this is an air inlet design to duct air to whatever component you wish to supply.

PARC FERMÉ
The parking area where the cars have to be placed at various times through the weekend under the surveillance of the FIA. During this time, teams are only allowed to perform routine checks on the car, with no alteration or maintenance that has not had prior FIA approval.

POWER-TO-WEIGHT RATIO
The power of the engine in horsepower divided by the weight of the car, including driver, in kilograms. Formula One cars have typically been in the area of 1.2hp per kilogram over recent years.

PULLROD SUSPENSION
A way of transmitting the motion of the wheel to spring damper units mounted inside the chassis at the front and at the side of the gearbox at the rear. A pull-rod runs diagonally from the upper wishbone at the wheel end, down to the bottom of the spring damper unit at the inboard end.

PUSHROD SUSPENSION
Essentially the same as pull-rod suspension, except that the rod runs from the lower wishbone at the wheel end, up to the top of the spring damper unit at the inboard end.

RIDE-HEIGHT
The proximity of the car to the ground. Downforce and the balance of downforce between the front and rear axles change as the ride height changes, and therefore ride-height is a key set-up consideration when adjusting a car to suit a particular circuit.

ROLL BAR STIFFNESS
Responsible for controlling the car's roll. A stiff roll bar will mean the car

will roll very little, which is good for response and aerodynamic platform control but poor for the ride over bumps and kerbs. The balance of stiffness between the front and rear is known as mechanical balance; a very stiff front bar and soft rear, for instance, will lead to a very stable car that has a lot of understeer.

SPACER

This is often used by chassis designers as a slang term for the engine; i.e. the bit that joins the back of the chassis to the front of the gearbox. It is also a term used in long-distance racing for inserts fitted into the seat of the chassis to reduce its size for smaller teammates.

SPRING RATES

This refers to the stiffness of the suspension system, which seeks to find the optimum compromise between being very stiff for aerodynamic platform control and much softer for load fluctuation and the ride over bumps and kerbs. It is another key set-up variable between individual circuits.

TIP VORTEX

The vortex formed when the high pressure on one side of the wing tries to leak around the tip of the wing to the low pressure on its opposite side.

TOE-IN/TOE-OUT

The angle of the wheels when the steering wheel is straight ahead. Viewed from above, the wheels are angled slightly inwards when they are toe-in, and slightly outwards for toe-out.

TRACK ROD

The suspension member that controls the steering on the front wheels and prevents steering of the rear wheels.

TRACTION CONTROL

Considered a driver aid after the regulation changes of 1993, this system is designed to modulate the power of the engine to prevent the rear wheels from spinning up at a corner exit. It needs no input from the driver and is instead controlled by the ECU.

UNDERWING

A term originally used in the late 1970s to describe the huge wing shapes that were placed underneath the sidepods of the cars, with sliding skirts attached to the tips of the wing to prevent leakage and the consequent tip vortices.

WING

The most important part of an F1 car is the front wing, the reasons for which I go into in more detail in the main text. The front wing is responsible not only for generating most of the front downforce of the car but also for controlling the wake off the front wheels behind it.

YAW

When a car brakes, it 'pitches forward'; when it accelerates, it 'pitches rearwards'; and when it corners, it 'rolls'. But also it rotates in 'yaw', which describes the rotation of the entire car as it follows the steering of the front wheels.

ACKNOWLEDGEMENTS

I am not normally one to look back and reflect, so writing an autobiography has been a different, surprisingly emotional experience. I even surprised myself how much I could remember.

I say 'write', but that is a misnomer. The credit for taking my ramblings and putting them down into some sort of ordered and elegant structure goes to my ghost writer, Andrew Holmes. Andrew has been an absolute pleasure to work with; prior to meeting me he knew nothing of motor racing and that has worked well, forcing me to explain myself. Also to Nicole Carling for typing up my edits of the first draft.

I would also like to thank Jack Fogg of HarperCollins. This book was his idea and baby, including the format and title.

I owe a huge debt of gratitude to the people who have supported and believed in me through thick and thin: my parents, family and close friends – you know who you are. Thank you. You have been real rocks of support when I have needed it.

Also, my tutor at university, the late Ken Burgin, then Robin Herd at March.

In truth, career paths happen as a series of coincidences and luck. Had the late Harvey Postlethwaite not rang and subsequently offered me that opportunity at Fittipaldi then my first job would have been at Lotus Cars and my career would doubtless have followed a different path. But Harvey did make that call and did take a chance on a kid fresh out of university, and gave me that foot in the door. Thank you, Harvey.

Finally, to Mandy, for being my partner in our next series of adventures.

INDEX